The Making of the Modern Body

The Making of
the Modern Body

**Sexuality and Society
in the Nineteenth Century**

EDITED BY
Catherine Gallagher and Thomas Laqueur

University of California Press
Berkeley · Los Angeles · London

University of California Press
Berkeley and Los Angeles, California

University of California Press, Ltd.
London, England

Originally published as REPRESENTATIONS, no. 14, Spring 1986

Library of Congress Cataloging-in-Publication Data

The Making of the modern body.

    "Originally published as Representations, no. 14,
Spring 1986"—T.p. verso.
    1. Sex—Miscellanea.   2. Sex—History—19th
century.   3. Sex—Social aspects.   I. Gallagher, Catherine.
II. Laqueur, Thomas Walter. III. Representations
(Berkeley, Calif.)
QP251.S4828   1987   305.3   86–19361
ISBN 0-520-05960-3 (alk. paper)
ISBN 0-520-05961-1 (pbk. : alk. paper)

Printed in the United States of America

1 2 3 4 5 6 7 8 9

Contents

Introduction   PAGE vii

THOMAS LAQUEUR
Orgasm, Generation, and the Politics
of Reproductive Biology   PAGE 1

LONDA SCHIEBINGER
Skeletons in the Closet: The First
Illustrations of the Female Skeleton in
Eighteenth-Century Anatomy   PAGE 42

CATHERINE GALLAGHER
The Body Versus the Social Body
in the Works of Thomas Malthus
and Henry Mayhew   PAGE 83

D. A. MILLER
Cage aux folles: Sensation and Gender in
Wilkie Collins's *The Woman in White*   PAGE 107

MARY POOVEY
"Scenes of an Indelicate Character":
The Medical "Treatment"
of Victorian Women   PAGE 137

LAURA ENGELSTEIN
Morality and the Wooden Spoon: Russian
Doctors View Syphilis, Social Class, and
Sexual Behavior, 1890–1905   PAGE 169

ALAIN CORBIN
Commercial Sexuality in Nineteenth-
Century France: A System of Images
and Regulations   PAGE 209

CHRISTINE BUCI-GLUCKSMANN
Catastrophic Utopia: The Feminine
as Allegory of the Modern   PAGE 220

List of Contributors   PAGE 231

INTRODUCTION

SCHOLARS HAVE ONLY RECENTLY DISCOVERED that the human body itself has a history. Not only has it been perceived, interpreted, and represented differently in different epochs, but it has also been lived differently, brought into being within widely dissimilar material cultures, subjected to various technologies and means of control, and incorporated into different rhythms of production and consumption, pleasure and pain. The eight articles in this volume support, supplement, and explore the significance of these insights. They belong to a new historical endeavor that derives partly from the crossing of historical with anthropological investigations, partly from social historians' deepening interest in culture, partly from the thematization of the body in modern philosophy (especially phenomenology), and partly from the emphasis on gender, sexuality, and women's history that large numbers of feminist scholars have brought to all disciplines.

Michel Foucault, of course, did much to deepen the significance and widen the appeal of historical considerations of the body, but he was only the most visible of a large number of investigators in many disciplines who have lately pointed to the centrality of the body, and particularly of sexuality, in the social discourses and practices of the nineteenth century. Building on such studies, the articles in this book both show how representations and routines of the body were transformed during the late eighteenth and early nineteenth centuries and explain how those transformations were linked to the emergence of modern social organizations. They provide multiple perspectives on the new discourse of the body that dominated the nineteenth century, a discourse that not only attributed a new set of social, political, and cultural meanings to bodies but also placed them at the very center of social, political, and cultural signification.

The nineteenth century's expansion and elaboration of the discourse of the body are difficult to reconcile with our twentieth-century stereotypes of Victorian culture. We often imagine that the previous century was a time when the body had no place in public discussion and sexuality was considered a dirty secret. The essays in this volume do not seek any simplistic overturning of such clichés. Rather, they describe in detail how the Victorians managed to win for themselves the reputation of the most sexually, and indeed physically, repressive society in history precisely by bringing the body ever more fully into discourse.

In "Orgasm, Generation, and the Politics of Reproductive Biology," the first essay, Thomas Laqueur articulates several of the volume's recurrent themes. He argues that the late eighteenth century witnessed a revolutionary reinterpretation of sexual difference. Put briefly, the model of hierarchical difference, based on a set of homologies between male and female reproductive systems (which mirrored the sexes' places in the great chain of being), gave way to a model of complementary difference, which stressed the binary oppositions between the two physiologies. The hierarchical model that held sway from ancient times until the eighteenth century, Laqueur demonstrates, interpreted the female body as merely an inferior and inverted version of the male body, all of the woman's reproductive organs simply underdeveloped homologues of male organs. The theory of homologues allowed a strict hierarchical ordering of the sexes, for it claimed that women had no truly unique parts, only lesser ones. Such a view assumed, moreover, that female orgasm, just like male orgasm, was necessary for generation and that orgasm derived from pleasurable stimulation. Laqueur traces the breakdown of this hierarchical model—which stressed the generative importance of female sexual pleasure—and its replacement by a reproductive biology stressing the opposition of male and female bodies, the woman's automatic reproductive cycle, and her lack of sexual feeling.

Laqueur demonstrates that the new model of sexual incommensurability could not have been simply the result of advances in scientific knowledge. He goes on to show that the reinterpretation of women's reproductive biology solved ideological problems inherent in eighteenth- and nineteenth-century social and political practices. As he interlaces the political and medical debates about gender, Laqueur emphasizes that the binary model of sexual difference served no one social ideology exclusively. Rather, it allowed the emergence of the full spectrum of nineteenth-century social thought, from reactionary reassertions of "natural" hierarchies to feminist advocacy of cooperative society. Thus, he concludes, the revision of female sexuality and reproductive biology was fundamental to modern social and political discourse.

Nevertheless, as Laqueur points out, that revision was itself full of contradictions, one of which emerges frequently as a topic in this collection. Women's reproductive biology, now conceived as a system opposite to men's, is increasingly seen as the key to women's nature. That is, the essence of Woman becomes ever more elaborately sexually embodied. At the same time, however, women are increasingly conceptualized as people without strong sexual feelings. The new opposition of male and female turns into an opposition of desire and nondesire. Whereas it was thought normal for women to be ruled in all of their mental states by activities of their reproductive organs, it was also thought abnormal for them to have pleasurable sexual sensations. Hence, the old clichés about the Victorian woman derive from only one half of the discourse. She was conceptually disembodied, but only to the extent that she was biologized; she was denied sexual feeling, but only to the extent that she was often imagined as wholly sexually determined.

In "Skeletons in the Closet: The First Illustrations of the Female Skeleton in Eighteenth-Century Anatomy," Londa Schiebinger, like Laqueur, finds that before the eighteenth century there was little interest in portraying the female body as in any essential way different from that of the male. Normally, the male skeleton was thought to represent the general form of the body's foundation. Indeed, no one had bothered to publish an illustration of a female skeleton, explicitly labeled as such, until 1733.

In the eighteenth century, however, as part of a much broader cultural mandate to illustrate the fundamental differences between the sexes, French and German anatomists produced what they took to be canonical versions of the female frame, of the "groundplan" of women's bodies. As a result, by the early nineteenth century the bones of the body had taken on distinct auras of masculinity and femininity. Schiebinger demonstrates that despite the claims made for their "exactitude" by contemporaries, these anatomists' representations were in fact "laden with cultural values"—not because they are inaccurate but rather because they, like all anatomical illustration, reflect an anatomist's ideal of the structure being depicted, whether it be an eye, an internal organ, or a skeleton. The "ideal" woman's skeleton was thus constructed with as wide a pelvis as could be found, narrow neck, small rib cage, and relatively tiny skull. Cultural ideals thus masqueraded as the facts of nature.

While Laqueur argues that a biology of difference is politically ambivalent, Schiebinger emphasizes this biology's oppressive mode. The female skeleton was shown to be in some ways like that of the child, and women were therefore proven to be relatively "childlike." In general, scientists welcomed nature as the basis for social inequality and, according to Schiebinger, constructed through their research a view of it detrimental to women. Because of the smallness of their skulls and the special adaptation of their pelvises for childbearing, women were, in the depths of their bones, regarded as unsuitable for intellectual labor (especially for science) and were thus unable to gain access to the dominant discourse of their subjugation.

Schiebinger argues here neither against science in general nor for the proposition that there are no differences between men and women. Rather, she, like the other contributors to this volume, maintains that the language of naturalistic description does not exist in a cultural vacuum but is itself deeply embedded in the culture from which it comes.

Catherine Gallagher's essay, "The Body Versus the Social Body in the Works of Thomas Malthus and Henry Mayhew," is concerned less specifically with the sexuality of the female body than are most of the essays in this volume; at the same time, it provides the most comprehensive framework in which to understand how women's bodies came to represent *the* body, both individual and social, during the nineteenth century. In the first place, she argues, the body is both absolutely central *and* absolutely problematic in nineteenth-century social and economic discourse. She shows that the vindication of the power of the body in Thomas Malthus's *Essay on Population,* one of the founding texts of political economy, renders it at once the source of value and the source of misery. In Gallagher's account, Malthus destroys the old homology between a healthy body and a healthy social order by showing that it is precisely in its most vigorous and strongest forms that the body is most problematic. Untranscendable and by its nature unreformable, the body is no longer available for its accustomed metaphorical roles.

Instead, it becomes the arena in which society's anxieties about decay, about corruption, and, most importantly, about the nature of economic life itself are expressed. The costermongers described by Mayhew are both healthy in their bodies and dangerous in their mobility; they are outside the social body as they seem to circulate parasitically through the economy, but they are also central to that economy's workings as they distribute its products.

Gallagher shows why the body was imagined to be both the source of value in the productive process and a sign of the sterility of exchange (as in the mechanical movement of Mayhew's costermongers or in Malthus's "fatted beast of circulation"). Hence, the Victorians came to take "mere biological being" as the object of obsessive representations full of loathing. Sexuality, in her account, is shown to be problematic not because of some supposed Victorian prudery but because the reproducing body in Malthusian social thought is a Janus-faced sign that stands for fecundity, health, pleasure, and productivity and simultaneously for misery, starvation, and sterile exchange. She thus sets the stage for understanding a whole range of problematic Victorian images of the body—the literal absorption of the factory child's body into a machine while she is in the process of producing something of value, the prostitute's association with usury and other forms of pure exchange—the vast cluster of images that swirl around bodies valuable, because weak and productive, and dangerous, because strong and capable only of exchange.

Mary Poovey's essay, "'Scenes of an Indelicate Character': the Medical 'Treatment' of Victorian Women," also concerns the nineteenth-century preoccupation with reproduction and shows the connection between that preoccupation and the theme of our first two articles: the biological construction of femininity. Analyzing the midcentury English debate over the use of chloroform in childbirth, Poovey shows that doctors on both sides of the controversy (those for and those against the use of chloroform) sought to enhance or protect the prestige of their profession by equating the "nature of Woman" with her reproductive function. Poovey interweaves the various determinants of this construction. She shows, for example, that the singling out of the uterus not only as the most important female organ but also as the most important organ of the "Race" ("the uterus is to the Race what the heart is to the Individual," as one doctor put it) had as much to do with obstetricians' anxiety about their status inside the medical profession as with the need to elevate the value of women's reproductive organs as a prelude to making reproduction the essence and telos of Woman. She reads in this debate the process by which the nature of Woman becomes Nature itself, but a Nature peculiarly demanding of interpretive medical authority and intervention. Chloroform represented, paradoxically, both an instance of that interventionist authority and a challenge to it, for Poovey's research reveals that attempts to anesthetize women during childbirth, to make them unconscious of their sensations, threatened to uncover a sensational unconscious. Women were reported to have become flirtatious, improper, even obscene in their words and gestures, and such behavior was unreconcilable with nineteenth-century ideas of maternity.

Once again we note the close but contradictory relationship between the obsessive biologization of femininity, centered on the reproductive function, and the denial that women normally experience sexual pleasure. The contradictions inherent in interpreting women as essentially sexual beings who lack sexual sensations are displayed in the chloroform debate. Poovey concludes that in their very attempts turn the female into a passive and mute object of interpretation and control, obstetricians created a disturbingly "indeterminate" body, as likely to reflect the interpreter's projected anxieties as his conscious beliefs. The insensible woman refused to make sense and thus defied the mastery that called her into being.

D. A. Miller's "*Cage aux folles:* Sensation and Gender in Wilkie Collins's *The Woman in White*" also takes up the themes of gender construction, sensation, and interpretation. Like Poovey, Miller is interested in the relationship between femininity read as and through a somatic state (the Woman as neuropathic body) and the anxieties of the male who reads her in this way. For Miller, however, the creation of gender in bodies is a circuitous process that establishes masculine/feminine, subject/object dichotomies only by deeply, in the very somatic responses of the reader, unsettling them. Thus his analysis of Wilkie Collins's sensation novel, *The Woman in White,* occasions a compelling and startling account of how anxiety about the unboundedness, the elusiveness, of Woman becomes not (as in Poovey's article) a defiance of mastery but a strategy for enforcing self-regulating gender distinctions in both women and men. This article complicates the implicit assumption of the other essays—that the construction of femininity is an imposition of male power on women—by detailing the elaborate procedures of power that create the properly masculine subject.

Miller shows that the nervousness that is both the result and cause of reading the sensation novel stems in particular from a fear of "catching" femininity, from being "touched" or invaded by the neuropathic body of the Woman. To become nervous in or through the sensation novel is to become feminine inside; hence, the state of nervousness coincides, if one is a man, with the nineteenth century's classic definition of the homosexual: a woman's soul trapped in a man's body. It follows that the homosexual is already a confined (trapped) subjectivity: the homosexual is by definition his own jailor and is, therefore, already enacting, through his very essence, society's homophobic urge to incarcerate him.

The sensational effects of *The Woman in White* also serve simultaneously to unsettle and reinforce binary gender distinctions, for these effects include hysterical defenses against the significance of feelings. That is, the "sensational" quality of the feelings is their hystericization, which is also the very means of containing them, by rendering them insignificant. Similarly, freeing the Woman in White from an asylum and empowering her to make men nervous is the novel's necessary prelude to and justification for the final reincarceration of her double in the "normalized" sanctuary of the home. This incarceration, Miller explains, operates on men and women alike: "the sequestration of the woman takes for its object not just women, who need to be put away in safe places or asylums, but men as well, who must monitor and master what is fantasized as the 'woman inside' them."

With Laura Engelstein's "Morality and the Wooden Spoon: Russian Doctors View Syphilis, Social Class, and Sexual Behavior, 1890–1905," we return to the relationship between scientific evidence and cultural assumptions about sexuality. Like Mary Poovey, Engelstein is analyzing a debate among doctors, but her protagonists are late-nineteenth-century Russians using the distinction between venereal and congenital syphilis in their battle with the state for some degree of professional autonomy. Engelstein does not claim that there is no difference between the two forms of the disease, or that their clinical signs were, or are, clear to any honest observer. She does argue, though, that political and cultural considerations, rather than some set of clinical indicators, determined which form of the disease was most frequently diagnosed by the Russian physicians. Moreover, she shows that their propensity to favor the nonvenereal diagnosis and their reluctance to extend their professional authority to empower the state (as Western physicians did) by defining sexuality as a medical question reflect, as she puts it, "basic issues separating state and society in the fifteen years preceding the revolution of 1905."

Peasants, Russian doctors believed, were not sexual, and peasant women were the least sexual of all. They worked, bore children, and embodied the virtues of tradition. Prostitution, which was seen as the vector of venereal disease, simply did not—and could not, in the doctors' view—exist in rural Russia except perhaps as a small pocket of social infection in some towns or villages opened to railroads or industry. Syphilis in the countryside thus had to be regarded as the result of unhygienic eating practices, poor sanitation and ventilation around dwellings, and other environmental factors; that is, it had to be nonvenereal.

The moral power of the peasant community seemed to extend to the city, where doctors refused to identify cankers on the mouths of urban artisans, still regarded as members of their villages, as being of sexual origin. Although the doctors ultimately had to admit that peasant women who migrated to the city were capable of contracting and transmitting venereal disease, Engelstein demonstrates that peasants, even when removed from their original context, were generally regarded as not sexual. The fact that in one study army officers had three times the rate of venereal syphilis as did enlisted men was read as a sign of the common man's preference for marriage and family life—even in the army, the peasant male preferred innocent diversions.

Thus, the relationship between class and moral contagion in Russia was just the reverse of what it was in western Europe. There the lower classes were seen as sewers of contagion, especially venereal, because they had broken the bonds of traditional society. In Russia, venereal disease within the peasantry was regarded as infrequent precisely because the degree of individuation necessary for sexual life was deemed impossible in the village community. Moreover, far from making the common western European assumption that morality and bad sanitation were linked, Russian doctors used the unsanitary conditions of peasant life (signified by the supposed relative frequency of nonvenereal syphilis) to confirm the peasant's peculiar asexuality (as signified by the concomitant relative infrequency of the veneral form).

Engelstein likewise shows that the relationship between the professional authority of doctors and the power of the interventionist state was the reverse of what it was in western Europe. Rather than seizing on syphilis as an occasion to intervene on behalf of the state, doctors used it as an occasion to preach "enlightenment," thus morally neutralizing syphilis and discrediting repressive state measures. They believed that only knowledge, and not government power, would make the peasant give up carriers of disease such as the common wooden spoon. Doctors as professionals thus sought autonomy from the state, although the question of how to accomplish their ends without destroying the traditional framework of rural life was never resolved.

Engelstein thus shows in greater detail than exists anywhere else in the literature how diagnostic categories and understanding of disease are embedded in other discourses. But more to the point of this volume, she shows that a discourse about the sexual body is part of much broader currents in the political and cultural life of a society.

Alain Corbin, in "Commercial Sexuality in Nineteenth-Century France: A System of Images and Regulations," is engaged in the same enterprise but in a very different context. Throughout the nineteenth century, France stood at the very opposite end of the spectrum from Russia in the matter of state control of prostitution. France was the home of state regulation. This difference between Russia and France cannot, as Engelstein's piece makes clear, be explained simply in the terms customarily invoked to explain the differences between England and France on these matters; unlike the English, the Russians had a highly interventionist state and virtually no ideology of laissez-faire. But neither is the difference explicable in terms of the "monotonously repeated arguments or denotative discourses" generally hauled out to justify it. Rather, Corbin argues, the prostitute became an archetype of the sexualized female body, and a "series of images and perceptual schemas" surrounding her came to inspire deep-seated fears and the need for regulation—indeed, the very forms that regulation took.

The prostitute is a body that smells bad; it has rotten blood. Intimately related to this image is her body as the sewer in which the social body excretes its excess— the "seminal drain," as one nineteenth-century physician put it. She is in this way symbolically linked to death and to corpses, to disease—especially syphilis—and to that other set of potentially dangerous resigned female bodies at the disposal of the bourgeoisie, the bodies of servants.

This particular cultural understanding of the prostitute suggests that she is a necessary danger to society. The connection between sex and sanitation is, however, as it was in Engelstein's essay, a complex one, for the prostitute is not by her nature unsanitary. Rather, she is "filthy" because she is part of the very apparatus of sanitation. Hence, she must be tolerated for the role she fills, and at the same time she must be carefully controlled, subjected to isolation, surveillance, concealment, and incorporation into a network of medical observation and treatment.

These images and strategies of control were, Corbin shows, historically specific. A new link between prostitution and desire, a new eroticization of prostitution in which the bourgeois male could imagine himself, in having sex with a prostitute, as seducing his neighbor's wife, involved changing the fantasized class of the prostitute, shifting to bordello-based prostitution with a new set of governing regulations. In short, Corbin describes the making and unmaking during the nineteenth century of particular "female bodies" and of the connection of these bodies to social discourse.

Christine Buci-Glucksmann's "Catastrophic Utopia: The Feminine as Allegory of the Modern" focuses also on nineteenth-century Parisian prostitution but refracts it through a series of lenses different from Corbin's. She analyzes Walter Benjamin's writings on Baudelaire's reflections about prostitution in order to illustrate how the prostituted body was turned into an allegory of modernity itself. Indeed, the prostitute stands for the very obverse of corporeal immanence—she represents (like the poet himself) the loss of the actual and immediate, the derealization of the body and its petrification into nonvital signification. As allegory of the modern, the prostitute is linked to abstraction; she becomes a pure commodity. As Benjamin indicates, when one buys a prostitute's time, one buys the pervasiveness of the marketplace itself. But precisely through this abstraction, this allegorizing, which is the essence of prostitution, the prostitute's body is infused with a new reality. Its very petrification and fragmentation become for the modernist new modes of plenitude. With Buci-Glucksmann's essay, then, our collection concludes by reflecting on modernism's links to many of the phenomena the other articles analyze: modes of imaging the connections between bodies and marketplaces; the simultaneous impulse to equate women with their bodies and render them insensible; the self-defeating attempts of male interpreters to differentiate themselves from Woman, the object of their interpretations.

As this brief excursion into the modernist sensibility suggests, twentieth-century thinkers have not really taken up a position outside the nineteenth century's discourses of the body and sexuality. Women have been reassigned orgasms; syphilis is no longer a pressing social problem. But other diseases have come to occupy the same discursive place. Women's pleasure inside an increasingly commercialized psycho-sexual economy remains a controversial topic, even in feminist circles. Inside and outside feminism, moreover, the impulse to fix the true essence of Woman in a set of characteristics that differentiates her from Man continues. Populations are more than ever seen as entities to control. Many of the details of the discourse outlined here may seem bizarre, outrageous, or even comically absurd, but we cannot deny the continuity between its governing assumptions and our own.

THOMAS LAQUEUR

Orgasm, Generation, and the Politics of Reproductive Biology

SOMETIME IN THE LATE EIGHTEENTH CENTURY human sexual nature changed, to paraphrase Virginia Woolf. This essay gives an account of the radical eighteenth-century reconstitution of female, and more generally human, sexuality in relation to the equally radical Enlightenment political reconstitution of "Man"—the universalistic claim, stated with starkest clarity by Condorcet, that the "rights of men result simply from the fact that they are sentient beings, capable of acquiring moral ideas and of reasoning concerning these ideas. [And that] women, having these same qualities, must necessarily possess equal rights."[1]

Condorcet moves immediately to biology and specifically to reproductive biology. Exposure to pregnancy, he says, is no more relevant to women's political rights than is male susceptibility to gout. But of course the facts or supposed facts of female physiology were central to Condorcet, to Mill, to feminists as well as antifeminists, to liberalism in its various forms and also to its enemies. Even the political pornography of Sade is grounded in a theory of generation. The body generally, but especially the female body in its reproductive capacity and in distinction from that of the male, came to occupy a critical place in a whole range of political discourses. It is the connection between politics and a new disposition of male and female that concerns me here.[2]

Near the end of the century of Enlightenment, medical science and those who relied upon it ceased to regard the female orgasm as relevant to generation. Conception, it was held, could take place secretly, with no tell-tale shivers or signs of arousal. For women the ancient wisdom that "apart from pleasure nothing in mortal kind comes into existence" was uprooted. We ceased to regard ourselves as beings "compacted in blood, of the seed of man, and the pleasure that [comes] with sleep." We no longer linked the loci of pleasure with the mysterious infusing of life into matter. Routine accounts, like that in a popular Renaissance midwifery text of the clitoris as that organ "which makes women lustful and take delight in copulation," without which they "would have no desire, nor delight, nor would they ever conceive," came to be regarded as controversial if not manifestly stupid.[3]

Sexual orgasm moved to the periphery of human physiology. Previously a deeply embedded sign of the generative process—whose existence was no more open to debate than was the warm, pleasurable glow that usually accompanies a good meal—orgasm became simply a feeling, albeit an enormously charged one, whose existence was a matter for empirical inquiry or armchair philosophizing. Jacques Lacan's provocative characterization of female orgasm, "la jouissance, ce qui ne sert a rien," is a distinctly modern possibility.[4]

The new conceptualization of the female orgasm, however, was but one formulation of a more radical eighteenth-century reinterpretation of the female body in relation to that of the male. For several thousand years it had been a commonplace that women have the same genitals as men, except that, as Nemesius, bishop of Emesa in the sixth century, put it: "Theirs are inside the body and not outside it." Galen, who in the second century A.D. developed the most powerful and resilient model of the homologous nature of male and female reproductive organs, could already cite the anatomist Herophilus (third century B.C.) in support of his claim that a woman has testes with accompanying seminal ducts very much like the man's, one on each side of the uterus, the only difference being that the male's are contained in the scrotum and the female's are not.[5]

For two millennia the organ that by the early nineteenth century had become virtually a synecdoche for woman had no name of its own. Galen refers to it by the same word he uses for the male testes, *orchis*, allowing context to make clear with which sex he is concerned. Regnier de Graaf, whose discoveries in 1672 would eventually make the old homologies less plausible, continues to call the ovaries he is studying by their old Latin name, *testiculi*. A century later the Montpelierian physiologist Pierre Roussel, a man obsessed with the biological distinctiveness of women, notes that the two oval bodies on either side of the uterus "are alternatively called ovaries or testicles, depending on the system which one adopts." As late as 1819, the *London Medical Dictionary* is still somewhat muddled in its nomenclature: "Ovaria: formerly called female testicles; but now supposed to be the recepticles of ova or the female seed." Indeed, doggerel verse of the nineteenth century still sings of these hoary homologies after they have disappeared from learned texts:

> . . . though they of different sexes be,
> Yet on the whole they are the same as we,
> For those that have the strictest seachers been,
> Find women are but men turned outside in.

By 1800 this view, like that linking orgasm to conception, had come under devastating attack. Writers of all sorts were determined to base what they insisted were fundamental differences between male and female sexuality, and thus between man and woman, on discoverable biological distinctions. In 1803, for example, Jacques Moreau de la Sarthe, one of the founders of "moral anthropology," argued passionately against the nonsense written by Aristotle, Galen, and their modern followers on the subject of women in relation to men.[6] Not only are the sexes different, they are different in every conceivable respect of body and soul, in every physical and moral aspect. To the physician or the naturalist the relation of woman to man is "a series of oppositions and contrasts." Thus the old model, in which men and women were arrayed according to their degree of metaphysical perfection, their vital heat, along an axis whose telos was male, gave way by the late eighteenth century to a new model of difference, of biological divergence. An anatomy and physiology of incommensurability replaced a metaphysics of hierarchy in the representation of women in relation to men.[7]

But neither the demotion of female orgasm nor the biology of incommensurability of which it was a part follow simply from scientific advances. True, by the 1840s it had become clear that, at least in dogs, ovulation could occur without coition and thus presumably without orgasm. And it was immediately postulated that the human female, like the canine bitch, was a "spontaneous ovulator," producing an egg during the periodic heat that in women was known as the menses. But the available evidence for this half truth was at best slight and highly ambiguous. Ovulation, as one of the pioneer twentieth-century investigators in reproductive biology put it, "is silent and occult: neither self-observation by women nor medical study through all the centuries prior to our own era taught mankind to recognize it." Indeed until the 1930s standard medical advice books recommended that to *avoid* conception women should have intercourse during the middle of their menstrual cycles—i.e., during days twelve through sixteen, now known as the period of *maximum* fertility. Until the 1930s even the outlines of our modern understanding of the hormonal control of ovulation were unknown. Thus, while scientific advances might in principle have caused a change in the understanding of the female orgasm, in fact the reevaluation of pleasure occurred a century and a half before reproductive physiology came to its support.[8]

The shift in the interpretation of the male and female body, however, cannot have been due, even in principle, primarily to scientific progress. In the first place the "oppositions and contrasts" between the female and the male have been self-evident since the beginning of time: the one gives birth and the other does not, to state the obvious. Set against such momentous truths, the discovery, for example, that the ovarian artery is not, as Galen would have it, the homologue of the vas deferens is of relatively minor significance. Thus, the fact that at one time male and female bodies were regarded as hierarchically, that is vertically, ordered and that at another time they came to be regarded as horizontally ordered, as opposites, as incommensurable, must depend on something other than one or even a set of real or supposed "discoveries."

In addition, nineteenth-century advances in developmental anatomy (germlayer theory) pointed to the common origins of both sexes in a morphologically androgenous embryo and thus not to their intrinsic difference. Indeed the Galenic homologies were by the 1850s reproduced at the embryological level: the penis and the clitoris, the labia and the scrotum, the ovary and the testes shared common origins in fetal life. Finally, and most tellingly, no one was very interested in looking at the anatomical and concrete physiological differences between the sexes until such differences became politically important. It was not, for example, until 1797 that anyone bothered to reproduce a detailed female skeleton in an anatomy book so as to illustrate its difference from the male. Up to this time there had been one basic structure for the human body, the type of the male.[9]

Instead of being the consequence of increased scientific knowledge, new ways of interpreting the body were rather, I suggest, new ways of representing and indeed of constituting social realities. As Mary Douglas wrote, "The human body is always treated as an image of society and . . . there can be no natural way of considering the body that does not involve at the same time a social dimension." Serious talk about sexuality is inevitably about society. Ancient accounts of reproductive biology, still persuasive in the early eighteenth century, linked the experiential qualities of sexual delight to the social and indeed the cosmic order. Biology and human sexual experience mirrored the metaphysical reality on which, it was thought, the social order too rested. The new biology, with its search for fundamental differences between the sexes and its tortured questioning of the very existence of women's sexual pleasure, emerged at precisely the time when the foundations of the old social order were irremediably shaken, when the basis for a new order of sex and gender became a critical issue of political theory and practice.[10]

The Anatomy and Physiology of Hierarchy

The existence of female sexual pleasure, indeed the necessity of pleasure for the successful reproduction of humankind, was an unquestioned commonplace well before the elaboration of ancient doctrines in the writings of Galen, Soranus, and the Hippocratic school. Poor Tiresias was blinded by Juno for agreeing with Jove that women enjoyed sex *more* than men. The gods, we are told in the *Timaeus,* "contrived the love of sexual intercourse by constructing an animate creature of one kind in us men, and another in women"; only when the desire and love of the two sexes unite them are these creatures calmed. Galen's learned texts, *On the Seed* and the sections on the reproductive organs in *On the Usefulness of the Parts of the Body,* are intended not to query but rather to explain the obvious: "why a very great pleasure is coupled with the exercise of the generative parts and a raging desire precedes their use."[11]

Heat is of critical importance in the Galenic account. It is, to begin with, the sign of perfection, of one's place in the hierarchical great chain of being. Humans are the most perfect of animals, and men are more perfect than women by reason of their "excess of heat." Men and women are, in this model, not different in kind but in the configuration of their organs; the male is a hotter version of the female, or to use the teleologically more appropriate order, the female is the cooler, less perfect version of the male.[12]

4   THOMAS LAQUEUR

Understanding the machinery of sex thus becomes essentially an exercise in topology: "Turn outward the woman's, turn inward, so to speak, and fold double the man's, and you will find the same in both in every respect." Galen invites his readers to practice mentally the admittedly difficult inversions.

Think first please, of the man's [external genitalia] turned in and extending inward between the rectum and the bladder. If this should happen, the scrotum would necessarily take the place of the uterus with the testes lying outside, next to it on either side.

The penis in this exercise becomes the cervix and vagina; the prepuce becomes the female pudenda and so forth, continuing on through the various ducts and blood vessels. Or, he suggests, try it backwards:

Think too, please, of the converse, the uterus turned outward and projecting. Would not the testes [ovaries] then necessarily be inside it? Would it not contain them like a scrotum? Would not the neck [the cervix], hitherto concealed inside the perineum but now pendant, be made into the male member?[13]

In fact, Galen argues, "You could not find a single male part left over that had not simply changed its position." And, in a blaze of rhetorical virtuosity, he elaborates a stunning and unsuspected simile to make all this more plausible: the reproductive organs of women are like the eyes of the mole. Like other animals' eyes, the mole's have "vitreous and crystalline humors and the tunics that surround [them]"; yet, they do not see. Their eyes do not open, "nor do they project but are left there imperfect." Likewise, the womb itself is an imperfect version of what it would be were it projected outward. But like the eyes of a mole, which in turn "remain like the eyes of other animals when these are still in the uterus," the womb is forever as if still in the womb![14]

If the female is a replica of the male, with the same organs inside rather than outside the body, why then, one might ask, are women not men? Because they have insufficient heat to extrude the organs of reproduction and, as always for Galen, because form befits function. Nature in her wisdom has made females cooler, allowing their organs to remain inside and providing there a safe, guarded place for conception and gestation. Moreover, if women were as hot as men, semen planted in the womb would shrivel and die like seed cast upon the desert; of course, the extra nutriment needed by the fetus would likewise burn off. The fact remains that women, whatever their special adaptations, are but variations of the male form, the same but lower on the scale of being and perfection.[15]

In this model, sexual excitement and the "very great pleasure" of climax in both men and women are understood as signs of a heat sufficient to concoct and comingle the seed, the animate matter, and create new life. Friction heats the body as it would two objects rubbing together. The chafing of the penis, or even its imagined chafing in a nocturnal emission, warms the male organ and, through its connections to veins and nerves, every other part of the body. As warmth and

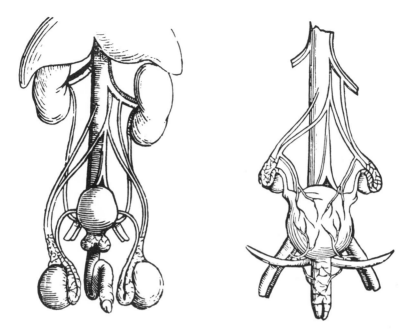

FIGURES 2 and 3. Andreas Vesalius, male and female reproductive organs, *Tabulae Sex.* From *The Anatomical Drawings of Andreas Vesalius,* ed. Charles D. O'Malley and J. B. de C. M. Saunders (New York, 1982).

Ancient medicine bequeathed to the Renaissance a physiology of flux and corporeal openness, one in which blood, mother's milk, and semen were fungible fluids, products of the body's power to concoct its nutriment. Thus, not only could women turn into men, as writers from Pliny to Montaigne testified (see below), but bodily fluids could turn easily into one another. This not only explained why pregnant women, who, it was held, transformed food into nourishment for the fetus, and new mothers, who transformed the catamenial elements into milk, did not menstruate; it also accounted for the observation that obese women, who transformed the normal plethora into fat, and dancers, who used up the plethora in exercise, did not menstruate either and were thus generally infertile. Menstrual blood and menstrual bleeding were, moreover, regarded as no different than blood and bleeding generally. Thus Hippocrates views nosebleed and the onset of menstruation as equivalent signs of the resolution of fevers. A woman vomiting blood will stop if she starts to menstruate, and it is a good sign if epistaxis occurs in a woman whose courses have stopped. Similarly, bleeding in men and in women is regarded as physiologically equivalent. If melancholy appears "after the suppression of the catamenial discharge in women," argues Araeteus the

Cappadocian, "or the hemorrhoidal flux in men, we must stimulate the parts to throw off their accustomed evacuation."[19]

Indeed, the menses, until one hundred years before its phantasmagoric nineteenth-century interpretations by Michelet and others, was still regarded, as it had been by Hippocrates, as but one form of bleeding by which women rid themselves of excess materials. Brazilian Indian women "never have their flowers," writes an eccentric seventeenth-century English compiler of ethnographic curiosities, because "maids of twelve years old have their sides cut by their mothers, from the armpit down unto the knee . . . [and] some conjecture they prevent their monthly flux in this manner." Albrecht von Haller, the great eighteenth-century physiologist, argues that in puberty the plethora "in the male, vents itself frequently through the nose . . . but in the female the *same* plethora finds a more easy vent downward." Herman Boerhaave, the major medical teacher of the generation before Haller, cites a number of cases of men who bled regularly through the hemorrhoidal arteries, the nose, or the fingers or who, if not bled prophylactically, developed the clinical signs, the tenseness of the body, of amenorrhea. Even the enlightened Frederick the Great had himself bled before battle to relieve tension and facilitate calm command.[20]

The fungibility of fluids thus represented in a different register the anatomical homologies described earlier. The higher concoction of male semen with respect to that of the female and the fact that males generally rid themselves of nutritional excesses without frequent bleeding bore witness both to the essential homology between the economies of nutrition, blood, and semen in men and women, and to the superior heat and greater perfection of the male. Sexual heat was but an instance of the heat of life itself, and orgasm in both sexes the sign of warmth sufficient to transform one kind of bodily fluid into its reproductively potent forms and to assure a receptive place for the product of their union. In this context, it is not difficult to see why Galen's clinical judgments on the relationship between pleasure and fertility, or between the absence of pleasure and barrenness, should have become commonplace in both learned and popular Renaissance medical literature.

Avicenna, the eleventh-century Arab writer who served as a conduit to the West for much ancient medicine, writes in some detail of how a woman may not "be pleased by" the smallness of her mate's penis "wherefore she does not emit sperm; and when she does not emit sperm a child is not made." "Pleasure induces a hasty emission of sperm"; conversely, if women delay in emitting "and do not fulfill their desire . . . the result is no generation." The midwife and physician Trotulla in the twelfth century describes how barrenness can well be the sad consequence of too little or too much heat, though she does not distinguish sexual heat from its more mundane varieties. Of course, it is argued in a great body of Renaissance literature that barrenness might well be due to anatomical defects and arguably to witchcraft, but either a lack of passion or an excess of

FIGURE 4. Vesalius, uterus, vagina, and external pudenda from a young woman, *De humani corporis*. This illustration was not made to illustrate homologies with the male organ. From *Anatomical Drawings of Vesalilus*.

FIGURES 5 and 6 (*opposite*). Frontal cross section of female genitals (*left*); front wall of the vagina (*right*); from Jakob Henle, *Handbuch der systematischen Anatomie des Menschen*, vol. 2 (Braunschweig, 1866). These illustrations show that the geometric relations depicted in fig. 4 are not intrinsically implausible.

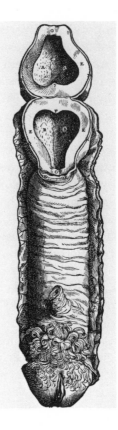

lust had to be considered in any differential diagnosis. In men, insufficient heat manifested by a lack of sexual desire could be remedied by rubbing the loins with heat-producing drugs. Still other drugs—in addition to lascivious talk, coquetry, and the like—could cure "defect of spirit," the inability to have an erection when desire was present. In women adversity and indisposition "to the pleasures of the lawful sheets" or "no pleasure and delight" in intercourse, along with a slow pulse, little thirst, thin urine, scant pubic hair, and similar signs, were almost certain indicators of insufficient heat of the testicles to concoct the seed. As Jacob Rueff puts it in discussing the problem of cold, "The fruitfulness of man and wife may be hindered very much for want of desire to be acquainted with Venus." Conversely, too much desire (prostitutes were thought seldom to conceive); curly, dark, and plentiful hair (marks of the virago, the virile, unnaturally warm woman); a short or absent menses (the hot body burning off the excess materials that in normal women were eliminated through the monthly courses) indicated excessive heat, which will consume or shrivel up the seed.[21]

Thus, to ensure "generation in the time of copulation," the right amount of heat, made manifest by normal sexual pleasure and in the end by orgasm, must be produced. Talk and teasing, several books suggest, were the first resort. Women should be prepared with lascivious words, writes John Sadler, having pointed out earlier the importance of mutual orgasm; sometimes the problem is neither the womb nor other impediments in either spouse,

except only in the manner of the act as when in the emission of the seed, the man is quicke and the woman too slow, whereby there is not a concourse of both seeds at the same instant as the rules of conception require.

He further recommends wanton behavior, "all kinde of dalliance" and "allurement to venery." Then, if the man still found his mate "to be slow, and more cold, he much cherish, embrace, and tickle her." He must

handle her secret parts and dugs, that she may take fire and be enflamed in venery, for so at length the wombe will strive and waxe fervent with desire of casting forth its own seed, and receiving the man's seed to be mixed together therein.

The womb, as another writer notes almost a century later, "by Injoyment Naturally receives Seed for Generation . . . as Heat [attracts] Straws or Feathers." Be careful, warn Ambroise Pare and others, not to leave a woman too soon after her orgasm, "lest aire strike the open womb" and cool the seeds so recently sown.[22] If all this fails, the Renaissance pharmacopoeia was full of useful drugs that worked either directly or by sympathetic magic. Pare recommends "fomenting her secret parts with a decoction of hot herbes made with muscadine, or boiled in other good wine," and rubbing civet or muske into the vagina. Submerge the privates in a warm sitz bath of junipers and chamomile, advises another authority. The heart of a male quail around the neck of a man and the heart of

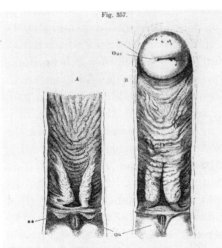

Fig. 357.

Vagina, Ansicht der vorderen Wand nach Wegnahme der hinteren. A mit aufwärts, B mit abwärts divergirenden Wülsten der Columna vaginalis anterior. *Ou* Orificium uretrae. *Oue* Ost. uterinum ext. * Durchschnitt des Fornix vaginae. ** Carunculae hymenales.

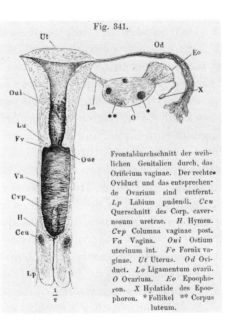

Fig. 341.

Frontaldurchschnitt der weiblichen Genitalien durch das Orificium vaginae. Der rechte Oviduct und das entsprechende Ovarium sind entfernt. *Lp* Labium pudendi. *Ccu* Querschnitt des Corp. cavernosum uretrae. *H* Hymen. *Cvp* Columna vaginae post. *Va* Vagina. *Oui* Ostium uterinum int. *Fv* Fornix vaginae. *Ut* Uterus. *Od* Oviduct. *Lo* Ligamentum ovarii. *O* Ovarium. *Eo* Epoophoron. *X* Hydatide des Epoophoron. *Follikel ** Corpus luteum.

The Politics of Reproductive Biology   11

a female around the neck of a woman were said to enhance love, presumably because of the lecherous character of birds generally and perhaps of quails in particular; a concoction of ale hoof and pease straw was also indicated.[23]

In the Renaissance, as in late antiquity, an unbreakable bond between orgasm and fulfillment of the command to be fruitful and multiply linked personal experience to a greater social and cosmic order. On the one hand concupiscence and the irresistible attractions of sexual rapture stood as marks in the flesh of mankind's fall from grace, of the essential weakness of the will. But on the other hand pleasure was construed as precisely what compelled men and women to reproduce themselves, despite what prudence or individual interest might dictate. The import of the *Timaeus*'s account of creation was that in both men and women brazenly *self-willed* genitals assured the propagation of the species through their love of intercourse even if reason might urge abstinence. This notion is elaborated with an especial poignancy for women in the popular Renaissance literature. Only "ardent appetite and lust" prevented the "bitter decay in short time of mankind"; only the fact that a mercifully short memory and an insatiable desire made women forget the dangerous agonies of childbirth allowed the human race to continue. Women, with clinched fists "in the great pain and intolerable anguish" of the time of their travail, "forswear and bind themselves never to company with a man again." Yet time after time, the "singular natural delight between men and women" causes them to forget "both the sorrow passed and that which is to come." If the bearing of children was God's offer of consolation for the loss of eternal life, the lethean pleasures of sex were a counterweight to its pain. The biological "invisible hand" of delight made them cooperate in assuring the immortality of the species and the continuity of society.[24]

Male and female bodies in these Renaissance accounts were, as is perhaps obvious, still very much those of Galen. Consider Leonardo's drawings (fig. 1), or the far more influential engravings in Andreas Vesalius' epoch-marking *De humani corporis fabrica* and his more popular *Tabulae sex,* all of which reinforce the hoary model through striking new representations. When Vesalius is self-consciously trying to emphasize the homologies between male and female organs of generation (figs. 2 and 3) and, even more telling, when he is not (fig. 4), he is firmly in the camp of the "ancients," however much he might rail against the authority of Galen in other contexts. But the anatomical accuracy of Galen is not what at issue here. The female reproductive system can be, and indeed on occasion was still in the late nineteenth century, "accurately" rendered in the manner of Vesalius long after the old homologies had lost their credibility (figs. 5 and 6). But after the late seventeenth century and the collapse of the hierarchical model there was, in general, no longer any reason to draw the vagina and external pudenda in the same frame with the uterus and the ovaries. Bodies did not change, but the meanings of the relationship between their parts did.[25]

Seventeenth-century audiences still gave credence to a whole collection of tales, going back at least to Pliny, that illustrate the structural similarities and thus the mutability of male and female bodies. Sir Thomas Browne, in his *Enquiries into Vulgar and Common Errors* (1646), devotes an entire chapter to the question of whether "every hare is both male and female." He concludes that "as for the mutation of sexes, or transition of one into another, we cannot deny it in Hares, it being observable in Man." Some pages later, in an exegesis of Aristotle and the schoolmen, he continues on this subject: "As we must acknowledge this Androgynal condition in Man, so can we not deny the like doth happen in beasts." Ambroise Pare, the great sixteenth-century surgeon, recounts the case of one Germain Garnier, christened Marie, who was serving in the retinue of the king. Germain was a well-built young man with a thick, red beard who until he was fifteen had lived and dressed as a girl, showing "no mark of masculinity." But then, in the heat of puberty,

as he was in the fields and was rather robustly chasing his swine, which were going into a wheat field, [and] finding a ditch, he wanted to cross over it, and having leaped, at that very moment the genitalia and the male rod came to be developed in him, having ruptured the ligaments by which they had been held enclosed.

Marie, soon to be renamed, hastened home to his/her mother, who consulted physicians and surgeons, all of whom assured her that her daughter had become her son. She took him to the bishop, who called an assembly that decided that indeed a transformation had taken place. "The shepard received a man's name: instead of Marie . . . he was called Germain, and men's clothing was given him." (Some persisted in calling him Germain-Marie as a reminder that he had once been a girl.) Montaigne tells the same story, "attested to by the most eminent officials of the town." There is still, he reports, in the area "a song commonly in the girls' mouths, in which they warn one another not to stretch their legs too wide for fear of becoming males, like Marie Germaine."[26]

How were transformations like Marie's possible? Pare offers the following account:

The reason why women can degenerate into men is because women have as much hidden within the body as men have exposed outside; leaving aside, only, that women don't have so much heat, nor the ability to push out what by the coldness of their temperament is held bound to the interior. Wherefore if with time, the humidity of childhood which prevented the warmth from doing its full duty being exhaled for the most part, the warmth is rendered more robust, vehement, and active, then it is not an unbelievable thing if the latter, chiefly aided by some violent movement, should be able to push out what was hidden within.

The learned Caspar Bauhin explains more succinctly how "women have changed into men," namely, "The heat having been rendered more vigorous, thrusts the testes outward." Such transformations, however, seem to work only up the great chain of being.

We therefore never find in any true story that any man ever became a woman, because Nature tends always toward what is most perfect and not, on the contrary, to perform in such a way that what is perfect should become imperfect.[27]

Moreover, the Galenic structure survived the discovery of a new, and one would think totally incompatible, homology: that of the clitoris to the penis. This organ first was described accurately by Readolus Colombus, Vesalius' successor in the chair at Padua, and was called in various sixteenth-century learned texts the *mentula muliebris* (female penis or woman's yard, to use the English vernacular), *columnella* (column), *crista* (cock's comb), *nympha* (the term used by Galen presumably to refer to this organ), *dulcedo amoris* or *oestrum veneris* (*taon de Venus* in French, referring to a frenzy, the *oestrum* metaphorically linked to the *taon*, i.e., "gadfly" or "oxfly"). Jane Sharp, whose 1671 midwifery guide was last reprinted in 1728, could happily argue at one point in her work that the vagina, "which is the passage for the yard, resembleth it turned inward," while arguing two pages later and with no apparent embarrassment, that the clitoris is the female penis. "It will stand and fall as the yard doth and makes women lustful and take delight in copulation," thus helping to assure the conditions necessary for conception. The labia thus fit nicely into both systems of analogies. They give women great pleasure in copulation and, as the ancients said, defend the matrix from outward violence, but they are also, as John Pechey puts it, "that wrinkled membranous production, which clothes the Clitoris like a foreskin." This left open the question of whether the vagina or the clitoris were to be thought of as the female penis, though both could be regarded as erectile organs. One midwifery manual notes that "the action of the clitoris is like that of the yard, which is erection" and, on the very same page, that "the action of the neck of the womb [the vagina and cervix] is the same with that of the yard; that is to say, erection." Thus, until the very end of the seventeenth century there seemed no difficulty in holding that women had an organ homologous, through topological inversion, to the penis inside their bodies, the vagina, and another one morphologically homologous to the penis, outside, the clitoris.[28]

Perhaps the continued power of the systemic, genitally unfocused account of sex inherited by Renaissance writers from antiquity—the view of the sexually excited body as a great boiler heating up to blow off steam—explains why mutually incompatible interpretations of male and female genitals caused so little consternation. Seventeenth-century writers seem to have welcomed the idea that male and female pleasure was located in essentially the same kind of organ. They remain undisturbed by the clitoris's supposed dual function—licit pleasure in heterosexual intercourse and illicit pleasure in "tribadism." They elaborate the penis/clitoris homology with great precision: the outward end of the clitoris, one physician writes, is like the glans of the penis, and like it "the seat of the greatest pleasure in copulation in women." According to another, the tip of the clitoris is,

FIGURE 7. Jacobo Pontormo, *Alabardiere* (1529–30). The codpiece in this picture very much resembles, contrary to what Jacques Duval suggests, "a large-mouthed bottle . . . whose mouth rather than base would be attached to the body." Frick Museum, New York.

therefore, also called the "amoris dulcedo." They would have found very curious Marie Bonaparte's contention that "clitoroidal women" suffer from one of the stages of frigidity or protohomosexuality. Rather, as Nicholas Culpepper writes without the fanfare of controversy: "It is agreeable both to reason and authority, that the bigger the clitoris in a woman, the more lustful they are."[29]

The ancient account of bodies and sexual pleasures was not ultimately dependent for its support simply on facts or supposed facts about the body, even though it was articulated in the concrete language of anatomy and physiology. Were it otherwise, the system of homologies would have fallen well before its time from the sheer weight of readily apparent difficulties. The recognition of the clitoris is a case in point. The word *clitoris* makes its first known English appearance in 1615 when Helkiah Crooke argues that it *differs* from the yard: "[It] is a small body, not continued at all with the bladder, but placed in the height of the lap. The clitoris hath no passage for the emission of seed; but the virile member is long and hath a passage for seed." Yet, one can easily set beside this quite correct list of facts equally unexceptional observations supporting the contrary view. The clitoris, for example, is called the *tentigo* in Thomas Vicary's enormously popular *The Anatomie of the Body of Man* (1586), a term borrowed from the eleventh-century Arab medical writer Albucasis meaning in Latin "a tenseness or lust; an erection." It *is*, of course, erectile and erotogenous, and thus a "counterfeit yard," if one chooses to emphasize these features.[30]

The homological view survived not only the potential challenge posed by the anatomist Colombus's discovery of the clitoris, but other expressions of scepticism as well. Crooke, in the text cited above, attacks the Galenic homologies in general, pointing out that the scrotum of a man is thin-skinned while the base of the womb, its homologue, is "a very thicke and tight membrane." Again, this is scarcely a telling point when compared with the self-evident fact that the womb carries a baby while the penis does not. Moreover, the topological inversions suggested by Galen are, and were known to be, manifestly implausible if taken literally. Recall the mind-bending metaphor of the womb as a penis inside itself, like the eyes of a mole, or perfectly formed but hidden within, like the eyes of other animals *in utero*. Jacques Duval, another seventeenth-century physician, proposes trying Galen's "thought experiment" and concludes quite rightly that it does not work: "If you imagine the vulva completely turned inside out . . . you will have to envisage a large-mouthed bottle hanging from a woman, a bottle whose mouth rather than base would be attached to the body and which would bear no resemblance to what you had set out to imagine." But in fact, a bottle shaped like the vagina and womb hanging by its mouth does resemble a penis; indeed it is the precise form of the codpiece (fig. 7).[31]

The fact that criticisms of the Galenic model are not only self-evident but were also sprinkled throughout the literature is a reminder that the cultural construction of the female in relation to the male, while expressed in terms of the body's concrete realities, was more deeply grounded in assumptions about the nature of politics and society. It was the abandonment of these assumptions in the Enlightenment that made the hierarchically ordered system of homologies hopelessly inappropriate. The new biology, with its search for fundamental differences between the sexes and between their desires, emerged at precisely the time when the foundations of the old social order were irremediably shaken. Indeed, as Havelock Ellis discovered, "It seems to have been reserved for the nineteenth century to state that women are apt to be congenitally incapable of experiencing complete sexual satisfaction and are peculiarly liable to sexual anaesthesia." But what happened to the old biology, to its complex of metaphors and relations? In some respects nothing happened to it; or, in any case, nothing happened very fast.[32]

Politics and the Biology
of Sexual Difference

When in the 1740s the young Princess Maria Theresa was worried because she did not immediately become pregnant after her marriage to the future Hapsburg emperor, she asked her physician what she ought to do. He is said to have replied:

Ceterum censeo vulvam Sanctissimae Majestatis ante coitum esse titillandum [Moreover I think the vulva of Her Most Holy Majesty is to be titillated before intercourse].

The advise seems to have worked as she bore more than a dozen children. Similarly, Albrecht von Haller, one of the giants of eighteenth-century biological science, still postulated an erection of both the external and the internal female reproductive organs during intercourse and regarded woman's orgasm as a sign that the ovum has been ejaculated from the ovary. Although he is well aware of the existence of the sperm and the egg and of their respective origins in the testes and ovaries, and has no interest in the Galenic homologies, the sexually aroused female in his account bears a remarkable resemblance to the male under similar circumstances.

When a woman, invited either by moral love, or a lustful desire of pleasure, admits the embraces of the male, it excites a convulsive constriction and attrition of the very sensible and tender parts; which lie within the contiguity of the external opening of the vagina, after the same manner as we observed before of the male.

The clitoris grows erect, the nymphae swell, venous blood flow is constricted, and the whole external genitalia become turgid as the system works "to raise the pleasure to the highest pitch." A small quantity of lubricating mucous is expelled in this process, but

the same action which, by increasing the heights of pleasure, causes a greater conflux of blood to the whole genital system of the female, occasions a much more important alteration in the interior parts.

The uterus becomes turgid with inflowing blood; likewise the fallopian tubes become erect "so as to apply the ruffle or fingered opening of the tube to the ovary." Then, at the moment of mutual orgasm, the "hot male semen" acting on this already excited system causes the extremity of the tube to reach still further until, "surrounding and compressing the ovarium in fervent congress, [it] presses out and swallows a mature ovum." The extrusion of the egg, Haller points out finally to his learned readers, who would probably have read this torrid account in the original Latin,

is not performed without great pleasure to the mother, nor without an exquisite unrelatable sensation of the internal parts of the tube, threatening a swoon or fainting fit to the future mother.[33]

The problem with which this essay began thus remains. Neither advances in reproductive biology nor anatomical discoveries seem sufficient to explain the dramatic revaluation of the female orgasm that occurred in the late eighteenth century and the even more dramatic reinterpretation of the female body in relation to that of the male. Rather, a new model of incommensurability triumphed over the old hierarchical model in the wake of new political agendas. Writers from the eighteenth century onward sought in the facts of biology a justification for cultural and political differences between the sexes that were crucial to the articulation of both feminist and antifeminist arguments. Political theorists beginning with Hobbes had argued that there is no basis in nature for any specific sort of authority—of a king over his people, of slaveholder over slave, nor, it followed, of man over woman. There seemed no reason why the universalistic claims made for human liberty and equality during the Enlightenment should exclude half of humanity. And, of course, revolution, the argument made in blood that mankind in all its social and cultural relations could be remade, engendered both a new feminism and a new fear of women. But feminism itself, and indeed the more general claims made by and for women to public life—to write, to vote, to legislate, to influence, to reform—was also predicated on difference.

Thus, women's bodies in their corporeal, scientifically accessible concreteness, in the very nature of their bones, nerves, and, most important, reproductive organs came to bear an enormous new weight of cultural meaning in the Enlightenment. Arguments about the very existence of female sexual passion, about women's special capacity to control what desires they did have, and about their moral nature generally were all part of a new enterprise seeking to discover the anatomical and physiological characteristics that distinguished men from women. As the natural body itself became the gold standard of social discourse, the bodies of women became the battleground for redefining the most ancient, the most intimate, the most fundamental of human relations: that of woman to man.

It is relatively easy to make this case in the context of explicit resistance to the political, economic, or social claims of women. Prominent male leaders in the French Revolution, for example, strenuously opposed increased female participation in public life on the grounds that women's physical nature, radically distinguished from that of men and represented most powerfully in the organs of reproduction, made them unfit for public life and better suited to the private sphere. Susanna Barrows maintains that fears born of the Paris Commune and of the new political possibilities opened up by the Third Republic generated an extraordinarily elaborate physical anthropology of sexual difference to justify resistance to change. In the British context the rise of the women's suffrage movement in the 1870s elicited a similar response. Tocqueville argues that in the United States democracy had destroyed the old basis for patriarchal authority and that consequently it was necessary to trace anew and with great precision "two clearly distinct lines of action for the two sexes." In short, wherever boundaries were threatened arguments for fundamental sexual differences were shoved into the breach.[34]

But reinterpretations of the body were more than simply ways of reestablishing hierarchy in an age when its metaphysical foundations were being rapidly effaced. Liberalism postulates a body that, if not sexless, is nevertheless undifferentiated in its desires, interests, or capacity to reason. In striking contrast to the old teleology of the body as male, liberal theory begins with a neuter body, sexed but without gender, and of no consequence to cultural discourse. The body is regarded simply as the bearer of the rational subject, which itself constitutes the person. The problem for this theory then is how to derive the real world of male dominion of women, of sexual passion and jealousy, of the sexual division of labor and cultural practices generally from an original state of genderless bodies. The dilemma, at least for theorists interested in the subordination of women, is resolved by grounding the social and cultural differentiation of the sexes in a biology of incommensurability that liberal theory itself helped bring into being. A novel construal of nature comes to serve as the foundation of otherwise indefensible social practices.

For women, of course, the problem is even more pressing. The neuter language of liberalism leaves them, as Jean Elshtain recently argues, without their own voice. But more generally the claim of equality of rights based on an essential identity of the male and female, body and spirit, robs women both of the reality of their social experience and of the ground on which to take political and cultural stands. If women are indeed simply a version of men, as the old model would have had it, then what justifies women writing, or acting in public, or making any other claims for themselves as women? Thus feminism, too—or at least historical versions of feminisms—depends upon and generates a biology of incommensurability in place of the teleologically male interpretation of bodies on the basis of which a feminist stance is impossible.[35]

Rousseau's essentially antifeminist account is perhaps the most theoretically elaborated of the liberal theories of bodies and pleasures, but it is only one of a great many examples of how deeply a new biology is implicated in cultural reconstruction. In the state of nature, as he imagined it in the first part of *A Discourse on Inequality,* there is no social intercourse between the sexes, no division of labor in the rearing of young, and, in a strict sense, no desire. There is, of course, brute physical attraction between sexes, but it is devoid of what he calls "moral love," which "shapes this desire and fixes it exclusively on one particular object, or at least gives the desire for this chosen object a greater degree of energy." In this world of innocence there is no jealousy or rivalry, no marriage, no taste for this or that woman; to men in the state of nature "every woman is good." Rousseau is remarkably concrete in specifying the reproductive physiology of women that must, in his view, underlie this condition. Hobbes, he argues, erred in using the struggle of male animals for access to females as evidence for the natural combativeness of the primitive human state. True, he concedes, there is bitter competition among beasts for the opportunity to mate, but this is because for much of the year females refuse the male advance. Suppose they were to make themselves available only two months out of every twelve: "It is as if the population of females had been reduced by five-sixth." But women, he points out, have no such periods of abstinence and are thus not in short supply:

No-one had ever observed, even among savages, females having like those of other species fixed periods of heat and exclusion. Moreover, among several of such animals, the whole species goes in heat at the same time, so that there comes a terrible moment of universal passion, a moment that does not occur in the human species, where love is never seasonal.

Reproductive physiology and the nature of the menstrual cycle bear an enormous weight here; the state of nature is in large measure conceptualized as dependent on the supposed biological differences between women and beasts.[36]

But what happened to this primitive state of desire? Rousseau gives an account of the geographical spread of the human race, of the rise of the division of labor, of how in developing a dominion over animals man "asserted the priority of his species, and so prepared himself from afar to claim priority for himself as an individual." But the individuation of desire, the creation of what he calls the moral part of love ("an artificial sentiment"), and the birth of imagination ("which causes such havoc amongst us") are construed as the creation of women and, specifically, as the product of female modesty. The *Discourse* presents this modesty as volitional, as instrumental: "[It is] cultivated by women with such skill and care in order to establish their empire over men, and so make dominant the sex that ought to obey." But in *Emile* modesty is naturalized: "While abandoning women to unlimited desires, He [the Supreme Being] joins modesty to these desires in order to constrain them." And somewhat later in a note Rousseau adds: "The timidity of women is another instinct of nature against the double risk they run during their pregnancy." Indeed, throughout *Emile* he argues that natural differences between the sexes are represented and amplified in the form of moral differences that society erases only at its peril.[37]

Book 5 begins with the famous account of sexual difference and sameness. "In everything not connected with sex, woman is man. . . . In everything connected with sex, woman and man are in every respect related but in every respect different." But, of course, a great deal about women *is* connected with sex: "The male is male only at certain moments. The female is female her whole life. . . . Everything constantly recalls her sex to her." "Everything," it turns out, is everything about reproductive biology: bearing young, suckling, nurturing, and so on. Indeed the chapter becomes a catalogue of physical and consequently moral differences between the sexes; the former, as Rousseau says, "lead us unawares to the latter." Thus, "a perfect woman and a perfect man ought not to resemble each other in mind any more than in looks." From the differences in each sex's contribution to their union it follows that "one ought to be active and strong, the other passive and weak." "One must necessarily will and be able; it suffices that the other put up little resistance." The problem with Plato, Rousseau argues, is that he excludes "families from his regime and no longer knowing what to do with women, he found himself *forced to make them men*." It is precisely this sameness of "the exercises" Plato gives men and women, this "civil promiscuity which throughout confounded the two sexes in the same employments and the same labors and which cannot fail to engender the most intolerable abuses," to which Rousseau objects. But what are these objectionable abuses?

I speak of that subversion of the sweetest sentiments of nature, sacrificed to an artificial sentiment which can only be maintained by them—as though there were no need for a natural base on which to form conventional ties; as though the love of one's nearest were not the principle of the love one owes the state; as though it were not by means of the small fatherland which is the family that the heart attaches itself to the large one; as though it were not the good son, the good husband, and the good father [all males of course] who make the good citizen.

Finally, returning to the ostensible subject of the book, Rousseau concludes that "once it is demonstrated that man and woman are not and ought not to be constituted in the same way in either their character or temperament, it follows that they ought not to have the same education."[38]

For Rousseau a great deal depends, it turns out, on the natural modesty of women and on their role, distinct from the male's, in reproducing the species. Indeed, all of civilization seems to have arisen in consequence of the secular fall from innocence when the first woman made herself temporarily unavailable to the first man. But Rousseau is simply pushing harder on a set of connections that are commonplace in the Enlightenment—although by no means always so antifeminist in their interpretation. In his article on "jouissance," Diderot locates the creation of desire, of marriage and the family if not of love itself, at the moment *women* first came to withhold themselves from just any man and chose instead one man in particular,

when women began to discriminate, when she appeared to take care in choosing between several men upon whom passion cast her glances. . . . Then, when the veils that modesty cast over the charms of women allowed an inflamed imagination the power to dispose of them at will, the most delicate illusions competed with the most exquisite of senses to exaggerate the happiness of the moment . . . two hearts lost in love vowed themselves to each other forever, and heaven heard the first indiscreet oaths.[39]

Most prominently among the figures of the Scottish Enlightenment, John Millar argues for the critical role of women and their virtues in the progress of civilization. Far from being lesser men, they are treated in his *Origin of the Distinctions of Ranks* as both a moral barometer and as an active agent in the improvement of society. Millar's case begins with the claim that sexual relations, being most susceptible "to the peculiar circumstances in which they are placed and most liable to be influenced by the power of habit and education," are the most reliable guide to the character of a society. In barbarous societies, for example, women accompanied men to war and were scarcely different from them; in peaceful societies that had progressed in the arts, a woman's "rank and station" were dictated by her special talents for rearing and maintaining children and by her "peculiar delicacy and sensibility," whether these derived from her "original constitution" or her role in life. Thus civilization in Millar's account leads to an increasing differentiation of male and female social roles; this greater differentiation of roles—and specifically what he takes to be improvements in the lot of women—are signs of moral progress. But women themselves in more civilized societies are also the engines of further advance. "In such a state, the pleasures which nature has grafted upon love between the sexes, become the source of an elegant correspondence, and are likely to have a general influence upon the commerce of society." In this, the highest state—he is thinking of French salon society and of the *femme savant*—

[women are] led to cultivate those talents which are adapted to the intercourse of the world, and to distinguish themselves by polite accomplishments that tend to heighten their personal attractions, and to excite those peculiar sentiments and passions of which they are the natural objects.

Thus, desire among civilized men, and indeed modern civilization, is inextricably bound up in Millar's moral history with feminine accomplishment.[40]

It is hardly surprising in the context of Enlightenment thought that the moral and physical differentiation of women from men is also critical to the political discourse of women writers—from Anna Wheeler and early socialists at one end of the political spectrum through the radical liberalism of Mary Wollstonecraft to the domestic ideology of Hannah More and Sarah Ellis. For Wheeler and others, as Barbara Taylor argues, the denial or devaluation of female passion is to some degree part of a more general devaluation of passion. Reason, they dare to hope, would be triumphant over the flesh. Wheeler and early utopian socialists are, after all, writing out of the tradition that produced William Godwin's argument that civilization would ultimately eliminate destructive passions, that the body finally would be curbed by Enlightenment and be subsumed under the captaincy of the mind. It is against this view, as Catherine Gallagher argues, that Thomas Malthus rehabilitates the body and insists upon the absolute irreducibility of its demands, especially its sexual demands.[41]

But the nature of female passion and of the female body is unresolved in Wheeler's work. Her book, *An Appeal of One-Half the Human Race, Women, Against the Pretensions of the Other Half, Men, To Retain Them in Political and Thence in Civil and Domestic Slavery,* jointly written with William Thompson, is a sustained attack on James Mill's argument that the interests of women and children are subsumed—i.e., are virtually represented by—the interests of husbands and fathers. This "moral miracle," as they call it, would be credible were Mill right in holding that women are protected against abuse because men "will act in a kind way toward women in order to procure from her those gratifications, the zest of which depends on the kindly inclinations of one party yielding them." Since women are themselves free from sexual desire, they are in an excellent bargaining position vis à vis men, who are decidedly not liberated from their bodies. Nonsense, say Wheeler and Thompson. If women are "like the Greek Asphasia," cold and sexless, the argument might have force. But not only are they, like men, sexed and desirous but, in the current state of affairs, "Woman is more the slave of man for gratification of her desires than man is to woman." The double standard allows men to seek gratification outside of marriage but forbids it to women.[42]

Both Wheeler and Thompson's analysis of the sorry shape of the male world and their need to claim some political ground for women lead them dramatically to change their emphasis and make almost the opposite case as well. In a chapter entitled "Moral Aptitude for Legislation More Probable in Women than Men," woman is represented not as equally passionate as man but as more moral, more empathetic, and generally better able to act in accord with the common interest and not merely out of self-interest. Whether women had these traits in some hypothetical state of nature or acquired them through a kind of moral Lamarckianism is unclear, but in the modern world they demonstrate a greater susceptibility to pain and pleasure, a more powerful desire to promote the happiness of others, and a more developed "moral aptitude" than men. These, Wheeler and Thompson argue, are the most important qualities in a legislator. It is, moreover, precisely women's inferior strength and her inability to oppress others through superior force as men are wont to do that will ensure that they rule fairly and justly. Moreover, women as mothers and as the weaker sex need a world at peace far more than men, and they would thus be constitutionally more likely to legislate ways to obtain it. Wheeler and Thompson's arguments are more poignantly put than this summary suggests, but they contribute to a construction of woman not very different from that of the domestic ideologists. Whether through inherent nature—because they have more sensitive nervous systems, as many eighteenth- and nineteenth-century doctors held—or through centuries of suffering, women are construed as less passionate and hence morally more adept than men.[43]

As a radical liberal, Mary Wollstonecraft is caught in much the same dilemma. On the one hand, liberal theory pushes her to declare that the neutral, rational subject has in essence no sex. On the other hand, she was in her own life only too aware of the power, indeed the destructive violence, of sexual passion. Moreover she seems to have held, with Rousseau, that civilization increases desire and that "people of sense and reflection are most apt to have violent and constant passions and to be preyed on by them." Finally, as Zillah Eisenstein argues, for Wollstonecraft to subscribe to the notion of the subject as genderless would be to deny what to her were manifestly present, the particular qualities of women's experiences.[44]

Her solution was to take for women the moral high ground. Blessed with a unique susceptibility "of the attached affections," women's special role in the world is to civilize men and raise up children to virtue. In the *Female Reader,*

Wollstonecraft lays on a heavy dose of religion, which she says will be "the solace and support" of her readers when they find themselves, as they often will, "amidst the scenes of silent unobserved distress." "If you wish to be loved by your relations and friends," she counsels without detectable irony, "prove that you can love them by governing your temper." Good humor, cheerful gaity, and the like are not to be learned in a day. Indeed, as Barbara Taylor argues, Wollstonecraft shares with early socialist feminists a commitment to "passionlessness," whether out of some sense of its political possibilities, an acute awareness of passion's dangers, or a belief in the special undesiring qualities of the female body.[45]

In any case, Wollstonecraft's arguments for the differences between the sexes begin to sound very much like Sarah Ellis's, however profound the political chasm that divided the two women. In *Wives of England,* one of the canonical works of domestic ideology, Ellis argues that from the wife and mother, "as head of a family and mistress of a household, branch off in every direction trains of thought, and tones of feeling, operating upon those more immediately around her, but by no means ceasing there . . . extending outwards in the same manner, to the end of all things." This influence is born of the heightened moral sensibilities with which the female organism seems blessed. Though women are to have no role in the world of mundane politics, they are to confront issues

such as extinction of slavery, the abolition of war in general, cruelty to animals, the punishment of death, temperance, and many more, on which, neither to know, nor to feel, is almost equally disgraceful.

In short, women's politics must be the politics of morality.[46]

All of this is not intended as an argument that writers from Hobbes, through Sade and Rousseau, and on to Ellis were all engaged in precisely the same theoretical or political undertaking. Rather, I have sought to display the wide range of apparently unrelated political agendas in which a new differentiation of the sexes occupied a critical place. Desire was given a history, and the female body distinguished from the male's, as the seismic transformations of European society between the seventeenth and the nineteenth centuries put unbearable pressure on old views of the body and its pleasures. A biology of hierarchy grounded in a metaphysically prior "great chain of being" gave way to a biology of incommensurability in which the relationship of men to women, like that of apples to oranges, was not given as one of equality or inequality but rather as a *difference* whose meaning required interpretation and struggle.

Reproductive Biology and
the Cultural Reconstruction of Women

I want now to turn from political and moral theory to the sciences of reproductive biology, to the seemingly unpromising domain of ovarian and uterine histology and the clinical observation of menstruation and fertility. Aldous Huxley's remark that "the sciences of life can confirm the intuitions of the artist, can deepen his insights and extend the range of his vision" could as well be said of those who produced what he takes to be a prior and culturally pure knowledge. The dry and seemingly objective findings of the laboratory and the clinic become, within the disciplines practiced there, the stuff of art, of new representations of the female as a creature profoundly different from the male. And this "art," clothed in the prestige of natural science, becomes in turn the specie, the hard currency of social discourse.[47]

But I do not want to give the impression that reproductive biology or clinical gynecology are simply exercises in ideology. I will therefore begin by describing a critically important discovery of the early nineteenth century: that some mammals—nineteenth-century researchers believed all mammals—ovulate spontaneously during regularly recurring periods of heat, independently of intercourse, conception, pleasure, or any other subjective phenomena. Until the early 1840s the question of when and under what conditions ovulation took place was as obscure as it had been in 1672 when de Graaf argued that what he called the female testicle actually produced eggs. In the first place no one had observed a mammalian egg until 1827, when Karl Ernst von Baer, in a brilliant piece of research, definitively demonstrated its existence, first in the ovarian follicle and subsequently in the fallopian tubes of a dog. Until then, direct evidence for ovulation was lacking. At the time of his great discovery, von Baer still believed that an animal ovulated only when sexually stimulated; he therefore used a bitch that he knew to have quite recently mated. This was only reasonable, since the late eighteenth-century researches of the Englishmen William Cruickshank and John Haighton, on which von Baer relied, had shown that rabbits do *not* generally ovulate without intercourse; indeed they had claimed that ovulation is dependent on conception.[48]

In humans, the evidence for spontaneous ovulation was, in the early nineteenth century, highly ambiguous. Numerous anecdotal clinical reports, based on increasingly available autopsy material, claimed that cicatrices—scars remaining after a wound, sore, or ulcer has healed—can be demonstrated on ovaries of virgins and that these are left there by the release of an ovum and, more to the point, by the release of numerous ova corresponding to the number of menstrual cycles that the woman had had. But what, if anything, did this prove? Very little. Johann Friederich Blumenbach, professor of medicine at Göttingen and one of the most distinguished physicians of Europe, for example, had been among the first to notice by the late eighteenth century that ovarian follicles burst without the presence of semen or even "without any commerce with the male." But he concluded from these cases only that, on occasion, "venereal ardour alone . . . could produce, among the other great changes in the sexual organs, the enlargement of the vesicles" and even their rupture.

On this point I find it difficult in the present state of knowledge to make up my mind; but I think it pretty evident that, although semen has no share in bursting the ovarium, the high excitement that occurs during the heat of brutes and the lascivious states of the human virgin is sufficient frequently to effect the discharge of the ova. It is perhaps impossible otherwise to explain the fact that ova are so commonly expelled from the ovaria, and impregnated whenever a connection is arbitrarily or casually brought about.

Johannes Muller, professor of physiology at Berlin, a leading proponent of biological reductionism, concludes that scars on the ovaries of virgins mark anomalous ovulations. Thus, while the exact forces causing the egg to be thrust into the fallopian tube remained unknown, the evidence until the 1840s was by no means sufficient to establish the normal occurrence of ovulation independent of coition, venereal arousal, or even conception.[49]

The critical experiment establishing spontaneous ovulation in dogs and by extension other mammals was elegantly simple. In the novelistic style that characterizes so much early nineteenth-century scientific reporting, Theodor L. W. Bischoff tells his reader that on 18 and 19 December 1843 he noted that a large bitch in his possession had begun to go into heat. On the 19th he allowed her contact with a male dog, but she refused its attentions. He kept her securely imprisoned for two more days and then brought on the male dog again; this time she was interested but the animals were separated before coition could take place. At ten o'clock two days later, i.e., on the morning of the 23rd, he cut out her left ovary and fallopian tubes and carefully closed the wound. The Graafian follicles in the excised ovary were swollen but had not yet burst. Five days later he killed the dog and found in the remaining ovary four developing corpus lutei filled with serum; careful opening of the tubes revealed four eggs. He concludes:

I do not think it is possible to demonstrate with any more thoroughness the whole process of the ripening and expulsion of the eggs during heat, independently of coition, than through this dual observation on one and the same animal.

And of course if ovulation occurs independently of coition it must also occur independently of fecundation. Indeed, F. A. Pouchet considered the later discovery in itself so major that he formulated it as his "fifth" and critical law of reproductive biology, "le point capital" of his 476-page *magnum opus*. The historian Michelet was enraptured and hailed Pouchet for having formulated the entire science of reproductive biology in a definitive work of genius, a monument of daring grandeur.[50]

Granted that dogs and pigs go into heat and during this period ovulate whether they mate or not, what evidence was there that women's bodies behave in a similar manner? No one prior to the early twentieth century had claimed to have seen a human egg outside the ovary. Bischoff admitted that, in the absence of such a discovery, there was no direct proof for the extension of his theory to women, but he was sure that an egg would be found soon enough. In 1881, V.

Hensen, professor of physiology at Kiel, notes in L. Hermann's standard *Hand-buch der Physiologie* that except for two probably spurious reports, human eggs still eluded investigators, though he adds, in a curiously optimistic footnote, that "it can not be so difficult to find a [human] egg in the [fallopian] tubes." In fact, an unfertilized egg was not reported until 1930, and then in the context of an argument against the nineteenth-century view relating heat to menstruation. Thus, the crucial experimental link—the discovery of the egg—between menstruation on the one hand and the morphology of the ovary on the other was lacking in humans. Investigators could only note in the cases that came their way that women were menstruating or that they were at some known point in their menstrual cycles and then attempt to correlate these observations with the structural characteristics of the ovary removed in surgery or autopsy. They lacked as a biological triangulation point the actuai product of the ovary, and the results of their studies were manifestly unsatisfactory. Evidence for the timing of ovulation based on pregnancy from a single coition whose occurrence in the menstrual cycle was supposedly known was likewise increasingly ambiguous. The role of the ovaries in the reproductive cycle of mammals was very imperfectly understood until the publication of a series of papers beginning in 1900, while the hormonal control of ovulation by the ovary and the pituitary remained unknown until the 1930s.[51]

But despite the paucity of evidence in humans, the discovery of spontaneous ovulation in dogs and other mammals was of enormous importance in the history of representating women's bodies. Beginning in the middle of the nineteenth century, the ovaries came to be regarded as largely autonomous control centers of reproduction in the female animal, and in humans they were thought to be the essence of femininity itself. "Propter solum ovarium mulier est id quod est," as the French physician Achilles Chereau puts it; it is only because of the ovary that woman is what she is. Moreover, menstruation in women came to be interpreted as the precise equivalent of the heat in animals, marking the only period during which women are normally fertile. Widely cited as Pouchet's eighth law, the view was that "the menstrual flow in women corresponds to the phenomena of excitement which manifests itself during the rut [*l'époque des amours*] in a variety of creatures and especially in mammals." The American physician Augustus Gardner drew out the implications of the menstruation/rut analogy less delicately: "The bitch in heat has the genitals tumified and reddened, and a bloody discharge. The human female has nearly the same." "The menstrual period in women," announces the *Lancet* in 1843, "bears a strict physiological resemblance" to the heat of "brutes."[52]

With these interpretations of spontaneous ovulation the old physiology of pleasure and the old anatomy of sexual homologies were definitively dead. The ovary, whose distinction from the male testes had only been recognized a century earlier, became the driving force of the whole female economy, with menstruation the outward sign of its awesome power. As the distinguished British gynecologist Mathews Duncan put it, in an image too rich to be fully teased apart here: "Menstruation is like the red flag outside an auction sale; it shows that something is going on inside." And that something, as will become clear, was not a pretty sight; the social characteristics of women seemed writ in blood and gore. The silent workings of a tiny organ weighing on the average seven grams in humans, some two to four centimeters long, and the swelling and subsequent rupture of the follicles within it, came to represent synecdochically what it was to be a woman.[53]

But why would anyone believe that menstruation was in women what heat was in the dog? The answer lies outside the bounds of science in a wide range of cultural demands on the enterprise of interpretation. Consider, for example, the answer Bischoff himself offers: the equivalence of menstruation and heat is simply common sense. If one accepts spontaneous ovulation during periods of heat in mammals generally, it "suggests itself." In any case there is much indirect evidence for the equation of heat and menstruation, in addition to the authority of the "most insightful physicians and naturalists" from the earliest times on.

In fact the analogy was far from evident, and most of those from antiquity to Bischoff's day who gave their views on the subject repudiated it. Haller's *Physiology* is quite explicit on the point that, while there are "some animals, who, at the time of their venal copulation, distil blood from their genitals," menstruation is peculiar "to the fair sex [of] the human species." Moreover, in contrast to bleeding in animals, menstruation for Haller is quite independent of the periodicity of sexual desire. Intercourse neither increases nor decreases the menstrual flux; women deny a heightened "desire of venery" during their periods and report rather being "affected by pain and languor." Finally, sexual pleasure is localized "in the entrance of the pudendum" and not in the uterus, from which the menses flow. Blumenbach, among the most widely reprinted and translated texts of the next generation, joins Pliny in arguing that only women menstruate, though cautioning his readers that the investigation of the "periodical nature of this hemorrhage is so difficult that we can obtain nothing beyond probability" and should thus be careful not to offer mere conjecture as fact.[54]

What scant facts there were seemed more anthropological than biological, and these came under severe attack. In a masterful review of the literature up to 1843, Robert Remak, professor of neurology at Posen, argues that even if one grants that, as do healthy women, all or some mammals have regularly recurring periods of bleedings and that the bleeding in animals originates in the uterus and not from the turgescent external genitalia—neither concession being warranted by the evidence—there remains "one further circumstance on which to ground the most radical difference between menstruation and the periodical flow of blood from the genitals of animals":

In female animals the bleeding accompanies heat [*brunst*], the period of the most heightened sexual drive, the only time the female will allow the male access, and the only time she will conceive. Quite to the contrary, in women the menstrual period is scarcely at all connected to increased sexual desire nor is fecundity limited to its duration; indeed a kind of instinct keeps men away from women during the menses—some savage people like certain African and American tribes isolate menstruating women in special quarters—and experience shows that there is no time during the inter-menstrual period when women can not conceive. It follows therefore that the animal heat is totally missing in women. . . . Indeed the absence of menstruation in animals is one of the features that distinguish man from the beasts.

Johannes Muller, in his 1843 textbook, comes to similar conclusions. He modestly points out that neither the purposes nor the causes of the periodical return of the menses are known. Quite probably, however, it exists to "*prevent* in the human female the periodical return of sexual excitation [*brunst*]" that occurs in animals. Common sense, in short, does not explain why nineteenth-century investigators would want to view the reproductive cycle of women as precisely equivalent to that of other animals.[55]

Professional politics and the imperatives of a particular philosophy of science offer perhaps part of an answer. As Jean Borie points out, Pouchet's is "une gynaecologie militante"; the same can be said of that of many of his colleagues, especially his French ones. Their mission was to free women's bodies from the stigma of clerical prejudice and centuries of popular superstition and, in the process, to substitute the physician for the priest as the moral preceptor of society. Sexuality would shift from the realms of religion to those of science triumphant. At the heart of the matter lay the faith that reproduction, like nature's other mysteries, was in essence susceptible to rational analysis. Thus, in the absence of specific evidence of human ovulation, "logic" for Pouchet would dictate that women functioned no differently from the bitch, sow, or female rabbit, who in turn followed the same fundamental laws as mollusks, insects, fishes, or reptiles. He explicitly calls his readers' attention to the pristinely scientific, experimentally grounded, character of his work and its avoidance of metaphysical, social, and religious concerns. Thus, there were considerable professional and philosophical attractions to the position that menstruation was like heat and that a sovereign organ, the ovary, ruled over the reproductive processes that made women what they were.[56]

But this radical naturalization, this reduction of women to the organ that differentiates them from men, was not in itself a claim for their association with nature as against culture and civilization. The argument for the equation of heat and menstruation could be just as easily used to prove women's moral elevation as to prove the opposite. Indeed the very fact that women, on account of their recurrent cycles of rut, were more bound to their bodies than were men was evidence on some accounts for their superior capacity to transcend the brutish state. Arguing against those who held that the lack of animal-like lust or behavioral disturbances in women belied the new theory of spontaneous ovulation, one noted authority draws attention to "the influence exercised by moral culture on the feelings and passions of humanity." Observe "the marvellous power exercised by civilization on the mind of her who, from her social position, is rendered the charm of man's existence." Is it a wonder that the creature who can subjugate her own feelings, simulate good cheer when her heart is rent in agony, and in general give herself up to the good of the community can exercise control "the more energetically, at a time [menstruation] when she is taught that a stray thought of desire would be impurity, and its fruition pollution." But then, as if to back off from this model of woman as being simultaneously a periodically excited time bomb of sexuality and a model for the power of civilization to keep it from exploding, G. F. Girdwood concludes that "to aid her in her duty, nature has wisely provided her with the sexual appetite slightly developed."[57]

The interpretive indigestion of this passage, its sheer turning in on itself, bears witness to the extraordinary cultural burden that the physical nature of women—the menstrual cycle and the functions of the ovaries—came to bear in the nineteenth century. Whatever one thought about women and their rightful place in the world could, it seemed, be mapped onto their bodies, which in turn came to be interpreted anew in the light of these cultural demands. The construal of the menstrual cycle dominant from the 1840s to the early twentieth century rather neatly integrates a particular set of discoveries into a biology of incommensurability. Menstruation, with its attendant aberrations, became a uniquely and distinguishingly female process. Moreover, the analogy now assumed between heat and menstruation allowed evidence hithertofore used against the equivalence of the reproductive cycles of women and brutes to be reinterpreted to mean the opposite. Behavior hidden in women, just as ovulation is hidden, could be made manifest by associating it with the more transparent behavior of animals.

Thus, for example, the author of one of the most massive compilations of moral physiology in the nineteenth century could argue that the quite mad behavior of dogs and cats during heat, their flying to satisfy the "instinct which dominates all else," leaping around an apartment and lunging at windows, repeated "so to speak indefinitely" if the venereal urge were not satisfied, is but a more manifest version of what the human female too experiences. Since both women and brutes are thought to be subject to the same "orgasme de l'ovulation," and since the bursting of the ovarian follicle was marked by the same deluge of nervous excitement and bleeding in both, whatever discomfort adolescent girls might feel at the onset of menstruation and whatever irritability or tension a woman might experience during her menses could be magnified through the metaphors of this account and reinterpreted as but the tip of a physiological volcano. Menstruation, in short, was a minimally disguised heat. Women would behave like brutes were it not for the thin veneer of civilization. Language, moreover, adjusted to the new science. The whole cultural baggage of *brunst, rut, heat*—words hith-ertofore applied only to animals—and the neologism *estrous,* derived from the Latin *oestrum,* "gadfly," meaning a kind of frenzy and introduced to describe a process common to all mammals, was subtly or not so subtly laden on the bodies of women.[58]

Menstrual bleeding thus become the sign of a periodically swelling and ulti-mately exploding ovarian follicle whose behavioral manifestation is an "estrous," "brunst," or "rut." But what one saw on the outside was only part of the story; the histology of the uterine mucosa and of the ovary revealed much more. Described in seemingly neutral scientific language, the cells of the endometrium or corpus luteum became re-presentations, rediscriptions of the social theory of sexual incommensurability. Walter Heape, the militant antisuffragist and reader in zool-ogy at Cambridge University, for example, is absolutely clear on what he thinks of the female in relation to the male body. Though some of the differences between men and women are "infinitely subtle, hidden" and others "glaring and forceful," the truth of the matter, he argues, is that

the reproductive system is not only structurally but functionally fundamentally different in the Male and the Female; and since all other organs and systems of organs are affected by this system, it is certain that the Male and Female are essentially different throughout.

They are, he continues, "complementary, in no sense the same, in no sense equal to one another; the accurate adjustment of society depends on proper observa-tion of this fact." A major set of these facts were evident, for Heape and many others, in the uterus. It should be noted, however, that the basic histology of menstruation—let alone its causes—was not established until the classic 1908 paper of L. Adler and F. Hitschmann. Previous descriptions, as these two young Viennese gynecologists noted, were demonstrably inadequate. The point here is less that so little was known about menstruation than that it was described in a way that created, through an extraordinary leap of the synecdochic imagination, a cellular correlative to the socially distinguishing characteristics of women. His-tology mirrored with uncanny clarity what it meant to be female.[59]

Today, the uterus is described as passing through two stages, rather color-lessly designated "secretory" and "proliferative," during each menstrual cycle. In the nineteenth and early twentieth centuries it was said to proceed through a series of at least four and as many as eight stages. Its "normal" stage was con-strued as "quiescence," followed by "constructive" and "destructive" stages and a stage of "repair." Menstruation, as one might surmise, was defined as occurring at the destructive stage, when the uterus gave up its lining. As Heape puts it, in an account redolent of war reportage, the uterus during the formation of the menstrual clot is subject to "a severe, devastating, periodic action." The entire ephithelium is torn away at each period, leaving behind a ragged wreck of tissue, torn glands, ruptured vessels, jagged edges of stroma, and masses of blood corpuscles, which it would seem hardly possible to heal satisfactorily without the aid of surgical treatment.

Mercifully, this is followed by the recuperative stage and a return to normalcy. Little wonder that Havelock Ellis, steeped in this rhetoric, would conclude that women live on something of a biological roller coaster. They are, "as it were, periodically wounded in the most sensitive spot in their organism and subjected to a monthly loss of blood." The cells of the uterus are in constant, dramatic flux and subject to soul-wrenching trauma. Ellis concludes, after ten pages of still more data on the physiological and psychological periodicity in women, that the establishment

of these facts of morbid psychology, are very significant; they emphasize the fact that even in the healthiest woman a worm however harmless and unperceived, gnaws periodically at the roots of life.[60]

A gnawing worm is by no means the only metaphor of pain and disease employed to interpret uterine or ovarian histology. The bursting of the follicle is likened by Rudolph Virchow, the father of modern pathology, to teething, "accompanied with the liveliest disturbance of nutrition and nerve force." For the historian Michelet, woman is a creature "wounded each month," who suffers almost constantly from the trauma of ovulation, which in turn is at the center, as Thérèse Moreau has shown, of a physiological and psychological phantasmagoria dominating her life. Less imaginatively, a French encyclopedia likens follicular rupture to "what happens at the rupture of an acute abscess." The German physiologist E. F. W. Pfluger likens menstruation to surgical debridement, the creation of a clean surface in a wound, or alternatively, to the notch used in grafting a branch onto a tree, to the "innoculationschnitt." Imperatives of culture or the unconscious, not positive science, informed the interpretations of the female body more or less explicitly in these accounts.[61]

While all of the evidence presented so far is by men and produced in a more or less antifeminist context, image making, the construction of the body through science, occurs in feminist writers as well. Mary Putnam Jacobi's *The Question of Rest for Women During Menstruation* (1886), for example, is a sustained counter-attack against the view that "the peculiar changes supposed to take place in the Graafian vesicles at each period . . . involve a peculiar expenditure of nervous force, which was so much dead loss to the individual life of the woman." Women were therefore unfit for higher education, a variety of jobs, and other activities that demand large expenditures of the mental and physical energy that was thought to be in such short supply. Since the "nervous force" was commonly associated in higher animals and in women with sexual arousal, Jacobi's task becomes one of severing the sexual from the reproductive life of women, of breaking the ties between the two postulated in the ovarian theory of Bischoff, Pouchet, Adam Raciborski, and others.[62]

Much of her book is taken up with a compilation of the real or supposed empirical failings of this view. Neither menstruation nor pregnancy, she argues for example, are tied to the time of ovulation; indeed as several hundred cases of vicarious menstruation in women suggest, menstruation itself is only statistically, not in any more fundamental way, bound to ovulation and thus to reproduction. The amount of blood that flows to the uterus even in women who feel particular pelvic heaviness is but a tiny proportion of the body's blood and far less than the proportion transferred to the stomach and intestines during the obviously normal daily processes of digestion. There is no evidence, Jacobi continues, that the uterus, ovaries, or their appendages become turgid during the menstrual period, and thus the effort to link a sort of histological tension of the reproductive organs to sexual tension, to the excitement of heat, must come to naught. But though many of her criticisms are well taken, she neither offers a more compelling new theory of the physiology of ovulation nor gives a clearer picture of cellular changes in the uterine mucosa during the menstrual cycle than do those she is arguing against.[63]

Jacobi does, however, offer a new metaphor: "All the processes concerned in menstruation converge, not toward the sexual sphere, but the *nutritive*, or one department of it—the reproductive." The acceleration of blood flow to the uterus "in obedience to a *nutritive* demand" is precisely analogous to the "afflux of blood to the muscular layer of the stomach and intestines after a meal." Jacobi, like her opponents, tended to reduce woman's nature to woman's reproductive biology. But for her, the essence of female sexual difference lay not in periodically recurring nervous excitement nor in episodes of engorgement, rupture, and release of tension but rather in the quiet processes of nutrition. Far from being periodical, ovulation in Jacobi's account is essentially random: "The successive growth of the Graafian vesicles strictly resembles the successive growth of buds on a bough." Buds, slowly opening into delicate cherry or apple blossoms and, if fertilized, into fruit, are a far cry from the wrenching and sexually intense swellings of the ovary imagined by the opposing theory.[64]

Indeed, Jacobi's woman is in many respects the inverse of that of Pouchet, Raciborski, or Bischoff. For these men the theory of spontaneous ovulation demanded a woman shackled to her body, woman as nature, as physical being, even if the tamed quality of her modern European avatar spoke eloquently of the power of civilization. For Jacobi, on the other hand, spontaneous ovulation implied just the opposite. Biology provides the basis for a radical split between woman's mind and body, between sexuality and reproduction. The female body carries on its reproductive functions with no mental involvement; conversely, the mind can remain placidly above the body, free from its constraints. Jacobi's first effort at a metaphorical construction of this position uses fish whose ova are extruded without "sexual congress, and in a manner analogous to the process of defecation and micturation." In higher animals sexual congress is necessary for conception, but ovulation remains spontaneous and independent of excitement. From this, it follows, according to Jacobi, that *the superior contribution of the nutritive element of reproduction made by the female is balanced by an inferior dependence upon the animal or sexual element: in other words, she is sexually inferior.*[65]

Of course, Jacobi cannot deny that in lower animals female sexual instinct is tied exclusively to reproduction and that a ruptured follicle or follicles are invariably found during the rut. She nevertheless maintains that there is no proof of anything but a coincidental relationship between the state of the ovaries and the congested state of the external and internal genitalia that seems to signal sexual readiness. But in women, she adamantly maintains, "the sexual instinct and reproductive capacity remain distinct; there is no longer any necessary association between sexual impulse, menstruation, and the dehiscence of ova." Indeed, her entire research program is devoted to showing that the menstrual cycle may be read as the ebb and flow of female nutritive rather than sexual activity, that its metabolic contours are precisely analogous to those of nutrition and growth. And this brings one back to the metaphor of the ovary as fruit blossom. The woman buds as surely and as incessantly as the "plant, continually generating not only the reproductive cell, but the nutritive material without which this would be useless." But how, given that women generally eat less than men, do they obtain a nutritive surplus? Because "it is the possibility of making this reserve which constitutes the *essential peculiarity* of the female sex."[66]

The point here is not to belittle Jacobi's scientific work but rather to emphasize the power of cultural imperatives, of metaphor, in the production and interpretation of the rather limited body of data available to reproductive biology during the late nineteenth century. At issue is not whether Jacobi was right in pointing out the lack of coincidence between ovulation and menstruation in women and wrong in concluding that there is therefore no systematic connection between the two. Rather, both she and her opponents emphasized some findings and rejected others on largely extrascientific considerations. In the absence of an accepted research paradigm, their criteria were largely ideological—seeing woman either as civilized animal or as mind presiding over a passive, nutritive body.

But perhaps even the accumulation of fact, even the coherent and powerful modern paradigm of reproductive physiology in contemporary medical texts, offers but slight restraint on the poetics of sexual difference. Indeed, the subject itself seems to inflame the imagination. Thus, when W. F. Ganong's 1977 *Review of Medical Physiology*, a standard reference work for physicians and medical students, allows itself one moment of fancy it is on the subject of women and the menstrual cycle. Amidst a review of reproductive hormones, of the process of ovulation and menstruation described in the cold language of science, one is quite unexpectedly hit by a rhetorical bombshell, the only lyrical moment linking the reductionism of modern biological science to the experiences of humanity in 599 pages of compact, emotionally subdued prose:

Thus, to quote an old saying, "Menstruation is the uterus crying for lack of a baby."

Cultural concerns have free license here, however embedded they may be in the language of science. As in nineteenth-century texts, synecdochic leaps of the imagination seem to view woman as the uterus, which in turn is endowed, through the by now familiar turn of the pathetic fallacy, with feelings, with the capacity to cry. The body remains an arena for the construction of gender even though modern research paradigms do, of course, isolate the experimental and interpretive work of reproductive biology from extrascientific pressures far more than was possible in the essentially preparadigmatic research of the nineteenth century.[67]

Scientific advances, I have argued, did not destroy the hierarchical model that construed the female body as a lesser, turned-inward version of the male, nor did it banish female orgasm to the physiological periphery. Rather, the political, economic, and cultural transformations of the eighteenth century created the context in which the articulation of radical differences between the sexes became culturally imperative. In a world in which science was increasingly viewed as providing insight into the fundamental truths of creation, in which nature as manifested in the unassailable reality of bones and organs was taken to be the only foundation of the moral order, a biology of incommensurability became the means by which such differences could be authoritatively represented. New claims and counterclaims regarding the public and private roles of women were thus contested through questions about the nature of their bodies as distinguished from those of men. In these new discursive wars feminists as well as antifeminists sacrificed the idea of women as inherently passionate; sexual pleasure as a sign in the flesh of reproductive capacity fell victim to political exigencies.

Notes

1. Condorcet, "On the Admission of Women to the Rights of Citizenship" (1791), in *Selected Writings,* ed. Keith Michael Baker (Indianapolis, 1976), 98.
2. Ibid., 98; see, for example, Sade's *Philosophy in the Bedroom,* trans. Richard Seaver and Austryn Wainhouse (New York, 1965), 206 and passim.
3. Wisdom of Solomon 7.2 and Philo *Legum allegoriae* 2.7, cited in Peter Brown, "Sexuality and Society in the Fifth Century A.D.: Augustine and Julian of Eclanum," in *Tria corda: Scritti in onore di Arnaldo Momigliano,* ed. E. Gabba (Como, 1983), 56; Mrs. Jane Sharp, *The Midwives Book* (1671), 43–44.
4. "There is a *jouissance* proper to her, to this 'her' which does not exist and which signifies nothing"; Jacques Lacan, "God and the *Jouissance* of T̶h̶e̶ Woman," in *Feminine Sexuality,* ed. Juliet Mitchell and Jacqueline Rose (New York, 1982), 145.

5. Nemesius of Emesa, *On the Nature of Man* (Philadelphia, 1955), 369; Galen *De semine* 2.1, in *Opera omnia*, ed. C. G. Kuhn, 20 vols. (1821–33), 4:596.

6. Regnier de Graaf, *A New Treatise Concerning the Generative Organs of Women*, translation of *De mulierum organis generationi inservientibus tractatus novus* (1672) by H. D. Jocelyn and B. P. Setchell, *Journal of Reproduction and Fertility*, suppl. no. 17 (1972), 131–35; Pierre Roussel, *Système physique et moral de la femme* (1775; Paris, 1813), 79–80. On Roussel who, through Pierre-Jean-Georges Cabinis, was to influence significantly the discourse on sexual politics during the French Revolution, see Paul Hoffmann, *La Femme dans la pensée des Lumières* (Paris, n.d.), 142–52; Bartholomew Parr, ed., *The London Medical Dictionary*, vol. 2 (Philadelphia, 1819), 88–89; *Aristotle's Masterpiece* (1803; reprint ed., New York, 1974), 3.

7. Jacques Moreau de la Sarthe, *Histoire naturelle de la femme*, vol. 1 (Paris, 1803), 15, which sounds the theme of the entire volume.

8. George W. Corner, "The Events of the Primate Ovarian Cycle," *British Medical Journal*, no. 4781 (23 August 1952): 403. On older views of the fertile period of the menstrual cycle see, for example, the Roman Catholic authority Carl Capellmann, *Fakultativ Sterilität ohne Verletzung der Sittengesetze* (Aachen, 1882), who taught that days fourteen to twenty-five are "safe" while fertility rises just before the menses and continues until day fourteen. Marie Stopes, in her immensely popular manuals *Married Love* (10th ed., London, 1922), 191, and *Contraception* (London, 1924), 85, advised that maximum fertility occurs just after cessation of the menses. For the popularity of these views well into the 1930s see Carl G. Hartman, *Time of Ovulation in Women* (Baltimore, 1936), 149 and passim.

9. For an early and clearly presented table of embryological homologies, see Rudolf Wagner, ed., *Handwörterbuch der Physiologie*, vol. 4 (Braunschweig, 1853), s.v. "Zeugung," 763. Regarding skeletons, see Londa Schiebinger, "Skeletons in the Closet: The First Illustrations of the Female Skeleton in Eighteenth-Century Anatomy," in the current issue. 1759 is an alternative date for the first representation of the female skeleton; see ibid.

10. Mary Douglas, *Natural Symbols* (New York, 1982), 70.

11. Plato *Timaeus* 91A–C, Loeb Classical Library, ed. R. G. Bury (Cambridge, Mass., 1929), 248–50; Galen, *On the Usefulness of the Parts of the Body*, ed. and trans. Margaret May, 2 vols. (Ithaca, N.Y., 1968), 2:640.

12. Ibid., 1:382 and n. 78; 2:628, 630.   13. Ibid., 2:628–29.

14. Ibid., 2:629.   15. Ibid., 2:630–31 and, more generally, 636–38.

16. Ibid., 2:640–43. The allusion to Democritus is probably the following: "Coition is a slight attack of apoplexy: man gushes forth from man, and is separated by being torn apart with a kind of blow"; 68B.22, in *Die Fragmente der Vorsokratiker*, ed. Diels-Kranz (Berlin, 1956). Galen is clearly in sympathy here with the Hippocratic treatise *The Seed*, in *Hippocratic Writings*, ed. G. E. R. Lloyd (London, 1978), 317–21. Aristotle argues that the emission of semen in men is due "to the penis being heated by its movement"; in addition, "maturation" or a final concoction of the semen takes place through the heating of copulation. See Aristotle *Generation of Animals* 717b24 and 717a5, in *The Complete Works of Aristotle*, ed. Jonathan Barnes, 2 vols. (Princeton, N.J., 1984).

17. Hippocrates, *The Seed*, 319; for Galen on wet dreams in women see *De semine* 2.1, in *Opera omnia*, 4:599. There is no space in this paper to argue for the basic compatibility of Aristotle's views with what became the dominant Galenic model. Despite Aristotle's denial of female semen, he nevertheless construed the catamenia, i.e., the female

contribution to generation, as a less highly concocted version of semen and conversely argued that men who had copulated too frequently, and thus had spent their vital heat, ejaculated blood, of which semen was a higher concoction; both blood and semen are interpreted as residues of the concoction of food. Aristotle's hierarchy of fluids based on vital heat is thus congruent with Galen's, and their differences concern the efficacy of the female contribution; *Generation of Animals* 726b1–15, 35; 737a27–29. Though Aristotle argues that neither female orgasm nor the emissions of women in dreams are proof of female semination, he nevertheless holds that female pleasure normally is a sign of heat sufficient for generation; women can conceive without pleasure if "the part chance to be in heat and the uterus to have descended." These are not normal circumstances; ibid., 739a20–35. For an extraordinarily lucid account of these matters see Michael Boylan, "The Galenic and Hippocratic Challenges to Aristotle's Conception Theory," *Journal of the History of Biology* 17, no. 1 (Spring 1984): 83–112.

18. Galen, *On the Usefulness of Parts,* 2:640–44; Avicenna, *Libri in re medica omnes . . . id est, libri canonis* (Venice, 1564), 3.21.1.25.
19. This is all quite commonplace in classical medicine. See, for examples, Aristotle *Generation of Animals* 727a3–15, 776a15–33 on milk and *History of Animals* 581b30–583b2 on semen and menstrual blood as plethora and on menstrual blood finding its way to the breasts and becoming milk; Aetius of Amida, *Tetrabiblion,* trans. James V. Ricci (Philadelphia, 1950); Hippocrates *Aphorisms* 32 and 33 and *Epidemics* 1.16, in *The Medical Works of Hippocrates,* ed. and trans. John Chadwick and W. N. Mann (Oxford, 1950). Renaissance texts, both popular and learned, repeated much of this lore; see, for example, Patricia Crawford, "Attitudes to Menstruation in Seventeenth-Century England," *Past and Present,* no. 91 (1981): 48–73.
20. The earliest version of the hemorrhoidal bleeding/menstruation equivalency I have encountered is in Aristotle *Generation of Animals* 27a10, where he notes that women in whom the menstrual discharge is normal are not troubled with hemorrhoidal bleeding or nosebleeds. See J. B. [John Bulwer], *Anthropometamorphosis: Man Transformed of the Artificial Changling* (1653), 390; and Albrecht von Haller, *Physiology: Being a Course of Lectures,* vol. 2 (1754), paragraph 816, p. 293, my emphasis. For further clinical notes on the connection between menstrual and other bleeding see John Locke, *Physician and Philosopher . . . with an Edition of the Medical Notes,* Wellcombe History of Medicine Library, n.s., vol. 2 (London, 1963), 106, 200. Herman Boerhaave, *Academical Lectures on the Theory of Physic* (1757), paragraph 665, p. 114, cites the case of "a certain merchant here at Leyden, a Man of Probity, who discharges a larger Quantity of Blood every Month by the haemorrhoidal arteries than is discharged from the Uterus of the most healthy woman"; John Keegan, *The Face of Battle* (London, 1976), 337.
21. Avicenna *Canon* 3.20.1.44; Trotulla of Salerno, *The Diseases of Women,* ed. Elizabeth Mason-Huhl (Los Angeles, 1940), 16–19; on witchcraft and barrenness see Nicholas Fontanus,*The Woman's Doctour* (1652), 128–37, for a discussion of barrenness generally and the signs of too much or too little heat; Jacob Rueff, *The Expert Midwife* (1637), book 6, p. 16 (on witchcraft) and p. 55 (quote). Leonard Sowerby, *The Ladies Dispensatory* (1652), 139–40, gives a list of materials to "cause standing of the yard"; see Lazarus Riverius, *The Practice of Physick* (1672), 503 (on lack of lust being sign of cold and unreceptive womb) and 502–9 (generally on the diagnosis and cure of barrenness).
22. John Sadler, *The Sicke Woman's Private Looking Glass* (1636), 118 and 110–18 more

generally; Pierre Dionis, *A General Treatise of Midwifery* (1727, from a late seventeenth-century French text), 57 (on the importance of the imagination); Ambroise Pare, "Of the Generation of Man," in *The Workes of the Famous Chirurgion* . . . , trans. Thomas Johnson (1634), book 24, pp. 889–90; Robert Barrett, *A Companion for Midwives* (1699), 62.

23. Pare, "Of the Generation of Man," 889; Trotulla, *Diseases of Women*, 16; William Sermon, *The Ladies Companion or the English Midwife* (1671), 13; Sadler, *Looking Glass*, 118ff.

24. Euchar Roesslin, *The Byrth of Mankynde* (1545), fol. 28. This text, or thinly disguised versions of it, was widely reprinted in large numbers of vernacular and Latin editions; the trope of a succession of children as a merciful God's comfort for the sting of death was often attributed to St. John Chrysostom, presumably to Homily XVIII on Gen. 4.1, "And Adam Knew Eve as His Wife."

25. J. B. de C. M. Saunders and Charles D. O'Malley, *The Anatomical Drawings of Andreas Vesalius* (New York, 1982), point out that figs. 2 and 3 were drawn to illustrate the Galenic homologies while the penis-like vagina in fig. 4 is simply an artifact of having to remove the organs in a great hurry. A useful table of the homologies Vesalius sought to illustrate are given in L. R. Lind, ed., *The Epitome of Andreas Vesalius* (New York, 1949), 87. These representations became the standards for more than a century in both popular and learned tracts; see for example Alexander Read, *A Description of the Body of Man* (1634), 128, for an English version; and Fritz Weindler, *Geschichte der gynäkologische-anatomischen Abbildung* (Dresden, 1908).

26. Sir Thomas Browne, *Pseudodoxia Epidemica or Enquiries into Very Many Received Tenents and Commonly Presumed Truths*, vol. 2 of *The Works of Sir Thomas Browne*, ed. Geoffrey Keynes (London, 1928), book 3, chap. 17, pp. 212–13, 216; Browne denies the vulgar belief in the annual alteration of sex in hares; Ambroise Pare, *On Monsters and Marvels*, ed. and trans. by Janis L. Pallister (Chicago, 1982), 32; *Montaigne's Travel Journal* (San Francisco, 1983), 6.

27. Pare, *On Monsters*, 32–33; Caspar Bauhin, *Theatrum Anatomicum* (Basel, 1605), as cited in William Harvey, *Lectures on the Whole Anatomy* (1616), ed. and trans. C. D. O'Malley, F. N. L. Poynter, and K. F. Russell (Berkeley, 1961), 132 and 467n.

28. On the discovery of the clitoris see Renaldo Colombo, *De re anatomica* (1572), book 2, chap. 16, pp. 447–48; for synonyms see Joseph Hyrtl, *Onomatologia anatomica* (Vienna, 1880), s.v. "clitoris"; Sharp, *Midwives Book*, 44–45; John Pechey, *Complete Midwives Practice* (London, 1698), 49.

29. Thomas Gibson, *The Anatomy of Humane Bodies Epitomized* (4th ed., 1694), 99; Marie Bonaparte, *Female Sexuality* (New York, 1953), 3, 113–15; for more recent psychoanalytic thought on this subject see *Journal of the American Psychoanalytic Institute* 14 (1966): 28–128 and 16 (1968): 405–612; Nicholas Culpepper, *A Dictionary for Midwives; or, A Guide for Women* (1675), part 1, p. 22. The "spermatical vessels," or as Philip Moore, *The Hope of Health* (1565), called them, the "handmaidens to the stones," were thought to carry the excitation from the external organs, i.e., the penis and clitoris/labia, to the male and female testes respectively.

30. Helkiah Crooke, *A Description of the Body of Man* (1615), 250; Thomas Vicary's work is also known as *The Englishman's Treasure* (1585), 53.

31. Crooke, *Description*, 250; Jacques Duval, *Des Hermaphrodites, accouchemens des femmes* . . . (1612), 375, cited in Stephen Greenblatt, "Fiction and Friction," an unpublished paper he has generously let me read.

32. Havelock Ellis, *Studies in the Psychology of Sex*, vol. 3 (Philadelphia, 1923), 194; the phenomenon Ellis observes is, I suggest, of eighteenth-century origins.

33. Cited in V. C. Medvei, *A History of Endocrinology* (Boston, 1982), 357; Haller, *Physiology*, paragraphs 823–26, pp. 301–3. Haller, at the time he wrote these passages, was an ovist; that is, he believed that the egg contained the new life and that the sperm merely activated its development. But the same sorts of accounts were also written by spermaticists.

34. See for examples Jane Abray, "Feminism in the French Revolution," *American Historical Review* 80, no. 1 (February 1975): 43–62; Susanna Barrows, *Distorting Mirrors* (New Haven, 1981), chap. 2; Susan Sleeth Mosedale, "Science Corrupted: Victorian Biologists Consider 'The Woman Question,'" *Journal of the History of Biology* 11, no. 1 (Spring 1978): 1–55; Elizabeth Fee, "Nineteenth-Century Craniology: The Study of the Female Skull," *Bulletin of the History of Medicine* 53, no. 3 (Fall 1979): 915–33; Lorna Duffin, "Prisoners of Progress: Women and Evolution," in Sara Delamont and Lorna Duffin, eds., *Woman: Her Cultural and Physical World* (New York, 1978), 56–91. For two contemporary English articulations of these themes see Grant Allen, "Plain Words on the Woman Question," *Fortnightly Review*, n.s., 46 (October 1889): 274; and W. L. Distant, "On the Mental Differences Between the Sexes," *Journal of the Royal Anthropological Institute* 4 (1875): 78–87. Alexis de Tocqueville, *Democracy in America*, ed. Phillips Bradley, vol. 2 (New York, 1945), 223.

35. Jean Elshtain, *Public Man, Private Woman* (Princeton, N.J., 1981), chap. 3.

36. Jean-Jacques Rousseau, *A Discourse on Inequality*, trans. Maurice Cranston (Harmondsworth, 1984), 104.

37. Ibid., 102–3, 110; *Emile; or, On Education*, trans. Allan Bloom (New York, 1979), book 5, pp. 359 and 362n.

38. Ibid., 357–58, 362–63; my emphasis.

39. Denis Diderot, *Encyclopédie*, s.v. "jouissance"; I have taken the translation with some modifications from *The Encyclopedia*, ed. and trans. Stephen J. Gendzier (New York, 1967), 96; *jouissance* is translated here as "enjoyment," but it is perfectly clear that Diderot means by it sexual pleasure and passion.

40. John Millar, *Origin of the Distinctions of Ranks* (Basel, 1793), 14, 32, 86, 95–96.

41. Barbara Taylor, *Eve and the New Jerusalem: Socialism and Feminism in the Nineteenth Century* (New York, 1983), esp. chap. 2 and passim; Catherine Gallagher, "The Body Versus the Social Body in the Works of Thomas Malthus and Henry Mayhew," in this issue.

42. Anna Wheeler and William Thompson, *An Appeal of One-Half the Human Race, Women, Against the Pretensions of the Other Half, Men, to Retain Them in Political and Thence in Civil and Domestic Slavery* (London, 1825), 60–61, emphasis in text.

43. Ibid., 145 and part 2, question 2, generally.

44. Zillah Eisenstein, *The Radical Future of Liberal Feminism* (New York, 1981), chap. 5, pp. 89–112; Mary Wollstonecraft, *Thoughts on the Education of Daughters . . .* (1787), 82.

45. Ibid., *Female Reader* (1789), vii; Taylor, *Eve*, 47–48. I take the term *passionlessness* and an understanding of its political meaning in the early nineteenth century from Nancy Cott's pioneering article "Passionlessness: An Interpretation of Victorian Sexual Ideology, 1790–1850," *Signs* 4, no. 21 (1978): 219–36.

46. Sarah Ellis, *The Wives of England* (London, n.d.), 345; and *The Daughters of England, Their Position in Society, Character & Responsibilities* (London, 1842), 85. Mitzi Myers, "Reform or Ruin: A Revolution in Female Manners," *Studies in the Eighteenth Century* 11 (1982): 199–217, makes a persuasive case for considering writers as far apart

politically as the domestic ideologists and Mary Wollstonecraft as engaged in the same moral enterprise.

47. Aldous Huxley, *Literature and Science* (New York, 1963), 67; quoted in Peter Morton, *The Vital Science: Biology and the Literary Imagination, 1860–1900* (London, 1984), 212.

48. Karl Ernst von Baer, "On the Genesis of the Ovum of Mammals and of Man," trans. C. D. O'Malley, *Isis* 47 (1956): 117–53, esp. 119; John Haighton, "An Experimental Inquiry Concerning Animal Impregnation," reported by Maxwell Garthshore, *Philosophical Transactions of the Royal Society of London* 87, part 1 (1797): 159–96; and William Cruickshank, "Experiments in Which, on the Third Day After Impregnation, the Ova of Rabbits Were Found in the Fallopian Tubes . . . ," reported by Everard Home, ibid., 197–214, esp. 210–11; on the difficulties of discovering the mammalian ovum see A. W. Meyer, *The Rise of Embryology* (Stanford, Calif., 1939), chap. 8.

49. For references to some of the English and French clinical reports see William Baly, *Recent Advances in the Physiology of Motion, the Senses, Generation, and Development* (London, 1848), 46n.; Johann Friedrich Blumenbach, *The Elements of Physiology*, trans. John Elliotson (1828), 483–84; Johannes Muller, *Handbuch der Physiologie des Menschen*, vol. 2 (Coblenz, 1840), 644–45 and 643–49 generally on the release of the ovum.

50. Theodor L. W. Bischoff, *Beweis der von der Begattung unabhängigen periodischen Reifung und Loslösung der Eier der Säugethiere und des Menschen* (Giesen, 1844), 28–31; F. A. Pouchet, *Théorie positive de l'ovulation spontanée et de la fécondation des Mammifères et de l'espèce humaine* (Paris, 1847), 104–67 (for the evidence supporting this claim), 452; Jules Michelet, *L'Amour* (Paris, 1859), xv.

51. Bischoff, *Beweis*, 43; V. Hensen, in L. Hermann, *Handbuch der Physiologie*, vol. 6 (Leipzig, 1881), part 2, p. 69; Q. U. Newell, et al., "The Time of Ovulation in the Menstrual Cycle as Checked by Recovery of the Ova from the Fallopian Tubes," *American Journal of Obstetrics and Gynaecology* 19 (February 1930): 180–85; on the discovery of the reproductive hormones see A. S. Parkes, "The Rise of Reproductive Endocrinology, 1926–1940," *Journal of Endocrinology* 34 (1966): xx–xxii; Medvei, *History*, 396–411; and George W. Corner, "Our Knowledge of the Menstrual Cycle, 1910–1950," *The Lancet* 240, no. 6661 (28 April 1951): 919–23.

52. Achilles Chereau, *Memoires pour servir a l'étude des maladies des ovaires* (Paris, 1844), 91; Pouchet, *Théorie positive*, 227; Augustus Gardner, *The Causes and Curative Treatment of Sterility, with a Preliminary Statement of the Physiology of Generation* (New York, 1856), 17; *Lancet*, 28 January 1843, 644.

53. Duncan is cited as the epigraph of chapter 3, "The Changes That Take Place in the Non-Pregnant Uterus During the Oestrous Cycle," in F. H. A. Marshall, *The Physiology of Reproduction* (New York, 1910), 75.

54. Bischoff, *Beweis*, 40 and 40–48 generally on this point; Haller, *Physiology*, paragraph 812, p. 290 (p. 419 of the 1803 English edition); Blumenbach, *Elements*, 461–62; the oft-repeated allusion to Pliny is from his *Natural History* 7.15.63.

55. Robert Remak, "Über Menstruation und Brunst," *Neue Zeitschrift für Geburtskunde* 3 (1843): 175–233, esp. 176; Muller, *Handbuch*, 640.

56. Jean Borie, "Une Gynecologie passionée," in Jean-Paul Aron, ed., *Misérable et glorieuse: La Femme du XIX siècle* (Paris, 1980), 164ff.; Angus McLaren, "Doctor in the House: Medicine and Private Morality in France, 1800–1850," *Feminist Studies* 2, no. 3 (1974–75): 39–54; Pouchet, *Théorie positive*, introduction, 12–26 (on the use of "logic" in the absence of hard evidence see his discussion of the first law, esp. 15), 444–46 (summary of his programmatic statement).

57. G. F. Girdwood, "On the Theory of Menstruation," *Lancet*, 7 October 1844, 315–16.

58. Adam Raciborski, *Traité de la menstruation* (Paris, 1868), 46–47 and 43–47 generally; his *De la puberté et de l'âge critique chez la femme* (Paris, 1844) was often cited, along with Bischoff, as having established the existence of spontaneous ovulation in humans; *orgasme* was primarily a medical term in the nineteenth century meaning an increase of vital energy to a part often associated with turgescence (see *Littre*, s.v. "orgasme"); the first use I have found of the term *estrous* to refer to the reproductive cycle of humans as well as other mammals is in Walter Heape, "The 'Sexual Season' of Mammals and the Relation of the 'Proestrum' to Menstruation," *Quarterly Journal of the Microscopical Society*, 2nd ser., 44, no. 1 (November 1900): 1–70 and esp. 29–40.

59. Walter Heape, *Sex Antagonism* (London, 1913), 23; F. Hitschmann and L. Adler, "Der Bau der Uterusschleimhaut des geschlechtsreifen Weibes mit besonderer Berucksichtigung der Menstruation," *Monatsschrift für Geburtshulfe und Gynäkologie* 27, no. 1 (1908): 1–82, esp. 1–8, 48–59.

60. Walter Heape's account of the stages of menstruation is in his "The Menstruation of *Semnopithecus entellus*," *Philosophical Transactions of the Royal Society of London*, ser. B, 185, part 1 (1894): 411–66 plus plates, esp. 421–40; the quotation is from Marshall's summary *Physiology*, 92; Havelock Ellis, *Man and Woman: A Study of Human Secondary Sexual Characteristics* (London, 1904), 284, 293.

61. Rudolph Virchow, *Der puerperale Zustand: Das Weib und die Zelle* (1848), 751, as cited in Mary Jacobi, *The Question of Rest for Women During Menstruation* (New York, 1886), 110. According to Michelet (*L'Amour*, 393), the ovary was of course not the only source of woman's fundamental sickness: "Ce siècle sera nommé celui des maladies de la matrice," he argues, having identified the fourteenth century as that of the plague and the sixteenth as that of syphilis (iv). See Thérèse Moreau, *Le Sang de l'histoire* (1982); A. Charpentier, *Cyclopedia of Obstetrics and Gynaecology*, trans. Egbert H. Grandin (New York, 1887), part 2, p. 84; for Pfluger see Hans H. Simmer, "Pfluger's Nerve Reflex Theory of Menstruation: The Product of Analogy, Teleology and Neurophysiology," *Clio Medica* 12, no. 1 (1977): 57–90, esp. 59.

62. Jacobi, *Question of Rest*, 1–25, 81, and 223–32 passim.

63. Ibid., section 3, pp. 64–115, is devoted to laying out and criticizing the so-called ovarian theory of menstruation.

64. Ibid., 98–100.   65. Ibid., 83, 165; emphasis is in the text.

66. Ibid., 99, 167–68.

67. W. F. Ganong, *Review of Medical Physiology*, 8th ed. (Los Altos, Calif., 1977), 332 and 330–44 passim.

Skeletons in the Closet: The First Illustrations of the Female Skeleton in Eighteenth-Century Anatomy

Introduction

IN 1796 THE GERMAN ANATOMIST Samuel Thomas von Soemmerring published in a separate folio what he claimed to be the first illustration of a female skeleton.[1] This was a remarkable claim since Andreas Vesalius and modern anatomists had drawn human skeletons from observation and dissection since the sixteenth century. Though Soemmerring's claim to originality was a bit exaggerated, he was, indeed, among the first illustrators of a distinctively female skeleton. But the importance of his illustration goes beyond the fact that it was one of the first. With his drawing of a female skeleton, Soemmerring became part of the eighteenth-century movement to define and redefine sex differences in every part of the human body. It was in the eighteenth century that the doctrine of humors, which had long identified women as having a unique physical and moral character, was overturned by modern medicine. Beginning in the 1750s, doctors in France and Germany called for a finer delineation of sex differences; discovering, describing, and defining sex differences in every bone, muscle, nerve, and vein of the human body became a research priority in anatomical science. It was as part of this broader search for sex differences that the drawings of the first female skeletons appeared in England, France, and Germany between 1730 and 1790.

What sparked interest in the female skeleton in the eighteenth century? Did portrayals of female bones follow the "clean cut" of scientific objectivity? Or was interest in female anatomy molded by broader social movements? Was there a connection between eighteenth-century movements for women's equality and attempts on the part of anatomists to discover a physiological basis for female "inequality"?

I want to argue here that it was in the context of the attempt to define the position of women in European society that the first representations of the female skeleton appeared in European science. The interests of the scientific community were not arbitrary: anatomists focused attention on those parts of the body that were to become politically significant. When the French anatomist Marie-

Geneviève-Charlotte Thiroux d'Arconville published drawings of the female skeleton in 1759, she portrayed the female skull as smaller than the male skull, and the female pelvis as larger than the male pelvis.[2] This was not, however, simply the product of the growth of realism in anatomy. The depiction of a smaller female skull was used to prove that women's intellectual capabilities were inferior to men's. This scientific measure of women's lesser "natural reason" was used to buttress arguments against women's participation in the public spheres of government and commerce, science and scholarship. The larger female pelvis was used in parallel fashion to prove that women were naturally destined for motherhood, the confined sphere of hearth and home.

"Nature" played a pivotal role in the rise of liberal political thought. In the seventeenth and eighteenth centuries, natural-law philosophers such as Locke and Kant sought to found social convention on a natural basis.[3] Appeals to "the natural reason and dignity of man" provided important philosophical underpinnings for arguments in favor of individual freedom and equality. Yet, when women asked for equality, they were denied it.

It is important to understand how the eighteenth-century denial of civil rights to women could be justified within the framework of liberal thought. To the mind of the natural-law theorist, an appeal to natural rights could be countered only by proof of natural inequalities.[4] In his *Lettres Persanes,* Montesquieu, for example, framed the crucial question: "Does natural law [*loi naturelle*] submit women to men?"[5] Nature and its law were considered above human politics. According to this view, there exists an order in nature that underlies the well-ordered *polis.*[6] If social inequalities were to be justified within the framework of liberal thought, scientific evidence would have to show that human nature is not uniform but differs according to age, race, and sex.

In the course of the eighteenth and nineteenth centuries, the study of the "nature" of woman became a priority of scientific research. The increasing tendency to look to science as an arbiter of social questions depended on the promise that hotly debated social issues—such as women's rights and abilities—could be resolved in the cool sanctuaries of science. When modern science first turned an "impartial" eye to the study of women, however, there emerged a paradox that still plagues women's relationship to science. The "nature" and capacities of women were vigorously investigated by a scientific community from which women (and the feminine) were almost entirely absent.[7] As a consequence, women had little opportunity to employ the methods of science in order to revise or refute the emerging claims about the nature of women. As science gained social prestige in the course of the nineteenth century, those who could not base their arguments on scientific evidence were put at a severe disadvantage in social debate. Thus emerged a paradox central to the history of modern science: women (and what women value) have been largely excluded from science, and the results of science often have been used to justify their continued exclusion.

FIGURES 1 and 2 (*opposite*). Andreas
Vesalius, male and female nudes,
in *The Epitome* (Basel, 1543).

44   LONDA SCHIEBINGER

I want to stress from the outset that it is not my purpose to explain away physical differences between men and women but to analyze social and political circumstances surrounding the eighteenth-century search for sex differences. This study of the first representations of the female skeleton is intended to serve as a case study of more general problems. Why does the search for sex differences become a priority of scientific research at particular times, and what political consequences have been drawn from the fact of difference? As we will see, the fact of difference was used in the eighteenth century to prescribe very different roles for men and women in the social hierarchy. In the course of the eighteenth century, some anatomists were even moved to believe that women held a lowly rank in the natural hierarchy; it became fashionable to find in women the qualities of children and "primitives." By locating woman's social worth in her physical nature, anatomists hoped to provide a sure and easy solution to the "woman" problem.

Sex Differences and the Rise of Modern Anatomy, 1600–1750

> L'esprit n'a point de sexe.
> —François Poullain de la Barre[8]

The identification of sex differences in the human body is not unique to modern times. In the ancient world, Hippocrates, Aristotle, and Galen drew a picture of the nature of woman that provided a thoroughgoing justification of women's inferior social status.[9] Aristotle argued that women are colder and weaker than men, and that women do not have sufficient heat to cook the blood and thus purify the soul. Galen, following the Hippocratic doctrine of the four humors, believed that women are cold and moist while men are warm and dry; men are active, women are indolent. The medical assumptions of these ancients were incorporated into medieval thinking with few revisions and dominated much of Western medical literature until well into the seventeenth century.[10]

The new science of anatomy that emerged in the sixteenth century had the potential to challenge ancient views of women's physical and moral nature. Paul Hoffmann and Ian Maclean have argued that there was a limited feminist movement in sixteenth- and seventeenth-century medicine.[11] In 1645, J. P. Lotichium, professor of medicine at the German University of Rinteln, reviewed this feminist literature and stressed that women are perfect in their physical creation and should be considered completely human.[12] In 1673, the French feminist Poullain de la Barre used explicitly medical arguments to buttress pleas for the social equality of women. Women, he wrote, have the same sense organs as men—their eyes see as clearly, their ears hear with the same degree of accuracy, their hands are as dexterous. And their heads, he continued, are the same as men's. "The

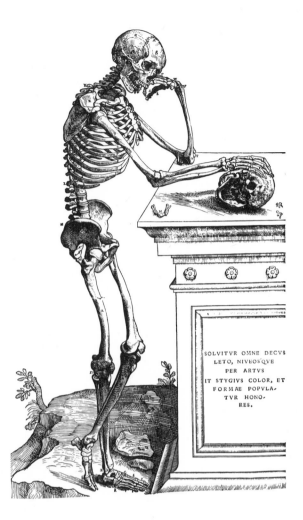

FIGURE 3. Vesalius, bones of the human body, drawn to same scale as figs. 1 and 2, in *The Epitome*.

SOLVITVR OMNE DECVS
LETO, NIVEOS'QVE
PER ARTVS
IT STYGIVS COLOR, ET
FORMAE POPVLA-
TVR HONO-
RES.

most exact anatomy has not discovered any difference in that part [the head] between men and women; the brain is the same in both, as are memory and imagination."[13] The English feminist Mary Astell defended the rational capabilities of women in a similar vein:

If there be any defect in women it cannot be in the Body, (if I may credit the Report of learned Physicians) for there is no difference in the Organ of those Parts, which have any relation to, or influence over the Minds.[14]

Though there were feminist stirrings in Renaissance and early modern medical circles, they were small. By and large, anatomists of the sixteenth and seventeenth centuries did not focus attention on the question of sex difference. As Hilda Smith has pointed out, those whom we today identify as leading figures in seventeenth-century English medicine—Thomas Willis, Thomas Sydenham, William Harvey—had very little to say about women or sex differences in the human body. The issue of sex differences was taken up only by the more marginal writers of gynecological treatises who continued to rely on the Galenic tradition.[15] Maclean has further pointed out that although Renaissance doctors saw themselves as attacking all ancient authority, they actually merely combined Galenism with enlightened views of women. The continued reliance on ancient authority made difficult any real change in attitudes toward women.[16] Anatomists of this period did not fully challenge the views of women contained in the Galenic corpus, nor did they formulate fundamentally new views of sex differences.

Andreas Vesalius, widely recognized as the founder of modern anatomy, typifies this meshing of old and new attitudes.[17] For Vesalius, sex differences were only skin deep. Vesalius did not believe that sex differences derived from the humors (as had the ancients); nor did he believe that sex differences penetrated the skeleton (as would the moderns). In the *Epitome* of his great work on the fabric of the human body, Vesalius drew a male and female nude where he pointed out differences in the curves and lines of the two bodies and the two sets of reproductive organs (figs. 1 and 2).[18] To accompany his male and female nudes, Vesalius drew a single skeleton that he labeled a "human" skeleton (fig. 3). By believing that one "human" skeleton gives shape to both the male and the female body, Vesalius did not sexualize the bones of the "human" body. Though he made clear in textual notes that the skeleton was drawn from a seventeen- or eighteen-year-old male, Vesalius did not give a sex to his skeleton.

In Vesalius' view, sex differences between male and female bodies are limited to differences in the outline of the body and the organs of reproduction. In his *Epitome*, Vesalius drew two manikins or paper dolls that were to be cut out by medical students and "dressed" with their organs; this was an exercise designed to teach medical students the position and relation of the various viscera. One manikin represented a female form and displayed the system of nerves; the other represented a male figure and showed the muscles. Vesalius presented both the male and female manikins in order to demonstrate the position and nature of the organs of generation. Apart from the reproductive organs, Vesalius considered all other organs interchangeable between the two figures. In his instructions for construction of the manikins Vesalius made this explicit: "The sheet [of organs to be attached to the male manikin] differs in no way from that containing the figures to be joined to the last page [the drawing of the female manikin] except for the organs of generation."[19]

Though Vesalius rejected the ancient view that sex differences pervade the body, he did accept ancient views on the inferior nature of women's reproductive organs. In his *De corporis humani fabrica,* Vesalius adopted Galen's view of female sex organs as analogous to men's but imperfect because they were inverted and internal.[20] Vesalius not only accepted Galen's view of women's reproductive organs, he also provided the best visual rendering of Galen's conception (see p. 10, fig. 4).

The relative indifference of early modern anatomists to the question of sex differences did not derive from an ignorance of the female body. A look at anatomical illustrations from the fourteenth through the seventeenth centuries shows that women were, in fact, dissected. The Montpellier Codex of 1363 includes an illustration showing the dissection of a female body.[21] A statute enacted in France in 1560 required midwives to attend the dissection of female bodies so that they would know enough about female anatomy to be able to testify in abortion cases.[22] The frontispiece of Vesalius' 1543 *De corporis humani fabrica* depicts a public dissection in a theater teeming with men, dogs, and one lone monkey; on the table, under the knife, is a woman.[23] Vesalius based his drawings of female organs of reproduction on dissections of at least nine female bodies. Vesalius did not procure these bodies without difficulties, however; at least one was stolen. Hearing that a woman who had been the mistress to a certain monk had died, Vesalius and his helpers snatched her body from the tomb.[24] This remained a common practice for quite some time: William Cheselden, an English physician, reported in 1713 that he procured female bodies for dissection from "executed bodies and . . . a common whore that died suddenly."[25]

The indifference of early modern anatomists to the question of sex differences did not, however, lead them to "desexualize" the bodies they studied. On the contrary, until the nineteenth century the sex of the bodies used for dissection was explicitly portrayed either by genitalia or breasts, or by a wisp of hair falling over the shoulder in the case of a woman or a prominent beard in the case of a man.[26] The Dutch anatomist Godfried Bidloo produced a set of plates in the late seventeenth century unique for their explicit portrayal of the sex of the body dissected. Bidloo's "true to life" drawings always portrayed the sex of the cadavers being dissected. Male and female bodies were used indiscriminately to illustrate various parts of the body. In William Cowper's 1697 publication of Bidloo's plates, a woman model appears in a series of plates describing the muscles in the upper half of the human body (fig. 4).[27]

Bidloo and Cowper, like Vesalius, focused on two major differences between men and women: external bodily form and reproductive organs. In 1697, Cowper reproduced the Bidloo drawings of the Apollo-Pithius and Medici Venus, in order to portray differences in symmetry and proportion between man and woman (figs. 5 and 6). Cowper found that

most remarkably the shoulders of the woman are narrower; the man having Two Length or Faces in the Breadth of his Shoulders, and one and a Half in his Hips; whereas Woman, on the contrary, has but one Face and a Half in her Shoulders, and Two in her Hips. Secondly, the Clavicule or Channel-bones, and Muscles in general do not appear in Women as in Men; whence it is, the out Line of the one, as Painters call it, differs very much from the other.[28]

These three Bidloo figures were drawn not from life but from classical statues; Bidloo claimed these figures exhibited "the most beautiful proportions of a man and woman as they were fixed by the ancients." Venus' distinctive parts (labeled A and B) are the breasts and genitalia. Cowper did not attribute differences in the male and female outline to any deep structural differences between men and women "either in their whole frame, or in the intimate Structure of their Parts." Rather, the differences in appearance between men and women emanate from "the great quantity of Fat placed under the skins of women."[29]

It is true of course that throughout the sixteenth and seventeenth centuries anatomists in the vanguard of science—Vesalius, Bidloo, Cowper—made passing remarks about differences in male and female bodies apart from differences in exterior form or sex organs. Cowper, for example, noted that the skin is softer in women and the thyroid gland is larger. Yet few attempts were made to delineate sex differences throughout the body. Drawings of skeletons, although most often done from male bodies, were thought to represent the bones of the human body.

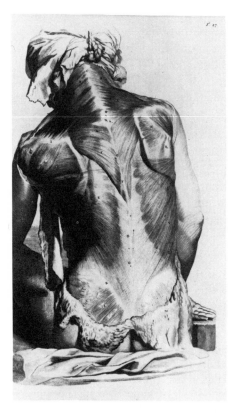

FIGURE 4 (*left*). William Cowper, muscles of the back, in *The Anatomy of Humane Bodies* (1697; London, 1737), plate 27.

FIGURES 5 and 6 (*opposite*). Cowper, male and female nudes, in Andrew Bell, *Anatomia Brittanica: A System of Anatomy* (Edinburgh, 1798), plates 42, 43.

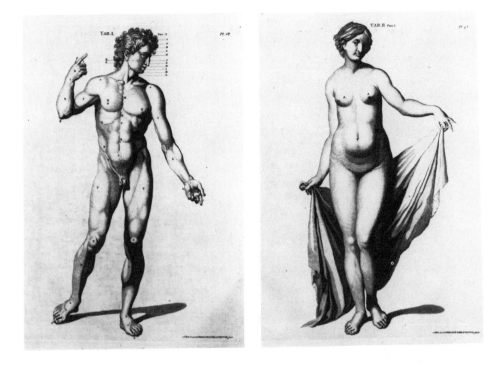

Sex Is More Than Skin Deep

Sexual differences are not restricted merely to the organs of reproduction but penetrate the entire organism. The entire life takes on a feminine or masculine character.
—J. J. Sachs[30]

A fundamental shift in the definition of sex differences emerged in the course of the eighteenth and early nineteenth century. Beginning in the 1750s, a body of literature appeared in France and Germany calling for a finer delineation of sex differences. In 1750, Edmond Thomas Moreau published a slim book in Paris entitled *A Medical Question: Whether Apart from Genitalia There Is a Difference Between the Sexes?*[31] In 1775, the French physician Pierre Roussel reproached his colleagues for considering woman similar to man except in sexual organs. "The essence of sex," he explained, "is not confined to a single organ but extends, through more or less perceptible nuances, into every part."[32] In 1788, German anatomist Jakob Ackermann stated that the present definition of sex differences was inadequate. The great physiologists, he complained, have neglected the description of the female body. "Indeed, sex differences," he emphasized, "have always been observed, but their description has been arbitrary."[33] In his two-hundred-page book on sex differences in bones, hair, mouths, eyes, voices, blood vessels, sweat, and brains, Ackermann called for a "more essential" descrip-

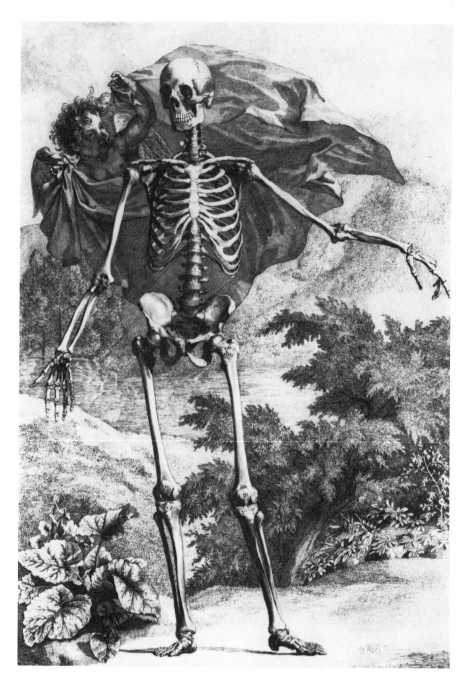

FIGURE 7. Bernhard Albinus, bones of the human body, in
Tabulae sceleti et musculorum corporis humani (Leyden,
1747), plate 1.

tion of sex differences and encouraged anatomists to research the most basic parts of the body to discover "the essential sex difference from which all others flow."[34]

These anatomists' interest in the female body was shaped, in part, by changes in the broader culture. Mercantilist interests in population growth played a role in the rise of the eighteenth-century ideal of motherhood.[35] The ideal of motherhood, in turn, profoundly changed medical views of the uterus.[36] Prior to the eighteenth century, the uterus was much maligned in natural philosophy. Plato thought it an animal with independent powers of movement.[37] Democritus cited the uterus as the cause of a thousand sicknesses. Baglio thought that women suffer each sickness twice, because of the uterus.[38] Galen and even (for a time) Vesalius reported that horns bud from the sides of the womb (see p. 8, fig. 3).[39] As the ideal of motherhood gained acceptance, however, anatomists rejected the view that women are "imperfect men" or monsters of nature.[40] Rather anatomists such as Jacques-Louis Moreau found women uniquely equipped to contribute to the propagation of the human race—even more so, in fact, than men.[41] Reviewing the history of women's medicine in 1829, Carl Ludwig Klose rejected the comparison of men's and women's sex organs that had, he maintained, occupied natural scientists from Aristotle to Albrecht von Haller. Klose argued that the uterus, woman's most important sex organ, has no analogue in man; hence the comparison with men's organs is worthless.[42]

The eighteenth-century ideal of motherhood encouraged doctors to view women as sexually perfect. Yet, if the uterus was to be viewed as perfect, did this mean that women were physiologically perfect beings? Certainly this hypothesis left the door open for those who, like Poullain de la Barre or Astell in the seventeenth century, argued that the physically perfect woman could be considered the social equal of man. Yet the debate did not end here. If the uterus was to be considered a unique and perfect organ in its own right, perhaps there were other sex differences that revealed a natural inferiority of women to men.

It was as part of this broader investigation of sex differences that drawings of the first female skeletons appeared in England, France, and Germany between 1730 and 1790. The skeleton, as the hardest part of the body, was thought to provide a "ground plan" upon which muscles, veins, and nerves were to be drawn. In 1749, anatomist Bernhard Siegfried Albinus wrote:

I must pitch upon something . . . as the base or foundation to build my figures upon. And this is the skeleton: which being part of the body, and lying below the muscles, the figures of it ought first to be taken off as certain and natural direction for the others.[43]

If sex differences could be found in the skeleton, then sexual identity would no longer be a matter of sex organs appended to a neutral human body, as Vesalius had thought, but would penetrate every muscle, vein, and organ attached to and molded by the skeleton.

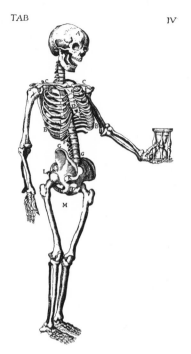

TAB   IV

FIGURE 8. Gaspard Bauhin,
"Sceleton of the Bones and
Gristles of a Woman," in
Theatrum anatomicum
(Frankfurt, 1605), table 4.

In 1734, Bernhard Albinus produced the definitive illustration of the human skeleton, which remained unsurpassed for at least three quarters of a century (fig. 7).[44] The work was laborious, taking three months to complete. Albinus drew the skeleton from three different perspectives—front, side, and back—"not free hand as is customary, but from actual measure . . . and by collecting data from one body after another, and making a composite according to rules so that actual truth will be displayed. . . . All [drawings] have been measured, brought down to scale . . . as architects do."[45] Having produced the most perfect possible drawing of the human skeleton (which Albinus made clear was drawn from a male body), Albinus lamented, "We lack a female skeleton."[46]

Albinus had good grounds for complaining that the study of female anatomy was inadequate before 1740. The standard studies of the human skeleton by Vesalius and Bidloo had been of the male. Only one "crude" illustration of a female skeleton published by Gaspard Bauhin in 1605 had appeared before the eighteenth century (fig. 8).[47] Within fifty years of Albinus' plea, however, basic anatomical descriptions of the female body had been established. One of the first drawings of a female skeleton appeared in England in 1733 (William Cheselden). Two appeared in France: one in 1753 (Pierre Tarin),[48] and another in 1759 (d'Arconville). One appeared in Germany in 1796 (Soemmerring). Even though

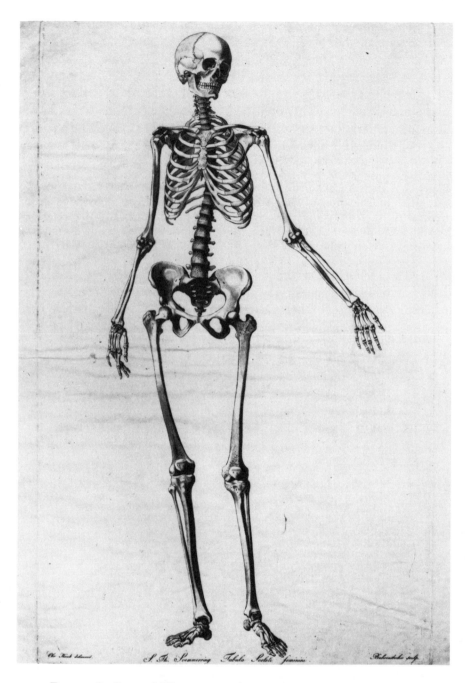

FIGURE 9. Samuel Thomas von Soemmerring, female skeleton, in *Tabula sceleti feminini* (Frankfurt, 1796).

each of these drawings purported to represent *the* female skeleton, they varied greatly from one another.

In 1726, Alexander Monro, professor of anatomy in Edinburgh, appended to his text on *The Anatomy of the Humane Bones* one of the earliest descriptions of the bones of the female. To "finish the Description of the Bones . . . [so] that no part of this Subject might be left untouched," he wrote, "it [is] necessary to subjoin the distinguishing Marks of the Male and Female Sceletons." Following a pattern well established since the time of Aristotle, Monro described the female as incomplete and deviant, using the male body as a standard of measure:

The Bones of Women are frequently incomplete, and always of a Make in some Parts of the Body different from those of the robust Male, which agree to the Description already delivered, unless where the proper Specialities of the Female were particularly remarked, which could not be done in all Places where they occur, without perplexing the Order of this Treatise: Therefore I chose rather to sum them up here by Way of *Appendix*.[49]

Monro used a functionalist argument to explain how three "causes" shaped the "specialities of the female Bones": A weak constitution makes "the bones of women . . . smaller in Proportion to their Length than those of Men, because the Force

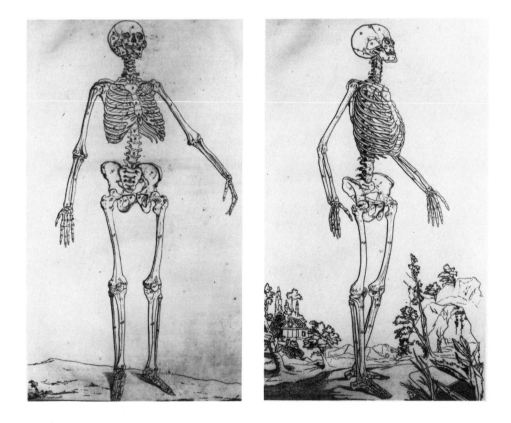

of their Muscles is not so great." A sedentary life makes "their *Clavicles* less crooked, because their Arms have been less forcibly pulled forewards, which indeed in our *European* Women, especially those of Distinction, is more hindred by their Garb." And a frame proper for their procreative functions makes women's pelvic area larger and stronger "to afford Lodging and Nourishment to their tender *Fetus's*." In particular, Monro found:

The Os sacrum is more turned outwards for enlarging the Pelvis. The Os Coccygis is more moveable, and less bended forwards, to facilitate the Birth. . . . The conjoined Surfaces of the Ossa pubis, and of the Offa innominata and sacrum are less, that with the straighter Os sacrum, a larger Passage might be left for the Exclusion of the Child in Birth.[50]

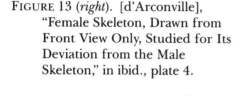

FIGURE 13 (*right*). [d'Arconville], "Female Skeleton, Drawn from Front View Only, Studied for Its Deviation from the Male Skeleton," in ibid., plate 4.

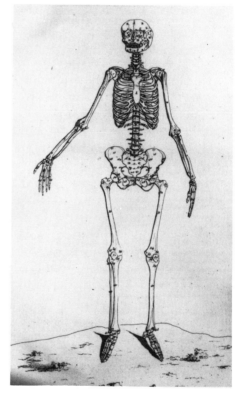

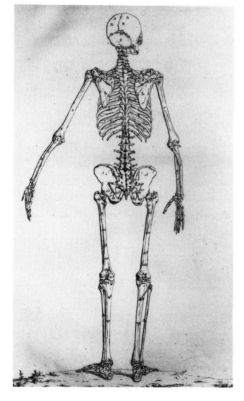

FIGURES 10, 11, and 12 (*opposite and left*). [Marie-Geneviève-Charlotte Thiroux d'Arconville], "Male Skeleton Studied from Front, Side, and Back," from Jean-J. Sue, *Traité d'ostéologie* (Paris, 1759), plates 1–3.

Monro provided one of the first descriptions of the bones of the female body in his four-page appendix, but he did not supplement his description with any illustrations.

One of the earliest drawings of a female skeleton was done by William Cheselden in 1733. This was a new interest of his in 1733; the 1713 edition of his *Anatomy* did not include an illustration of a female skeleton. Cheselden's matched set of male and female skeletons followed the Bidloo tradition of comparing idealized male and female figures drawn from art. His female skeleton is drawn in the "same proportion as the Venus of Medicis"; his male skeleton is drawn in the same proportion and attitude as the Belvedere Apollo.[51]

Text and image came together in the French rendering of a female skeleton that made its debut in 1759, capturing the imagination of medical doctors for more than half a century. The skeleton appears to be one of the very few drawn by a woman anatomist. Marie-Geneviève-Charlotte Thiroux d'Arconville, who studied anatomy at the Jardin du Roi, directed the drawing of illustrations from dissections for her French translation of Monro's *Anatomy*.[52] D'Arconville's plates were published under the protection of Jean-J. Sue, member of the Académie royale de Chirurgie. D'Arconville's name does not appear in the volume, and the illustrations were generally attributed to Sue.[53]

In 1796, the German anatomist Samuel Thomas von Soemmerring produced a rival female skeleton (fig. 9).[54] Although d'Arconville's (Sue's) work was known in Germany, Soemmerring's reviewers praised his female skeleton for "filling a gap which until now remained in all anatomy."[55] Directly answering Albinus' plea, Soemmerring spent years perfecting his portrayal of the female skeleton, and he considered his female to be of such "completeness and exactitude" that it made a perfect mate for the great Albinus male. As a model, he selected the skeleton of a twenty-year-old woman from Mayence who had borne a child.[56] Soemmerring also checked his drawing against the classical statues of the Venus di Medici and Venus of Dresden to achieve a universal representation of woman. Soemmerring intended that his skeleton represent not an individual woman but (as Ludwig Choulant put it) "the most beautiful norm as it was imagined to exist in life, with all the carefully observed minutiae of the differential sexual characters of the entire bony structure of woman."[57]

Although d'Arconville and Soemmerring applied the same criteria of exactitude in drawing the female skeleton from nature, the skeletons differ greatly from one another. D'Arconville/Sue depicted the skull (incorrectly) as smaller in proportion to the body than a man's, the hips as much broader than men's, and the ribs as extremely narrow and confining. In the commentary to her plate, d'Arconville described the chest of the female as narrower, the spine more curved, and the haunches and pelvis larger in women than in men.[58] Soemmerring, by contrast, portrayed his female skeleton with the ribs as smaller in proportion to

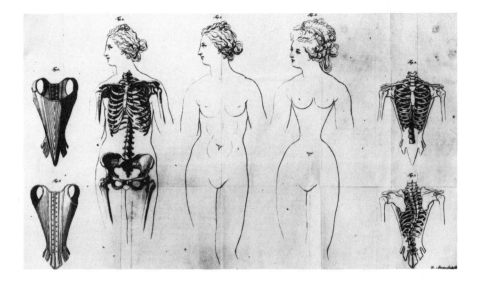

FIGURE 14. Soemmerring, "Effects of the Corset," in *Über die Wirkungen der Schnürbruste* (1785; Berlin, 1793).

the hips, but not remarkably so. Ackermann argued that women's hips appear larger than men's because their upper bodies are narrower, which by comparison makes the hips seem to protrude on both sides.

The d'Arconville skeleton is, in fact, remarkable for its proportions. The skull is drawn extremely small, the ribs extremely narrow, making the pelvis appear excessively large (figs. 10, 11, 12, and 13). D'Arconville apparently either intended to emphasize the cultural perception that narrow ribs are a mark of femininity, or she chose as the model for her drawing a woman who had worn a corset throughout her life (fig. 14).

Great debate erupted over the exact character of the female skeleton. Despite its exaggerations, the d'Arconville/Sue skeleton became the favored drawing in Britain.[59] Soemmerring's skeleton, by contrast, was attacked for its "inaccuracies." John Barclay, the Edinburgh physician, wrote, "although it be more graceful and elegant [than the Sue skeleton] and suggested by men of eminence in modeling, sculpture, and painting, it contributes nothing to the comparison [between male and female skeletons] which is intended."[60] Soemmerring was attacked, in particular, for showing the incorrect proportion of the ribs to the hips:

Women's rib cage is much smaller than that shown by Soemmerring, because it is well known that women's restricted life style requires that they breathe less vigorously. . . . The pelvis, and it is here alone that we perceive the strongly-marked and peculiar characters of the female skeleton, is shown by Soemmerring as improperly small.[61]

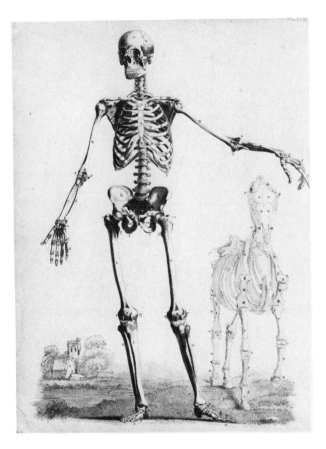

Anatomists concluded that Soemmerring was an artist, but no anatomist. The French doctor Jacques-Louis Moreau, however, found Soemmerring's portrayal of the female skeleton the most sublime and, in his two-volume work on the natural history of women, modeled his skeleton on Soemmerring's.[62]

What are we to make of this controversy? Did even the most exact illustrations of the female skeleton represent the female body accurately? The ideal of anatomical representation in the eighteenth century was exactitude. In his "Account of the Work," Albinus recounted how he prepared his male skeleton carefully with water and vinegar so that it would not lose moisture and change appearance over the three months of drawings. Though anatomists attempted to represent nature with precision, they also intended to represent the body in its most beautiful and universal form. Albinus quite consciously strived to capture the details not of a particular body but of a universal and ideal type. "I am of the opinion," he stated, "that what Nature, the arch workman . . . has fashioned must be sifted

FIGURES 15 (*opposite*) and 16 (*right*). John Barclay, "Male Skeleton Compared to the Horse" and "Female Skeleton Compared to the Ostrich," in *The Anatomy of the Bones of the Human Body* (Edinburgh, 1829), plate 1.

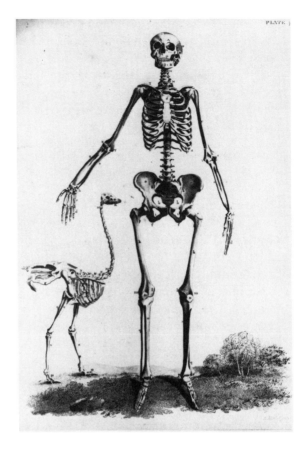

with care and judgment, and that from the endless variety of Nature the best elements must be selected."[63]

The supposedly "universal" representations of the human body in eighteenth-century anatomical illustrations were, in fact, laden with cultural values. The two sets of male and female skeletons shown in figures 7 and 9, 10–12 and 13 represent not merely the bones of the male and the female body; they also serve to produce and reproduce contemporary ideals of masculinity and femininity. For his illustrations, Albinus collected data from "one body after another." He then selected one "perfect" skeleton to serve as his model. Albinus also revealed the criteria by which he "sifted" nature in the drawing of his male skeleton:

As skeletons differ from one another, not only as to the age, sex, stature and perfection of the bones, but likewise in the marks of strength, beauty and make of the whole; I made choice of one that might discover signs both of strength and agility: the whole of it elegant, and at the same time not too delicate; so as neither to shew a juvenile or feminine roundness and slenderness, nor on the contrary an unpolished roughness and clumsiness.[64]

In his preface to Ackermann's book on sex differences, Joseph Wenzel discussed the difficulties anatomists have in choosing models for their work. He noted that a sharp physiological delineation between the sexes is impossible because the great variation among individual men and women produces continuity between the sexes. In fact, he wrote, one can find skulls, brains, and breast bones of the "feminine" type in men. Wenzel then defined a standard of femininity that he used as the basis of his own work:

I have always observed that the female body which is the most beautiful and womanly in all its parts, is one in which the pelvis is the largest in relation to the rest of the body.[65]

Soemmerring strived, like Albinus, for exactitude and universality in his illustrations. He made every possible effort to "approach nature as nearly as possible." Yet, he stated, the physiologists should always select the most perfect and most beautiful specimen for their models.[66] In identifying and selecting the "most beautiful specimen," Soemmerring intended to establish norms of beauty. According to Soemmerring, without having established a norm by means of frequent investigations and abstractions, one is not able to decide which cases deviate from the perfect norm.[67] Soemmerring chose the "ideal" model for his illustration of the female skeleton with great care:

Above all I was anxious to provide for myself the body of a woman that was suitable not only because of her youth and aptitude for procreation, but also because of the harmony of her limbs, beauty, and elegance, of the kind that the ancients used to ascribe to Venus.[68]

In their illustrations of the female body, anatomists followed the example of those painters who "draw a handsome face, and if there happens to be any blemish in it, they mend it in the picture."[69] Anatomists of the eighteenth century "mended" nature to fit emerging ideals of masculinity and femininity.

In the nineteenth century, the bones of the human body took on more overtones of masculinity and femininity. In 1829, John Barclay, the Edinburgh anatomist, brought together the finest illustrations from the European tradition for the sake of comparison. As the finest example of a male skeleton Barclay chose the Albinus drawing. Then looking to the animal kingdom, Barclay sought an animal skeleton, one that would highlight the distinctive features of the male skeleton. The animal he found as most appropriate for comparison to the male skeleton was the horse, remarkable for its marks of strength and agility (fig. 15). As the finest representation of the female skeleton Barclay chose the delicate d'Arconville/Sue rendition. This he compared to an animal noted for its large pelvis and long, narrow neck—the ostrich (fig. 16).

Man (White and European)
the Measure of All Things: Women
as Children and Primitives

In approaching puberty, woman seems to distance herself less than man from her primitive constitution. Delicate and tender, she always conserves something of the temperament characteristic of children.

—Pierre Roussel[70]

The flood of medical literature on sex differences did not subside in the course of the nineteenth century. As the century progressed, some anatomists came to believe that differences between male and female bodies were so vast that women's development had been arrested at a lower stage of evolution. Measurement of the distinguishing characteristics of the skeleton—the skull and pelvis—led some anatomists to conclude that white women ranked below European men in the scales of both ontogeny and phylogeny. Neither in the development of the species nor in the development of the individual were women thought to attain the full "human" maturity exemplified by the white male.[71] In terms of both physical and social development, these anatomists classified women with children and "primitive" peoples.

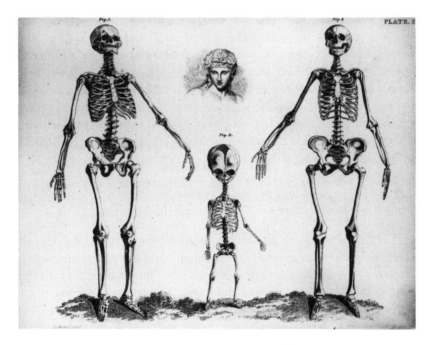

FIGURE 17. Barclay, "Skeleton Family," in ibid., plate 32.

In the course of the late eighteenth and nineteenth centuries, categories of sex and race increasingly came to define standards of social worth. At the same time, these standards came to reflect the structure of the scientific community. Those who possessed the tools of science took themselves as the standard of excellence. In the absence of women, the largely male scientific community studied women using male anatomy as the norm against which to measure female anatomy. In similar fashion, in the absence of blacks, the white scientific community studied blacks using the white male as the standard of excellence.[72] Excluded from the practice of science, women and blacks (not to mention other groups) had little opportunity to dispute the findings of scientists.

The illustrations of female skeletons by d'Arconville/Sue and Soemmerring sparked a protracted debate about the size of the female skull. The question of intelligence was becoming more and more important; "natural reason" was increasingly conceived to be a prerequisite for many political rights and social opportunities.[73] In this context, the skull became an important focus for providing an objective measure of intelligence. Hegel, following F. J. Gall, held that the brain "molded the skull—here pressing it out around, there widening or flattening it."[74] Craniologists analyzed the size and shape of the skulls of men and women, whites and blacks, hoping to answer the much debated question: whether or not the intellectual capacities of women and "primitive peoples" were equivalent to those of white men.

The assumption fueling the debate over skull size was that intelligence, like sexual identity, is innate and not dependent on educational opportunities. Soemmerring repudiated d'Arconville's findings and portrayed the female skull as larger in proportion to the body than the male skull. Soemmerring found that women's skulls are actually *heavier* than men's in the sense that the female skull occupies a greater proportion of total body weight (1/6 for women; 1/8 or 1/10 for men).[75] From this Ackermann (Soemmerring's student) concluded that women's brains are larger than men's:

Since women lead a sedentary life, they don't develop large bones, muscles, blood vessels and nerves as do men. Since brain size increases as muscle size decreases, it is no surprise that women are more adept in intellectual pursuits than men.[76]

The debate among anatomists about the correctness of d'Arconville/Sue's or Soemmerring's representation of women's skull size found one resolution in Barclay's work in the 1820s. Women's skulls were larger in relation to their body size than men's—but then, so were children's. According to Barclay, one needn't conclude that women's larger skulls are loaded with heavy and high-powered brains. Rather than a mark of intelligence, large skulls signal women's incomplete growth. In 1829 Barclay, using d'Arconville/Sue's plates, presented a skeleton family (fig. 17). Although anatomical drawings of children and fetuses had been published since the early eighteenth century, skeletons of man, woman, and child were brought together for the first time by Barclay "for sake of comparison." In his commentary, Barclay upbraided Soemmerring for drawing comparisons between only the male and female skeleton; Barclay introduced the child's skeleton "to shew that many of those characteristics, which he [Soemmerring] has described as peculiar to the female, are more obviously discernible in the fetal skeleton."[77] Barclay pointed out that along with equivalent skull sizes, both women and children have the fissure separating the frontal skull bone; both have smaller bones compared to men; the rib cage, jaw shape, and feet size of women are more similar to those of children than to men. Woman's one distinguishing characteristic, Barclay argued, is her pelvis:

It is there [in the pelvis] that we cease to trace the analogies between its [the female skeleton's] proportions and those of the foetus: or in other words, it is there that, in deviating from those characters which at one time were common to both [male and female], we regularly find it [the pelvis] deviating farther than that of the male—the pelvis of the foetus being always proportionally the smallest of the three, and that of the female proportionally the largest.

By mid-century, the image of the childlike woman had become common. In *Das Weib und das Kind* (1847) the German doctor E. W. Posner gave one of the clearest statements of the physical similarities between women and children:

Women's limbs are short and delicate ... and the shortness of the limbs determines the smaller size of the female body and proves the similarity of the female body with the child's body. ... As is true in the child, the woman has a larger and rounder abdomen in relation to her breast. ... The entire trunk, which in man forms a pyramid with the base turned upward, is reversed in woman with the point of the pyramid at the shoulders which are smaller and narrower, while the stomach is the broad base from which the even broader hips and strong thighs proceed. ... Women's heads also tend toward the childish type. The finer bone structure, the tender, less sharply developed facial features, the smaller nose, the larger childish roundness of the face clearly show this similarity. ... The nerves and blood vessels of women are also as delicate and fine as those of children ... and the skin with its layer of rich fat is childish.[78]

Posner accounted for these similarities between women's and children's bodies by arguing that since "the female sex ends its growth earlier than men before reaching full individual maturity [at age fourteen rather than eighteen] ... the woman retains her childish roundness." While the comparison of women to children is not in itself negative (children in the nineteenth century also represent innocence, freshness, and youth), Posner's explanation implied that women have failed to reach full human maturity. Like Charles Darwin, Posner assumed that there is one unified, natural hierarchy of physical, intellectual, and cultural development within which every category of human being has its place. Posner made it clear that the European male body type was the norm of maturity against which women, blacks, and children were to be measured.

It should be noted that the comparison of women with children was by no means new to the nineteenth century. By drawing parallels between the anatomy of women and children, anatomists restated in the language of modern science an ancient prejudice against women. The ancients—Zenocrates, Galen, and Hermagoras—commonly held that a woman can never be more than a child.[79] Galen thought that both women and children suffered from cold and moist humors that accounted for their lack of self-control. Aristotle grouped women, children, and slaves together in the three states of *consilium*.[80] In the biblical tradition the man was the head of the household, since God gave Adam dominion over women and children. The supposed evidence emerging in the early nineteenth century that women were physiologically linked to children served to translate these traditional prejudices into the language of modern science. The physical image of the childlike woman also reflected certain aspects of European custom. In the late eighteenth century, middle-class wives were on average ten years younger than their husbands;[81] it is not surprising that middle-class women should have appeared "childish" in comparison to their husbands.

I want to mention again that it has not been my purpose here to minimize physical differences between men and women but rather to analyze the social and political circumstances surrounding the search for sex differences. While identifiable differences between the sexes do exist, they have often been exaggerated. It is important to remember what Wenzel stressed in 1789, namely that "individual members of each sex differ significantly from one another; one can find male bodies with a feminine build, just as one can find female bodies with a masculine build."[82] Moreover, many physical differences among human beings are not absolute but relative to social conditions.[83] Eighteenth-century anatomists repeatedly pointed to the fact that women are shorter and smaller than men. Women's smallness, they thought, was dependent on bone size, which provided an absolute index of women's weakness and delicacy. As current studies show, however, the difference in average height between European men and women has decreased over the last century. Height is, in part, determined by nourishment. In many cultures, it is customary for the woman to eat what remains after the man has eaten, or to give the man the best portion.[84]

Even if we do away with the exaggerations that have plagued studies of sex differences in Western medicine, however, we cannot do away with the fact of difference. Yet it is unclear what difference difference makes. Why should a set of physical differences be used to underwrite a system of social inequality? Why has the argument that physical difference implies intellectual and moral difference been so persuasive to so many for so long?

"Social Inequality as Natural Law"

The laws of divine and natural order reveal the female sex to be incapable of cultivating knowledge, and this is especially true in the fields of natural sciences and medicine.

—Theodor L. W. von Bischoff[85]

Why did the comparative anatomy of men and women become a research project for the medical community in the late eighteenth century?[86] I want to argue here that it was the attempt to define the position of women in bourgeois European society at large and in science in particular that spawned the first representations of the female skeleton. One powerful assumption underlying much of nineteenth-century social theory was that physical evidence—nature—provided a point of certainty from which social theory could depart. A look at how the findings of anatomists were used will illuminate the role that the study of anatomical sex differences played in underwriting the increasing polarization of gender roles in European society.[87]

The growth of democratic tendencies brought about a reshuffling of the social order. In the eighteenth century it was not yet clear what women's role in the new social order was to be. Certainly, throughout the seventeenth and eighteenth centuries there was a struggle between those advocating full social equality for women and those advocating the continued subordination of women.[88] Some philosophers, such as Rousseau, hoped to lay a solid foundation for the theory of natural rights by disentangling the natural from the social in human nature. In his *Emile,* Rousseau appealed to a hypothetical state of nature, and to the nature of the human body as defined by comparative anatomy in his search for the natural relation between the sexes.[89]

Rousseau's pedagogical writings opened the flood gates of modern prescriptive literature on the proper character and education of the sexes.[90] Rousseau abhorred the public influence he saw in French women and the stirrings of feminism in the French Revolution. He took on proponents of women's equality by arguing that woman is not man's equal but his complement. Rousseau was instrumental in initiating the view that the inherent physical, moral, and intellectual differences of women suited them for roles in society vastly different from those of men.[91] To Rousseau's mind, it was the purpose of natural philosophy to read in the book of nature "everything which suits the constitution of her [woman's] species and her sex in order to fulfill her place in the physical and moral order."[92]

There were also those who opposed Rousseau's argument of women's different nature and argued instead for the social equality of women. Among French philosophes, Helvétius, d'Alembert, and Condorcet traced the inferior intellectual achievement of women to their inferior education.[93] This line of argument was also promoted by Mary Wollstonecraft in England, Olympe de Gouges in France, and Theodor von Hippel in Germany, to name a few.[94] It was in the eighteenth century that debates about women's character were framed by the modern opposition of "nurture" versus "nature." Those who found women's weakness a matter of "nurture" envisioned social and educational reform as the brightest path toward social equality of the sexes. Those who traced women's weakness to women's "nature" assumed that "whatever is, is right."

Many, however, were to apply the new findings of anatomy to the "woman" question. In French medical camps in particular, the physical became tied to the moral in such a way that medical arguments from "nature" increasingly penetrated social theory. The *Encyclopédie* article of 1765 on the "skeleton" devoted half its text to a comparison of the male and female skeleton. In great detail the differences are laid out between the male and female skull, spine, clavicle, sternum, coccyx, and pelvis. The article ends with one prescriptive phrase: "All of these facts prove that the destiny of women is to have children and to nourish them."[95]

In 1775, the medical doctor Pierre Roussel expanded upon this message. He claimed that differences in the male and female skeleton were of great importance. "Nature," he wrote, "has revealed through that special form given to the bones of woman that the differentiation of the sexes holds not only for a few superficial differences, but is the result perhaps of as many differences as there are organs in the human body."[96] Spirit or mind were among the organs Roussel listed. To Roussel's mind, moral and intellectual qualities were as innate and as enduring as the bones of the body. Roussel argued against "writers" who insisted that differences between men and women resulted from custom, education, or climate.[97] It was, he believed, rather the unerring findings of medicine that provided a certain ground for ethics. Philosophy, he wrote, cannot determine the moral powers of human beings without taking into consideration the influence of the bodily organization.[98]

In Germany, Soemmerring also believed that gender differences were to be traced to "nature," not to "nurture." In his book on the comparative anatomy of the "Negro" and European, Soemmerring reported his observations on the physical and moral character of woman:

A boy will always dominate a girl, without knowing that he dominates, and knowing even less that he dominates because of his solid, strong body. He will dominate even when he has received the same nourishment, love and clothing as a girl. I have had the rare opportunity of seeing definite proof of this fact. From his earliest youth, Prince D . . . G was raised alongside his sister. Their training in all moral and physical matters was equivalent in every way. And yet, differences of masculinity and femininity in physical and moral character were always conspicuous. This is a fact of experience.[99]

Johann Ziegenbien propagated Soemmerring's ideas in German schools. Reading to the parents of a girls' school, Ziegenbien opened his lecture on "Female

Nature, Character, and Education" with Soemmerring's findings that "already in the earliest stages of the embryo one finds sex differences. That boys will seize a stick while girls will take up a doll ... that men rule the affairs of state while women govern the affairs of the home reflects nothing other than what is already in the seed of the embryo."[100]

Medical manuals for women that appeared in France and Germany between the 1780s and 1830s also made use of the new findings on sex differences. These health manuals emphasized that physical differences between men and women must be taken into account for the proper treatment of their illnesses. These manuals also emphasized that the well-being of each sex depended on establishing a lifestyle appropriate to its particular physiology.[101] The authors of these manuals spoke of the physiological and moral character of woman in one and the same breath.[102]

Those who thought that social life in "harmony" with nature ensured individual well-being also thought that such a life ensured social stability. In his 1806 book on the character of the female sex, Carl Friedrich Pockels asserted that differences in bodily strength are "designed by nature as a necessary basis to ensure the social order between man, woman, and the family."[103] Drawing from Rousseau, Roussel, and Georges Cuvier, Pockels found man and woman perfect but complementary beings. In 1830, medical doctor J. J. Sachs explained how physical complementarity led to complementary social roles for men and women:

The male body expresses positive strength, sharpening male understanding and independence, and equipping men for life in the State, in the arts and sciences. The female body expresses womanly softness and feeling. The roomy pelvis determines women for motherhood. The weak, soft members and delicate skin are witness of woman's narrower sphere of activity, of home-bodiness, and peaceful family life.[104]

The French father of positivism, Auguste Comte, also considered the proper relation between the sexes the foundation of solid social order. Comte believed that the strength of the family rested on the natural subordination of the female to the male. Thus in his epic *Cours de philosophie positive*, Comte reasserted the growing belief that the proper social role of women is a question not of politics but of biology:

The sound philosophy of biology, especially the important theories of Gall, begins to offer a scientific resolution to the much acclaimed equality of the sexes. The study of anatomy and physiology demonstrates that radical differences, at once physical and moral ... profoundly separate the one [sex] from the other.[105]

J. S. Mill's moral arguments for women's equality were unable to sway Comte from this view. Comte persisted in his belief that biology "has established the hierarchy of the sexes."[106]

One important aspect of the definition of women's nature emphasized women's inability to do intellectual work or science of any kind. This view, expressed by Wilhelm von Humboldt but stretching back to Rousseau, held that women's physical weakness results in intellectual weakness. According to Humboldt, women are incapable of analytical or abstract thought. Women, he wrote, are given to subjective impressions; they reveal their inner life, they think in wholes, but don't ground their information in empirical data.[107] Hegel strengthened the growing association of masculinity with reason and science, and of femininity with feeling and the moral sphere of the home. Woman's ethical and intellectual character, he argued, made her inherently incapable of philosophy or science:

> Women are capable of education, but they are not made for the more advanced sciences, philosophy and certain forms of artistic production, all of which require a universal faculty. Women may have quick wit, taste, and elegance, but they cannot attain the ideal. . . . Women regulate their actions not by the demands of universality, but by arbitrary inclinations and opinions . . . they follow the dictates of subjectivity, not objectivity.[108]

It is important to look at these texts on women's nature—medical and philosophical—in the context of women's participation in medicine. The search for sex differences on the part of anatomists also coincided with changes in the structure of seventeenth- and eighteenth-century medical care. Anatomists' interest in the distinctive character of women's body build came at a time when the professionalization of medical sciences was taking women's health care out of the hands of female midwives.[109] On the one hand, doctors stressed their concern for distinctively female problems in health care. Ackermann, for example, appended a chapter on women's health to his book on sex differences and argued that traditional medicine did not take into account differences in body build that might influence the cause and course of a sickness.[110] In order to treat an illness properly a physician was to take into account women's distinctive anatomy. The implication here was, of course, that midwives did not have the proper training to care for women's health. On the other hand, women were not thought capable of getting that training. They were not to work in the increasingly public realm of medicine but to remain in the home.[111] Women were defined as incapable of doing science by a medical community that was itself attempting to become more scientific.

At the same time that the idea of the "unscientific" woman drove a final nail in the coffin of midwifery, scientists presented their findings as "objective" or "value neutral." In the course of the nineteenth century, there emerged an increasing tendency to look to science as an arbiter of social questions. The promise of objectivity inspired hope that the "woman question" could be resolved by science. Anatomists stressed the "impartial" nature of their work. In his work on the comparative anatomy of the "Negro" and European, for example, Soemmerring concluded that the Negro was "somewhat nearer the ape, particularly in respect to the brain, than the European."[112] Yet Soemmerring argued that his work reflected what he called the "cold-blooded" findings of science and did not take a "moral" stand.[113] In a similar manner, Pockels insisted that his four-volume study of the character of woman was "impartial," "purely empirical," and following the "principles of reason."[114]

If the scientific argument against women in science played a role in removing women from the medical profession, it was also invoked repeatedly to keep them out. In 1872, Professor Theodor Bischoff argued against the admission of women to the medical profession.[115] Using, as he said, the "impartial and certain" methods of science, he promised to prove that the "pure and unadulterated feminine nature" of woman is not a scientific one.[116] Bischoff's central argument against women's equal participation in medicine rested on scientific definitions of sex differences. Anyone who is familiar with the physical and mental differences between man and woman as discovered in anatomy and physiology, he wrote, could never support the equal participation of men and women in medicine.[117] Equality, he stated, can only be achieved where initial conditions are equal. He then spun off the (by then) familiar list of sex differences—in bones, muscles, nerves, and skulls—relying heavily on the work of Soemmerring and citing the supporting passages from Kant's *Anthropologie*.[118]

Opposition to these and similar views on women came largely from outside the medical community. Already in 1744, Eliza Haywood reported in her journal, *The Female Spectator*, that anatomists were finding women to be physiologically incapable of deep thought. She believed this to be incorrect, and argued that the supposed delicacy of the female brain does not necessarily render it less "strong" than the male brain:

The Delicacy of those numerous Filaments which contain, and separate from each other what are call'd the Seats of Invention, Memory, and Judgment, may not, for anything they [the anatomists] can prove to the contrary, render them [women's brains] less strong.

Haywood was not a natural philosopher, however, and qualified her authority to speak of such matters; she wrote that "as I am not Anatomist enough to know whether there is really any such Difference or not between the Male and Female Brain, I will not pretend to reason on this Point."[119] Like others of her time, Haywood bowed to claims of science to have a privileged access to truth.[120]

Asymmetries in social power forced adversaries on either side of the "woman question" to use markedly different forms of arguments to state their case.[121] Barred from science, women used what were essentially *moral* arguments to demand education and voting rights; scientists (by and large male) used the findings of anatomy and other sciences to argue that women were incapable of scientific endeavor. As science gained in social prestige, those who could not base their arguments on scientific evidence were put at a disadvantage in social debate. Nineteenth-century feminist Hedwig Dohm, for example, was not reticent in her critique of science. Yet even she qualified her rebuttal of anatomist Theodor Bischoff with the words "I am no physiologist."

Because Dohm wrote from outside the academy and not under the guise of science, her work was commonly viewed as merely polemical.[122] In 1875, an Austrian minister of health, Friedrich W. H. Ravoth, made explicit a common conception of the relationship between feminism of any kind and science. In a speech to the Assembly of German Scientists and Doctors, Ravoth stated:

Competent and qualified scientific research can and must face the dialectical, or rather, sophistical talk about the so-called woman question with a categorical imperative, and uphold unchangeable laws.[123]

Thus in the absence of women (one might say in opposition to women) nineteenth-century science defined feminine nature as essentially incommensurate with masculine nature. The "natural" inequalities between men and women seemed to justify social inequalities between the two sexes. Many believed that the social order parallels the natural order. Cultural historian Wilhelm Riehl, for example, held that the incommensurate nature of men and women shows that inequalities of society are based in natural law.[124] Scientific definitions of human "nature" were thus used to justify the channeling of men and women (as well as whites and blacks) into vastly different social roles. It was thought "natural" that men, by virtue of their "natural reason," should dominate public spheres of government and commerce, science and scholarship, while women, as creatures of feeling, fulfilled their natural destiny as mothers, conservators of custom in the confined sphere of the home.

The consequences of this story, however, go beyond the exclusion of various groups—women or ethnic minorities—from the scientific community. Along with women, scientists excluded from science a specific set of moral and intellectual qualities defined as feminine. It was woman's distinctive moral qualities—feeling and instinct —that were thought to dull her abilities to practice science. The true scientist was to be a man of "reason and truth."

The femininization of feeling and the masculinization of reason was produced and reproduced by specific divisions of labor and power in European society. At the same time, it should be recognized that the "nature" of science is no more innate than the moral "nature" of man or woman. Science too has been shaped by social forces. One of those forces has been the persistent desire to distance science from the feminine, and to identify it with the masculine. The irony in the case of the female skeleton is that as modern science plunged headlong into the study of sex differences in the eighteenth century, it helped construct its own gender.

Notes

1. Samuel Thomas von Soemmerring, *Tabula sceleti feminini juncta descriptione* ([Utrecht], 1796). My thanks to the staff of the Rare Book Collection of the Boston Medical Library in the Francis A. Countway Library, Harvard University, for their kind assistance with materials for this article. I also thank the Charlotte Newcombe Fellowship Program of the Woodrow Wilson Foundation, which provided support for the preparation of this manuscript. To those friends and critics who read earlier drafts—Robert Proctor, Margaret Rossiter, and Hal Cook—my thanks.

2. D'Arconville was one of a small number of women working in anatomy in eighteenth-century France. She published her work under the name and protection of Jean-J. Sue.

3. See Ernst Cassirer, *The Philosophy of the Enlightenment*, trans. F. C. A. Koellen and J. P. Pettegrove (Princeton, N.J., 1951), 234–52. See also Maurice Bloch and Jean Bloch, "Women and the Dialectics of Nature in Eighteenth-Century French Thought," in *Nature, Culture and Gender*, ed. Carol P. MacCormack and Marilyn Strathern (Cambridge, 1980), 25–41.

4. Although the need to reconcile an appeal to "natural equality of men" and the realities of slavery and the subordination of women became pressing only after the French and American revolutions, the dilemma first posed itself in the work of Locke. See Marvin Harris, *The Rise of Anthropological Theory* (New York, 1968), 80–107; William Stanton, *The Leopard's Spots* (Chicago, 1960), 1–15.

5. Charles Louis de Secondat, Baron de Montesquieu, *Lettres Persanes* (Paris, 1721), letter 38.

6. On this point see Steven Rose, Leon Kamin, and Richard Lewontin, *Not in Our Genes: Biology, Ideology and Human Nature* (London, 1984), 63–81; Ruth Bleier, *Science and Gender: A Critique of Biology and Its Theories on Women* (New York, 1984), 49ff.

7. See Londa Schiebinger, *Women and the Origins of Modern Science* (Ph.D. diss., Harvard University, 1984).

8. François Poullain de la Barre, *De l'égalité des deux sexes: Discours physique et moral* (Paris, 1673), 59.

9. See Sarah Pomeroy, *Goddesses, Whores, Wives, and Slaves* (New York, 1975); M. C. Horowitz, "Aristotle and Woman," *Journal of the History of Biology* 9 (1976): 183–213; G. E. R. Lloyd, *Science, Folklore and Ideology* (Cambridge, 1983), 58–111.

10. On the continuity in medical views from the ancient to the medieval worlds see Vern L. Bullough, "Medieval Medical and Scientific Views of Women," *Viator* 4 (1973): 487; Julia O'Faolain and Lauro Martines, *Not in God's Image: Women in History* (London, 1973), 130–39; Lester S. King, "The Transformation of Galenism," *Medicine in Seventeenth-Century England*, ed. Allen Debus (Berkeley, 1974), 7–32; Ian Maclean, *The Renaissance Notion of Woman: A Study in the Fortunes of Scholasticism and Medical Science in European Intellectual Life* (Cambridge, 1980).

11. Paul Hoffmann, *La Femme dans la pensée des lumières* (Paris [1977]); Maclean, *Renaissance Notion of Woman*.

12. J. P. Lotichium, *Gynaecologia, das ist: grund- und ausführlicher Discurs von Perfection, und Fürtrefligkeiten des löblichen Frawenzimmers: So allen und jeden ihren Feinden entgegen gesetzet* (Frankfurt, 1645), first dedication and p. 15.

13. Poullain de la Barre, *De l'égalité des deux sexes*, 60.

14. [Mary Astell], *An Essay in Defence of the Female Sex* (London, 1696), 12–13.
15. Hilda Smith, "Gynecology and Ideology in Seventeenth-Century England," in *Liberating Women's History*, ed. Berenice A. Carroll (Chicago, 1976), 98. On Harvey's discussion of the female role in reproduction see Carolyn Merchant, *The Death of Nature: Women, Ecology and the Scientific Revolution* (San Francisco, 1980), 155–62.
16. Maclean, *Renaissance Notion of Woman*, 29. Maclean notes that even though physiologists abandon Aristotle's woman-as-imperfect-male theory, they retain the belief that woman had a less perfect mental faculty than man (35).
17. Other examples of the meshing of the old and new include: André du Laurens, *Anatomica humani corporis historia* (Paris, 1593); Gaspard Bauhin, *Institutiones anatomicae corporis virilis et muliebris historiam exhibentes* (Basel, 1604); Helkiah Crooke, *A Description of the Body of Man* (London, 1615).
18. Andreas Vesalius, *De corporis humani fabrica* (Basel, 1543).
19. J. B. Saunders and C. D. O'Malley, *The Illustrations from the Works of Andreas Vesalius* (New York, 1950), 222–23.
20. In Galen's view, women's sex organs were analogous to men's but "imperfect and, as it were, mutilated." Women lacked sufficient heat to propel their sex organs outward.

    Consider first [Galen wrote] whichever ones you please . . . think of the man's turned in and extending inward between the rectum and the bladder. If this should happen, the scrotum would necessarily take the place of the uteri *[sic]*, with the testes lying outside, next to it on either side; the penis of the male would become the neck of the cavity that had been formed; and the skin at the end of the penis, now called the prepuce, would become the female pudendum itself. . . . In fact, you could not find a single male part left over that had not simply changed its position; for the parts that are inside in the woman are outside in the man. . . . Now just as mankind is the most perfect of all animals, so within mankind, the man is more perfect than the woman, and the reason for his perfection is his excess heat, for heat is Nature's primary instrument. . . . The woman is less perfect than the man in respect to the generative parts. For the parts were formed within her when she was still a foetus, but could not because of the defect in heat emerge and project on the outside.

    On the Usefulness of the Parts of the Body, trans. Margaret May, vol. 2 (Ithaca, N.Y., 1968), 628–30. See also Esther Fischer-Homberger, *Krankheit Frau und andere Arbeiten zur medizingeschichte der Frau* (Bern, 1979).
21. See Fritz Weindler, *Geschichte der gynäkologisch-anatomischen Abbildung* (Dresden, 1908), fig. 37, p. 41. See also G. Wolf-Heidegger and Anna Maria Cetto, *Die anatomische Sektion in bildlicher Darstellung* (Basel, 1967).
22. Kate Campbell Hurd-Mead, *A History of Women in Medicine* (Haddam, Conn., 1938), 358–59.
23. Vesalius, *De corporis humani fabrica*, frontispiece.
24. Saunders and O'Malley, *Illustrations from the Works of Vesalius*, 170. Female bodies were hard to come by, but then so were male bodies. The story is told that Vesalius saw a body of a male who had been executed swinging from a tree. Waiting until nightfall, he returned and cut it down.
25. William Cheselden, *Anatomy of the Bones* (1713; Boston, 1795), 276.
26. The illustrator merely drew what he or she saw. In addition to beards and breasts, illustrators often drew the ropes used to hold the body during dissection.
27. William Cowper, *The Anatomy of Humane Bodies* (London, 1737).

28. Cowper, *Anatomy of Humane Bodies*, commentary to plate 2.

29. Ibid. Harvey also noted that women are clad "as with a furred mantle." The abundant layer of fat under women's skin explains their good humor. "Men," he wrote, "are lean . . . and they are of a melancholic disposition. Fat is useful in many ways. . . . It is the result of abundant nutrition and promotes health"; William Harvey, *Lectures on the Whole of Anatomy on the Male and Female Body* (1616), trans. Gweneth Whitteridge (London, 1964), 53.

30. J. J. Sachs, *Ärztliches Gemälde des weiblichen Lebens im gesunden und krankhaften Zustände aus physiologischem, intellektuellem und moralischem Standpunkte: Ein Lehrbuch für Deutschlands Frauen* (Berlin, 1830), 1.

31. Edmond Thomas Moreau, *Quaestio medica: An praeter genitalia sexus inter se discrepent?* (Paris, 1750).

32. Pierre Roussel, *Système physique et moral de la femme, ou tableau philosophique de la constitution, de l'état organique, du tempérament, des moeurs, & des fonctions propres au sexe* (Paris, 1775), 2. This became a common theme. Dr. G. Jouard made a similar point in his *Nouvel essai sur la femme* (Paris, 1804), 3 and 36. The German physician Carl Ludwig Klose also argued that it is not the uterus that makes woman what she is. Even women from whom the uterus has been removed, he stressed, retain feminine characteristics; *Über den Einfluss des Geschlechts-Unterschiedes auf Ausbildung und Heilung von Krankheiten* (Stendal, 1829), 28–30.

33. Jakob Ackermann, *De discrimine sexuum praeter genitalia* (Mainz, 1788); *Über die körperliche Verschiedenheit des Mannes vom Weibe ausser Geschlechtstheilen*, trans. Joseph Wenzel (Koblenz, 1788), 2–5. The German edition is used throughout.

34. Ibid. Anatomists were not alone in their search for differences between the sexes. Physiologists, too, attempted to identify fundamental chemical components underlying differences between men and women. Sexual differences were deduced from the proportion of oxygen and hydrogen in the blood (Ackermann); from the proportion of acids in the body (Mitchill); from the balance of oxygen to carbon (Karl Burdach). At times modern definitions of sexual differences bore striking resemblance to the older Galenic tradition. In 1808, Dr. Johann Christian Rosenmüller read a paper to the Physikalisch-Medicinischen Societät zu Erlangen emphasizing that in the earliest development of the fetus, sex organs are neither masculine nor feminine. According to Rosenmüller, this continuity between the sexes meant that there must be great similarity between male and female sex organs; "Über die Analogie der männlichen und weiblichen Geschlechtstheile," *Abhandlungen der physikalisch-medicinischen Societät zu Erlangen* 1 (1810), 47–51. Rosenmüller coupled this view with a revised theory of humors. In Galen's view, heat determined sexuality—the right testicle being warmer than the left generated males. At the end of the eighteenth century, the burning of oxygen in the blood had been discovered to produce heat. Rosenmüller believed that sex is determined by the amount of oxygen in the fetus. The egg contains a preponderance of oxygen; the sperm has an excess of hydrogen. If, when they merge, oxygen predominates, the "sexless seed" will develop into a male; if hydrogen predominates it will develop into a female. If the proportions are equal, a hermaphrodite will develop. See Johann Christian Jörg, *Handbuch der Krankheiten des Weibes, nebst einer Einleitung in die Physiologie und Psychologie des weiblichen Organismus* (Leipzig, 1831), 6ff. Rosenmüller used the oxygen/hydrogen ratio to explain the external or internal development of sex organs. "The surplus of oxygen," he believed, "causes the external development of male sex organs, while the overproduction of hydrogen causes the internal development of female organs."

35. Yvonne Knibiehler and Catherine Fouquet, *La Femme et les médecins* (Paris, 1983), 124. See also Elisabeth Badinter, *L'Amour en plus* (Paris, 1980).

36. On the rise of the ideal of motherhood, see Marlene LeGates, "The Cult of Womanhood in Eighteenth-Century Thought," *Eighteenth-Century Studies* 10, no. 1 (1976): 21–39; Margaret Darrow, "French Noblewomen and the New Domesticity, 1750–1850," *Feminist Studies* 5, no. 1 (1979): 41–65; Silvia Bovenschen, *Die imaginierte Weiblichkeit: Exemplarische Untersuchungen zu kulturgeschichtlichen und literarischen Präsentationsformen des Weiblichen* (Frankfurt, 1979); Barbara Corrado Pope, "Revolution and Retreat: Upper-Class French Women After 1789," in *Women, War and Revolution*, ed. Carol Berkin and Clara Lovett (New York, 1980), 215–36; Susanne Risse-Stumbries, *Erziehung und Bildung der Frau in der zweiten Hälfte des 18. Jahrhunderts* (Tübingen, 1980); Badinter, *L'Amour en plus;* Mitzi Myers, "Reform or Ruin: A Revolution in Female Manners," *Studies in Eighteenth-Century Culture* 11 (1982).

37. "The animal within them [the womb or matrix within women] is desirous of procreating children, and when remaining unfruitful beyond its proper time, gets discontented and angry, and wandering in every direction through the body, closes up the passages of breath, and by obstructing respiration, drives them to extremity, causing all varieties of disease"; Plato *Timaeus* 91c, in *The Collected Dialogues of Plato*, ed. Edith Hamilton and Huntington Cairns (Princeton, N.J., 1961). Throughout the ancient period the uterus was portrayed in a variety of forms—a tortoise, a newt, a crocodile; Harold Speert, *Iconographia Gyniatrica: A Pictorial History of Gynecology and Obstetrics* (Philadelphia, 1973), 8.

38. Ackermann, *Über die körperliche Verschiedenheit des Mannes vom Weibe ausser Geschlechtstheilen*, appendix.

39. For Vesalius see the six plates originally printed without title, now known as *Tabulae anatomicae sex* (1538), plate 87, figs. 2–4.

40. Ian Maclean dates the reevaluation of women's sex organs much earlier. He found that after 1600, one sex is no longer thought to be an imperfect and incomplete version of the other, and that by the end of the sixteenth century, most anatomists abandon Galenic parallelism; *Renaissance Notion of Women*, 33. Nonetheless the Galenic view persisted well into the eighteenth century in the works of writers such as Diderot in France and Rosenmüller in Germany. Important naturalists such as Georges-Louis Buffon held that women's ovaries were testicles as late as 1749; *Histoire naturelle*, vol. 3 (Paris, 1749), 264.

41. Jacques-Louis Moreau, *Histoire naturelle de la femme, suivie d'un traité d'hygiène appliquée à son régime physique et moral aux différentes époques de sa vie*, vol. 1 (Paris 1803), 68–69.

42. Klose, *Über den Einfluss des Geschlechts-Unterschiedes*, 28–33.

43. Bernhard Albinus, "Account of the Work," in *Table of the Skeleton and Muscles of the Human Body* (London, 1749).

44. In the seventeenth and eighteenth centuries, the number of existing anatomical plates was small and well known within the community of European anatomists. Once a part of the human body had been adequately rendered, the plate was reproduced and used by other anatomists.

45. Bernhard Albinus, *Annotationes academicae* (1754–68), 7, 11–14, 30–50; quoted in Ludwig Choulant, *History and Bibliography of Anatomic Illustration*, trans. Mortimer Frank (Chicago, 1920), 277.

46. Albinus gave a description of a female skeleton in his *De sceleto humano* but does not provide an illustration; B. S. Albini, *De sceleto humano* (Leiden, 1762), chap. 126.

47. Gaspard Bauhin, *Theatrum anatomicum* (Frankfurt, 1605), plate 4, p. 247.

48. Pierre Tarin, *Ostéo-graphie, ou description des os de l'adulte, du foetus* (Paris, 1753), plate 23.

49. Alexander Monro, *The Anatomy of the Humane Bones* (Edinburgh, 1726), appendix, 341.

50. Ibid., 340–44.

51. William Cheselden, *Osteographia or the Anatomy of the Bones* (London, 1733), plates 34 and 35.

52. D'Arconville (1720–1805) was well known by her contemporaries. She published widely; her works include *Essai pour servir à l'histoire de la putréfaction; Vie de Marie de Médicis, reine de France et de Navarre;* the French translation of Peter Shaw's work on chemistry. See Louis-Gabriel Michaud, *Biographie universelle ancienne et moderne*, vol. 41 (Paris, 1843).

53. D'Arconville's role in the publication of the *Ostéologie* remains unclear. The title page attributes the work to Sue: *Traité d'Ostéologie, traduit de l'Anglois de M. Monro, Où l'on ajouté des Planches en Taille-douce, qui représentent au naturel tous les Os de l'Adulte & du Foetus, avec leurs explications, Par M. Sue, Professeur & Démonstrateur d'Anatomie aux Ecoles Royales de Chirurgie, de l'Académie Royale de Peinture & de Sculptur* (Paris, 1759). Sue's son, Jean-J. Sue, reproduced the plates under his own name in 1788; *Elémens d'anatomie, à l'usage des peintres, des sculpteurs, et des amateurs* (Paris, 1788). In Britain, Andrew Bell and John B. Barclay also attributed the plates to Sue. See Andrew Bell, *Anatomica Britannica: A System of Anatomy; Illustrated by Upwards of Three Hundred Copperplates, from the Most Celebrated Authors in Europe* (Edinburgh, 1798), and John Barclay, *The Anatomy of the Bones of the Human Body, Represented in a Series of Engravings, Copied from the Elegant Tables of Sue and Albinus* (Edinburgh, 1829). Current literature, such as Paule Dumaitre's *Histoire de la medicine et du livre medical* (Paris, 1978), 285, credits d'Arconville with the translation but Sue with the illustrations.

Though I have been unable to find manuscripts or letters that might solve the mystery of d'Arconville's contribution to the *Ostéologie*, I believe that d'Arconville should be credited with the translation and with overseeing the drawing of the illustrations. I draw this conclusion for two reasons. First, in the introduction to the *Ostéologie*, the voices of the translator and the illustrator are one and the same. Speaking in the first person, the translator states, "The plates were drawn under my eyes, and there were many that I had redone many times in order to correct the slightest fault." A second piece of evidence pointing to a leading role for d'Arconville in the *Ostéologie* is that the introduction to the work is reprinted in a collection of works attributed to her.

The confusion about d'Arconville's role arises from the fact that, as Pierre-Henri-Hippolyte Bodard tells us, she was careful always to guard her anonymity; *Cours de botanique médicale comparée*, vol. 1 (Paris, 1810), xxvi–xxx. D'Arconville was a sharp critic of society women of her day, in particular those who (in her view) vainly paraded their literary achievement; see her essay "Sur les Femmes" in *Mélanges de littérature, de morale et de physique*, 7 vols. (Amsterdam, 1775) 1:368–83.

54. Soemmerring, *Tabula sceleti feminini*. 1797 is the date given for the publication of this plate in Choulant, *History of Anatomic Illustration*; Adolph Callisen, *Medicinisches Schriftsteller-Lexicon*, vol. 18 (Copenhagen, 1843), 353; and *The Dictionary of Scientific Biography* article on Soemmerring. There is, however, a 1796 first edition at the Countway Library, which is the one I have used. The two editions or printings are nearly identical.

55. *Journal der Empfindungen: Theorien und Widersprüche in der Natur- und Artzneiwissen-*

schaft 6, no. 18 (1797): 17–18.

56. It was thought that a woman did not reach maturity with the onset of menstruation but only with age eighteen or twenty, after the birth of her first child; see Jörg, *Handbuch der Krankheiten des Weibes*, 6ff.

57. Choulant, *History and Bibliography of Anatomic Illustration*, 306–7.

58. Sue, *Ostéologie*, text to plate 4.

59. Bell, *Anatomica Britannica*; Barclay, *Anatomy of the Bones of the Human Body*.

60. Ibid., commentary to plate 32. Barclay gives the date of Soemmerring's publication incorrectly as 1787.

61. Ibid.

62. Although Moreau praised Soemmerring's work, the illustration of the female skeleton in his own work bears no resemblance to Soemmerring's. In its exaggerations of the width of the pelvis, Moreau's skeleton is interestingly similar to d'Arconville's. See Moreau, *Histoire naturelle de la femme*, 1:95.

63. Quoted in Choulant, *History and Bibliography of Anatomic Illustration*, 277.

64. Albinus, "Account of the Work."

65. Quoted in Ackermann, *Über die Verschiedenheit*, 5–7.

66. Choulant, *History and Bibliography of Anatomic Illustration*, 302.

67. Ibid.

68. Soemmerring, *Tabula sceleti feminini*, commentary to plate.

69. Albinus, "Account of the Work."

70. Roussel, *Système physique et moral de la femme*, 6.

71. See Stephen Jay Gould, *Ontogeny and Phylogeny* (New York, 1977).

72. Both J. F. Blumbach and Pierre de Maupertuis took Caucasian skin to be the norm of which black skin was a degenerate form; see John C. Greene, *The Death of Adam*, (Ames, Ia., 1959), 224 and 231.

73. As early as 1615, Helkiah Crooke had rejected Galen's notion that the testicles should rank as the most noble part of the human body. He also rejected Aristotle's notion that the heart should be honored as the most able part of the human body and ascribed superiority instead to the brain because its functions are more "divine and noble" than those of the heart. Crooke judged the brain in terms of the new philosophy as the "seate of the intelligible or understanding faculty": "We are enforced to yeelde the superiority to the braine. . . . All sense and voluntary motion proceede from it, the habitation it is of Wisedome, the Shrine of Memory, Judgement and Discourse, which are the prerogatives of Man above all other Creatures. This is the Prince of the Family, the head is the head of the tribe . . . yea all were created onely for his use and behoofe"; *Description of the Body of Man*, 45.

74. Georg Wilhelm Friedrich Hegel, *Phänomenologie des Geistes* (1807), in *Werke*, ed. Eva Moldenhauer and Karl Michel, 20 vols. (Frankfurt, 1969–1971), 3:248.

75. Samuel Thomas von Soemmerring, *Vom Baue des menschlichen Körpers*, 5 Vols. (1796; Frankfurt, 1800), vol. 1, section 61, p. 82. Soemmerring believed that larger skulls hold larger brains, that larger brains are capable of greater intellectual activity, and, consequently, that intellectual ability is innate (5:392).

76. Ackermann, *Über die Verschiedenheit*, 146.

77. Barclay, *Anatomy of the Bones of the Human Body*, text to plate 32.

78. E. W. Posner, *Das Weib und das Kind* (Glogau, 1847), 9–10.

79. Ruth Kelso, *The Doctrine of the Renaissance Lady* (Chicago, 1978), 213.

80. "For the free rules the slave, the male the female, and the man the child [each] in a different way." Aristotle justified the subordination of slaves, women, and children

in terms of the supposedly lesser degree of rationality each possesses: "All possess the various parts of the soul, but possess them in different ways; for the slave has not yet got the deliberative part at all, and the female has it, but without full authority, while the child has it, but in an undeveloped form"; Aristotle, *The Politics*, trans. H. Rackham (London, 1932), 63.

81. Heidi Rosenbaum, *Formen der Familien* (Frankfurt, 1982), 288–89.

82. Quoted in Ackermann, *Über die Verschiedenheit*, 5.

83. On this point see Marian Lowe, "The Dialectic of Biology and Culture," *Woman's Nature: Rationalizations of Inequality*, ed. Marian Lowe and Ruth Hubbard (New York, 1983), 39–62.

84. In the nineteenth century, poor women consistently had more deficient diets than their husbands, because they allowed their men and children more and better food; Mary Chamberlain, *Old Wives' Tales: Their History, Remedies and Spells* (London, 1981), 107.

85. Theodor L. W. von Bischoff, *Das Studium und die Ausübung der Medicin durch Frauen* (Munich, 1872), 45.

86. On "social inequality as natural law" see Wilhelm Riehl, *Die Naturgeschichte des Volkes als Grundlage einer deutschen Socialpolitik*, vol. 3 (1856; Stuttgart, 1956), 3.

87. On the polarization of gender roles, see Karin Hausen, "Die Polarisierung der Geschlechtscharaktere," *Sozialgeschichte der Familie in der Neuzeit*, ed. Werner Conze (Stuttgart, 1976), 363–93; Barbara Duden, "Das schöne Eigentum: Zur Herausbildung des bürgerlichen Frauenbildes an der Wende vom 18. zum 19. Jahrhundert," *Kursbuch* 47 (1977): 125–40; Ruth Bloch, "Untangling the Roots of Modern Sex Roles: A Survey of Four Centuries of Change," *Signs* 4, no. 2 (1978): 237–57.

88. See Sheila Rowbotham, *Women, Resistance and Revolution* (London, 1972); Maïte Albistur and Daniel Armogathe, *Histoire du féminisme français*, 2 vols. (Paris, 1977); Bloch and Bloch, "Women and the Dialectics of Nature," 25–41; Joan Kelly, "Early Feminist Theory and the Querelle des Femmes, 1400–1789," *Signs* 8, no. 1 (1982): 4–28; Katharine Rogers, *Feminism in Eighteenth-Century England* (Chicago, 1982); Hilda Smith, *Reason's Disciples: Seventeenth-Century English Feminists* (Chicago, 1982); Dale Spender, *Women of Ideas and What Men Have Done to Them: From Aphra Behn to Adrienne Rich* (London, 1982); Susan Bell and Karen Offen, eds., *Women, the Family and Freedom: The Debate in Documents*, vol. 1, *1750–1880* (Stanford, Calif., 1983).

89. Jean-Jacques Rousseau, *Emile* (1762), in *Oeuvres complètes*, ed. Bernard Gagnebin and Marcel Raymond, 4 vols. (Paris, 1959–69), 4:693.

90. Rousseau's views are so well known that I have chosen to focus here on less well-known followers of Rousseau. On Rousseau see Susan Moller Okin, *Women in Western Political Thought* (Princeton, N.J., 1979); Bovenschen, *Die imaginierte Weiblichkeit*; Zillah Eisenstein, *The Radical Future of Liberal Feminism* (New York, 1981), esp. chap. 4; Jean Elshtain, *Public Man, Private Woman: Women in Social and Political Thought* (Princeton, N.J., 1981); Joel Schwartz, *The Sexual Politics of Jean-Jacques Rousseau* (Chicago, 1984).

91. Bloch and Bloch, "Women and the Dialectics of Nature," 35.

92. Rousseau, *Emile*, 692.

93. C. Helvétius, *De l'esprit* (Paris, 1758); Jean le Rond d'Alembert, *Lettre de M. d'Alembert à M. J.-J. Rousseau* (Amsterdam, 1759); M.-J. Condorcet, *Esquisse d'un tableau historique des progres de l'esprit humain* (Paris, 1794).

94. Mary Wollstonecraft, *Vindication of the Rights of Woman* (London, 1792); Olympe de Gouges, "Declaration of the Rights of Woman and Citizen in 1791," in Bell and Offen,

Women, the Family and Freedom, 1:105–9; [Theodor von Hippel], *Über die bürgerliche Verbesserung der Weiber* (Berlin, 1792).

95. *Encyclopédie ou Dictionnaire Raisonné des Sciences, des Arts, et des Métriers* (Neuchatel, 1765), s.v. "squelette."

96. Roussel, *Système physique et moral de la femme,* 12.

97. Ibid., 22–23. For the relationship between environmentalists of the Enlightenment and sex differences, see L. J. Jordanova, "Natural Facts: A Historical Perspective on Science and Sexuality," *Nature, Culture and Gender,* ed. Carol P. MacCormack and Marilyn Strathern (Cambridge, 1980), 42–69.

98. Roussel, *Système physique et moral de la femme,* xvi. Roussel may well have picked up this sentiment from Voltaire. Jacques-Louis Moreau quotes Voltaire saying that "the physical always rules the moral" in his *Histoire naturelle de la femme,* 42. On Roussel see also Michèle Le Doeuff, "Pierre Roussel's Chiasmas: From Imaginary Knowledge to the Learned Imagination," *I & C* 9 (Winter 1981–82): 39–63.

99. Samuel Thomas von Soemmerring, *Über die körperliche Verschiedenheit des Negers vom Europäer* (Frankfurt, 1785), ix. That Soemmerring wrote about women in a book on race is not surprising, for Soemmerring viewed race in the same way he viewed sex: as penetrating the entire life of the organism. He wrote: "If skin is the only difference then the Negro might be considered a black European. The Negro is, however, so noticeably different from the European that one must look beyond skin color" (2).

100. Johann Wilhelm Heinrich Ziegenbien, *Aussprüche über weibliche Natur, weibliche Bestimmung, Erziehung und Bildung* (Blankenburg, 1808), 1.

101. A number of manuals on the illnesses of women appeared in the late eighteenth and early nineteenth centuries; among them are: Jean Astruc, *Traité des maladies des femmes,* 2 vols. (Avignon, 1768); [Anonymous], *Der Arzt der Frauenzimmer, oder die Kunst, dieselben gesund zu erhalten* (Leipzig, 1773); Jörg, *Handbuch der Krankheiten des Weibes* (1832); Sachs, *Ärztliches Gemälde des weiblichen Lebens* (1830).

102. On the relation between the moral and physical characteristics of woman see Knibiehler and Fouquet, *La Femme et les médecins,* esp. chap. 4.

103. Carl Friedrich Pockels, *Versuch einer Charakteristik des weiblichen Geschlechts,* vol. 1 (Hanover, 1806), 6 and 8. For other literature of this type, see Antoine-Léonard Thomas, *Essai sur le charactère, les moeurs, et l'esprit des femmes dans les différents siècles* (Paris, 1773); [Ernst Brandes], *Über die Weiber* (Leipzig, 1787) and *Betrachtungen über das weibliche Geschlecht und dessen Ausbildung in dem geselligen Leben* (Hanover, 1802); C. Meiners, *Untersuchungen über der Naturgeschichte der Menschenspecies* (Tübingen, 1811); Immanuel Kant, *Anthropologie* (Königsberg, 1798); A. F. Nolde, *Momenta quaedam circa sexus differentiam* (Göttingen, 1788); Gabriel Jouard, *Nouvel essai sur la femme considérée comparativement à l'homme* (Paris, 1804); K. F. Burdach, *Die Physiologie als Erfahrungswissenschaft* (Leipzig, 1826).

104. Sachs, *Ärztliches Gemälde des weiblichen Lebens,* 25, 47.

105. Auguste Comte, *Cours de philosophie positive,* vol. 4 (Paris, 1839), 569–70.

106. Auguste Comte to J. S. Mill, 16 July 1843, in *Lettres inédites de J. S. Mill à A. Comte avec les résponses de Comte,* ed. L. Lévy-Bruhl (Paris, 1899), 231.

107. Wilhelm von Humboldt, "Über den Geschlechtsunterschied und dessen Einfluss und die organische Natur" and "Über die männliche und weibliche Form," in *Neudrücke zur Psychologie,* ed. Fritz Giese, vol. 1 (1917), 110.

108. Georg Wilhelm Friedrich Hegel, *Grundlinien der Philosophie des Rechts* (1821), in *Werke,* 7:319–20.

109. Midwives held a traditional monopoly on the certification of virginity and on birthing until the seventeenth century. Midwives received certification from other midwives, or they merely went into practice after serving an apprenticeship with an experienced midwife. On midwifery, see Barbara Ehrenreich and Deirdre English, *For Her Own Good: 150 Years of the Experts' Advice to Women* (New York, 1978); G. Elmeer, "The Regulation of German Midwifery in the Fourteenth, Fifteenth, and Sixteenth Centuries" (M.D. thesis, Yale University School of Medicine, 1963); Richard L. Petrelli, "The Regulation of French Midwifery During the *Ancien Régime*," *Journal of the History of Medicine and Allied Sciences* 16, no. 3 (July 1971), 276–92; Thomas R. Forbes, "The Regulation of English Midwives in the Sixteenth and Seventeenth Centuries," *Medical History* 8, no. 3 (July 1964): 235–44; H. R. Spencer, *The History of British Midwifery from 1650 to 1800* (London, 1927); A. G. Debus, *Medicine in Seventeenth-Century England* (Berkeley, 1974); Jean Donnison, *Midwives and Medical Men* (New York, 1977); Toby Gelfand, *Professionalizing Modern Medicine: Paris Surgeons and Medical Science and Institutions in the Eighteenth Century* (Westport, Conn. 1980).

110. Ackermann, "Krankheitslehre der Frauenzimmer," appendix to *Über die Verschiedenheit.*

111. Hilda Smith, "Gynecology and Ideology in Seventeenth-Century England," 98.

112. Soemmerring, *Über die körperliche Verschiedenheit des Negers vom Europäer,* xiv.

113. Ibid., xix.

114. Pockels, *Versuch einer Charakteristik des weiblichen Geschlechts,* 1:viii–xviii.

115. For a similar story in England and the United States, see Joan Burstyn, "Education and Sex: The Medical Case Against Higher Education for Women," *Proceedings of the American Philosophical Society* 117 (1973): 79–89; Janet Sayer, *Biological Politics: Feminist and Anti-Feminist Perspectives* (London, 1982); Louise Newman, ed., *Men's Ideas/Women's Realities: Popular Science, 1870–1915* (New York, 1985).

116. Bischoff, *Das Studium und die Ausübung der Medicin durch Frauen,* 47.

117. Ibid., 14 and 48.

118. Ibid., 15 and 20.

119. Eliza Haywood, *The Female Spectator* 2 (1744): 240–41.

120. In her 1802 book *On the Appropriateness of the Admission of Women to Higher Education,* Amelia Holst argued that no anatomist had ever proved that women's brains are organized differently from men's; *Über die Bestimmung des Weibes zur höhern Geistesbildung* (Berlin, 1802), 91. This is, of course, exactly what craniologists set out to do.

121. For the changing relation of scientific and moral discourse see Robert N. Proctor, "The Politics of Purity: Origins of the Ideal of Neutral Science" (Ph.D. diss., Harvard University, 1984).

122. Hedwig Dohm, *Die wissenschaftliche Emancipation der Frauen* (Berlin, 1874). On Dohm see Renate Duelli-Klein, "Hedwig Dohm: Passionate Theorist," in *Feminist Theorists: Three Centuries of Women's Intellectual Traditions,* ed. Dale Spender (London, 1983), 165–83. Nor did training in science remove the taint of "moralism" from opposition to the mainstream. In France, Jenny d'Héricourt, a woman well trained in physiology, raised her voice in opposition to the prevailing wisdom; *A Woman's Philosophy of Woman; or, Woman Affranchised* (New York, 1864). I thank Karen Offen for information about Héricourt. In the United States, Antoinette Brown Blackwell also refuted Darwin's claim that women represented a primitive stage of evolution; *The Sexes Throughout Nature* (New York, 1875).

123. Friedrich W. T. Ravoth, "Über die Ziele und Aufgaben der Krankenpflege," quoted

in Helga Rehse, "Die Rolle der Frau auf den Naturforscherversammlungen des 19. Jahrhunderts," *Die Versammlung deutscher Naturforscher und Ärzte im 19. Jahrhundert,* ed. Heinrich Schipperges, in *Schriftenreihe der Bezirksärztekammer Nordwürttemberg* 12 (1968): 126.

124. Riehl, *Die Naturgeschichte des Volkes,* 3:3−5.

CATHERINE GALLAGHER

The Body Versus the Social Body in the Works of Thomas Malthus and Henry Mayhew

WITH THE PUBLICATION OF Thomas Malthus's first *Essay on the Principles of Population* in 1798, the social and economic significance of the vigorous body was radically reconceptualized. By insisting that healthy bodies eventually generate a feeble social organism, Malthus departed from nearly all his contemporaries.[1] Such predecessors as Adam Smith and David Hume, who also wrote of the "power of population" and its "checks," were certainly cognizant of population size as an important factor in social well-being. However, they maintained a two-millennia-old tradition of seeing the individual body as sign—both as metaphor and as source—of the health or infirmity of the larger social body. Hence they viewed rapid reproduction as simply an index of a healthy state. Hume writes, "For as there is in all men, both male and female, a desire and power of generation more active than is ever universally exerted, the restraints . . . must proceed from some difficulties in men's situation, which it belongs to a wise legislature carefully to observe and remove."[2] Thus, he continues, "Every wise, just and mild government, by rendering the condition of its subjects easy and secure will always abound most in people, as well as in commodities and riches." Hume is typical of eighteenth-century writers in seeing no apparent contradiction, either actual or latent, between individual physical potency and social vitality. In this one particular, his social vision is uncharacteristically static ("Every wise, just and mild government . . . will always abound most in people") and based on the assumption that human biological nature itself is not at fault ("the restraints . . . must proceed from some difficulties in men's situations").

For Enlightenment utopians, the link between healthy individual and social bodies was even more direct; in the works of Condorcet and William Godwin, whom Malthus explicitly takes as antagonists, hopes of the perfect society were often founded on the possibility of biological perfectability. Malthus's *Essay* is the first work to counter this utopianism, not with reminders of the fallen state of the human race, its imperfections and frailties, but with a far more devastating evocation of its most redoubtable power, the power it shares with all other animal species and that exercises itself almost automatically as a biological function: "the power of population." The fact that populations have a tendency to increase beyond their means of subsistence and are only held in check by misery or vice is the single principle on which Malthus tries to erect a "juster philosophy" of social questions. His aim is to avoid the "mere conjectures" of both the "advocate for the present order of things" and the "advocate for the perfectibility of man,"[3] and his means is a revaluation of the social meaning of the healthy body, a revaluation fundamental to nineteenth-century social discourses and practices.

Malthus's theory destroyed the homological relationship between individual and social organisms by tracing social problems to human vitality itself. For him, the human body is a profoundly ambivalent phenomenon. He admits that Hume and even such utopians as Godwin are right to see the rate of increase in the number of human bodies as a sign of *present* physical prosperity and even healthy, "innocent" social institutions. But Malthus simultaneously sees the unleashed power of population, the reproducing body, as that which will eventually destroy the very prosperity that made it fecund, replacing health and innocence with misery and vice.

Thus, for example, he asks what would be the effect on population of the actualization of Godwin's utopian society and, in turn, what would be the effect on his utopia of the power of population. Malthus hypothesizes almost all the elements of Godwin's perfectly rational society, even granting the supposition that marriage could be abolished without immediately causing social chaos: "Each man would probably select himself a partner to whom he would adhere as long as that adherence continued to be the choice of both parties" (68). Everything else in the society likewise both attests to and promotes equality, rationality, and health. Malthus makes no claims for any *a priori* weakness or depravity in human nature when he supposes

all the causes of misery and vice in this island removed. War and contention cease. Unwholesome trades and manufactories do not exist. . . . The greater part of the happy inhabitants of this terrestrial paradise live in hamlets and farm-houses scattered over the face of the country. Every house is clean, airy, sufficiently roomy, and in a healthy situation. . . . The necessary labours of agriculture are shared amicably among all. The number of persons, and the produce of the island, we suppose to be the same as at present. The spirit of benevolence, guided by impartial justice, will divide this produce among all the members of the society according to their wants. Though it would be impossible that they should all have animal food every day, yet vegetable food, with meat occasionally, would satisfy the desire of a frugal people and would be sufficient to preserve them in health, strength, and spirits. (68)

Malthus begins his demonstration, therefore, by granting the time-honored homology: healthy individual bodies represent a healthy social organism. Unlike Hume's scheme, however, Malthus's is temporally dynamic; the strong body entails a present and a future social condition: first a society of innocence and health and then one of vice and misery. The degeneration from one society to the next, moreover, is effected neither by inner corruption nor by external adversity. It is solely a product of the vigor of the body itself.

The spirited health and strength of the utopian body leads within two generations to social chaos, want, warfare, and, finally, starvation. For within fifty years, the very felicities of Godwin's utopia would overpopulate it: "The irremediableness of marriage, as it is at present constituted, undoubtedly deters many from entering into that state. An unshackled intercourse on the contrary would be a most powerful incitement to early attachments, and as we are supposing no anxiety about the future support of children to exist, I do not conceive that there would be one woman in a hundred, of twenty-three, without a family" (68). Thus in half a century the population would quadruple (according to Malthus's famous dictum that animal populations increase geometrically) while the stock of food to support them could only—under nearly miraculous conditions—triple (following his maxim that increase in the vegetable kingdom takes place according to an "arithmetic" ratio). The healthy, and consequently *reproducing*, body thus is the harbinger of the disordered society full of starving bodies: "Provisions no longer flow in for the support of the mother with a large family. The children are sickly from insufficient food. The rosy flush of health gives place to the pallid cheek and hollow eye of misery" (70).

By rhetorically melting one generation into another in this way, Malthus occludes the possibility of using the healthy body to signify the healthy society. The healthy body here has lost, in the very power of its fecundity, the integrity of its boundaries, and hence comes to be a sign of its opposite. The blooming body is only a body about to divide into two feebler bodies that are always on the verge of becoming four starving bodies. Hence, no state of health can be socially reassuring. Malthus's argument ruptures the healthy body/healthy society homology. Simultaneously, by making the body absolutely problematic, he helps place it in the very center of social discourse.

At the end of his argument, Malthus actually uses the same body/society analogy he has been rendering so untenable, and his use of it exposes its accumulated difficulties. Predictably, he centers the metaphor on the instability of vigorous physical states. Also predictably, he imagines the social body as female, since only the number of women of child-bearing age in a society gives an indication of its rate of increase. The relationship of the social theorist to the society, then, is that of an anxious lover to the body of the beloved:

A person who contemplated the happy state of the lower classes of the people in America twenty years ago, would naturally wish to retain them for ever in that state, and might think, perhaps, that by preventing the introduction of manufactures and luxury he might effect his purpose; but he might as reasonably expect to prevent a wife or mistress from growing old by never exposing her to the sun or air. The situation of new colonies, well governed, is a bloom of youth that no efforts can arrest. There are, indeed, many modes of treatment in the political, as well as animal body, that contribute to accelerate or retard the approaches of age, but there can be no chance of success, in any mode that could be devised, for keeping either of them in perpetual youth. (114–15)

At first glance, the analogy seems to work; social bodies, like individual bodies, are subject to decay. But the sentence "The situation of new colonies, well governed, is a bloom of youth that no efforts can arrest" betrays the paradoxical nature of even this negative body/society homology. The sentence's ambiguity reveals Malthus's double vision, for the woman's bloom of youth is both the prized thing that one wants to "arrest," in the sense of fixing forever, and the culprit whose "arrest" would be necessary to stop the enfeebling process of reproduction. The ambiguity points to the underlying paradox that would immediately strike any careful reader of the preceding argument: the social body is growing "old" precisely insofar as the actual demographic proportions of the society are increasingly weighted toward youth, since, under optimal conditions, each generation would be twice as large as the generation preceding it. To be comprehensible in the terms of Malthus's argument, this body/society homology can only be read as a body/society opposition. The social body is an "old woman" insofar as it is populated by young women.

Malthus, thus, turns the body into an absolute social problem. All individual bodily states, without exception, mean trouble for the state of society. This problematization of the body does not in itself, however, completely account for its centrality in the social discourse of the nineteenth century. The body, after all, had been problematized before in both classical and Christian ascetic traditions that had made the flesh into a treacherous enemy of man's "ultimate" good. If Malthus had stopped at merely making all states of the body problematic, we might be able to see him as just a secularizer of those older traditions, one who substituted "social good" for "spiritual good." But Malthus breaks definitively with those traditions by accomplishing the problematization of the body in the context of its complete valorization. Indeed, the body can only become absolutely problematic when it is completely valued.

Far from making war on the body and its appetites, as earlier enumerators of its dangers had done, Malthus casts himself in the role of the body's champion. Instead of following the lead of conservative contemporaries by accusing Enlightenment utopians of crass materialism, of the denial of the spiritual dimension of human nature, Malthus launches an attack from the opposite quarter, accusing the "advocates for the perfectibility of man" of being indifferent, indeed hostile, to the just claims of the body. It is these claims that his essay sets out to vindicate. His two opening postulates set the direction for the entire argument:

First, That food is necessary to the existence of man. Secondly, That the passion between the sexes is necessary and will remain nearly in its present state. (19)

Despite the seeming obviousness of these propositions, even despite the fact that he calls them "postulates," Malthus actually spends some time justifying them. For it is the most basic facts of biological existence that he finds denied in the works of Condorcet and Godwin, his two examples of utopian thought.

In the *Essay*, these two writers represent different aspects of a single utopian desire to alter radically human biological nature. Condorcet is presented as a biological engineer, planning organic perfectibility through selective breeding. Malthus's task is to belittle this scheme without belittling the body itself by concentrating on its imperfections and without appearing to be an "advocate for the present order of things" who dismisses all novelty and scientific experimentation. He must expose, under the desire for a scientifically perfected body, a blatantly unscientific disregard for the body as it is. He accomplishes this by harnessing a Swiftean satiric rhetoric to a rigorous methodological argument.

Malthus ostensibly centers his attack on Condorcet's faulty induction. From the evidence of biological improvement noted in plant and animal breeding, Condorcet concludes (according to Malthus) that species might be perfected even to the point of producing the feature of physical immortality. Malthus leaves aside the disastrous effects on population of such an "improvement" as too obvious to need mentioning, and explicitly concentrates on the fallacy in Condorcet's reasoning: the latter has failed to distinguish between "an unlimited progress and a progress where the limit is merely undefined" (63). That is, the fact that no limit has been reached in the development of a certain feature does not imply that no limit exists. Indeed, it does not even imply that (taking into account the known rules of the physical universe) one cannot predict "a point at which [improvement] will not arrive" (63).

Although this argument seems to question only Condorcet's logical failures and to leave untouched his devaluation of the empirical body, Malthus uses this logical structure as a framework for a satirical rhetoric that implicitly accuses Condorcet of contempt for the whole of biological nature. In illustrating "points at which improvement will not arrive," Malthus creates a series of grotesque forms of life, biological absurdities, that, although entirely of his own fabrication, seem somehow the perverse results not just of his opponent's faulty reasoning but of the underlying desire to direct biological progress:

In the famous Leicestershire breed of sheep, the object is to procure them with small heads and small legs. Proceeding upon [the maxim that you might breed to any degree of nicety you please], it is evident that we might go on till the heads and legs were evanescent quantities, but this is so palpable an absurdity that we may be quite sure that the premises are not just and that there really is a limit, though we cannot see it or say exactly where it is. . . . I should not scruple to assert that were the breeding to continue for ever, the head and legs of these sheep would never be so small as the head and legs of a rat. (63)

Monsters proliferate in this section of the argument; counterfactual beings are created as the possibilities of their existence are denied. We see a carnation "increased to the size of a large cabbage" (63), human bodies with four eyes and four legs, and trees that grow horizontally (83). The very comic grotesqueness of these bodies implies that Condorcet is attempting a ridiculous and impertinent interference with nature. Malthus thus manages to incorporate the satirical rhetoric of a Swiftean antiscientific tradition into a defense of proper empirical reasoning. Without ever directly attacking the validity of Condorcet's aims or the morality of his means, Malthus is able to cast his opponent as an overreaching distorter of the harmonies of the natural world. Consequently, Malthus fashions himself the protector of the "delicate materials of a carnation stalk" and a friend of heads and legs that are more than "evanescent quantities."

Malthus is even more obviously the vindicator of the rights of the body in his critique of Godwin. When, for example, he duplicates Godwin's utopia, he refuses to grant one of his opponent's central hypotheses: the hypothesis that "the passion between the sexes will become extinct" (76). He denies this hypothesis, moreover, not on the grounds that man's fallen nature makes him incapable of rising above base, animal instincts, but rather on the grounds that the instincts are not base. Healthy sexual passion, he insists, "seems to be that sort of mixture of sensual and intellectual enjoyment particularly suited to the nature of man, and most powerfully calculated to awaken the sympathies of the soul and produce the most exquisite gratifications" (77). Just as Condorcet had been indirectly characterized as an impertinent disrupter of nature's course, Godwin becomes the dessicated, heartless repressor of the body's just demands:

Men in the decline of life have in all ages declaimed a passion which they have ceased to feel, but with as little reason as success. Those who from coldness of constitutional temperament have never felt what love is, will surely be allowed to be very incompetent judges with regard to the power of this passion to contribute to the sum of pleasurable sensations of life. (76)

Malthus even indulges in passages of lyrical rhapsody in defense of these pleasures:

Perhaps there is scarcely a man who has once experienced the genuine delight of virtuous love, however great his intellectual pleasures may have been, that does not look back to the period as the sunny spot in his whole life, where his imagination loves to bask, which he recollects and contemplates with the fondest regrets, and which he would most wish to live over again. (76)

To be sure, the vindication of sexual passion as a rational pleasure is an essential component of the grand design of Malthus's argument, for it allows him to class sexual abstinence under the category of "misery," one of the two categories (misery and vice) into which he tries to fit all checks to population growth. The vindication of sexual passion is made within the assumption that any practice severing sexual pleasure from reproduction would be classed as vice. These points, however, only remind us that Malthus's argument must continually valorize the body's needs and natural reproductive processes. Its structure demands the re-iteration of his central and distinguishing claim: the human body is unfit for utopia not by its weaknesses but by its strengths, not by its vices but by its virtues. The intensity of misery in the body deprived of sexual pleasure (and thus non-reproducing) is directly proportional to the healthiness and legitimacy of the pleasure it lacks.[4]

Malthus's attack on Godwin, furthermore, carries his vindication of the body beyond the confines of sexual pleasure. He presents all of Godwin's schemes for self-discipline, for the exercise of the "power of mind over the body," as so many recipes for enfeeblement. Just as Condorcet seemed the creator of many monsters, Godwin seems the deviser of many tortures. Malthus takes Godwin to be arguing that the body is only "real" insofar as the mind experiences it. Thus, a man who had just walked twenty miles but who did not feel tired because he was enlivened by some urgent purpose would not, in Godwin's argument, be admitted to have any "real" muscular fatigue. Godwin, according to Malthus, holds that the mind's ability to render the body "unreal" and thus overcome its exigencies is practically limitless. Denying this, Malthus argues that the experiences of the body are real regardless of the mind's cognizance. As in his argument against Condorcet, Malthus attempts not to define the positive limits of bodily endurance but to infer them from the existence of impossible feats: "A motive of uncommon power acting upon a frame of moderate strength, would, perhaps make the man kill himself by his exertions, but it would not make him walk an hundred miles in twenty-four hours" (79–80). Similarly,

When a horse of spirit is nearly half tired, by the stimulus of the spur, added to the proper management of the bit, he may be put so much upon his mettle, that he would appear to a stander-by as fresh and as high spirited as if he had not gone a mile. Nay probably the horse himself, while in the heat and passion occasioned by this stimulus, would not feel any fatigue; but it would be strangely contrary to all reason and experience to argue from such an appearance that if the stimulus were continued, the horse would never be tired. (80)

Thus Godwin's line of reasoning seems to implicate him in the crimes of walking men to death and spurring on exhausted horses. As Malthus's argument advances, Godwin seems guilty of depriving people of food and sleep, and even of inhumanely denying the reality of Malthus's very own toothache, which he happens to have at the exact moment of composing this argument even though "in the eagerness of composition, I every now and then, for a moment or two, forget it" (80). Malthus once again emerges as a defender of the body, preventing its subjection to such a "utopian" regime. Coming to rest once again on the power of even the most exhausted body, he concludes, "The brightest and most energetic intellects, unwilling as they may attend to the first or second summons, must ultimately yield the empire of the brain to the calls of hunger, or sink with the exhausted body in sleep" (81). Malthus, in short, exults in the body's power to triumph over every insolent scheme to improve, rearrange, suppress, or discount it.

Completely untranscendable, the body is thus absolutely problematic. For a body that could and should be overcome would provide its own means of displacement from the center of social discourse. Absolute problematization, thus, relies on complete valorization. These, then, are the two fast interlocking elements of the nineteenth-century's discourse of the body that place it at the heart of so much Victorian social thought. They are the features that mark a definitive break with earlier European thought on the subject, even that of the Enlightenment. As we are about to see, the Victorians often tried to overcome the discourse's ambivalence by categorizing bodies as either valuable or problematic. But this categorical differentiation nevertheless preserved the paradox it set out to avoid. Unavailable as a metaphor of order and harmony, equally untranscendable and unperfectible, the body came to occupy the center of a social discourse obsessed with sanitation, with minimizing bodily contact and preventing the now alarmingly traversable boundaries of individual bodies from being penetrated by a host of foreign elements, above all the products of other bodies. Medical doctors became the most prestigious experts on social problems. Society was imagined to be a chronically, incurably ill organism that could only be kept alive by the constant flushing, draining, and excising of various deleterious elements. These dangerous elements, moreover, were often not themselves unhealthy but rather were overly vigorous and fecund individuals, such as these urban wanderers:

There are the urban and suburban wanderers, or those who follow some itinerant occupation, in and round about the large towns. Such are . . . the pickpockets—the beggars—the prostitutes—the street-sellers—the street-performers—the cabmen—the coachmen—the watermen—the sailors and such like. In each of these classes—according as they partake more or less of the purely vagabond, doing nothing whatsoever for their living, but moving from place to place preying upon the earnings of the more industrious portions of the community, so will the attributes of the nomade [sic] tribes be more or less marked in them. Whether it is that in the mere act of wandering, there is a greater determination of blood to the surface of the body, and consequently a less quantity sent to the brain, the muscles being thus nourished at the expense of the mind, I leave physiologists to say. But certainly be the physical cause what it may, we must all allow that in each of the classes above mentioned, there is a greater development of the animal than of the intellectual or moral nature of man, and that they are all more or less distinguished for their high cheek-bones and protruding jaws—for their use of a slang language—for their lax ideas of property—for their general improvidence—their repugnance to continuous labour—their disregard of female honour—their love of cruelty—their pugnacity—and their utter want of religion.[5]

Here, in the opening pages of perhaps the most famous Victorian work of social investigation, *London Labour and the London Poor*, Henry Mayhew lightly draws on the same body/society metaphor that had informed social discourse for millennia when he calls the wanderers parasites who prey on what can only be a social organism. The relationship of metaphoric correspondence between the body and society is present, but it is submerged, barely perceptible, beneath the more striking relationship the passage develops between the individual and social bodies: a relationship, as in Malthus, of opposition. Although the opposition seems at first to locate the wanderers outside the social body, they are very quickly internalized and equated with society's circulatory system. Mayhew's description is typical of Victorian social discourse: society is still imagined as a body, but as a corporate body menaced by those very overly physical individual bodies that distribute its sustenance.

Mayhew's costermongers, coach drivers, prostitutes, and sailors, then, although they clearly represent the problematic nature of the strong body, seem to deny its social or economic value. Mayhew, however, does not deny the value of bodies in general; rather, he tends to split their problematic and valuable aspects, seeking to locate them in separate economic functions. The vigorous bodies, distinguished from those of "honest workers," are not valuable in the common nineteenth-century economic sense of that term: through their labor they do not alter some portion of the material world in such a way as to increase its exchangeable value. The nomads, Mayhew says, have grown strong by "preying" on the "productive" portion of the population. Victorian works of social reportage and social investigation often present these two distinct although complexly related lower-class physiques: the enfeebled bodies of productive workers (the proletariat, properly speaking), and the excessively hardy bodies of the nomads (people explicitly associated with the circulation and exchange, rather than the production, of commodities). Briefly, as I will illustrate in the final section of this essay, the Victorians often seem to desire a radical disjunction dividing the working class into productive bodies out of which value is extracted and nonproductive bodies onto which it is added. However, the productive/nonproductive distinction often collapses when confronted with the ubiquitousness of the marketplace, and at those moments Victorian social discourse begins to nauseate itself with its biological obsessions.

The attempt to distinguish between productive and nonproductive bodies does not begin with the Victorians. We can find a version of it also in Malthus's *Essay*, which suggests that it might be a part of the overall logic of this discourse when applied to modern society. As we will see, Malthus's way of framing the problem certainly differs from that of the Victorians, for he partly denies the labor theory of value on which they based their distinction. Nevertheless, when he turns from his general argument about the relationship between human biological and social orders to make a specific analysis of the physical state of the lower classes in modern times, Malthus, like Mayhew, imagines workers' bodies to be enfeebled by a bloated apparatus of circulation. If, in the first part of his essay, the body in general seemed both indomitable and valuable, in this more detailed contemporary analysis, in which the problem of specifically economic value dominates, the bodies of workers who contribute by their labor to what he calls the "essential part of the riches of the state" (111) are consumed by the constant displacement onto other bodies of the value they create.

Despite the importance of Malthus's contributions to political economy, his *Essay* reveals a profound distrust of several of that nascent discipline's most basic assumptions. Indeed, in his analysis of contemporary problems, Malthus might almost be said to put Adam Smith in the place formerly filled by Condorcet and Godwin, the place of the enemies of the body. For, according to Malthus, Smith's theories supported a system of circulation and distribution that tended to separate labor and value from the valuable, laboring body. The concept effecting this separation was the labor theory of value itself, a theory that Malthus questioned because it conflated value and exchangeable value, determining both by the amount of labor embodied in a commodity.

Malthus's objections to this conflation uncover an ambivalence toward human biology at the heart of political economy. On the one hand, the discipline takes labor to be the source of all value and measures the value of labor by the value of the commodities (food, clothing, lodging) necessary to replenish the body for the hours of labor expended on another commodity. Thus the exchange value of any commodity seems rooted in biological need; the worker's body is the primary nexus of exchange through which the value of those commodities that replenish its labor power largely determine the value of all other commodities. Moreover, since labor is itself a commodity, its value will be partly determined by its abundance or scarcity in relationship to demand, that is, by the size of the working population. Hence, like Malthus, the labor theorists of value place biological sustenance and reproduction at the center of their system. But on the other hand, the very ability to calculate, through the common measure of labor, the relative values of commodities led away from a hierarchy of commodities based on ultimate biological usefulness. The labor theory of value could "equate" a bushel of corn, for example, with a bit of lace, even though, from another biological point of view, the corn would seem more intrinsically valuable. Thus Malthus can argue that it is precisely the *bodies* of laborers, their collective biological needs, that the labor theory of value allows one to discount or overlook. This paradoxical treatment of biology by political economists—making biology simultaneously central and irrelevant to discussions of value—helps account for the fact that, in the nineteenth century, issues of bodily well-being and of economic circulation are frequently articulated both on and against each other.

Malthus, for example, blames the labor theory of value for conflating value in general with exchange value and hence encouraging the growing use of money by all classes; for proliferating nonagricultural enterprises; and ultimately for lowering the overall standard of living for the working population. Against these pernicious tendencies, Malthus, we will see, opposes a theory that allows him to maintain his emphasis on the body as the only sure locus of value by distinguishing between commodities on the basis of their "usefulness," by which he means their direct capacity to sustain human life. Finally, this leads him to imply that the labor involved in the production of wheat is the only form of productive labor. Hence, as we will also see, his rethinking of the issue of economic value solely in terms of the body directs him around in a logical circle that actually cuts off the possibility of valuing strong bodies *per se*, adding a further complication to that already posed by the threat of overpopulation. In this part of the argument, Malthus's tendency to locate value in the body severely restricts his definition of productive labor and finally, paradoxically, denies value to whole sections of the laboring population because their labor is not directly productive enough of laboring bodies.

One might say that in this section of the *Essay*, Malthus gives in to a latent utopianism of his own and comes close to indulging the dream of a painless equilibrium between food and population. His analysis shifts its emphasis from inevitable biological drives to alterable market forces, and this shift is accompanied by a movement away from the topic of sexual reproduction to that of food production. Whereas earlier in the *Essay* sexual pleasure always eventuated in the pain of overpopulation or the sins of its prevention, the claim for inevitable, biologically rooted misery and vice is significantly qualified in this section. To be sure, reproduction remains automatic; indeed, it is so automatic that it altogether disappears as a discrete event. However, it does not appear to be automatically out of proportion to the increase in food production. Here the oppositions earlier seen to be inherent in biological drives (the sexual instinct versus misery and vice) are reconceived in economic categories (productive labor versus unproductive labor or production versus exchange). And once reconceived in this way, the problem of overpopulation appears ameliorable.

Population increase in itself was not seen by Malthus as a particularly severe contemporary problem; he was unaware of the rapid growth that we now know was taking place in England in the late eighteenth century. He thought, rather, that population had increased rather slowly since the revolution. Nevertheless, he believed that working people were living on less and less, not because they were increasing too rapidly but because the fund out of which they were supported was either stationary or dwindling. The money economy, however, was hiding this fact from view and misrepresenting the size of the fund for the support of labor. The false promises of the money economy were, in Malthus's view, tricking the feeble poor into reproducing themselves beyond the country's present ability to support them. To this new ability of a society to misrepresent the size of its fund for the support of labor Malthus attributes a new steady state of working class misery: "The increasing wealth of the nation has had little or no tendency to better the condition of the labouring poor. They have not, I believe, a greater command of the necessaries and conveniences of life, and a much greater proportion of them than at the period of the revolution is employed in manufactures and crowded together in close and unwholesome rooms" (105–6). Malthus argues that the more a society believes that exchangeable value equals value in general, the more it believes in the abstract equivalencies of monetary value, the more enfeebled the body of labor becomes.

He was not, to be sure, so naive as to think that exchangeable value was always to be discounted or that money was mere misrepresentation. In arguing against Godwin's claim that the miser locks up "nothing" when he locks up his money, for example, Malthus asserts,

Having defined therefore wealth, very justly, to be the commodities raised and fostered by human labour, [Godwin] observes that the miser locks up neither corn, nor oxen, nor clothes, nor houses. Undoubtedly he does not really lock up these articles, but he locks up the power of producing them, which is virtually the same. . . . But supposing, for a moment, that the conduct of the miser did not tend to check any really useful produce, how are all those who are thrown out of employment to obtain patents which they may shew in order to be awarded a proper share of the food and raiment produced by the society? (101)

Money here represents both things that might be and things that are. The miser's money box "virtually" contains any and every actual or potential commodity up to a certain exchangeable value. In this insistence on the abstract "reality" of money, Malthus is in accord with Adam Smith.

Mathus's critique of the "Speenhamland system" poor laws is also wholly in keeping with the dominant assumptions of political economy, but in this critique the dark side of the relationship between money and human bodies begins to emerge. Money is mainly a representation of wealth that can have both productive and unproductive uses. When money is distributed gratis to the poor, it makes them physically miserable in the long run. First, such a distribution impedes the production of real wealth since the inclination to labor decreases in proportion to the increase in parish aid. Second, parish aid "lowers the real price of labour." Finally, it increases "population without increasing the food for its support. A poor man may marry with little or no prospect of being able to support a family in independence. [Funds for parish relief] may be said therefore in some measure to create the poor which they maintain" (39). More parish aid, then, means more bodies, at least temporarily, but punier bodies producing and consuming even less than they would have without the interference of the money. Parish aid thus makes paupers themselves less valuable. The money becomes a kind of false representation, unable to be exchanged for the sufficiency of provisions it first seemed to promise: "Each man's patent would be diminished in value or the same number of pieces of silver would purchase a smaller quantity of subsistence" (39).

Malthus departs altogether from the normal assumptions of political economy, however, when he implies that money is deceptive in ways that have nothing to do with its elasticity. Indeed, the very thing that makes money "real"—its ability to represent accurately the relations of exchange between commodities—is precisely what makes it "false" as a gauge of how many laboring bodies a country can adequately sustain. By allowing the relations between commodities to be imagined purely as relative exchange values, money becomes a great deceiver and enemy to physical well-being. The equation of value with exchangeable value is deceptive in Malthus's view because it blurs what he sees as crucial distinctions between kinds of commodities, and it even reproportions biological nature to the detriment of the masses of mankind. At this stage in his argument, Malthus necessarily takes issue with Adam Smith. In keeping with his tendency to root all value in the very body he finds problematic, Malthus insists that Smith has committed a fundamental error in "representing every increase of the revenue or stock of a society as an increase in the funds for the maintenance of labour" (103). He argues that a stock or revenue "will not be a real and effectual fund for the maintenance of an additional number of labourers, unless the whole, or at least a great part of this increase . . . be convertible into a proportional quantity of provisions; and it will not be so convertible where the increase has arisen merely from the produce of labour, and not from the produce of land" (104). In other words, the only stock whose increase is truly destined for the maintenance of labor is the stock of working-class food, that which can be converted *most directly and immediately* into working-class bodies.

Malthus claims that the habit of always thinking in terms of exchangeable values has destroyed a real basis for distinguishing between productive and unproductive labor: "It appears to me that it is with some view to the real utility of the produce that we ought to estimate the productiveness and unproductiveness of different sorts of labour" (110). Most forms of manufacturing are "unproductive" for Malthus in this sense: "The consumable commodities of silks, laces, trinkets, and expensive furniture are undoubtedly a part of the revenue of the society; but they are the revenue only of the rich and not of the society in general. An increase in this part of the revenue of the state cannot therefore be considered of the same importance as an increase of food, which forms the principal revenue of the great mass of the people" (112). Expensive furniture and lace simply bear too attenuated or frivolous a relationship to the bodies of producers to be easily converted back into those bodies. Hence only the fiction of the abstract equivalence of exchange allows them to be imagined as part of the general society's wealth, as things that are convertible into working-class sustenance.

The obvious answer to Malthus on this point is that if the abstract notion of exchangeable value has created this "confusion," it has only been able to do so because, through the mediation of exchange, the lace really can become a certain quantity of food. The lace, for example, could be exchanged for money that, given the increased demand for food, could be used to expand agricultural enterprises and produce more food. But Malthus argues that food is not like mere wrought commodities that can be created on demand. The existence of an abundance of commodities that can be exchanged for food and the existence of an abundance of money with which to make the exchanges do not, according to Malthus, act as a stimulant to increase the overall quantity of food. Rather, as we will see, they may even tend to decrease the amount of human sustenance.

In making this argument, Malthus manifests a general distrust of far-ranging attenuated economic circuits. The process by which more land might be put under cultivation in England in response to a rise in the cost of provisions is depicted as slow and subject to various kinds of interference (105).[6] The possibility of importing a larger food supply is seen as too costly a process owing to the mere size of the country. In both cases, the longer the circuit of exchange leading from the laboring body in the form of a commodity and back to it in the form of food, whether that circuit be a certain number of exchanges or a certain amount of literal space traversed, the more inflated is the cost of food and the less productive is the labor.

Once again we note that it is the centrality of the literal body to Malthus's theory of value that causes his distrust of such elongated circuits. The most productive labor is that which can be converted back immediately into the laboring body. The habits of thought encouraged by the use of money and codified by Adam Smith in the labor theory of value abstract labor from the body itself. The abstracting mentality asks how much labor was required to produce the commodity and how much labor the commodity can command in the marketplace in order to define its value. But Malthus, resisting this tendency toward abstraction, asks instead into how many laboring bodies, or more precisely, how many pounds of laboring flesh the commodity can be easily converted? In the *Essay*, concrete laboring bodies, and not abstract units of labor, are the measures of value.

However, the short circuit of biological exchange favored by Malthus seems also to be the product of a circular logic. The body that labors is valuable insofar as its commodity can almost immediately be turned back into not just *a* body but another *valuable* body, that is, another body producing food. In other words, the value of bodies is not absolute but is rather based on their ability to create a commodity whose value is only defined in relationship to its ability to replenish the body. Food and the body, commodity and labor, thus constantly indicate each other as the source and gauge of their value.[7] And outside of this tight circle of production and consumption, a circle representing the most restrictive economy imaginable, is a network of exchanges that seems only to draw value away from its true site in order to dissipate it, often by attaching it to the bodies of those who have been rendered valueless by Malthus's logic.

A system that leaves out of account the commodity's contribution to working-class nutrition allows the pounds of healthy flesh, rightly destined for productive bodies, to get stuck in the wrong place. This is perhaps most graphically illustrated by Malthus's description of the way in which a surplus of money alters the very biological economy of a country to the detriment of the productive bodies. Money made in trade and manufacturing becomes an "increased demand for butcher's meat of the best quality, and . . . in consequence, a greater quantity of good land has annually been employed in grazing" (107). This new distribution of land has led to a "diminution of human subsistence, which . . . might have counterbalanced the advantages derived from the inclosure of waste lands and the general improvements in husbandry" (107). Thus money reshapes the relative proportions of the vegetable, animal, and human matter:

The present price will not only pay for fattening cattle on the very best land, but will even allow of the rearing many on land that would bear good crops of corn. The same number of cattle [as were formerly raised in waste lands] or even the same weight of cattle at the different periods when killed, will have consumed (if I may be allowed the expression) very different quantities of human subsistence. A fattened beast may in some respects be considered in the language of the French economists, as an unproductive labourer: he has added nothing to the value of the raw produce that he has consumed. The present system of grazing undoubtedly tends more than the former system to diminish the quantity of human subsistence in the country, in proportion to the general fertility of the land. (107)

The biological economy envisioned here is one in which cattle "eat" men. So many potential pounds of human flesh are converted (through the conversion of land from tillage to pasture) into so many pounds of animal flesh, which, by an undeniable caloric arithmetic, can never be converted back into an equal number of pounds of human flesh. That beast thus stands as an impediment to value as Malthus imagines it; or, more precisely, it stands for the displacement of value. Created by a surplus of money flowing from nonagriculture sources, it is the explicit embodiment of unproductive labor. It is the fatted beast of circulation.

One can thus see in Malthus's steer an ancestor of Mayhew's costermongers. The placement of the valuable, problematic body at the center of social discourse led, through the circular logic just outlined, to the division of the social organism into valuable (weak but productive) and problematic (strong but unproductive) bodies. Around this axis much nineteenth-century social criticism revolves. By breaking down the dilemma in this way, its parts come to seem ameliorable, while, in its entirety, it remains irresolvably paradoxical. Schemes for reform, for improvement and renewal can be endlessly generated out of the dissevered parts, which, when reassembled, become irremediable and hence endlessly generative.

Malthus's beast also allows us to understand the logic behind Mayhew's use of strong bodies to indicate a presently unhealthy social organism. The fatted body of circulation is an immediate threat to society's well-being, a threat that one does not need Malthus's time-lapse thinking in order to decipher. The social body, it turns out, is suffering from a distension, an overgrowth of its own circulatory system. Mayhew was not a sophisticated economic thinker. What we find in his work are not long thought-out theories but popularly held opinions. Like most nineteenth-century writers, he subscribed to Adam Smith's rather than Malthus's theory of value, including the producers of wrought goods inside the pale of "productive labour." In its simplest formulation, given by Smith in 1776, productive labor was that which would "fix or realize itself in any permanent subject, or vendible commodity, which endures after that labor is past, and for which an equal quantity of labour could afterwards be procured."[8] Material embodiment is necessary in this formulation, but the separation of the commodity from the producer and the abstract interchangeability of many kinds of labor are also stressed. There does not seem to be any anxiety in this passage about how the body, specifically, will eventually reclaim some portion of the value it produced.

One might argue that the refusal to narrow the definition of productive labor indicates a faith in the marketplace because it tolerates, even necessitates, extensive exchanges. But the broader definition of productive labor also makes production all the more dependent on such exchanges, and the dependence in itself becomes a source of anxiety. The expanded domain of productive labor also causes the onus of nonproductivity to fall, for the Victorians, more heavily because more exclusively on people who earn their living by circulating goods or selling services. Some kind of "fixed" embodiment remained central to the popular understanding of productive labor, attesting to the importance of physical being in economic thought, and leading writers like Mayhew to depict the economy in much the same way that Malthus had: by contrasting the fatted beasts of circulation to the puny bodies of production. Concurrently, however, Mayhew seems unable to imagine, as Malthus had, a proportional shrinkage (or "reabsorption") of the nonproductive sector. For circulation seems to him the basis as well as the opposite of production. Mayhew is not able to give any consistent economic reason for the opposition between the categories of productive and unproductive labor, and the more he denounces the creatures of circulation, the more it becomes clear that he does so because they embody not a marginal and dispensable economic condition but a central and essential one. The costermongers come to stand for the exchanges that underlie production. Their meaning expands to include the value of labor itself, and as this expansion occurs, Mayhew's loathing of their bodies becomes a loathing of the body in general.

Before returning to Mayhew's costermongers, though, we must briefly note some characteristics of their implied opposites. The weak bodies of productive workers, especially industrial workers, are such obvious and often-remarked figures in the Victorian social landscape that it would be superfluous to devote much time to them here. Malthus was not the only writer to depict them as creators of wealth that could not be taken back in as sustenance. The point had become a commonplace when Thomas Carlyle gave it its classic statement in 1844:

With unabated beauty the land of England blooms and grows; waving with yellow harvests; thick-studded with workshops, industrial implements, with fifteen millions of workers, understood to be the strongest, the cunningest and the willingest our Earth ever had; these men are here; the work they have done, the fruit they have realized is here, abundant, exuberant on every hand of us: and behold, some baleful fiat as of Enchantment has gone forth, saying, "Touch it not, ye workers . . . this is enchanted fruit."[9]

Ultimately this condition of "inanition" is spiritual in Carlyle's view; no one is really nourished by the fruits of England's wealth. But the physical condition of the working class is only available to Carlyle as a metaphor for the spiritual condition of the nation because Victorian social criticism is full of detailed physiological explanations for the weakness of labor.

One of these explanations is particularly striking as a basis of contrast between the bodies of productive and unproductive labor. The language of fixedness, which was often used to define productive labor and properly refers to the materialization of the work in a commodity, was often also applied to the condition of the laboring body. This very fixedness is enfeebling, as a medical doctor explained to a parliamentary committee on the labor of children in 1832. "In reference to the factory system," he was asked, "is not any employment, though it may be denominated light and easy, but being one of wearying uniformity and inducing much fatigue of mind as well as of body, more exhausting and injurious than moderate locomotive exercise though of a more strenuous nature, undergone for a reasonable length of time and with due intermission?" The doctor responds, "In my opinion, it certainly is; and I would add, that it becomes so more especially, in that wearisome exercise is to be undergone in a confined situation. Strenuous locomotive exercise . . . is not injurious at all, but on the contrary healthful."[10] Whereas the confined and stationary nature of factory work had been used to contrast it with agricultural work, by mid-century it also forms a contrast to the locomotive work of the pedlar. Thus it provides a physiological basis and analogue to the economic categories, an analogue that accords with but also goes beyond the mere issue of food distribution.

Mayhew contributes to this conversion of economic into physiological categories. He both assumes and develops the contrast incipient in the criticism of industrialism, and he also reveals how physical strength in itself can be made to seem socially dangerous. For Mayhew the opposite of productive labor that fixes itself is quite explicitly unproductive labor that moves about. Nonproductivity has for its sign "nomadic" movement, and movement has for its sign, as the paragraph quoted earlier in this essay makes clear, a strong body. But, as that passage further emphasizes, the bodies of the nomads are strong in sinister and distorted ways: "Whether it be that in the mere act of wandering, there is a greater determination of blood to the surface of the body, and consequently a less quantity sent to the brain, the muscles being thus nourished at the expense of the mind, I leave physiologists to say" (5). The physiological account of these bodies serves to make the costermongers (his first category of nomads) completely phenomena of circulation, internally and externally. The explanation thus bizarrely reconstitutes an implied analogy between social and individual bodies, even as it implies their opposition. The costermongers are an overly active economic circulatory system; they are carriers of goods who refuse to be controlled in any way. Each, at the same time, *contains* an overly active biological circulatory system, pumping a disproportionate amount of blood to the surface of the body. Instead of seeing the costermongers as parasites (his original depiction of them) or as bodies altogether foreign to the social organism, this new view establishes a more dangerous homology: just as the circulatory system of each costermonger both aggrandizes and distorts the individual bodies, the circulatory system they comprise seems also to vitiate the very core of the being it is supposed to be nourishing. Mayhew devotes pages to the uncontrollability of the costermongers, their "warfare" with the police and their hatred of all authority. A social body bursting with costermongers is, like the costermongers themselves, a body being "nourished at the expense of the mind."

Nevertheless, despite his allusions to the draining of executive powers and of a possible devolution to an animal state, Mayhew can never explain just what the costermonger is costing society. He admits that the costermonger is "simply a tradesman," like any other, "saving time, trouble, and inconvenience to, the [producers] in disposing of, and to the [consumers] in purchasing, their commodities"(8). Unlike Malthus's fatted beast, moreover, the costermonger is specifically associated with providing working-class food: "He brings the greengrocery, the fruit, the fish, the watercresses, the shrimps, the pies and puddings, the sweetmeats, the pine-apples . . . . Indeed, the poor man's food and clothing are mainly supplied to him in this manner" (9). Mayhew does not claim that the trade is particularly inflationary or that the costermonger does not deserve, for his trouble, "the penny profit out of the poor man's Sunday's dinner" (10). The fact that the costermonger did not grow what he sells is not consciously held against him, for Mayhew insists that someone must trade in the goods of others.

Thus he is deprived of any actual economic argument against these pedlars, and is reduced to accusing them of general immorality. At the outset, partly of course to justify the following volumes exposing social problems, Mayhew insists that, like all nomads with big muscles and small brains, costermongers are sexually promiscuous, lazy, and irreligious. As he details their lives, though, these charges evaporate. Strangely, this does not lead to any diminution of the writer's disgust; indeed, the more normal the costermongers turn out to be, the more their animalistic bodies represent nothing beyond walking the streets and selling food, the more they seem to bewilder and appall him.

The Irish women costermongers are a case in point. They are chaste, devout, and hardworking; Mayhew can find no morally deleterious effects of street selling on their characters. One woman explains that she became a costermonger to escape from the sexual perils of domestic service. But instead of accepting her conclusion that street peddling is independent and innocent, Mayhew attributes her preference for it to a kind of perversity:

> There is no doubt my informant was a modest, and, in her way, a worthy woman. But it may be doubted if any English girl, after seven years of domestic service, would have so readily adapted herself to a street calling. . . . I doubt if she, who had the virtues to resist the offers told of by my Irish informant, could have made the attempt to live by selling fruit. I do not mean that she would rather have fallen into immoral courses than honestly live upon the sale of stawberries, but that she would have struggled on and striven to obtain any domestic labour in the preference of a street occupation. (467)

The "street occupation" is in itself the vice that any normal (English) woman would strive to avoid.

But in what does its viciousness consist? The Irish woman's story gives a hint. As she stands there innocently selling strawberries, she is a visible and audible emblem of the sexual and economic exploitation that goes on behind doors and that has driven her into the street. If the costermongers as a group are guilty of anything in Mayhew's book, they are guilty of embodying and hence raising to the surface of consciousness a ruthless struggle for marketplace advantage that Mayhew thinks is going on everywhere unseen. Mayhew returns often to this theme: in their vivacity, their lurid physicality, the intensity of their appeal to the senses, the costermongers *force* on the city dweller the ubiquitousness of the competitive marketplace. Hence, they actually break down the very distinction between productive and unproductive labor that originally seemed to account for their stigmatization, for all life, they continually remind the writer, is a competitive struggle.

When the costermongers are gathered together at market, for Mayhew they are a veritable theater of the all-permeating principle of competitive exchange. Wearing their goods on their bodies, as if they were dressed in allegorical costumes, shouting and gesturing, they mean the universal economic and biological condition of mankind:

Such, indeed, is the riot, the struggle, and the scramble for a living, that the confusion and uproar of the Newcut on Saturday night have a bewildering and saddening effect upon the thoughtful mind.

Each salesman tries his utmost to sell his wares, tempting the passers-by with his bargains. The boy with his stock of herbs offers "a double 'andful of fine parsley for a penny;" the man with the donkey-cart filled with turnips has three lads to shout for him to their utmost, with their "Ho! ho! hi-i-i! What do you think of this here? A penny a bunch—hurrah for free trade! Here's your turnips!" Until it is seen and heard, we have no sense of the scramble that is going on throughout London for a living. (10)

Beneath the workplace, the home, and all other institutions is the "same shouting and the same struggling to get the penny out of the poor man's Sunday's dinner" (52).

The theater of circulation, precisely by presenting itself as the struggle of the poor man's dinner to turn itself into "profit," becomes an emblem not just of circulation *as opposed to* production but also of circulation *underlying* production. For Mayhew, as for Malthus, the poor man's food was the problematic hinge that joined production to exchange. But whereas for Malthus the problem was the actual or potential scarcity of food that laborers could afford, for Mayhew scarcity is not an issue. London seems to be overflowing with cheap food in his works. But that food, as the main portion of what the poor man got in exchange for his labor, is a commodity representing the complete interpenetration of exchange and production. The food is the reminder of the value of labor itself as a commodity. Moreover, the fact that it forms a locus of "struggle" is also a reminder that the value of labor as commodity (what the laborer gets in return for his labor) must be significantly less than the value generated by the laborer in production. Mayhew understood that the difference between the two values was not the "penny profit" of the costermonger but the much larger profit of the poor man's employer. The theater of struggling food thus both displaces and suggests the struggle over wages; hence it refers both to conflict within the working class and to conflict between the classes, a conflict situated at the basis of production.

Hence, unlike Malthus, Mayhew uses working-class food to stress the impossibility of separating exchange and production. By concentrating on the idea of labor as commodity, he emphasizes that the value of labor is itself not an invariable given but a problem and a generator of social conflict. The valuable and problematic aspects of the laboring body are thus combined, although never quite brought into a single focus, in the figure of the costermongers, who are not just the embodiment of the marketplace *as opposed to* productive labor. Since these strong bodies are themselves the very theater of the problematic nature of labor value, they cannot restrict to themselves, as could Malthus's steer, the devaluation of the bodies of circulation. Instead, in Mayhew's work, although physical welfare remains the central preoccupation, a general sense of the body's offensiveness spreads out from the costermongers and permeates the whole realm of organic matter.

Malthus had not been blind to the interpenetrations of exchange and production. The commodification of labor, its variable value, the difference between the value of the commodities produced by labor and those "destined for the support of labor," and the way in which biological reproduction and the value of labor as commodity reciprocally influence each other are all extensively discussed in his work. But because his *Essay* took the body as the locus of value, it also held out hope for as close an identity as possible (within the framework of capitalism) between overall wealth produced and that destined to replenish the bodies of the producers. Later, Malthus also expressed hope for a general rise in the overall market value of labor that would immediately transform itself into larger and healthier laboring bodies. Although he saw many of the same relationships between the body and economic exchange that Mayhew saw, Malthus implied that the problem could be diminished by making the production of productive bodies the telos of exchange, by shrinking economic circuits and centering them on biological needs.

As we have already seen, even in Malthus's *Essay* this wish begins to undercut its own assumptions and the body begins to lose its absolute value when it must produce food to be considered valuable. In the work of Mayhew, though, where the problematic and valuable bodies merge, Malthus's unstable solution, the centering of the marketplace on the body, seems the very basis of the problem. Malthus had personified the unfortunate priority of the marketplace as a dispensable beast, embodying precisely what was not meant for the consumption of labor. But Mayhew's personification, the costermonger, although indirectly representing what is subtracted in exchange from the value produced by labor, more directly and emphatically represents the fund for the maintenance of workers themselves.

Concentrating on working-class food, moreover, is only one of the steps Mayhew takes in turning the marketplace into a phenomenon of lower-class biology. He also physicalizes the motives of the costermongers; their animating principle is the mere need to move their muscles:

After a girl has once grown accustomed to street-life, it is almost impossible to wean her from it. The muscular irritability begotten by continued wandering makes her unable to rest for any time in one place, and she soon, if put to any *settled* occupation, gets to crave for the severe exercise she formerly enjoyed. . . . A gentleman of high literary repute, struck with the heroic strugglings of a coster Irish girl to maintain her mother, took her to his house, with a view of teaching her the duties of a servant. . . . But no sooner did she hear from her friends, that sprats were again in the market, than, as if there were some magical influence in the fish, she at once requested to be freed from the confinement, and permitted to return to her old calling. (44)

The costermonger's muscles move involuntarily in response to their own needs and to the fishes' need to be circulated and consumed. Her being is hence completely physical, determined entirely by the joint action of leg muscles and stomach. Mayhew has here entirely done away with strictly economic motives; he has completely physicalized the forces of the marketplace. The girl is no calculating *homo economicus* but merely a pair of legs that carry themselves back to the market for the sake of their own enjoyment and for the sake of the magically influential food that must find its way into the stomach of labor.

When Mayhew thus depicts the body as the telos of the marketplace he discredits both. The marketplace becomes merely an occasion for the exercise of inappropriate musculature and merely a means of filling bellies. The costermonger, in her complete physicality, suggests to Mayhew the appalling idea that the struggle to live is nothing beyond the struggle to live. Far from elevating the body to the standard of economic and social value, Mayhew's physicalization of the marketplace creates the fear that society is in danger of reducing human value to its most primitive biological needs:

Everything is sacrificed—as, indeed, under the circumstances it must be—in the struggle to live—aye! and to live *merely*. Mind, heart, soul, are all absorbed in the belly. The rudest form of animal life, physiologists tell us, is simply a locomotive stomach. Verily, it would appear as if our social state had a tendency to make the highest animal sink into the lowest. (43)

Reflections on the costermongers, that emblem of food in motion, that locomotive stomach, come to this: biological existence cannot be the measure of value in society; the point of living cannot be merely to stay alive, for if it were, we would soon have no way of distinguishing between one bit of protoplasm and another.

By thoroughly physicalizing the marketplace, therefore, Mayhew exposes the *reductio ad absurdum* of Malthus's implied theory of value and extends one vein of the earlier thinker's logic until it yields a recognizably Victorian disgust for the body. But this disgust cannot carry Mayhew beyond the problematic of the body already sketched in Malthus's work. Rather, Mayhew's work only helps us to understand the revisions leading to that peculiar Victorian discourse in which loathing "mere life" and obsessively examining it are parts of one impulse.

Hence, by stressing the all-pervasiveness of the marketplace and at the same time thoroughly physicalizing it, Mayhew both rewrites and extends the Malthusian problem. In the process, he assumes the characteristic pose of the Victorian middle-class exposer of the physical secrets of the working class.

It is impossible to contemplate the ignorance and immorality of so numerous a class as that of the costermongers, without wishing to discover the cause of their degradation. Let any one curious on this point visit one of these penny shows, and he will wonder that *any* trace of virtue and honesty should remain among the people. . . .

There was one scene . . . that was perfect in its wickedness. A ballet began between a man dressed up as a woman, and a country clown. The most disgusting attitudes were struck, the most immoral acts represented without one dissenting voice. . . . Here were two ruffians degrading themselves each time they stirred a limb, and forcing into the brains of the childish audience before them thoughts that must embitter a lifetime, and descend from father to child like some bodily infirmity. (40–42)

Mayhew stands transfixed before this spectacle in which the working-class body receives its ultimate degradation by acting a macabre pantomime of Malthus's most problematic but also most valuable act: the reproduction of country labor. Placed and parodied here, in the arena of exchange, the very idea of sexuality is overcome by associations of unproductive labor and sterile vice. Again, as in Mayhew's marketplace, one stage of the Malthusian dilemma is played out, and the vivacious depiction of the struggling, but somehow ultimately futile, life force becomes a disease of the social body.

Notes

1. In the second edition of the *Essay*, Malthus names the following eighteenth-century writers who had also noted "the poverty and misery arising from a too rapid increase of population": Montesquieu, Benjamin Franklin, James Stewart, Arthur Young, and Joseph Townsend. These writers, however, do not emphasize the connection Malthus makes between physical vigor and eventual social decline.
2. David Hume, "Of the Populousness of Ancient Nations," in *Essays, Moral, Political, and Literary*, vol. 1 (Edinburgh, 1825), 376.
3. Thomas Malthus, *An Essay on the Principle of Population: Text, Sources and Background, Criticism*, ed. Philip Appleman (New York, 1976), 17. My discussion of Malthus's argument is confined to the first edition of the *Essay* because that is its only coherent, and by far the most influential, version. I have tried in the footnotes to indicate where, in later works, Malthus revised or contradicted the first *Essay*. All quotations from the *Essay* are from the Norton Critical Edition, and subsequent page numbers are given in the text.
4. This aspect of Malthus's thought was highly controversial. Robert Southey, for example, berated Malthus for equating chastity and misery. Others accused him of having a purely utilitarian definition of sexual vice because he had argued that sexual offenses "can rarely or never be committed without producing unhappiness somewhere or other." The statement led some to conclude that Malthus did not consider sexual offenses to be particularly wrong in themselves. The controversy surrounding Malthus's extremely positive valuation of sexuality finally led him, in later editions, to remove sexual abstinence from the category of "misery," thereby severely weakening his own argument. For a discussion of the controversy, see Patricia James, *Population Malthus: His Life and Times* (London, 1979), 121–26.
5. Henry Mayhew, *London Labour and the London Poor; A Cyclopedia of the Condition and Earnings of Those That Will Work, Those That Cannot Work, and Those That Will Not Work*, vol. 1 (London, 1861), 2–3. All further references to this work are to volume 1, and page numbers are given in the text.
6. In both this section of the *Essay* and the earlier sections that concern the difficulties of increasing agricultural production, Malthus's arguments tend to be vague, for the Law of Diminishing Returns was not worked out until twenty years later.
7. See Ricardo's critique of Malthus's corn-labor standard of value in *The Principles of Political Economy and Taxation* (New York, 1973), 10–11. Malthus later returned to the

theory of value in two longer discussions that were generally considered unsuccessful, one in his *Principles of Political Economy and Taxation* (1820) and the other in *The Measure of Value Stated and Illustrated* (1823). In the latter, he came round to the labor theory of value, but in such a way that he remained outside the dominant Ricardian School.

8. Adam Smith, *The Wealth of Nations* (New York, 1970), 295.
9. Thomas Carlyle, *Past and Present* (London, 1960), 1.
10. *Report of the Select Committee of the House of Commons on Labour of Children in Factories,* 1831–32 (706.) XI. 542.

D. A. MILLER

Cage aux folles: Sensation and Gender in Wilkie Collins's *The Woman in White*

for E. K. S.

I

NOTHING "BORING" ABOUT the Victorian sensation novel: the excitement that seizes us here is as direct as the "fight-or-flight" physiology that renders our reading bodies, neither fighting nor fleeing, theaters of neurasthenia. The genre offers us one of the first instances of modern literature to address itself primarily to the sympathetic nervous system, where it grounds its characteristic adrenalin effects: accelerated heart rate and respiration, increased blood pressure, the pallor resulting from vasoconstriction, etc. It is not, of course, the last, and no less current than the phenomenon is the contradictory manner in which, following in the Victorians' footsteps, we continue to acknowledge it.[1] On the one hand, a vulgar salesmanship unblinkingly identifies hyperventilation with aesthetic value, as though art now had no other aim or justification than its successful ability to rattle what the French would call, with anatomical precision, our *cage.* That the body is compelled to automatism, that the rhythm of reading is frankly addictive—such dreary evidence of involuntary servitude is routinely marshaled in ads and on backcovers to promote entertainments whose Pavlovian expertise has become more than sufficient recommendation. On the other hand, an overnice literary criticism wishfully reassures us that these domineering texts, whose power is literally proved upon our pulses, are not worth a thought. By a kind of Cartesian censorship, in which pulp-as-flesh gets equated with pulp-as-trash, the emphatic physicality of thrills in such literature allows us to hold them cheap. Accordingly, the sensation novel is relegated to the margins of the canon of approved genres, and on the infrequent occasions when it is seriously discussed, "sensation"—the modern nervousness that is as fundamental to this genre as its name—is the first thing to be dropped from the discussion.[2] What neither view of sensation fiction questions—what both views, it might be argued, become strategies for not questioning—is the natural immediacy of sensation itself. The celebration of sensation (as a physical experience to be enjoyed for its own sake) merely *receives* it; the censure of sensation (granting it to the obviousness of something about which there is nothing to say) refuses to *read* it. In either case, sensation is felt to occupy a natural site entirely outside of meaning, as though in the breathless body signification expired.

To be sure, the silence that falls over the question of sensation seems first enjoined by the sensation novel itself, which is obsessed with the project of finding meaning—of staging the suspense of its appearance—in everything except the sensations that the project excites in us. Yet in principle the sensation novel must always at least imply a reading of these sensations, for the simple reason that it can mobilize the sympathetic nervous system only by giving it something to sympathize with. In order to make us nervous, nervousness must first be represented: in situations of character and plot that, both in themselves and in the larger cultural allusions they carry, make the operation of our own nerves significant in particular ways. The fiction elaborates a fantasmatics of sensation in which our reading bodies take their place from the start, and of which our physiological responses thus become the hysterical acting out. To speak of hysteria here, of course, is also to recall the assumption that always camouflages it—that what the body suffers, the mind needn't think. "So far as my own sensations were concerned, I can hardly say that I thought at all."[3] The efficacy of psychosomatisms as "defenses" presupposes a rigorously enforced separation in the subject between *psyche* and *soma,* and hysteria successfully breeches the body's autonomy only on the condition that this autonomy will be felt to remain intact. Reading the sensation novel, our hystericized bodies "naturalize" the meanings in which the narrative implicates them, but in doing so they also nullify these meanings as such. Incarnate in the body, the latter no longer seem part of a cultural, historical process of signification but instead dissolve into an inarticulable, merely palpable self-evidence. Thus, if every sensation novel necessarily provides an interpretation of the sensations to which it gives rise in its readers, the immediacy of these sensations can also be counted on to *disown* such an interpretation. It may even be that the nonrecognition that thus obtains between our sensations and their narrative thematization allows the sensation novel to "say" certain things for which our culture—at least at its popular levels—has yet to develop another language.

Wilkie Collins's *The Woman in White* (1860)—of all sensation novels considered the best and best known—seems at any rate an exemplary text for making this case. For what "happens" in this novel becomes fully clear and coherent only, I think, when one takes into account the novel's implicit reading of its own (still quite "effective") performative dimension and thus restores sensation to its textual and cultural mediations. For the reason given above, the attempt to do so must be prepared to seem rather "forced"—as unprovable as a connotation and as improbable as a latency—but it is worth undertaking for more than a better understanding of this particular text. The ideological valences with which sensation characteristically combines in the novel do not of course absolutely transcend the second half of the Victorian period in which they are elaborated—as though the social significance of nervousness (itself an historical construct) were fixed once for all; but neither are they restricted to this period. Collins's novel continues to be not just thoroughly readable but eminently "writable" as well. If it is still capable of moving readers to the edge of their seats (and how sharp a sense of this edge may be is suggested when one character starts from his own seat "as if a spike had grown up from the ground through the bottom of [his] chair" [41]), this is because its particular staging of nervousness remains cognate with that of many of our own thrillers, printed or filmed. It thus offers a pertinent, if not exhaustive, demonstration of the value, meaning, and use that modern culture—which in this respect has by no means broken radically with Victorian culture—finds in the nervous state.

Without exception, such a state affects all the novel's principal characters, who are variously startled, affrighted, unsettled, chilled, agitated, flurried. All sooner or later inhabit the "sensationalized" body where the blood curdles, the heart beats violently, the breath comes short and thick, the flesh creeps, the cheeks lose their color. No one knows what is the matter with Mr. Fairlie, but "we all say it's on the nerves" (61), and in widely different ways his niece Laura is "rather nervous and sensitive" (63). The "nervous sensitiveness" (127) of her double and half-sister Anne Catherick, the Woman in White, issues in the aneurism that causes her death. Characters who are not constitutionally nervous become circumstantially so, in the unnerving course of events. Unsettled by the mystery surrounding Anne, fearful that Laura may be implicated in it, suspecting that he is himself being watched, Walter Hartright develops a "nervous contraction" about his lips and eyes (178), which he appears to have caught from Laura herself, whose "sweet, sensitive lips are subject to a slight nervous contraction" (75). At first "perfect self-possession" (209), Sir Percival Glyde degenerates after his marriage to Laura into "an unsettled, excitable manner . . . a kind of panic or frenzy of mind" (417). And Marian Halcombe, Laura's other half-sister, has already lost the "easy inborn confidence in herself and her position" (60) that initially characterized her by the time of the first anxious and "sadly distrustful" extract (184) from her diary. In the course of keeping that diary, of gathering the increasingly less equivocal evidence of a "plot" against Laura, she literally writes herself into a fever. It is a measure of Count Fosco's control over these characters that he is said to be "born without nerves" (376), though his "eternal cigarettes" (252) attest that even here nervousness is not so much missing as mastered, and mastered only insofar as its symptoms are masked in the banal practices of civilized society.

Nervousness seems the necessary "condition" in the novel for perceiving its real plot and for participating in it as more than a pawn. The condition is not quite sufficient, as the case of the wilfully ignorant Mr. Fairlie shows, but otherwise those without the capacity to become nervous also lack the capacity to interpret events, or even to see that events require interpreting. The servants, for instance, also called (more accurately) "persons born without nerves" (69), are uniformly oblivious to what is or might be going on: the "unutterably tranquil" governess Mrs. Vesey (72), the maid who "in a state of cheerful stupidity" grins at the sight of Mrs. Catherick's wounded dog (229), the housekeeper Mrs. Michelson, whose Christian piety prevents her from advancing "opinions" (381). It is not exactly that the novel uses nervousness to mark middle-class status, since the trait fails to characterize the "sanguine constitution" of Mr. Gilmore, the family lawyer, who "philosophically" walks off his "uneasiness" about Laura's marriage (159). Rather the novel makes nervousness a metonymy for reading, its cause or effect. No reader can identify with unruffled characters like Gilmore or Mrs. Michelson, even when they narrate parts of the story, because every reader is by definition committed to a hermeneutic project that neither of these characters finds necessary or desirable. Instead we identify with nerve-racked figures like Walter and Marian who carry forward the activity of our own deciphering. We identify even with Anne Catherick in her "nervous dread" (134), though she is never capable of articulating its object, because that dread holds at least the promise of the story we will read. Nervousness is our justification in the novel, as Mrs. Michelson's faith is hers, insofar as it validates the attempt to read, to uncover the grounds for *being* nervous.

The association of nervousness with reading is complicated—not to say troubled—by its coincident, no less insistent or regular association with femininity. However general a phenomenon, nervousness is always gendered in the novel as, like Laura's headache symptom, an "essentially feminine malady" (59). Of the novel's three characters who seem "born" nervous, two are women (Anne and Laura) and the third, Mr. Fairlie, an effeminate. "I am nothing," the latter pronounces himself, "but a bundle of nerves dressed up to look like a man" (370). No one, however, is much convinced by the drag, and Walter's first impression— "He had a frail, languid-fretful, over-refined look—something singularly and unpleasantly delicate in its association with a man" (66)—never stands in need of correction. Even in the less fey male characters, nervousness remains a signifier of femininity. At best it declares Walter still "unformed," and Sir Percival's imposture—that he is not, so to speak, the man he is pretending to be—is already in a manner disclosed when Mrs. Michelson observes that "he seemed to be almost as nervous and fluttered . . . as his lady herself" (403). Fosco himself, Marian informs us, "is as nervously sensitive as the weakest of us [women]. He starts at chance noises as inveterately as Laura herself" (242).

The novel's "primal scene," which it obsessively repeats and remembers ("Anne Catherick again!") as though this were the trauma it needed to work through, rehearses the "origins" of male nervousness in female contagion—strictly, in the woman's touch. When Anne Catherick, in flight from the Asylum where she has been shut away, "lightly and suddenly" lays her hand on Walter Hartright's shoulder, it brings "every drop of blood in [his] body . . . to a stop" (47). Released from—and with—the Woman, nervousness touches and enters the Man: Anne's nervous gesture is at once sympathetically "caught" in Walter's nervous response to it. Attempting to recover himself, Walter tightens his fingers round "the handle of [his] stick," as though the touch—"from behind [him]" (47)—were a violation requiring violent counteraction, and what was violated were a gender identification that needed to be reaffirmed. Yet Anne Catherick impinges on him again: "The loneliness and helplessness of the woman touched me" (49). His formulation hopefully denies what is happening to him—Anne's weak femininity is supposed to evince *a contrario* his strong masculinity—but the denial seems only to produce further evidence of the gender slippage it means to arrest. Even in his classic gallantry, Walter somehow feels insufficiently manly, "immature": "The natural impulse to assist her and spare her got the better of the judgment, the caution, the worldly tact, which an older, wiser, and colder man might have summoned to help him in this strange emergency" (49). He is even "distressed by an uneasy sense of having done wrong" (54), of having betrayed his sex: "What had I done? Assisted the victim of the most horrible of all false imprisonments to escape; or cast loose on the wide world of London an unfortunate creature, whose actions it was my duty, and every man's duty, mercifully to control?" (55). Walter's protection has in fact suspended the control that is "every man's duty" to exercise over the activity of the neuropathic woman. Thanks to his help, Anne eludes a manifold of male guardians: the turnpike man at the entry gate of the city; the two men from the Asylum including its director; the policeman who, significantly, is assumed to be at their disposal; and even Walter himself, who puts her into a cab, destination unknown. "A dangerous woman to be at large" (177): the female trouble first transmitted to Walter will extend throughout the thick ramifications of plot to excite sympathetic vibrations in Laura and Marian, and in Sir Percival and even Fosco as well. And not just in them. "The reader's nerves are affected like the hero's," writes Mrs. Oliphant in a contemporary review of the novel; in what I have called the novel's primal scene, this means that "the silent woman lays her hand upon our shoulder as well as upon that of Mr. Walter Hartright."[4] As the first of the novel's sensation effects *on us*, the scene thus fictionalizes the beginning of our physiological experience of the sensation novel as such. Our first sensation coincides with—is positively triggered by—the novel's originary account of sensation. Fantasmatically, then, we "catch" sensation from the neuropathic body of the Woman who, no longer confined or controlled in an asylum, is free to make our bodies resonate with—like—hers.

Every reader is consequently implied to be a version or extension of the Woman in White, a fact that entails particularly interesting consequences when the reader is—as the text explicitly assumes he is—male.[5] This reader willy-nilly falls victim to an hysteria in which what is acted out (desired, repressed) is an essentially female "sensation." His excitements come from—become—her nervous excitability; his rib cage, arithmetically Adam's, houses a woman's quickened respiration, and his heart beats to her skittish rhythm; even his pallor (which of course he cannot see) is mirrored back to him only as hers, the Woman in White's. This reader thus lends himself to elaborating a fantasy of *anima muliebris in corpore virili inclusa*—or as we might appropriately translate here, "a woman's breath caught in a man's body." The usual rendering, of course, is "a woman's soul trapped. . . ," and it will be recognized as nineteenth-century sexology's classic formulation (coined by Karl Ulrichs in the 1860s) for male homosexuality.[6] I cite it, not just to anticipate the homosexual component given to readerly sensation by the novel, but also, letting the phrase resonate beyond Ulrichs's intentions, to situate this component among the others that determine its context. For if what essentially characterizes male homosexuality in this way of putting it is the woman-in-the-man, and if this "woman" is *inclusa,* incarcerated or shut up, her freedoms abridged accordingly, then homosexuality would be by its very nature homophobic: imprisoned in a carceral problematic that does little more than channel into the homosexual's "ontology" the social and legal sanctions that might otherwise be imposed on him. Meant to win a certain intermediate space for homosexuals, Ulrichs's formulation in fact ultimately colludes with the prison or closet drama—of keeping the "woman" well put away—that it would relegate to the unenlightened past. And homosexuals' souls are not the only ones to be imprisoned in male bodies; Ulrichs's phrase does perhaps far better as a general description of the condition of nineteenth-century women, whose "spirit" (whether understood as intellect, integrity, or sexuality) is massively interned in male corporations, constitutions, contexts. His metaphor thus may be seen to link or condense together 1) a particular fantasy about male homosexuality; 2) a homophobic defense against that fantasy; and 3) the male oppression of women that, among other things, extends that defense. All three meanings bear pointedly on Collins's novel, which is profoundly about enclosing and secluding the woman in male "bodies," among them institutions like marriage and madhouses. And the sequestration of the woman takes for its object not just women, who need to be put away in safe places or asylums, but men as well, who must monitor and master what is fantasized as the "woman inside" them.

II

Like *The Moonstone, The Woman in White* accords itself the status of a quasilegal document.

If the machinery of the Law could be depended on to fathom every case of suspicion, and to conduct every process of inquiry, with moderate assistance only from the lubricating influences of oil of gold, the events which fill these pages might have claimed their share of the public attention in a Court of Justice. But the Law is still, in certain inevitable cases, the pre-engaged servant of the long purse; and the story is left to be told, for the first time, in this place. As the Judge might once have heard it, so the Reader shall hear it now. . . . Thus, the story here presented will be told by more than one pen, as the story of an offence against the laws is told in Court by more than one witness—with the same object, in both cases, to present the truth always in its most direct and most intelligible aspect. (33)

The organizational device is a curious one, since nothing in the story ever appears to motivate it. Why and for whom does this story need to be thus told? At the end of the novel—after which Walter Hartright presumably gathers his narratives together—neither legal action nor even a paralegal hearing seems in the least required. And it is of course pure mystification to preface a mystery story with a claim to be presenting the truth "always in its most direct and most intelligible aspect." But the obvious gimmickiness of the device offers only the crudest evidence of the limited pertinence of the legal model that the text here invokes. On the face of it, despite its conventionally bitter references to oil of gold and the long purse, the text is eager to retain the Law—the juridical model of an inquest—for its own narrative. It simply proposes to extend this model to a case that it wouldn't ordinarily cover. The explicit ideal thus served would be a Law that fathomed every case of suspicion and conducted every process of inquiry. But what Law has ever done this, or wanted to? Certainly not the English law, which like all nontotalitarian legal systems is on principle concerned to limit the matters that fall under its jurisdiction. The desire to extend the Law as totally as the preamble utopically envisions—to *every* case of suspicion and *every* process of inquiry—would therefore supersede the legal model to which, the better not to alarm us, it nominally clings. For the project of such a desire makes sense only in a world where suspicion and inquiry have already become everyday practices, and whose affinities lie less with a given legal code or apparatus than with a vast, multifaceted network of inquests-without-end. Under the guise of a pedantic, legalistic organization, the novel in fact aligns itself with extra-, infra-, and supra-legal modern discipline.

Not, of course, that *The Woman in White* represents the world of discipline in the manner of either *Bleak House* or *Barchester Towers*. Its most important relationship to this world, at any rate, does not come at the level of an "objective" portrayal, either of institutions (like Court of Chancery and the Detective Police in Dickens) or of less formal means of social control (like "moderate schism" and the norm in Trollope).[7] It would be quite difficult to educe a sociological understanding of Victorian asylums from Collins's novel, which, voiding a lively contemporary concern with the private madhouse, describes neither its structure nor the (medicinal? physical? psychological?) therapies that may or may not be practiced within it.[8] Anne never says, and Laura finds it too painfully confusing to recall, what goes on there. The Asylum remains a very black "black box," the melodramatic site of "the most horrible of false imprisonments," where the sane middle class might mistakenly be sent. The Asylum, in short, is available to representation mainly insofar as it has been *incorporated:* in Walter's "unsettled state" when he first learns that Anne is a fugitive from there, in Anne's nervous panic at the very word, in the difference between Laura's body before she enters the place and after she leaves, in the way we are invited to fill in the blank horror of what she cannot remember with the stuff of our own nightmares. What the example may be broadened to suggest is that the novel represents discipline mainly in terms of certain general isolated effects on the disciplinary *subject*, whose sensationalized body both dramatizes and facilitates his functioning as *the subject/object of continual supervision.*

These effects, together with the juridical metaphor under which they are first inscribed, are best pursued in the contradiction between the Judge and the Reader who is supposed to take his place. "As the Judge might once have heard [the story], so the Reader shall hear it now." The pronouncement, of course, confers on the latter role all the connotations of sobriety and even serenity attached to the former. That "wretches hang that jurymen may dine" will always give scandal to our Western mythology of justice, in which the Judge—set above superstition, prejudice, "interest" of any kind—weighs the evidence with long and patient scruple before pronouncing sentence. Nothing, however, could be less judicial, or judicious, than the actual hermeneutic practice of the reader of this novel, whose technology of nervous stimulation—in many ways still the state of the art—has him repeatedly jumping to unproven conclusions, often literally jumping at them. Far from encouraging reflective calm, the novel aims to deliver "positive personal shocks of surprise and excitement" that so sensationalize the reader's body that he is scarcely able to reflect at all.[9] The novel's only character with strictly judicial habits of mind is the lawyer Gilmore, who judges only to misjudge. Hearing Sir Percival's explanation of his dealings with Anne Catherick, he says: "My function was of the purely judicial kind. I was to weigh the explanation we had just heard . . . and to decide honestly whether the probabilities, on Sir Percival's own showing, were plainly with him, or plainly against him. My own conviction was that they were plainly with him" (155). Characters who rely on utterly unlegal standards of evidence like intuition, coincidence, literary connotation get closer to what will eventually be revealed as the truth. In her first conversation with Walter, Anne Catherick nervously inquires about an unnamed baronet in Hampshire; Walter later learns that Laura is engaged to a baronet in Hampshire named Sir Percival Glyde. "Judging by the ordinary rules of evidence, I had not the shadow of a reason, thus far, for connecting Sir Percival Glyde with the suspicious words of inquiry that had been spoken to me by the woman in white. And yet, I did connect them" (101). Similarly, when after Sir Percival's explanation Gilmore wonders what excuse Laura can possibly have for changing her mind about him, Marian answers: "In the eyes of law and reason, Mr. Gilmore, no excuse, I dare say. If she still hesitates, and if I still hesitate, you must attribute our strange conduct, if you like, to caprice in both cases" (162). The competent reader, who does not weigh evidence so much as he simply assents to the ways in which it has been weighted, fully accepts the validity of such ungrounded connections and inexcusable hesitations: they validate, among other things, the sensations they make him feel. And this reader is capable of making what by the ordinary rules of evidence are comparably tenuous assumptions of his own. We can't know, just because Sir Percival's men are watching Somebody, and Walter may be being watched, that Walter is that Somebody, and yet we are convinced that we do know this. Or again, the loose seal on the letter that Marian recovers from the post-bag after she has seen Fosco hovering about it does not establish the fact that Fosco has opened and resealed her letter, but we take it firmly for granted nonetheless. Our judgments are often informed by no better than the silliest folk wisdom. Laura's pet greyhound shrinks from Sir Percival—"a trifle," Gilmore considers it (156), even though Nina later jumps eagerly enough into his own lap. In the strange court of justice over which we preside, we consider her evidence unimpeachable. Yet neither adhering to ordinary rules of evidence nor inhering in a decisive institutional context (except of course that provided by the conventions of this kind of novel), such "acts of judgment" are in fact only entitled to the considerably less authoritative status of *suspicions,* whose "uncertainty" in both these senses makes it easy to discredit them. Walter is the first to refer his hypotheses to their possible source in "delusion" and "monomania" (101, 105). Like the characters who figure him, the Reader becomes—what a Judge is never supposed to be—paranoid. From trifles and common coincidences, he suspiciously infers a complicated structure of persecution, an elaborately totalizing "plot."

What a Judge is never supposed to be? Yet the most famous paranoid of modern times *was* a judge, and his paranoia was triggered precisely when, at Dresden, he entered on his duties as Senatspräsident. Schreber's case suggests that paranoia is "born" at the moment when the Judge, without ceasing to be Judge, has also become the Accused, when he is both one and the other. It was, of course, his homosexuality that put Schreber in this institutionally untenable position, since the Law he was expected to administer would certainly include, as Guy Hocquengham has pointed out, interdictions against homosexuality itself.[10] Schreber's delusion does nothing so much as elaborate the paradoxical aspect of his actual situation as a judge who might well have to judge (others like) himself. The Rays of God, having constituted his monstrosity (literally: by feminizing his constitution via the nerves), taunt him with it thus: "So *this* sets up to have been a Senatspräsident, this person who lets himself be f——d!"[11] In *The Woman in White,* another case of feminization via the nerves, Mrs. Michelson's article of unsuspecting faith—"Judge not that ye be not judged" (381)—postulates an inevitable slippage between subject and object whenever judgment is attempted. The slippage is in fact far more likely to occur when judgment, no longer governed by an institutional practice with established roles and rules of evidence, has devolved into mere suspicion. Unlike legal judgment, suspicion presupposes the reversibility of the direction in which it passes. The novel abounds with suspicious characters, in the telling ambiguity of the phrase, for what Anne, Walter, and Marian all suspect is that *they are themselves suspected*. Why else would Anne be pursued, Walter watched, Marian's correspondence opened? They are suspected, moreover, precisely *for being suspicious*. For Walter to notice that Anne's manner is "a little touched by suspicion" is already to suspect her, as she instantly recognizes ("Why do you suspect me?" [48]). Hence the urgency, as well as the futility, of the suspicious character's obsessive desire *not to excite suspicion* (260, 275, 293, 311, 325), since the act of suspecting always already implies the state of being suspect. The whole vertiginous game (in which I suspect him of suspecting me of suspecting him) is meant to ward off—but only by passing along—the violation of privacy that it thus at once promotes and resists. In what Roland Barthes would call the novel's symbolic code, this violation connotes the sexual attack whose possibility "haunts" the novel no less thoroughly than the virginal presence—insistent like a dare—of the Woman in White. What stands behind the vague fears of Anne and Walter during their first encounter; what subtends Mr. Fairlie's malicious greeting of the latter ("So glad to possess you at Limmeridge, Mr. Hartright" [66]); what Sir Percival sadistically fantasizes when he invites his wife to imagine her lover "with the marks of my horsewhip on his shoulders" (283); and what Fosco finally accomplishes when he reads Marian's *journal intime*— is virtual rape. We might consider what is implied or at stake in the fact that the head game of suspicion is always implicitly transcoded by the novel into the body game of rape.

Perhaps the most fundamental value that the Novel, as a cultural institution, may be said to uphold is privacy, the determination of an integral, autonomous, "secret" self. Novel reading takes for granted the existence of a space in which the reading subject remains safe from the surveillance, suspicion, reading, and rape of others. Yet this privacy is always specified as the freedom to read about characters who oversee, suspect, read, and rape one another. It is not just that, strictly private subjects, we read about violated, objectified subjects but that, in the very act of reading about them, we contribute largely to constituting them as such. We enjoy our privacy in the act of watching privacy being violated, in the act of watching that is already itself a violation of privacy. Our most intense identification with characters never blinds us to our ontological privilege over them: they will never be reading about *us*. It is built into the structure of the Novel that every reader must realize the definitive fantasy of the liberal subject, who imagines himself free from the surveillance that he nonetheless sees operating everywhere around him.

The sensation novel, however, submits this panoptic immunity to a crucial modification: it produces repeated and undeniable evidence—"on the nerves"— that we are perturbed by what we are watching. We remain of course unseen but not untouched: our bodies are rocked by the same "positive personal shocks" as the characters' are said to be. For us, these shocks have the ambivalent character of being both an untroubled pleasure (with a certain "male" adventurism we read the sensation novel to *have* them) and a less tame and more painful *jouissance* (with a certain "female" helplessness we often protest that we can't *bear* them, though they keep on coming). The specificity of the sensation novel in nineteenth-century fiction is that it renders the liberal subject the subject of a *body*, whose fear and desire of violation displaces, reworks, and exceeds his constitutive fantasy of intact privacy. The themes that the liberal subject ordinarily defines himself against—by reading *about* them—are here inscribed into his reading body. Moreover, in *The Woman in White* this body is gendered: not only has its gender been *decided*, but also its gender identification is an active and determining *question*. The drama in which the novel writes its reader turns on the disjunction between his allegedly masculine gender and his effectively feminine gender identification (as a creature of "nerves"): with the result that his experience of sensation must include his panic at having the experience at all, of being in the position to have it. In this sense, the novel's initial assumption that its reader is male is precisely what cannot be assumed (or better, what stands most in need of "proof"), since his formal title—say, "a man"—is not or not yet a substantial entity—say, "a real man."

By far the most shocking moment in the reader's drama comes almost in the exact middle of the novel when the text of Marian's diary, lapsing into illegible fragments, abruptly yields to a postscript by the very character on whom its suspicions center. Not only has Count Fosco read Marian's "secret pages" (240), he lets her know it, and even returns them to her. In a fever that soon turns to typhus, Marian is in no condition even to take cognizance of this revelation, whose only immediate register is the reader's own body. Peter Brooks articulates our state of shock thus: "Our readerly intimacy with Marian is violated, our act of reading adulterated by profane eyes, made secondary to the villain's reading and indeed dependent on his permission."[12] It is not just, then, that Marian has been "raped," as both the Count's amorous flourish ("Admirable woman!" [258]) and her subsequent powerless rage against him are meant to suggest. We are "taken" too, taken by surprise, which is itself an overtaking. We are taken, moreover, from behind: from a place where, in the wings of the ostensible drama, the novelist disposes of a whole plot machinery whose existence—so long as it didn't oblige us by making creaking sounds (and here it is as "noiseless" as Fosco himself [242])—we never suspected. (We never suspected, though the novel has trained us to be nothing if not suspicious. Surprise—the recognition of what one "never suspected"—is precisely what the paranoid seeks to eliminate, but it is also what, in the event, he survives by reading as a frightening incentive: he can never be paranoid enough.) To being the object of violation here, however, there is an equally disturbing alternative: to identify with Fosco, with the novelistic agency of violation. For the Count's postscript only puts him in the position we already occupy. Having just finished reading Marian's diary ourselves, we are thus implicated in the sadism of his act, which even as it violates our readerly intimacy with Marian reveals that "intimacy" to be itself a violation. The ambivalent structure of readerly identification here thus condenses together—as simultaneous but opposite renderings of the same powerful shock—homosexual panic and heterosexual violence.

This is the shock, however, that, having administered, the novel (like any good administration) will work to absorb. The shock in fact proves the point of transition between what the narrative will soothingly render as a *succession:* on one side, a passive, paranoid, homosexual feminization; on the other, an active, corroborative, heterosexual masculine protest. Marian alerts us to this succession ("Our endurance must end, and our resistance must begin" [321]), but only toward the end of her narrative, since the moment of "resistance" will need to be effectively sponsored not just by a male agent but by an indefectibly composed male discourse as well. The master narrator and actor in the second half of the novel is therefore Walter: no longer the immature Walter whose nerve-ridden opening narrative seemed—tonally, at any rate—merely continued in Marian's diary, but the Walter who has returned from his trials in Central America "a changed man": "In the stern school of extremity and danger my will had learnt to be strong, my heart to be resolute, my mind to rely on itself. I had gone out to fly from my own future. I came back to face it, as a man should" (427). Concomitantly, the helpless paranoia of the first half of the novel now seeks *to prove itself*, as Walter aggressively attempts to "force a confession" from Sir Percival and Fosco "on [his] own terms" (470). Shocks decline "dramatically" in both frequency and intensity (our last sensation: its absence) as characters and readers alike come to get answers to the question that sensation could never do more than merely pose of the event occasioning it—namely, "What did it mean?" (99). Foremost on the novel's agenda in its second half is the dissolution of sensation in the achievement of decided meaning. What the narrative must most importantly get straight is, from this perspective, as much certain sexual and gender deviancies as the obscure tangles of plot in which they thrive. In short, the novel needs to realize the normative requirements of the heterosexual menage whose happy picture concludes it.

This conclusion, of course, marks the most banal moment in the text, when the sensation novel becomes least distinguishable from any other kind of Victorian fiction. Herein, one might argue, lies the "morality" of sensation fiction, in its ultimately fulfilled wish to abolish itself: to abandon the grotesque aberrations of character and situation that have typified its representation, which now coincides with the norm of the Victorian household. But the project, however successful, is nothing here if not drastic. In *Barchester Towers,* by contrast, the normative elements of heterosexual coupling—the manly husband, the feminine wife—are ready-to-hand early on, and the plot is mainly a question of overcoming various inhibitions and misunderstandings that temporarily prevent them from acknowledging their appropriateness for one another. In *The Woman in White*, however, these elements have to be "engendered" in the course of the plot through the most extreme and violent expedients. The sufficiently manly husband needs to have survived plague, pygmy arrows, and shipwreck in Central America, and the suitably feminine wife must have been schooled in a lunatic asylum, where she is half cretinized. Such desperate measures no doubt dramatize the supreme value of a norm for whose incarnation no price, including the most brutal aversion therapy, is considered too high to pay. But they do something else besides, something that Victorians, in thrall to this norm, suspected when they accused the sensation novel of immorality and that we, more laxly oppressed than they, are perhaps in a better position to specify. This is simply that, recontextualized in a "sensational" account of its genesis, such a norm risks appearing *monstrous*: as aberrant as any of the abnormal conditions that determine its realization.

III

"It ended, as you probably guess by this time, in his insisting on securing his own safety by shutting her up" (557). Male security in *The Woman in White* seems always to depend on female claustration. Sir Percival not only shuts up Anne in the Asylum but successfully conspires with Fosco to shut up Laura there as well. In a double sense, he also shuts up Anne's mother, whose silence he purchases with a "handsome" allowance and ensures by insisting she not leave the town where she has been shamed and where therefore "no virtuous female friends would tempt [her] into dangerous gossiping at the tea-table" (554–55). Thanks to "the iron rod" that Fosco keeps "private" (224), Madame Fosco, who once "advocated the Rights of Women" (255), now lives in a "state of suppression" that extends to "stiff little rows of very short curls" on either side of her face and "quiet black or grey gowns, made high round the throat" (238–39). She walks in a favorite circle, "round and round the great fish pond" (290)—the Blackwater estate is in any case already "shut in—almost suffocated . . . by trees" (220)—as though she were taking yard exercise. The novel does not of course approve of these restraining orders, which originate in unambiguously criminal depravity, but as we will see it is not above exploiting them as the stick with which to contrast and complement the carrot of a far more ordinary and acceptable mode of sequestration.

Sandra M. Gilbert and Susan Gubar have argued that "dramatizations of imprisonment and escape are so all-pervasive in nineteenth-century literature by women that . . . they represent a uniquely female tradition in this period." Male carceral representations, "more consciously and objectively" elaborated, tend to be "metaphysical and metaphorical," whereas female ones remain "social and actual."[13] Yet at least in the nineteenth-century novel, the representation of imprisonment is too pervasive to be exclusively or even chiefly a female property, and too consistent overall to be divided between male and female authors on the basis of the distinctions proposed. On the one hand, it is a commonplace that Dickens's carceral fictions are grounded in actual social institutions, and there is little that is metaphysical in Trollope's rendering of social control: what little there is, in the form of "religion" or "providence," merely sanctions the social mechanisms concretely at work. On the other, Charlotte Brontë's "dramatizations of imprisonment" do not deal with literal prisons at all, as Gilbert and Gubar themselves demonstrate. Insofar as these critics endorse a familiar series of oppositions (masculine/feminine = abstract/concrete = conscious/unconscious = objective/subjective) that, even graphically, keeps women behind a lot of bars, their attempt to isolate the essential paradigm of female writing unwittingly risks recycling the feminine mystique. We are nonetheless indebted to them for posing the question of the specific historical configuration, in the nineteenth-century English novel, of what might be called the "feminine carceral." As they convincingly show, this configuration centers on the representation, in varying degrees of alienation, of the "madwoman," and if this representation is not a uniquely female tradition, one readily grants that it is dominantly so. *The Woman in White*, however, with impressive ease incorporating the story of female "imprisonment and escape" (again, *anima muliebris inclusa*), suggests that there is a radical ambiguity about the "madwoman" that allows the feminist concerns she often voices to have already been appropriated in antifeminist ways. To the extent that novelists (or critics) underwrite the validity of female "madness" as virtually the only mode of its subject's authenticity, they inevitably slight the fact that it is also her socially given *role,* whose quasimandatory performance under certain conditions apotheosizes the familiar stereotypes of the woman as "unconscious" and "subjective" (read: irresponsible) that contribute largely to her oppression. The madwoman finds a considerable part of her truth—in the corpus of nineteenth-century fiction, at any rate—in being implicitly juxtaposed to the male *criminal* she is never allowed to be. If, typically, *he* ends up in the prison or its metaphorical equivalents, *she* ends up in the asylum or *its* metaphorical equivalents. (As a child perusing the shelves of a public library, I thought *The Woman in White* must be the story of a nurse: it at least proves to be the story of various women's subservience to "the doctor," to medical domination.) The distinction between criminal men (like Sir Percival and Fosco) and innocently sick women (like Anne and Laura) bespeaks a paternalism whose "chivalry" merely sublimates a system of constraints. In this light, the best way to read the madwoman would be not to derive the diagnosis from her social psychology ("Who wouldn't go crazy under such conditions?") but rather to derive her social psychology from the diagnosis: from the very category of Madness that, like a fate, lies ever in wait to "cover"—account for and occlude—whatever behaviors, desires, or tendencies might be considered socially deviant, undesirable, or dangerous.

The achievement of blowing this cover belongs to *Lady Audley's Secret* (1862), the novel where, writing under the ambiguous stimulus of *The Woman in White*, Mary Elizabeth Braddon demonstrates that the madwoman's primary "alienation" lies in the rubric under which she is put down. Not unlike Anne Catherick, "always weak in the head" (554), Lady Audley appears to have been born with the "taint" of madness in her blood. She inherits the taint from her mother, whose own madness was in turn "an hereditary disease transmitted to her from her mother, who died mad." Passed on like a curse through—and as—the woman, madness virtually belongs to the condition of being female. But the novel is not so much concerned to conjoin madness and femininity, each the "truth" of the other, as to display how—under what assumptions and by what procedures—such a conjunction comes to be socially achieved. For in fact the text leaves ample room for doubt on the score of Lady Audley's "madness." Her acts, including bigamy, arson, and attempted murder, qualify as crimes in a strict legal sense, and they are motivated (like crime in English detective fiction generally) by impeccably rational considerations of self-interest. When her nephew Robert Audley at last detects her, however, he simply arranges for her to be pronounced "mad" and imprisoned accordingly in a *maison de santé* abroad. The "secret" let out at the end of the novel is not, therefore, that Lady Audley is a madwoman but rather that, *whether she is one or not*, she must be treated as such. Robert feels no embarrassment at the incommensurability thus betrayed between the diagnosis and the data that are supposed to confirm it; if need be, these data can be dispensed with altogether, as in the findings of the doctor ("experienced in cases of mania") whom he calls in for an opinion:

"I have talked to the lady," [the doctor] said quietly, "and we understand each other very well. There is latent insanity! Insanity which might never appear; or which might appear only once or twice in a lifetime. It would be a *dementia* in its worst phase, perhaps; acute mania; but its duration would be very brief, and it would only arise under extreme mental pressure. The lady is not mad; but she has the hereditary taint in her blood. She has the cunning of madness, with the prudence of intelligence. I will tell you what she is, Mr. Audley. She is dangerous!"[14]

The doctor's double-talk ("the cunning of madness, with the prudence of intelligence") will be required to sanction two contradictory propositions: 1) Lady Audley is criminal—in the sense that her crimes must be punished; and 2) Lady Audley is not criminal—in the sense that neither her crimes nor her punishment must be made public in a male order of things. ("My greatest fear," Robert tells the doctor, "is the necessity of any exposure—any disgrace.") "Latent insanity, an insanity which might never appear" nicely meets the requirements of the case. At the same time that it removes the necessity for evidence (do Lady Audley's crimes manifest her latent insanity? or has the latter, quite independently of them, yet to make its appearance?), it adduces the grounds for confining her to a madhouse. Lady Audley is mad, then, only because she must not be criminal. She must not, in other words, be supposed capable of acting on her own diabolical responsibility and hence of publicly spoiling her assigned role as the conduit of power transactions between men.[15] Whatever doubts the doctor entertains in pronouncing her mad do not affect his certainty that she is, at all events, dangerous, and this social judgment entirely suffices to discount the ambiguities that the properly medical one need not bother to resolve.

Lady Audley's Secret thus portrays the woman's carceral condition as her fundamental and final truth. The novel's power as a revision of *The Woman in White* consists in its refusal of the liberal dialectic whereby the latter thinks to surpass this truth. Up to a certain point—say, up to the success of the conspiracy to confine Laura—Collins's novel is willing to tell the same story as Braddon's: of an incarceration whose patriarchal expediency takes priority over whatever humane considerations may or may not be invoked to rationalize it. (Anne's mental disorder, though real enough, is only a plausible pretext for confining her on other grounds, and Laura's confinement has no medical justification whatsoever.) But unlike Lady Audley, Lady Glyde *escapes* from her Asylum, and there fortunately proves somewhere else to go. The Asylum has an "alibi" in Limmeridge House (twice called an "asylum" in the text [367, 368]), where in the end Laura settles happily down with Walter. Whereas in the first movement of the novel the woman is shut up, in the second she is liberated, and it is rather the "feminine carceral" that is put away instead. Laura thus follows a common itinerary of the liberal subject in nineteenth-century fiction: she takes a nightmarish detour through the carceral ghetto on her way *home,* to the domestic haven where she is always felt to belong. Yet while her history plainly dichotomizes carceral and liberal spaces, the Asylum that keeps one inside and the "asylum" that keeps others out, it also gives evidence of continuities and overlappings between them. If her situation as Mrs. Hartright throws domesticity into relief as relief indeed from the brutalities of the Asylum, her state as Lady Glyde (at Sir Percival's "stifling" house [227]) merely anticipates the Asylum, which in turn only perfects Sir Percival's control over her. The difference between the Asylum-as-confinement and the "asylum"-as-refuge is sufficiently dramatic to make a properly enclosed domestic circle the object of both desire and—later—gratitude, but evidently it is also sufficiently precarious to warrant—as the means of maintaining it—a domestic self-discipline that must have internalized the institutional control it thereby forestalls. The same internment that renders Laura's body docile, and her mind imbecile, also fits her to incarnate the norm of the submissive Victorian wife. (Sir Percival might well turn in his grave to see his successor effortlessly reaping what, with nothing to show but acute frustration, *he* had sown.) Collins makes Laura's second marriage so different from her first that he has no reason to conceal the considerable evidence of its resemblance to what can be counted upon to remain its "opposite."

122   D. A. MILLER

This evidence comes as early as when, virtually at first sight, Walter falls in love with Laura. "Think of her," he invites the reader who would understand his feelings, "as you thought of the first woman who quickened the pulses within you" (76). As here, so everywhere else his passion declares itself in the language of sensation: of thrill and chill (86), of pang and pain (96), of "sympathies" that, lying "too deep for words, too deep almost for thoughts," have been "touched" (76). Concomitantly, in the associative pattern we have already established, his sensationalized body puts him in an essentially feminine position. His "hardly-earned self-control" (90) is as completely lost to him as if he had never possessed it, and "aggravated by the sense of [his] own miserable weakness" (91), his situation becomes one of "helplessness and humiliation" (92)—the same hendiadys that Marian will apply to herself and Laura at Blackwater Park (272). This is all to say that, notwithstanding Walter's implication, Laura Fairlie is *not* the first woman to quicken his pulses but rather the object of a repetition compulsion whose origin lies in his (sensationalizing, feminizing) first encounter with the Woman in White. Walter replays this primal trauma, however, with an important difference that in principle marks out the path to mastering it. He moves from an identification with the woman to a desire for her, heterosexual choice replacing homosexual surprise. The woman is once more (or for the first time) the other, and the man, who now at least "knows what he wants," has to that extent taken himself in charge.

Yet the sensational features of Walter's desire necessarily threaten to reabsorb it in the identification against which it erects itself as a first line of defence. Something more, therefore, is required to stabilize his male self-mastery, something that Walter does *not* know that he wants. "Crush it," Marian counsels him, "Don't shrink under it like a woman. Tear it out; trample it under foot like a man!" (96). But the eventual recipient of this violence will be as much the object of Walter's passion as the passion itself. From the very beginning of his exposure to it, Laura's "charm" has suggested to him "the idea of something wanting":

At one time it seemed like something wanting in *her;* at another, like something wanting in myself, which hindered me from understanding her as I ought. The impression was always strongest in the most contradictory manner, when she looked at me, or, in other words, when I was most conscious of the harmony and charm of her face, and yet, at the same time, most troubled by the sense of an incompleteness which it was impossible to discover. Something wanting, something wanting—and where it was, and what it was, I could not say. (76–77)

This is not (or not just) a Freudian riddle (Q.: What does a woman want? A.: What she is wanting), though even as such it attests the particular anxiety of the man responsible for posing it: who desires Laura "because" (= so that) she, not he, is wanting. For shortly afterward, with "a thrill of the same feeling which ran through [him] when the touch was laid upon [his] shoulder on the lonely highroad," Walter comes to see that the "something wanting" is "[his] own recognition of the ominous likeness between the fugitive from the asylum and [his] pupil at Limmeridge House" (86). Laura's strange "incompleteness" would thus consist in what has made this likeness imperfect—namely, that absence of "profaning marks" of "sorrow and suffering" which alone is said to differentiate her from her double (120). Accordingly, the Laura Walter most deeply dreams of loving proves to be none other than the Anne who has been put away. It is as though, to be quite perfect, his pupil must be taught a lesson: what is wanting—what Laura obscurely lacks and Walter obscurely wishes for—is her sequestration in the Asylum.

Courtesy of Sir Percival and Fosco, the want will of course be supplied, but long before her actual internment Laura has been well prepared for it at Limmeridge House, where—on the grounds that her delicacy requires protection—men systematically keep their distance from her. Rather than deal with her directly, Sir Percival, Mr. Gilmore, Mr. Fairlie, Walter himself all prefer to have recourse to the mannish Marian, who serves as their intermediary. "I shrank," says Walter at one point, "I shrink still—from invading the innermost sanctuary of her heart, and laying it open to others, as I have laid open my own" (90). His many such gallant pronouncements entail an unwillingness to *know* Laura, the better to affirm without interference the difference between him and her, man and woman. ("Me Tarzan, you Jane": notice how male solipsism overbears the very opposition that guarantees male difference. Laura is a closed sanctuary/Walter is an open book, but it is Walter here who empowers himself to decide, by his shrinking reticence, what Laura shall be.) More than anything else, this "respect" is responsible in the text for rendering Laura—even in terms of a genre that does not specialize in complex character studies—a psychological cipher. (An English translation of the French translation of the novel might be entitled, precisely, *The Woman as Blank*.) From turbid motives of her own, Marian is more than willing to do her part in drawing round Laura this *cordon sanitaire*. Like an efficient secretary in love with her boss, she spares Laura all troublesome importunities, and she is no less aggressive in forbidding an interview between Laura and Anne ("Not to be thought of for a moment" [131]) than in dispatching Walter from Limmeridge House "before more harm is done" (95). Laura's subsequent experience of the Asylum only further justifies the imperative to isolate her. "The wrong that had been inflicted on her . . . must be redressed without her knowledge and without her help" (456). And now a self-evident opposition between parent and child is available to overdetermine what had been the all-too-doubtful difference between man and woman. "Oh, don't, don't, don't treat me like a child!" Laura implores, but Walter immediately takes the plea for more evidence of her childishness and accordingly gives her some pretend-work to do. When she asks him "as a child might have" whether he is as fond of her as he used to be, he reassures her that she is dearer to him now than she had ever been in the past times (458). His profession carries conviction, and no wonder, since his passion for her, now become a part-parental, part-pedophilic condescension, no longer makes him feel like a woman. Though the text takes perfunctory notice of "the healing influences of her new life" with Walter (576), these have no power to produce a Laura who in any way exceeds men's (literal or "liberal") incarcerating fantasies about her. It is not just, as the text puts it, that the mark of the Asylum is "too deep to be effaced" but that it has always already effaced everything else.

The same could not be said of Marian Halcombe, whose far more "interesting" character represents the only significant variation on business-as-usual in the novel's gynaeceum. As the conspicuously curious case of a woman's body that gives all the signs of containing a man's soul, Marian figures the exact inversion of what we have taken to be the novel's governing fantasy. Yet we must not conceive of this inversion standing in opposition to what it inverts, as though it implied not just the existence of a rival set of matching *female* fears and fantasies but also the consequent assurance that, in the love and war between the sexes, all at least is fair: *così fan tutte*, too. No less than that of the woman-in-the-man, the motif of the man-in-the-woman is a function of the novel's anxious male imperatives ("Cherchez, cachez, couchez la femme") that, even as a configuration of resistance, it rationalizes, flatters, and positively encourages. Thus, however "phallic," "lesbian," and "male-identified" Marian may be considered at the beginning of the novel, the implicit structuring of these attributes is precisely what is responsible for converting her—if with a certain violence, then also with a certain ease—into the castrated, heterosexualized "good angel" (646) of the Victorian household at the end.

Our memorable first view of her comes in the disappointed appraisal of Walter's idly cruising eye:

The instant my eyes rested on her, I was struck by the rare beauty of her form, and by the unaffected grace of her attitude. Her figure was tall, yet not too tall; comely and well-developed, yet not fat; her head set on her shoulders with an easy, pliant firmness; her waist, perfection in the eyes of a man, for it occupied its natural place, it filled out its natural circle, it was visibly and delightfully undeformed by stays. She had not heard my entrance into the room; and I allowed myself the luxury of admiring her for a moment, before I moved one of the chairs near me, as the least embarrassing means of attracting her attention. She turned towards me immediately. The easy elegance of every movement of her limbs and body as soon as she began to advance from the far end of the room, set me in a flutter of expectation to see her face clearly. She left the window—and I said to myself, The lady is dark. She moved forward a few steps—and I said to myself, The lady is young. She approached nearer—and I said to myself (with a sense of surprise which words fail me to express), The lady is ugly!

Never was the old conventional maxim, that Nature cannot err, more flatly contradicted—never was the fair promise of a lovely figure more strangely and startlingly belied by the face and head that crowned it. The lady's complexion was almost swarthy, and the dark down on her upper lip was almost a moustache. She had a large, firm, masculine

since perhaps the most important fantasy feature of rape is the reaffirmation of the rapist's unimpaired capacity to withdraw, the integrity of his body (if not his victim's) recovered intact. (Fosco, we recall, returns to Marian the journal he has indelibly signed, and she, evidently, is stuck with it.)[18] As its sexual variant, seduction-and-abandonment would thus in both senses of the word "betray" the constitutive myth of the liberal (male) subject, whose human rights must include the freedom, as he pleases, to come and go.

The meaning of Marian's "rape" is of course further determined by another, better-known figure of the *anima virilis*: the lesbian. "She will be *his* Laura instead of mine!" (207), writes Marian of the bride of Limmeridge—having taken the precaution, however, of promoting rather this faint-hearted marriage to Sir Percival than the obvious love match with Walter, as if already anticipating the consolation that an unhappy Lady Glyde will not fail to bring to her closet: "Oh, Marian! . . . promise you will never marry, and leave me. It is selfish to say so, but you are so much better off as a single woman—unless—unless you are very fond of your husband—but you won't be very fond of anybody but me, will you?" (235). Important as it is not to censor the existence of erotic feeling between women in the text (in any of the ways this can be done, including a certain way of acknowledging it),[19] it is perhaps more important to recognize that what would also get absorbed here under the name of lesbianism is a woman's unwillingness to lend her full cooperation to male appropriations of her, as though Marian's "gayness" were the only conceivable key to passages like the following:

"Men! They are the enemies of our innocence and our peace—they drag us away from our parents' love and our sisters' friendship—they take us body and soul to themselves, and fasten our helpless lives to theirs as they chain up a dog to his kennel. And what does the best of them give us in return? Let me go, Laura—I'm mad when I think of it!" (203)

In general, the "lesbianism" contextualized in *The Woman in White* amounts mainly to a male charge, in which the accusation is hard to dissociate from the excitation. In particular, the novel most effectively renders Marian "lesbian" in the sense that it makes her suffer the regular fate of the lesbian in male representations: who defiantly bides her time with women until the inevitable and irrevocable heterosexual initiation that she, if no no else, may not have known that she always wanted. One recalls this exchange from *Goldfinger*, after James Bond has seduced Pussy Galore: "He said, 'They told me you only liked women.' She said, 'I never met a man before.' "[20] Not dissimilarly, Marian's "half-willing, half-unwilling liking for the Count" (246)—what in a rape trial would be called her "complicity"—provides the novel's compelling, compulsive proof of the male erotic power that operates even and especially where it is denied. "I am almost afraid to confess it, even to these secret pages. The man has interested me, has attracted me, has forced me to like him" (240). Fosco's eyes "have at times a clear, cold, beautiful, irresistible glitter in them which forces me to look at him, and yet causes me sensations, when I do look, which I would rather not feel" (241, repeated almost verbatim on 287). Like Pussy Bonded, Marian Foscoed (hearing the metathesis in the name of the "wily Italian" [264], we need not even consider resorting to what Freud called Schreber's "shamefaced" elision) is a changed woman. If it is not her ultimate destiny to roll up the Count's endless cigarettes "with the look of mute submissive inquiry which we are all familiar with in the eyes of a faithful dog" (239), as she abjectly fantasizes, he has nonetheless well trained her to be another man's best friend. "What a woman's hands *are* fit for," she tells Walter, whom she entrusts with her avengement, "early and late, these hands of mine shall do. . . . It's my weakness that cries, not me. The house-work shall conquer it, if *I* can't" (453–54). The old signs of Marian's "masculinity"—the hands that were "as awkward as a man's" (253), the tears that came "almost like men's" (187)— now realize what had always been their implied potential to attest a "weakness" that (like the housework she takes on "as her own right") refeminizes her. In the novel's last image, almost exactly according to the proper Freudian resolution of *Penisneid*, Marian is able to "rise" only on condition that she "hold up" Walter's son and heir "kicking and crowing in her arms" (646). Almost exactly, but not quite, since the child is not of course her own. It is as though the woman whom Fosco "rapes" and the woman whom Walter "neuters" prove finally one and the same odd thing—as though, in other words, a woman's heterosexuality ("hetero-" indeed) were no sexuality of hers.

Even as the victim of terrific male aggression, however, Marian is simultaneously the beneficiary of considerable male admiration. Walter aptly imagines that she "would have secured the respect of the most audacious man breathing" (60), and apart from Fosco, who eventually embodies that hypothetical man, apart even from Walter, who at once finds in the ugly lady an old friend (59), the novelist himself unexceptionally portrays Marian as a "positive," immensely likable character. Demonstrably, then, *The Woman in White* accords a far warmer welcome to the fantasy of the man-in-the-woman (which, fully personified, the novel works through to a narrative resolution) than to the apparently complementary fantasy of the woman-in-the-man (which, as we have seen, the novel only broaches obscurely, in the blind spot of "nonrecognition" between textual thematics and male reading bodies). This is doubtless because the *anima virilis* includes, in addition to the aspects aforementioned, a male identification. "I don't think much of my own sex," Marian admits to Walter on their first meeting; "No woman does think much of her own sex, though few of them confess it as freely as I do" (60). As though misogyny were primarily a female phenomenon and as such justified the male phenomenon that ventriloquially might go without saying, Marian's voice becomes the novel's principal articulation of that traditional code according to which women are quarrelsome, chattering, capricious, superstitious, inaccurate, unable to draw or play billiards. For all the pluck that it inspires, Marian's male identification consistently vouches for her female dependency.

Thus, determined "on justifying the Count's opinion of [her] courage and sharpness" (340), she bravely makes her night-crawl onto the eaves of the house at Blackwater to overhear Fosco's conversation with Sir Percival. But—perhaps because, as the male-identified woman necessarily comes to think, her "courage was only a woman's courage after all" (341–42)—this determination obliges her to remove "the white and cumbersome parts of [her] underclothing" (342) and so to prepare herself for the violation that, on one way of looking at it, follows soon afterward but that, on another, has already succeeded. If the woman-in-the-man requires his *keeping her* inside him, the man-in-the-woman takes for granted her *letting him* inside her. The sexual difference that the former endangers, the latter reaffirms: by determining a single view of women—men's—to which women accede in the course of constructing a male-identified femininity. Fosco "flatters" Marian's vanity "by talking to [her] as seriously and sensibly as if [she were] a man" (245), and she more than returns the favor by addressing Fosco, Walter, and the male reader on the same premise, reassuring all concerned that even the woman who speaks as "freely" as a man remains the prolocutor of a masculist discourse that keeps her in place. Finally, therefore, Marian may be taken to suggest how the novel envisions that *female* reader whom, though it nominally ignores, it has always taken into practical account. For the same sensation effects that "feminize" the male reading body also (the quotation marks are still indispensable) "feminize" the female: with the difference that this feminization is construed in the one case to threaten sexual identity and in the other to confirm it. Implicitly, that is, the text glosses the female reader's sensationalized body in exactly the terms of Marian's erotic responsiveness to Fosco: as the corporal confession of a "femininity" whose conception is all but exhausted in providing the unmarked term in opposition to a thus replenished "masculinity." If only on its own terms (though, when one is trembling, these terms may be hard to shake), the sensation novel constitutes proof of women's inability, as Marian puts it, to "resist a man's tongue when he knows how to speak to them" (278) and especially, we might add with Marian emblematically in mind, when he knows how to speak through them.

IV

Precisely insofar as it does not fail, the project of confining or containing the woman cannot succeed in achieving narrative quiescence or closure. Safely shut up in the various ways we have considered, women cease being active participants in the drama that nonetheless remains to be played out (for over a hundred pages) "man to man." For when the text produces the configuration of incarcerated femininity, it simultaneously cathects the congruent configuration of phobic male homoeroticism: thus, for instance, its "paradoxical" rendering of

Fosco, who is at once "a man who could tame anything" (239) and "a fat St. Cecilia masquerading in male attire" (250). Accordingly, the novel needs to supplement its misogynistic plot with a misanthropic one, in which it will detail the frightening, even calamitous consequences of unmediated relations between men, thereby administering to its hero an aversion therapy calculated to issue in a renunciation of what Eve Kosofsky Sedgwick has called "male homosocial desire," or in a liberation from what—with a more carceral but no less erotic shade of meaning—we might also call male bonds.[21] After Sedgwick's (here, actively) inspiring demonstration that men's desire for men is the very motor of patriarchally given social structures, it might seem implausible even to entertain the possibility of such a renunciation or liberation, which would amount to a withdrawal from the social *tout court*. Yet this is apparently what the endings of many nineteenth-century novels paradigmatically stage: the hero's thoroughgoing disenchantment with the (homo)social, from which he is resigned to isolate himself. By and large, nineteenth-century fiction is no less heavily invested than Sedgwick's analysis of it in luridly portraying the dysphoric effects—particularly on men—of homosocial desire, and this fact must raise the question of the status of such effects within the general rhetorical strategy of the fiction that cultivates them. If, for example, *The Woman in White* obligingly constitutes a "pathology" of male homosocial desire, this is evidently not because the novel shares, say, Sedgwick's ambition to formulate a feminist/gay critique of homophobically patriarchal structure; but neither is it because the novel so naively embraces this structure that it recounts-without-counting the latter's psychological costs. Rather, as we will see, the novel puts its homosocial pathology in the service of promoting a homosocial cure: a cure that has the effect of a renunciation of men's desire for men only because, in this treated form, and by contrast, such desire exists in a "normal" or relatively silent state.

The novel's most obvious specimen of an abnormal male homosocial *Bund*—the one it adduces at the end, as though at last to consolidate the freely floating homoerotics of the text and thus to name and contain them—is that secret Italian political association which (Walter is quite correct in saying) is "sufficiently individualized" for his purposes if he calls it, simply, "The Brotherhood" (595). The novel tolerates this exotic freemasonry on two ideological conditions, which, if they were not so inveterately combined in a policy of quarantine, might otherwise strike us as incompatible. On the one hand, The Brotherhood owes its existence to the political adolescence of Italy (595–96), to which, in case the point is lost, Pesca correlates his own immaturity when he became a member (597). The advanced nation as well as the enlightened parent may rest assured imagining that The Brotherhood is only a phase that in the normal course of political or personal development will be superseded. Yet on the other hand, no possible course of development can retrieve someone once he has been admitted into this society of fellows and bears its "secret mark," which, like his membership, lasts for life (596). Strange as it may be for Walter to learn that some one of his best friends belongs to the secret fraternity, the revelation occasions no alarm (lest, for instance, an attempt be made to initiate *him*), since the pathos of Pesca's case is well cultivated by Pesca himself, who admits to suffering still from those youthful impulses (" 'I try to forget them—and they will not forget *me*!' " [642]), which forever condemn him to consort in such dubious company. (In the usual distribution of roles, Walter's mother, but not his sullenly nubile sister, has welcomed Pesca into the household.) A congenial point is borne in the activities of The Brotherhood itself, whose in-house purges are the "outside" world's best protection against it. Walter's sword need never cross with Fosco's—a mercy given the impressive estimates we are invited to make of the "length" of the latter (611)—in the duel that "other vengence" has rendered unnecessary (642). The Brotherhood has mortally called the Count to "the day of reckoning" (642)—not for his offenses against Walter but for his all-too-promiscuous fraternizing within and without its organization. The wound struck "exactly over his heart" (643) hints broadly at the "passional" nature of the crime in which—for which—Fosco is murdered. Thus, at the exhibition of his naked and knifed corpse (the former "Napoleon" [241] now, as it were, the dead Marat, and the rueful Parisian morgue, also as it were, the gayer continental baths), we hear the curator's familiarly excited double discourse, in which a flushed moralism never quite manages to pacify the sheer erotic fascination that hence remains available to incite it: "There he lay, unowned, unknown, exposed to the flippant curiosity of a French mob! There was the dreadful end of that long life of degraded ability and heartless crime! Hushed in the sublime repose of death, the broad, firm, massive face and head fronted us so grandly that the chattering Frenchwomen about me lifted their hands in admiration, and cried in shrill chorus, 'Ah, what a handsome man!' " (643).

"And all men kill the thing they love": what is often taken for Wilde's gay depressiveness (though in Reading Gaol, what else is left to intelligence but to read its prison?) provides a not-so-oddly apt formula for the novel's pathology of male bonds, whose godforsaken expression coincides with its providential punishment in death. (Besides the murder of Fosco, we may cite the "suicide" of his boon companion: it is no accident that, having locked himself in the vestry, Sir Percival accidentally sets it on fire.) A couple of reasons obtain for bringing out, as I have pseudo-anachronistically been doing, the continuities between the novel's representation of "brotherhood" and our media's no less sensational staging of male homosexuality. One would be to begin measuring the extent to which nineteenth-century culture has contributed to the formation of the context in which an uncloseted gayness is popularly determined. (Thus, the homophobic virulence that dispreads in rivalrous response to homosexual immunodeficiency is "only" the most recent, extreme, and potentially catastrophic figure of an interpretative framework that precedes AIDS by well over a century.) Another would be to recognize that if our culture can only "think" male homosexual desire within a practice of aversion therapy, this is because—for a long while and with apparently greater efficiency—it has routinely subjected male homosocial desire to the same treatment.

Representationally, this treatment consists of a diptych in which the baleful images of homosocial apocalypse on one panel confront a comparatively cheering family portrait on the other. The fact that Fosco and Sir Percival are both married is far from making them what *The Woman in White* understands by family men. For as the novel's final tableau makes abundantly clear, what is distinctively cheering about the family portrait is less the connection between husband and wife (Marian, not Laura, holds up his son to Walter's charmed gaze) than the bond between father and son. Thus, the aim of what we have called aversion therapy is not to redirect men's desire for men onto women but, through women, onto boys: that is, to privatize homosocial desire within the middle-class nuclear family, where it takes the "normal" shape of an Oedipal triangle. Yet the twinned projects whose achievement the novel makes *precede* the establishment of a family curiously correspond to what, at least since Freud's summation of nineteenth-century culture, we may recognize as the family's own defining features: 1) shut up the woman—or, in the rivalry between father and son of which she is the object, keep mother from becoming the subject of a desire of her own; and 2) turn from the man—or, in that same rivalry, develop an aversion therapy for home use. The foundation of the Hartright family, therefore, cannot put an end to the brutalities of its prehistory, nor will these brutalities have dialectically prepared the way for a civilizing familialism, since the violent workings of an Oedipal family organization (Sir Percival is a much older man than Walter, and so forth) have implicitly generated the narrative that this organization is explicitly constituted to conclude. At the end, then, the novel has merely discovered its beginning, in the family matrix where such violence has acquired its specific structure and whence it has made its fearful *entrée dans le monde*. "And there is more where that came from," if only because where that came from is also where that eventually returns. As though refusing to cease shocking us, even where it least surprises us, *The Woman in White* "ends" only by recurring to that family circle which will continue to relay—with no end in sight—a plot that still takes many people's breath away.[22]

V

Note on the author's body: shortly after I began writing this essay, the muscles on my shoulders and back went into spasm. Referring this thoracic pain to other matters (excessive working out, an affair of the heart) than the work on which it continually interrupted my progress, I consulted physical and psychological therapists. Only when the former at last pronounced that a rib was out of place (which may have been what the latter was getting at when he diagnosed, on the insurance form, a personality disorder), was I willing to entertain the possibility that I had become, in relation to my own writing, an improbably pat case of hysteria. Now that a practiced hand has put the fugitive rib back into its cage, my spine tingles to have borne out my assumption of that "nonrecognition" which evidently also obtains between the somatics of writing and what is written about. I am less pleased (though still thrilled) to understand that, on the same assumption, what dumbfounds me also lays the foundation for my dumbness: too stupid to utter what has already been said in the interaction between body and text, and in the traces of that interaction within body or text; and too mute to do more than designate the crucial task of identifying in this writing the equivocal places where "sensation" has gone, not to say love.

Notes

This essay appears in *The Nineteenth-Century British Novel*, ed. Jeremy Hawthorn, Stratford-upon-Avon Studies, 2d series (London, 1986). Permission to reprint granted by Edward Arnold (Publishers) Ltd.

1. A valuable survey of Victorian responses to sensation fiction may be found in Elizabeth K. Helsinger, Robin Lauterbach Sheets, and William Veeder, *The Woman Question: Society and Literature in Britain and America, 1837–1883*, 3 vols. (New York, 1983), 3:122–44.

2. The omission is well exemplified in a recent article by Patrick Brantlinger entitled "What Is 'Sensational' About the Sensation Novel?" *Nineteenth-Century Fiction* 37 (June 1982): 1–28. Having posed the crucial question, the author elides its most obvious answer—namely, the somatic experience of sensation itself—by at once proceeding to considerations of "content" (murder, adultery, bigamy) and generic "mixture" (domestic realism, Gothic romance, etc.).

3. Wilkie Collins, *The Woman in White*, ed. Julian Symons (Harmondsworth, Eng., 1974), 47. Subsequent references to the novel are to this edition and are cited parenthetically in the text by page number.

4. Mrs. [Margaret] Oliphant, "Sensation Novels," *Blackwood's Magazine* 91 (May 1862), reprinted in Norman Page, ed., *Wilkie Collins: The Critical Heritage* (London, 1974), 118–19.

5. For example, Walter, the master narrator who solicits the others' narratives and organizes them into a whole, speaks of Laura to the reader: "Think of her as you thought of the first woman who quickened the pulses within you" (76). The same identification is also sustained implicitly, as in the equation between the reader and a judge (33).

6. See Jeffrey Weeks, *Coming Out: Homosexual Politics in Britain, From the Nineteenth Century to the Present* (London, 1977), 26–27. It does not seem altogether an historical "irony" that this intrinsically ambiguous notion—so useful to the apologists for homosexuality in the late nineteenth and early twentieth centuries—should popularly survive today as part of the mythological rationale for "vulgar" homophobia, which draws on an equally vulgar misogyny to oppress gay men.

   It may also be pertinent here to note that turn-of-the-century sexology is almost universally agreed on "a marked tendency to nervous development in the [homosexual] subject, not infrequently associated with nervous maladies"; Edward Carpenter, *The Intermediate Sex* (1908), in *Selected Writings,* vol. 1 (London, 1984), 209. Criticizing Krafft-Ebing for continuing to link homosexuality with " 'an hereditary neuropathic or psychopathic tendency'—*neuro(psycho)-pathische Belastung,*" Carpenter remarks that "there are few people in modern life, perhaps none, who could be pronounced absolutely free from such a *Belastung!*" (210). His ostensible point—that nervous disorders are far too widespread in modern life to be the distinctive mark of homosexuals, whose "neuropathic tendency" would bespeak rather a social than a metaphysical fatality—is still *(mutatis mutandis)* worth making. Yet in a discursive formation that insistently yokes male homosexuality and neuropathology together (in the femininity common to both), his observation might also be taken to conclude that this homosexuality *too* (if principally in its reactive, homophobic form) is a general modern phenomenon.

7. My understanding of the workings of discipline in Dickens and Trollope is elaborated in D. A. Miller, "Discipline in Different Voices: Bureaucracy, Police, Family, and *Bleak House,*" *Representations* 1 (February 1983): 59–89; and "The Novel as Usual: Trollope's *Barchester Towers,*" in *Sex, Politics, and Science,* ed. Ruth Bernard Yeazell (Baltimore, Md., 1985), 1–38.

8. See William Ll. Parry-Jones, *The Trade in Lunacy: A Study of Private Madhouses in England in the Eighteenth and Nineteenth Centuries* (Toronto, 1972).

9. Mrs. Oliphant, in *Wilkie Collins,* 112.

10. Guy Hocquengham, *Homosexual Desire,* trans. Daniella Dangoor (London, 1978), 42–43.

11. Quoted in Sigmund Freud, "Psycho-Analytic Notes on an Autobiographical Account of Paranoia," in *The Standard Edition of the Complete Works of Sigmund Freud,* ed. James Strachey, 24 vols. (London, 1953–74), 12:20.

12. Peter Brooks, *Reading for the Plot* (New York, 1984), 169.

13. Sandra M. Gilbert and Susan Gubar, *The Madwoman in the Attic* (New Haven, 1979), 85–86.

14. Mary Elizabeth Braddon, *Lady Audley's Secret* (New York, 1974), 249.

15. A Victorian reviewer, W. Fraser Ray, criticizes the characterization of Lady Audley thus: "In drawing her, the authoress may have intended to portray a female Mephistopheles; but if so, she should have known that a woman cannot fill such a part"; "Sensation Novelists: Miss Braddon," *North British Review* 43 (1865), quoted in Veeder, *The Woman Question,* 127. Ray might have spared himself the trouble (not to mention, in our hindsight, the embarrassment of failing to read the text that nonetheless proves quite capable of reading him), since his objection merely rehearses the same principle that, within the novel, Robert Audley victoriously carries in having Lady Audley confined.

16. Roland Barthes, *The Pleasure of the Text,* trans. Richard Miller (New York, 1975), 10.

17. The novel's elaborate canine thematics more than justify this slang usage, which of course postdates it. Marian's first lesson at Blackwater Park, for instance, involves being instructed in the destiny of dogs there. A housemaid thus accounts to her for the wounded dog found in the boathouse: " 'Bless you, miss! Baxter's the keeper, and when he finds strange dogs hunting about, he takes and shoots 'em. It's keeper's dooty, miss. I think that dog will die. Here's where he's been shot, ain't it? That's Baxter's doings, that is. Baxter's doings, miss, and Baxter's dooty' " (229). "Baxter's" doings indeed: if the keeper is little more than a name in the novel, the name nonetheless contains almost all the elements in the novel's representation of female containment. For one thing, the suffix *-ster* originally designates a specifically feminine agency (in

Old English a *baxter* means a female baker): whence perhaps Baxter's violence, as though he were protesting the femininity latently inscribed in his name. For another, in the context of the novel's insistence on "the touch from behind," the name would also signify the person who handles (its gender inflection keeps us from quite saying: man-handles) the hinder part of the body.

18. In this context one must read Fosco's dandiacal lament after the episode where—"to the astonishment of all the men" who watch him—he successfully intimidates "a chained bloodhound—a beast so savage that the very groom who feeds him keeps out of his reach": " 'Ah! my nice waistcoat! . . . Some of that brute's slobber has got on my pretty clean waistcoat!' " (243–44).

19. For example: "Does [Marian] . . . have Lesbian tendencies?" the editor of the Penguin edition boldly speculates, before prudently concluding that "it is doubtful whether such thoughts were in Collins's mind" (15). The response, which rationalizes its titillation as a sophisticated willingness to call things by their names and then rationalizes its disavowal of that titillation (and of those names) as scholarly caution, typifies the only acknowledgment that homoeroticism, female or male, is accustomed to receive in the criticism of nineteenth-century fiction. Here it does little more than faithfully reproduce—"Mind that dog, sir!" (243)—the novel's own equivocal structuring of the evidence for Marian's lesbianism. One may observe in passing how a similar fidelity entails that the editor who can mention lesbianism must fall entirely silent on the *male* homoerotics of the novel (see p. 129 above for why this should be so).

20. Ian Fleming, *Goldfinger* (1959; New York, 1982), 261.

21. Readers of Eve Kosofsky Sedgwick's *Between Men: English Literature and Male Homosocial Desire* (New York, 1985) will recognize how nearly its concerns touch on those of the present essay.

22. Like the woman's, or the homosexual's, or (for she has figured in both roles) Marian's: "Let Marian end our Story" (646), but—these are the text's last words, as well as Walter's—what follows is dead silence.

What also follows is my particular gratitude to those friends whom this essay did not leave speechless: Marston Anderson, Ann Bermingham, Mitchell Breitwieser, Carol T. Christ, Martin Cogan, Christopher Craft, Lizbeth Hasse, Caroline Newman, Mary Ann O'Farrell, Eve Kosofsky Sedgwick, and Alex Zwerdling.

"Scenes of an Indelicate Character": The Medical "Treatment" of Victorian Women

ON THE EVENING OF 4 November 1847, Dr. James Young Simpson, professor of midwifery at Edinburgh University, administered to himself and two colleagues yet another in the series of distillates, volatile fluids, and vapors he had been experimenting with throughout the summer and autumn of that year. Simpson was in search of the "perfect" anesthesia, an agent that could induce in patients the soporific state brought on by ether without ether's undesirable side effects. The vapor Simpson inhaled that night was chloroform, and its impact literally realized Simpson's ambition to "turn the world upside down" when it laid the three doctors under the table. As one of his contemporaries tells the story, Simpson awoke to find himself "prostrate on the floor," Dr. Duncan "beneath a chair . . . snoring in a most determined and alarming manner," and Dr. Keith's "feet and legs, making valorous efforts to overturn the supper table, or more probably to annihilate everything that was on it."[1]

Simpson lost no time in spreading news of his discovery to the medical community. On 8 November he first used chloroform in an obstetrical case; two days later he lectured on the subject to the Medico-Chirurgical Society; on 15 November he held the first public test of chloroform in the Edinburgh Infirmiry and published a pamphlet on the subject, which sold 1500 copies in less than two weeks. By the end of November he was using the anodyne constantly in his midwifery practice and urging all other medical men to follow his lead. But others were neither as enthusiastic nor as precipitate as Simpson. What he was later to call "the march of knowledge and science" was slowed by a debate that raged in the London medical journal *Lancet* and in a flurry of pamphlets published between 1847 and the mid fifties. The discussion abated somewhat after 1853, when Queen Victoria was administered chloroform for the birth of her eighth child, but it was still sufficiently vigorous in 1863 for the Royal Medical and Chirurgical Society of London to appoint a committee to study chloroform's physiological effects. The problem was that by that date, 123 fatalities had been positively assigned to chloroform—and this figure almost certainly fell far short of the actual number of deaths.[2] It had become apparent that no one actually understood how anesthesia worked, and by 1863 the medical community was sufficiently united to investigate the price some of its members were exacting for the relief from pain.

The anesthesia debate constitutes an important episode in the mid-Victorian discussion of the "woman question" because of the crucial role played by medicine in formulating a scientific justification for what was held to be woman's natural reproductive function and circumscribed social place. In naming or treating disease or disorders, medicine was intimately involved in the construction and regulation of norms that theoretically (and more or less actually) had a scientific basis but that also incorporated social assumptions into a vocabulary of physiology.[3] Beginning in the early eighteenth century with the disclosure of the Chamberlens' forceps,[4] technology enabled medical men to extend the domain of medicine into what had previously been seen as a natural territory presided over by women. The entry of the male accoucheur into the lying-in chamber transformed what had traditionally been a spiritual and physical trial endured within an enclave of women into a far more complex social scene, where concerns about women's modesty and physical well being intersected with anxieties about the doctor's reputation and his economic health, the status of his profession and the power of his tools.[5] Not incidentally, I will argue, the "drama" of childbirth—or, more specifically, the display staged by chloroform and theoretically directed by medical men—simultaneously justified confining women to a single social role and disclosed the ways in which the medical treatment of the female body rendered such confinement problematic.[6]

The story of anesthesia could be told in many ways; it *has* been told in many ways, in fact, ranging from the medical apologists' celebration of a "triumph over pain" to recent feminists' arguments that here, as elsewhere in the history of childbirthing practices, we see "hands of flesh" displaced by "hands of iron."[7] This political dispute is partly a function of the unevenness of the available historical record. The *Lancet*, for example, contains numerous charges that deaths from chloroform were not being reported and other accusations that their numbers were being exaggerated. It is impossible to choose between these claims on the basis of fact, because official inquests were not always held when a patient died, and what statistics do exist are blatantly contradictory.[8] But the contemporary debate about how to narrate the history of medicine—like the debate about the nature and propriety of anesthesia—has also emerged partly because all such debates are inevitably as bound up with the representation of reality as with material social relations and practices. As the arena for negotiating values, meanings, and identities, representation authorizes ethics and social practices; it stages the workings through of the dominant ideology. But opposition can *also* emerge within representation, in ways that I want to set out in this essay. As a consequence of the interpretation representation requires, the debates about how to tell this story and what it is about can both be seen as debates about authority—struggles to determine and legislate the "true" and who has the right to speak it. But while I am inevitably going to take a position in the current political debate, the issue I am centrally concerned with here is the mid-Victorian medical profession's representation of women; I do not address either contemporary versions of this history or how nineteenth-century women perceived themselves or medicine—except, of course, insofar as what was represented as public opinion shows up in the medical men's representations of themselves. My texts consist primarily of articles published between 1846 and 1856 in *Lancet,* the pamphlets either derived from or addressed to these articles, and a series of textbooks and medical manuals about women's physical and mental disorders written by medical men and published in or near this decade.

The debate about anesthesia first grew stormy in late 1847, when Dr. Simpson triumphantly announced in *Lancet* that chloroform could produce what ether could not: deep anesthesia without an initial prolonged period of excitation.[9] At least some of Simpson's claims were soon corroborated by others: because chloroform was more powerful than ether, less was necessary to produce the desired sleep; its odor and effects were more pleasant; it was less expensive, more portable, and required no special inhaler for application.[10] All of these properties made chloroform immediately attractive to surgeons in particular; like ether, chloroform helped transform surgery from a craft requiring speed and brute strength to a conservative practice in which careful dissection could preserve tissue that would otherwise be destroyed.[11]

In midwifery, however, the introduction of chloroform encountered vehement opposition, and practitioners remained divided over the advisability of its use. A twentieth-century obstetrician might offer many reasons for caution, beginning with the general level of ignorance among mid-nineteenth-century medical men about female and fetal physiology.[12] Unlike surgery, moreover, childbirth involves two patients with very different levels of tolerance to drugs; because the timing of delivery is nearly always unpredictable, the elaborate preparations possible in surgery are precluded; and, while surgery rarely lasts longer than four hours, labor may last for twenty hours or even more.[13] Yet such reasons rarely appear in the objections offered by mid-nineteenth-century medical men. Instead, the debate presented itself as an argument about the nature of women and medicine's proper relation to them.

The issues in this debate center around two, related, questions, although they were never given precisely this form. First, does the woman in labor properly belong to the realm of nature, which is governed by God, or to culture, where nature submits to man?[14] Second, how can a man know—so as to master—the female body, which is always other to his own? And what does he know when he has mastered it? The first question really involves the social place of medicine in relation to religion, although the position of women is the pivot of the dispute. Some doctors and clergymen argued, for example, that because God's curse upon Eve has fixed women's labor in the no man's land of "nature," for doctors to bring women into the social realm would be to "harden" society by attenuating this intermediary link between man and God. As one clergyman phrased it, chloroform is "a decoy of Satan, apparently offering itself to bless women; but in the end . . . it will harden society, and rob God of the deep earnest cries which arise in time of trouble for help."[15] Doctors who held this position tended to emphasize the transgression against nature rather than God, but their biblical imagery reveals the affinity of the two positions. "To be in natural labour is the culminating point of the female somatic forces," argued the American Dr. Meigs. "There is, in natural labour, no element of disease. . . . I should feel disposed to clothe me in sackcloth, and cast ashes on my head for the remainder of my days [if a patient were to die from such] meddlesome midwifery."[16]

Meigs yoked his complaint about "meddlesome midwifery" to the epistemological and practical question of how a doctor could read a woman's labors. As long as she was in a state of nature, presumably, her body would interpret its own condition more truthfully than could a doctor's medical expertise. When Meigs argued that the patient's responses to the question "Does it hurt you?" "are worth a thousand dogmas and precepts,"[17] he was simply adhering to the then traditional relation between a doctor and his patient, which privileged the patient's own experience of the body over any abstract theories the doctor might possess.[18]

Simpson's response to such arguments also linked religious issues to what amounts to a theory of interpretation. Written in December, one month after his discovery of chloroform, Simpson's "Answer to Religious Objections" offered seven counterarguments to his detractors. These range from an (inaccurate) etymological argument (the Hebrew word for "sorrow" means muscular effort, not physical pain), to a refutation of medicine's implicit double standard (if we take the Bible literally, God's curse on Adam's labor should make the steam engine sacrilege), to an assertion that God's *real* intention was to empower men to relieve women's pain ("The very fact that we have the power by human means to relieve the maternal sufferings, is in itself a sufficient criterion that God would rather that these sufferings be relieved and removed"),[19] to a reference to what Simpson calls "the first surgical operation ever performed on man," which, of course, showed God employing anesthesia ("And the Lord God caused a deep sleep to fall upon Adam; and he slept; and he took one of his ribs, and closed up the flesh instead thereof").[20] Each of these arguments assumes that women, like men, belong to the social realm, but each silences the patients and subjects them to a doctor's interpretive control. As the grounds of the debate rapidly shifted from theology to medical issues, Simpson, like Meigs, turned to a detailed consideration of how a doctor could read his patient's silenced body—particularly when the body was that of a woman.

Addressing Meigs directly, Simpson argues that the pain of childbirth is neither beneficial nor uncomplicated. As a condition of the patient's mind, labor pain has a prehistory in "anxiety and dread" and an afterlife in the "exhaustion and nervous depression which the pains and shock of delivery tend to produce." By eliminating anxiety and warding off "those secondary vascular excitements" labor indirectly causes, chloroform relieves the woman of all these forms of pain.[21] What chloroform actually does, Simpson argues, is to split pain into two separable components: the "severe muscular *efforts* and *struggles*" that the woman's body undergoes and the "*feelings* or *sensations* of pain" that her mind would otherwise experience.[22] Chloroform transfers to the doctor the *knowledge* of pain, as it renders the woman's body merely a sign, which he can read more accurately than she can.[23]

This argument has both practical and epistemological implications. Practically, removing pain from the patient's consciousness makes her more tractable and therefore a more passive object for the accoucheur. The "quiet and unresisting" body does not shrink from "the introduction of the hand into the maternal passages," as Simpson phrases it; "this state of relaxation and dilatability" therefore renders "the artificial extraction of the infant through those passages alike more easy for the practitioner, less dangerous for the child, and more safe for the structures of the mother."[24] Epistemologically, the "unresisting body" offers no impediment to the doctor's interpretation. Chloroform, therefore, enables the medical man simultaneously to conceptualize his necessarily intimate physical contact with a woman in abstract and euphemistic terms and to replace what Simpson described as the doctor's incapacitating vicarious suffering with a powerful feeling of having earned the thanks with which women rewarded his labor.[25] Additional letters, collected by Simpson and printed in one of his pamphlets, fairly exult in the power with which chloroform can "lay the most restless or ungovernable patient quiet on her pillow."[26] "Screams . . . audible across the street" are silenced, an unsuspecting patient is put under "in spite of herself," and even the most recalcitrant women express "sincere gratitude" "for saving them from their agonies."[27]

It is important to recognize that in none of these arguments are Simpson or Meigs arguing as scientists. While concern for the patient's safety appears in the controversy over chloroform, none of the arguments is based on anything remotely resembling what twentieth-century researchers would consider adequate or controlled experimentation. Some laboratory experiments were conducted, especially in England, but even those considered by opponents of chloroform to be decisive contained so many variables as to produce completely inconclusive results.[28] Doctors were quick to interpret—or dismiss—the results of experimentation according to the practitioner's convenience, not to base their practice on laboratory tests. Thus Dr. John Snow, who was certainly the most careful experimenter of all the practitioners who wrote upon the subject, judged ether to be safer than chloroform, yet continued to use chloroform himself because of its "ready applicability."[29] It was not unusual for correspondents to *Lancet* to argue for or against the safety of chloroform on the basis of one application to a parturient woman.[30]

There is one final issue in the chloroform debate, an issue that indicates the way in which what seems to be a debate about practice is actually a debate about the role of interpretation and definition in claiming authority. One version of this issue appears in a report Dr. Simpson delivered to the Medico-Chirurgical Society in July 1848, nine months after his enthusiastic adoption of chloroform. In this report, Simpson attributes the failure of English practitioners to achieve success commensurate with that of the Scots to a misreading of the anesthesized body. "Immediately before the chloroform produced anaesthesia," Simpson is reported saying, "more especially if there was any noise or disturbance, it not unfrequently excited the patient, who would talk incoherently for a moment or two, beg the inhalation to be suspended, perhaps struggle to get free of it, and have his [*sic*] arms and legs thrown into a state of strong clonic spasms. . . . In the English Journals such cases have been repeatedly and gravely recorded as instances of delirium, and spasms, and convulsions, and failure. They are not more anxious, or deserving of attention, than the same symptoms would be in a case of hysteria, and are quite transient if the inhalation is only persevered in."[31]

Simpson's passing reference to hysteria is telling, for what English journals repeatedly reported were not simply random "instances of delirium, and spasms, and convulsions," but specifically female displays of *sexual excitation*. Those few spasms that were reported in males were universally described as signs of fighting.[32] These reports had been appearing ever since the first successful inhalation of anesthesia, for ether, chloroform's immediate predecessor, had an even greater tendency than chloroform to stimulate motor and verbal responses. In an article published in 1847 and entitled "On the Utility and Safety of the Inhalation of Ether in Obstetrical Practice," W. Tyler Smith, an upstart from Bristol who was to become one of the founders of the Obstetrical Society, cited this excitation as a decisive barrier to ether's use. Smith claims to judge ether on a "physiological and pathological basis," but when he comes to "the occasional incitement of the sexual passion," it becomes clear that this, not physiology, is the heart of his objection. Here I want to quote Smith at some length.

In one of the cases observed by Baron Dubois, the woman drew an attendant towards her to kiss, as she was lapsing into insensibility, and this woman afterwards confessed to dreaming of coitus with her husband while she lay etherized. In ungravid women, rendered insensible for the performance of surgical operations, erotic gesticulations have occasionally been observed, and in one case, in which enlarged nymphae were removed, the woman went unconsciously through the movements attendant on the sexual orgasm, in the presence of numerous bystanders. . . . Viewed apart from the moral considerations involved, there is not, in the whole of the wonders related of this extraordinary agent, anything more wonderful than this exchange of the smarting of the knife and the throes of parturition, not for mere oblivion, but for sensations of an opposite kind, pain, in fact, being metamorphosed into its antithesis. Still, I may venture to say, that to the women of this country the bare possibility of having feelings of such a kind excited and manifested in outward uncontrollable actions, would be more shocking even to anticipate, than the endurance of the last extremity of physical pain.[33]

As Smith continues, his interpretation of such displays becomes more elaborate. "In many of the lower animals, we know that an erotic condition of the ovaria is present during parturition, and that sexual congress and conception may take place immediately upon delivery. It was, however, reserved for the phenomenon of etherization to show that, as regards sexual emotion, the human female may possibly exchange the pangs of travail for the sensations of coitus, and so approach to the level of the brute creation." In an article written a year later, Smith will argue, like Meigs, that labor pains are beneficial, and, in basing this position on what he considers a physiological fact, he asserts that that which facilitates the doctor's interpretation also eases the patient's suffering. Screaming, he writes in 1848, opens a woman's glottis, and thus "relieves the uterus of all extra-uterine pressure."[34] In this 1847 lecture, however, it is clear that what will become a physiological argument has its roots in an argument about propriety. "May it not be, that in woman the physical pain neutralizes the sexual emotions, which would otherwise probably, be present, but which would tend very much to alter our estimation of the modesty and retiredness proper to the sex, and which are never more prominent or more admirable than on these occasions?"

Implicit in Smith's description is the fear that, under ether, women will regress to a state of nature in which they are beyond recall or control. To counter this, he offers his paradoxical theory of a propriety "naturally" induced by pain—a theory, not incidentally, that ensures the doctor's ability to interpret what the woman really feels even when she "prominently" displays "admirable" modesty and retiredness. Smith has moved a step beyond Meigs here, for seeing sexuality where Meigs only saw pain prompts Smith to protect the doctor against being implicated in what he says the patient feels. Once more, Smith attributes this protectiveness to the "naturally" compliant woman: "Chastity of feeling, and, above all, emotional self-control, at a time when women are receiving such assistance as the accoucheur can render, are of far more importance than insensibility to pain. They would scarcely submit to the possibility of a sexual act in which their unborn offspring should take the part of excitor; and as the erotic condition has been chiefly observed in patients undergoing operations on the sexual organs, we must assign as the exciting cause, either the manipulations of the attendant or the passage of the child."[35]

Smith's complaint reappears repeatedly in the chloroform debate. Dr. G. T. Gream, physician-accoucheur to Queen Charlotte's Lying-In Hospital and one of the most fashionable obstetricians in London's West End, was particularly outspoken on this point, but he was certainly not alone. One of his lengthy complaints before the Westminster Medical Society in 1849 prompted a fellow medical man, Dr. Tanner, to cite an operation "in King's College Hospital on the vagina of a prostitute, in which ether produced lascivious dreams."[36] So general was the response that both John Snow and James Simpson rose to counter this charge. Snow simply pointed out that all "unpleasantness" could be avoided if a specialist administered chloroform;[37] Simpson flatly denied that such scenes could exist. "He had never seen, nor had he ever heard of any other person having seen, any manifestation of sexual excitement result from the exhibition of chloroform," he is reported to have said. "The excitement, he was inclined to think, existed not in the individuals anaesthesized, but was the result of impressions harboured in the minds of the practitioners." Collapsing Dr. Tanner's report with that of Baron Dubois, Simpson remarks that the experience of one "Parisian prostitute" with "lascivious dreams" should not be generalized to all women. "Surely it was," he retorted, "to say the least, very unbecoming to say that most English ladies should have sexual dreams (like one French prostitute) when under the influence of chloroform."[38]

The preventive Simpson recommended for an excitation so easily misconstrued was a "large, overwhelming dose" of the anodyne. By 1855, Dr. James Arnott had the temerity to suggest that Simpson's putatively scientific mode of application—the so-called Edinburgh method—had been developed, not for the patient's safety, but precisely to protect the practitioner from such " 'involuntary confidences' and emotions" as light anesthesia was apt to produce.[39] Whether Arnott was correct or not, his charge points out the extent to which Simpson and Smith actually agree about one essential fact: such "scenes of an indelicate character"[40] are undesirable and possibly dangerous for the patient, the practitioner, or the medical profession as a whole. I would like to suggest that this shared preoccupation with propriety reveals that, in at least one important sense, the chloroform debate was not really a debate at all. Or—more precisely—it *was* a debate but *not* about the issues it purported to address. Instead of disputing the nature or position of women, obstetricians on both sides actually agreed about what women were and where they should be. Their disagreement was really about tactics—about what treatment of women would consolidate the obstetricians' position within the profession and in society as a whole. I want to turn now to the model of the female body that both sides assumed to show how it could ground not only both sides of the chloroform debate but also the professional dispute of which this debate was only a part.

W. Tyler Smith's 1847–48 lecture series on obstetrics, which was the basis for his *Manual of Obstetrics,* was one of the most popular and influential nineteenth-century textbooks on midwifery.[41] Written at a time when Smith could have had little practical experience in obstetrics, these lectures nevertheless lament—and set out to correct—the current poverty of knowledge about the female body, and especially about parturition. "I venture without fear of contradiction," he states in the third lecture, "to assert, that nothing like a correct analysis or synthesis of the different forms of uterine motor action, no examination of the order in which the various uterine and extra-uterine actions of labour take place, or of the reasons why they follow each other in a certain definite and regular order, will be found in any of the works of British or Foreign writers on Obstetricy." The subject deserves more attention, Smith claims, because "the uterus is to the Race what the heart is to the Individual: it is the organ of circulation to the species." As Smith continues, individual women dissolve into one enormous, universal uterus—a disembodied, faintly threatening womb, continuously generating off-spring who seem dwarfed and shortlived in contrast to their great original. "Ages are the channels in which created beings circulate; and man passes continually from the womb of his mother onwards to the womb of time. . . . Parturition is the systole of the uterus, the unimpregnated state its diastole, and the living beings which flow on in countless numbers are as inconsiderable in the great stream of life as the myriads of globules revealed by the microscope are in the circulation of the blood."[42]

Smith's vision of a heart-like uterus has its counterpart in his assertion that, in any individual woman, this organ is "the largest, and perhaps the most important, muscle of the female economy."[43] Connected to all "distant parts of the economy . . . through the medium of the spinal marrow and its special incident excitor and reflex motor nerves," the uterus governs the entire female organism whether a woman is pregnant or not, and in spite of her mind, emotions, or will. "The uterus is altogether removed from the direct influence of Voluntary motion," Smith comments.[44] To quote another medical man, it is "as if the Almighty, in creating the female sex, had taken the uterus and built up a woman around it."[45]

The prominence of the uterus in representations of the female body belongs to the argument that women, more than men, are governed and defined by their reproductive capacity. "The character and position" of women—indeed, their "value"—are all directly related to the procreative function. "No life seems so valuable as that of a woman in childbirth," Smith asserts.[46] Most frequently, this conclusion is reached by reasoning from the visible influences of the female reproductive organs; but so resilient is it that it can also be reached the other way around. As Thomas Laycock remarked, the "influence which the generative organs must exert over the whole animal economy, may be easily inferred from the general fact, that the final cause of all vital action is the reproduction of the species."[47] Even if a woman did not bear children, her capacity to do so dictated her health—or rather, her lack of health; in the absence of reproduction, "some other demand for the unemployed functions must be established. Accumulated force must find an outlet, or disturbance first and weakness ultimately results."[48]

The physiological mechanism upon which Smith bases the influence and centrality of the uterus is what he and other medical men refer to as "reflex action." The model of the human body implicit in this physiology is that of a closed system containing a fixed quantity of energy; if stimulation or expenditure occurs in one part of the system, corresponding depletion or excitation must occur in another. In men, this theory anchors the so-called "spermatic economy";[49] in women, it grounds an economy that is perceived as being continuously internally unstable. This instability is a function of what medical men denominated female "periodicity," a state that is inaugurated by puberty, signaled by menstruation, and epitomized in childbearing. This periodicity has no counterpart in the male;[50] in the female it is so decisive because it is so pervasive. Thomas Laycock states, for example, that menstruation "is only a multiple of the hebdomadal period. . . . Changes occurring every three-and-a-half and every seven days, as well as every two, three, or four weeks, come under this head." Some moments in this ceaselessly changing organism are particularly critical to its stability: "The fourth day, and the seventh, eleventh, and fourteenth are critical days, and connect the doctrine of crisis with the menstrual period."[51]

The "doctrine of crisis" to which Laycock refers has to do with the recurrence in women of various nervous disorders, especially hysteria. Given a unified, self-regulating system subject to constant internal variation, the slightest irritation of any part of the system is liable to upset the balance. The likelihood of disorder is further enhanced by the greater delicacy and sensitivity thought to characterize female nerves.[52] Given the fact that "by universal consent the nervous system of the human female is allowed to be sooner affected by all stimuli, whether corporeal or mental, than that of the male," it hardly seems surprising that doctors thought women were subject to a bewildering array of physical and emotional disorders.[53]

This set of assumptions—that woman's reproductive function defines her character, position, and value, that this function is only one sign of an innate periodicity, and that this biological periodicity influences and is influenced by an array of nervous disorders—mandates the medical profession's superintendence of women. Parturition, Smith asserts, like menstruation, stands "at the boundary between physiology and pathology, being attended by more pain, and being liable to a greater number of accidents, than any other physiological act of the economy."[54] This set of assumptions is also the physiological basis offered for what was generally held to be woman's greater emotional volatility,[55] for the development of her artfulness or cunning,[56] and for the notion that woman is, by definition, disease or disorder.[57] It isn't far from Smith's statement that parturition and menstruation occupy the "boundary" of physiology and pathology to Dr. W. C. Taylor's notion that "these monthly returns [are] periods of ill health."[58] Even doctors who do not equate periodicity and disease argue for a causal connection. Smith, for example, states unequivocally that "a great part of the pathology of hysteria consists in interruptions of the catemenial [menstrual] cycle."[59]

In 1866, Dr. Issac Ray made explicit what was by then accepted as a medical "fact": "With women, it is but a step from extreme nervous susceptibility to downright hysteria, and from that to overt insanity. In the sexual evolution, in pregnancy, in the parturient period, in lactation, strange thoughts, extraordinary feelings, unseasonable appetites, criminal impulses, may haunt a mind at other times innocent and pure."[60] Seen in this way, hysteria is simultaneously the norm of the female body taken to its logical extreme and a medical category that effectively defines this norm as inherently abnormal. This representation provides an image of woman as always lacking and needing control—whether that control be exercised by the obstetrician, superintending her lying-in, or by the consulting physician, monitoring the disorder that makes her what she is.

The conceptual emergence of hysteria from childbearing, like the putative emergence of sexuality under anesthesia, reveals the contradictory implications of this representation of women. On the one hand, representing woman as an inherently unstable female body authorizes ceaseless medical monitoring and control. But on the other hand, this representation of woman as always requiring control *produces* her as always already exceeding the control that medicine can exercise. To understand the first of these—the benefits of this representation to the medical profession—I want to return to the chloroform debate. That will also take us, by an interesting detour, to the second implication—the dangerous excess built into the medical representation of the female body.

When W. Tyler Smith addresses the issue of anesthesia directly in his ninth lecture on obstetrics, he embroils himself in what turns out to be a characteristically circular logic. Once again, he is concerned about propriety and about whether "ordinary" women are "inferior animal[s]" or moral examples for men. "My own observation convinces me," Smith begins,

that sexual excitement is sometimes apparent during or after labour in a very high degree; indeed cases of this kind may pass into erotomania after parturition. . . . We should be bound to speak the truth in any case; but it would be most offensive to all the best feelings of our nature to suppose sexual excitement present during ordinary cases of labour, and it would certainly interfere very much with the confidence now placed in the obstetric practitioner. But no such suspicion need be entertained. Happily, human emotions are very much under moral control, and in women, almost universally, the utmost retiredness is preserved in everything which relates to childbearing and the puerperal state. . . . On a former occasion I pointed out that, in women, to whom ether-vapour had been administered during parturition, the signal orgasm had been substituted for their natural pains— an exchange which women of modesty would more shrink from, than the liveliest agony. Under the chloroform, too, I have been informed of instances in which the lying-in room has been defiled by the most painful and obscene conversation. There appears, therefore, apart from considerations of safety, to be a moral objection to the administration of the anaesthetic agents now in use—one which should unite against them all men who desire to uphold the respectability of the obstetric department of medicine; for most assuredly, the present kind of attendance could not continue if the facts were understood by parents and husbands.[61]

To underscore Smith's last concern, I cite in full this brief news item, which appeared in *Lancet* in 1854. It is entitled "Care in the Use of Chloroform."

An American practitioner at Philadelphia was lately tried and found guilty of violating a young lady while under chloroform. The jury recommended the prisoner to mercy, as it seemed probable the young lady was labouring under mental hallucinations from the chloroform. The case has created a great sensation in the hospitals and schools at the opposite side of the Atlantic, and suggests a word of caution to practitioners at home.[62]

The professional problem posed by this case had stalked male midwives ever since they had entered lying-in chambers. The mid-nineteenth-century version of this charge is set out at great length by two American brothers, Samuel and George Gregory. "Husbands have told me that they had no children," Samuel wwrites, "and wished to have none, if they must have a doctor to bring them into the world." Gregory turns to the French naturalist Count Buffon for an authoritative explanation of this fear. "In the submission of women to the unnecessary examinations of physicians," Buffon writes, "exposing the secrets of nature, it is forgotten that every indecency of this kind is a violent attack against chastity; that every situation that produces an internal blush is a real prostitution." "An imposition upon the credulity of women, and upon the fears of their husbands," the introduction of accoucheurs sets up a dangerous liaison between a volatile woman and a ready medical man. "Some women are attended by a half a dozen different doctors," Gregory moans, "How much 'affection' is left for the poor husband?"[63]

To allow such doubts to enter the minds of husbands, Smith suggests, would be to jeopardize obstetrics. More specifically, it would cost obstetricians ground in their continuing struggle against midwives and other doctors' prejudices against them. "It should be the steady aim of every man engaged in obstetric practice," Smith declares, "to discourage midwife practice. This department of the profession will never take its true rank until this reform has been effected."[64] Let me consider Smith's concerns one at a time.

Despite Smith's claim that "in Great Britain attendance by midwives is the exception,"[65] the vehemence of his attack upon them suggests that he feared them to be more numerous and threatening than he allowed.[66] The threat is partly practical: midwives, he says, too often hold posts in lying-in hospitals, where important advances in obstetric technique could otherwise be made. Such charity wards were necessary because only there could every doctor be assured that the women he attended would be of a socially inferior class and therefore tractable clinical material.[67] The threat is partly historical: the mere fact that a women's practice gave "birth" to modern obstetrics prompts Smith to rewrite obstetric history in terms of an exclusively male genealogy.[68] The magnitude of the threat midwives were thought to pose can also be measured by the fact that both proponents and opponents of anesthesia formulated part of their arguments so as to counter obstetrics' double association with midwives. Simpson, for example, held that anesthesia, like the forceps, was part of the technology that distinguished "scientific" obstetricians from untrained women, and Smith, like

Meigs, rejects anesthesia because it smacks of "meddlesome midwifery," the charge most often levied against women practitioners. Simpson and Smith agree that obstetrics should ground itself in "principles" rather than empiricism or what they called "practice" because practical experience was the area in which midwives justly claimed superiority.[69]

From one perspective, then, the entire anesthesia debate can be seen as displacing—although not completely containing—this older and more virulent debate. The erudite arguments about nature and (pseudo-) physiology that characterize discussions about anesthesia appear, from this point of view, as attempts on the part of all obstetricians to distinguish between themselves and midwives by moving the entire discussion of obstetrical practice onto spiritual, philosophical, and scientific terrain—terrain that women, equipped only with practical experience, could not enter.

But from another perspective, when Smith links the elimination of midwives to the "rank" of obstetrics, he reveals that *this* contest is itself displacing *another* struggle, that between obstetricians and other members of the medical profession for status and the concomitant right to dictate the grounds of medicine's social authority. This struggle raged partly because of the general level of ignorance within the medical community about physiology and natural science;[70] partly, it reflects the competing investments of various groups of medical men that flourished in this vacuum. Even at mid century, doctors still could not agree among themselves about how, and on what basis, the medical profession should be internally organized: should individual medical men operate in a free market economy, competing for the custom of patients on the basis of their medical expertise; should they derive their status from traditional social rank; or should they be granted a monopoly on the basis of some regularized training program required to enter the profession? One sign of this internal disarray was the fact that in 1850 there were nineteen medical licensing bodies in Great Britain with competing territories and qualifications and without sufficient power to enforce what sanctions they held.[71] Another was the fact that between 1840 and 1858, seventeen bills were introduced in Parliament in attempts to reorganize medical education and licensing; all but one of these bills failed.[72]

The crux of this professional dispute was that by mid century the traditional tripartite structure of the medical profession no longer accurately represented the way medicine was practiced in England. Legally, medicine was still divided into three branches: physicians, who were trained in the liberal arts as well as medicine and governed by the Royal College of Physicians; surgeons, who were descended from the old barber-surgeons and governed by the Royal College of Surgeons; and apothecaries, who were descended from shop-keeping druggists and governed by the Apothecaries' Society. Despite this legal organization, however, as early as 1830 it was generally agreed that very few "pure" physicians or surgeons remained. The vast majority of medical men practiced physic and surgery, regardless of which license they held, and most doctors dealt in midwifery and pharmacy as well. Those who practiced all these branches of medicine were increasingly denominated "general practitioners"; by 1848 they were estimated to number between fourteen and fifteen thousand. Over half of these general practitioners held licenses from both the Royal College of Surgeons and the Apothecaries' Society, but, because of restrictions that were fiercely defended, none of these men were allowed to sit on the powerful governing councils of the Royal Colleges.[73]

These councils were largely run by the so-called "consultants," physicians and surgeons who held appointments to the charity and special hospitals that had begun to proliferate in London in the eighteenth and nineteenth centuries. These elite consultants were at the top of the profession in terms of status, power, and income alike; their substantial earnings were assured, not only by teaching and lucrative supervisory work, but also by the patronage of the wealthy lay members of the hospitals' governing boards. These consultants, whether physicians or surgeons, had an enormous investment in preserving the traditional tripartite structure of the medical profession and the power of the Royal Colleges, for they wanted to protect their own privileged position by excluding from power all general practitioners, whose number was growing every day.[74]

The situation at mid century, then, was that the majority of medical men, who carried out the vast majority of medical work, had no representation in the organizations by which medicine was officially governed, no access to research facilities, and no guaranteed income or social rank. In an interesting way, this inequity was both maintained and challenged by the ways that the two sides represented—and treated—women. Practically, the difference between the two sides is clear: whereas general practitioners almost always practiced midwifery and frequently built their practices upon it, consultants almost never did.[75] The political ramification of this was that the Royal Colleges used the criterion of midwifery, along with that of pharmacy, as a principle of exclusion from their governing councils. The consultants' professed objection to midwifery was that it was manual labor, but their acceptance of surgery, along with such comments as that the practice was "dishonourable" because it involved the "humiliating events of parturition," reveal that the objection was not to manual labor but to this particular *kind* of labor.[76]

Consulting physicians and surgeons did not disdain the treatment of all female disorders, however. In fact, the nervous disorders I have discussed were the province *par excellence* of such expensive consultants. In order to authorize this treatment and not midwifery, consultants represented woman, not as a parturient body but as a delicate, moral creature whose modesty and secrets needed to be protected. So, for example, when Dr. George Burrows, President and Senior Censor of the College of Physicians, testified in 1847 before the Parliamentary Committee that had been appointed to adjudicate this quarrel, he argued that the reason for maintaining the tripartite structure was that only such a hierarchy could protect the public by singling out an elite body of doctors who could exercise "the highest honour and utmost fidelity" to those "secrets of families" that they were required to hear.[77] For this office, medical expertise was less important than discretion—or at least the respect one gentleman accorded to another.

Denied all the resources that accompanied hospital posts, general practitioners' only hope for reform was to challenge the traditional criteria of status and to argue that medical expertise, not social rank, should be the basis of medicine's social authority. To accomplish this, they, too, invoked women. Because their investment was in midwifery, however, they emphasized, not women's modesty, but the value of their reproductive capacity. Here is W. Tyler Smith again, addressing the relationship between the status of obstetrics, the status of women, and England's "standard of civilization." Notice what happens to the status of women.

The excellence of obstetric medicine is one of the most emphatic expressions of that high regard and estimation in which women are always held by civilized races. The state of the obstetric art in any country may be taken as a measure of the respect and value of its people for the female sex; and this, in turn, may be taken as a tolerably true indication of the standard of its civilization. It may be declared as a truism, that obstetric science must flourish most in countries where the marriage tie is most respected—where women are held in the highest esteem.

Long ago the philosophic Denman pointed out the influence which Christianity exerted on obstetric practice, by abolishing polygamy and enforcing a strict observance of the marriage tie—reforms which gave increased value and consequence to every means that science or art could devise for promoting the health and safety of individual women.[78]

Smith's claim that obstetrics *has* prestige is actually a plea *for* that status, and the key to that status is elevating the symbolic position of woman while fixing real women in their proper place—in relation to medical men in general and to obstetricians in particular. Woman could be both the basis of obstetric prestige and its effect, in other words, because the representation of woman has been detached from women's own narrations of their experience. In all the articles, lectures, and textbooks I have read about anesthesia, women are only quoted when their words support a medical man's position, and, even then, these passages emphasize primarily the difference between women's unsophisticated attitude toward what they call "the stuff" and the doctor's scientific understanding.[79] Part of this same controlling representation (which is actually a form of silencing) is the tendency of medical men to represent deliveries as "successful" even when the child is delivered "putrid" or, more horribly still, in pieces.[80] This silencing is simultaneously supported by and supports a set of related truisms—that women's biology dictates their proper social role and that the maternal instinct is physiologically linked to women's reproductive capacity.[81]

It is important to recognize that this silenced female body is the basis of all the debates I have set out—about the propriety of chloroform, the relative status of consultants and general practitioners, and the nature of medical authority. The point is that the silenced female body can be made the vehicle for any medical man's assumptions and practice because its very silence opens a space in which meanings can proliferate. Thus, consultants anxious to establish their territory as "moral feeling" can argue that woman is innately modest yet dangerously susceptible to the advances of unscrupulous men and to smoldering, internal fires; the doctor's calling is therefore to keep her secrets and to superintend her delicate modesty.[82] The general practitioner *cum* obstetrician lets the emphasis fall on woman's innately unstable, reproductive body, which periodically (but regularly) devolves to pathology; his role is also to protect her, but he does so with his instruments and by warding off "meddling" women. For obstetricians who oppose anesthesia, woman's body belongs to the realm of nature, which requires a man's monitoring; only Tyler Smith, for example, can recognize in her cries sexuality subdued through pain. For obstetricians who advocate chloroform, this same body must be stilled; only then can it be delivered from nature into the culture where, once so mastered, it properly belongs.

The debates provoked by chloroform, in other words, constitute a discourse of sexual politics in which the female body has been politicized—differently and in the service of divergent interests. Once silenced, this body can serve as a token in disputes both within the medical profession and between this male profession and the community of female midwives that gave birth to obstetrics. But the very silence that authorizes these different medical practices also produces at the site of the reproductive female body an undecidability that is dangerous to the medical profession and its controlling operations. The silence of the female body actually produces an excess of meanings, and the contradictions that emerge within this excess undermine the authority that medical men both claim and need.

The threat posed to the medical profession by the silenced female body takes three, related, forms. The first may be seen as a kind of promiscuity that attends the body's silence: if the female body is open to any man's definition, there is no ground to limit competition among the interpretations it will admit. Consultants may define woman as innately modest as a means of excluding from power any man who treats her as a reproductive animal, but in so doing they inadvertently align themselves with gentlemanly "quacks," who, as even Burrows had to admit, often obtained the patronage of the wealthy without bothering to purchase a license.[83] General practitioners may define woman as a reproductive creature and argue that empirical knowledge of her body should be the basis of medical authority, but as soon as they establish physiological expertise as the criterion for success, they risk eradicating the distinction between themselves and midwives, many of whom had not only experience of a female body no man could have but also years of informal apprenticeship as well. Both definitions construct woman so as to authorize medical control, but the two definitions are mutually exclusive and imply very different roles for medical men.

If the metaphorical promiscuity of the female body exacerbates competition among groups of medical men, her silence can also create an ambiguity that defies the entire medical community's attempts to maintain control. One version of this problem emerges in discussions of hysteria—a disorder that posed especially difficult, and irritating, problems even for specialists.[84] The source of this problem, as F. C. Skey pointed out, lay in the difficulty a doctor faced in identifying a disease whose symptoms could be feigned and whose organic origins (if any) were invisible and undetectable. Arguing that a doctor's first task is "to discriminate actual disease from no disease at all," Skey goes on to categorize hysteria as a disorder that, by definition, defies diagnostic categories.

> You would imagine this task an easy one, but it is not so. Diseases are feigned both wilfully and unconsciously; the first are generally detectable by a discriminating judgment; the second are imitated by the hand of Nature herself, and are not so readily detected. This factitious condition of the body, that mocks the reality of truth,—that not only invades the localities, but imitates the symptoms of real diseases in all the diversity of its forms, deluding the judgment and discrimination of men of even considerable experience in their profession,—is known under the term *hysteria*.[85]

The inherent duplicity of hysteria partially accounts for the hostility some medical men articulated toward their female patients. Jules Falret, for example, alienist at the Saltpetrière in Paris, railed savagely about the tendency of even genuine hysterics to "malinger" and deceive. "These patients are veritable actresses," he complained; "They do not know of a greater pleasure than to deceive. . . . In one word, the life of the hysteric is nothing but one perpetual falsehood; they affect the airs of piety and devotion and let themselves be taken for saints while at the same time secretly abandoning themselves to the most shameful actions."[86] Falret's hostility is aptly captured by Oliver Wendell Holmes's statement that "an hysterical girl is . . . a vampire who sucks the blood of the healthy people around her"—a phrase repeated by S. Weir Mitchell, a well-known American specialist on nervous diseases.[87]

One of these beset "healthy people" was, of course, the hysteric's attending medical man. The threat the hysteric posed in this sense was a threat to the doctor's authority—his authority to define the disease, to establish the course of treatment, to pronounce a "cure" when symptoms could so easily be feigned. The version of this threat that surfaces in the chloroform debate is suggested by medical men's anxiety that women who had received the "impregnation" of chloroform would become such "zealous missionaries" for the anodyne that they would override the doctor's judgment about whether chloroform was safe or advisable.[88] Simpson's pamphlets repeatedly refer to patients "eagerly," "insistently," "urgently" demanding "the stuff," and he even relates the story of one woman who, in the midst of labor, "secreted the handkerchief" so as to have control over her access to chloroform.[89]

Simpson and other pro-anesthesia obstetricians were reluctant to insist on medical authority in such cases because they needed to use the enthusiasm of patients to advertise chloroform; the argument that patients and doctors were simply obeying the logic of a free market economy helped authorize medical practice in this period because neither the relationship between empirical practice and scientific theory nor the reliability of scientific knowledge had yet been firmly established. Even the manner in which scientific lecture-experiments were sometimes conducted encouraged lay participation and suspended medical knowledge midway between science and entertainment. In 1848, for example, a lecture on ether and chloroform was held at the Royal Institute that "attracted a very large audience, amongst whom were not a few ladies." At the end of his lecture, Mr. Brande administered chloroform to a guinea pig, which—to the lecturer's dismay and the horror of the audience—promptly died. The correspondent to *Lancet*, lamenting the publicity of this debacle, asks rhetorically: "Who among that large assembly, if the inhalation of chloroform should be at any time proposed to them,—who would not remember the fate of that animal, and dread its application to themselves[?]"[90]

As this incident suggests, however, entrusting the adoption of anesthesia to the enthusiasm of the public was fraught with unforeseeable perils because, in the absence of any undisputed authority, the situation was too likely to get out of control. For opponents of chloroform, the very enthusiasm of the public constituted a danger for exactly this reason; obstetricians might well be "dragooned" into accepting this or any other technology just because "conceited or ignorant women of fashion [made] a pastime of this as of other quackeries."[91] Even Simpson suggests this danger when he warns that "medical men may oppose, for a time, the superinduction of anesthesia in parturition, but they will oppose it in vain; for certainly our patients themselves will force the use of it upon the profession."[92] In 1853, Dr. Robert Lee, who opposed chloroform, insisted that, by appealing to the public, the medical community had let the entire issue get out of its hands. The debate, he said, "had become almost an extra-professional question" in which "appeals were made to the natural timidity of women" alongside "a systematic concealment of truth by physicians." Lee explicitly pointed to the twofold consequence of Simpson's deference to consumers: "The cause of science and humanity [has been] placed in the hands of the most presumptuous and frivolous part of the community," he said, "while young and inexperienced mothers [are] decoyed to their destruction."[93]

The third danger that follows from the medical profession's silencing of the female body is suggested by Jules Falret's reference to the hysterics' "shameful actions" and by the metaphorical reference to the application of chloroform as "impregnation." One extreme version of the anxiety that underwrote this danger appears in Robert Brudenell Carter's objection to the speculum, "which he believed was avidly sought by women of all ages and situations as a means of sexual gratification."[94] The problem implicit in all these statements is the fact that medical practitioners, in capitalizing upon female sexuality as disorder, were inadvertently—but inevitably—ensnared by their own fantasies about it. As we have seen, medical men consistently tried to control female sexuality rhetorically—whether through the kind of spatial displacement by which Tyler Smith transforms the disembodied uterus into a heart, or through the consultants' relegation of all inappropriate female assertiveness into the category of deviance or disease. But such attempts were doomed to failure because the undecidability of the silenced female body solicits men to inscribe upon it their own anxieties about sexuality—especially, although not exclusively, female sexuality. These anxieties lie behind the concern repeatedly expressed about medical men attending women in labor. "Let it be known that [a woman] is accessible to the physician, and who that pays the least regard for virtue would notice her?"[95] The representations implicit in this statement are mirror images of each other. From one perspective, woman is a creature absolutely receptive, hence infinitely susceptible to any man's influence; the corresponding representation of man is of a creature absolutely sexual, unbound by social restraints, and desirous even of a woman in labor. Seen another way, however, woman incarnates unfettered, insatiable sexual appetite; before this creature, the attending physician stands impotent, deprived of professional authority and sexual power alike.

What medical men identified as woman's sexuality is obviously as thoroughly what they did not want to see in themselves as it was what real women actually felt.[96] Externalizing this distressing sexuality was, theoretically, one way of controlling fears about it. But in making anxieties about themselves dependent on their own definition and control, men set up an inherently unstable situation—in which they had to regulate both feelings and fears that were externalized because they could not regulate them when they were parts of themselves. In other words, the very instability of woman that mandated medical control also always exceeded that control—precisely, but paradoxically, because this instability was produced simultaneously as the condition, the origin, and the object of that control.[97] This is why doctors' representations of women always include representations of themselves as victims: the consultant is made complicitous by the secrets he must guard; the obstetrician becomes the guilty partner in the woman's sexual display.

To the extent that the undecidability of the silenced female body was connected to nineteenth-century medical men's anxieties about sexuality and their professional status, chloroform only exacerbated the problem. As a man-made technology that made visible both the organism's excitability and its susceptibility, anesthesia did not control the body so much as it disclosed its problematic capacity to produce meanings in excess of what the "exhibitors" of the technology intended. The debate about chloroform displays the extent to which medical men who used the technology were implicated in the "knowledge" it produced—just as it reveals the ways in which issues of gender could be invoked in disputes about power, authority, and professional competence and domains.

This revelation—the display chloroform produces—also begins to suggest how the vicious circle of representation finally opens. Even though the medical representation of woman silenced real women, even though representation is always the arena in which the dominant ideology reproduces itself by constructing knowledge and defining social practice, this ideology can never be totalizing because neither the representation nor its workings through is homogeneous. The representation of woman serves the interests, not of a monolithic entity called "patriarchy," but of various subgroups within the dominant group—of consultants against general practitioners or of husbands against all medical men.[98] The uneven developments within both institutional practice and the production of knowledge open spaces for opposition and analysis, even if that analysis lags behind the practices that call it forth. Requiring interpretation, which can never be disinterested, representation can never completely contain or master its subject. Even the silenced body acts out a language that defies mastery, that resists such simple treatment.

Notes

I would especially like to thank Leslie Katz for her help in conducting the original research for this essay and Barbara Taylor for offering particularly helpful suggestions about an earlier draft.

1. James Miller, *The Principles of Surgery* (1858), quoted in A. J. Youngson, *The Scientific Revolution in Victorian Medicine* (New York, 1979), 69.

2. Barbara M. Duncum, *The Development of Inhalation Anaesthesia, With Special Reference to the Years 1846–1900* (London, 1947), 253.

3. Ann Oakley, *Women Confined: Towards a Sociology of Childbirth* (New York, 1980), 13. See also L. J. Jordanova, "Natural Facts: A Historical Perspective on Science and Sexuality," in *Nature, Culture and Gender,* ed. Carol P. MacCormack and Marilyn Strathern (Cambridge, 1980), 42–45; and Barbara Ehrenreich and Deirdre English, *For Her Own Good: 150 Years of the Experts' Advice to Women* (Garden City, N.Y., 1979), 5.

4. For a history of the Chamberlens and their forceps, see James Hobson Aveling, *The Chamberlens and the Midwifery Forceps: Memorials of the Family and an Essay on the Invention of the Instrument* (London, 1892; reprint ed., New York, 1977).

5. John Hawkins Miller points out that before technological intervention, childbearing was often held to confer status upon a woman, both because it represented the achievement of her female "destiny" and because it was an opportunity for her to prove her physical and spiritual strength. See " 'Temple and Sewer': Childbirth, Pru-

dery, and Victoria Regina," in *The Victorian Family: Structure and Stresses*, ed. Anthony S. Wohl (New York, 1978), 24–26. One glimpse into the spiritual significance child-birth might have had in this period is provided by this extract from W. E. Gladstone's diary, written after watching the birth of his first child in 1840:

> This is to me a new scene & lesson in human life. I have seen her endure today—less than the average for first children, says Dr L, yet six times as much bodily pain as I have undergone in my whole life. . . . How many thoughts does this agony excite: the comparison of the termination with the commencement: the undergoings of another for our sakes: the humbling & sobering view of human relations here presented: the mixed & intricate considerations of religion which may be brought to bear upon the question of the continuation of our wayward race. Certainly the woman has this bless-ing that she may as a member of Christ behold in these pains certain espe-cially appointed means of her purification with a willing mind, & so the more cheerfully hallow them by willing endurance into a thank offering.

Quoted in F. B. Smith, *The People's Health, 1830–1910* (New York, 1979), 59, n. 20.

Queen Victoria's account of her daughter Alice's lying-in suggests how powerfully childbirth might encourage the identification of one woman with another and thus strengthen the sense of a community of women. Notice how Victoria's projection of herself changes from being the nurse to being the woman in labor.

> She is very calm and quiet [Victoria writes], but not as strong as I was. She reminded me so much during the labour and even now lying in bed of dearest Papa when he was ill. I was dreadfully shaken and agitated by it all. I was with her the greater part of the time and never got to bed till 1/4 to 6. To see good Louis, who behaved beautifully, hold her in his arms was so dreadful! It seemed a strange dream and as if it must be me and dearest Papa—instead of Alice and Louis! And then for me to direct every thing which beloved Papa always did and would have done! I had so wished for one other [baby] and had thought it very likely that Alice and I would have followed each other very closely! Then to see Mrs Lilly and Sir C. Locock both there seemed the same thing over again!

Quoted in Miller, " 'Temple and Sewer,' " 38.

6. Theatrical metaphors frequently appear in medical men's descriptions of their treat-ment of women. One example comes from W. Tyler Smith's fourteenth lecture on obstetrics. "Labour is a drama, painful to the individual, and exerting painful interest in those around her: in the great majority of cases it ends happily, and all the parties come forward with smiling faces at the close; but at any act or incident the curtain *may* fall upon a tragedy"; *London Lancet*, 1848, vol. 2: 208.

7. For one of the many examples of the former, see Frederick C. Cartwright, *The Devel-opment of Modern Surgery* (New York, 1968). Here Cartwright describes the discovery of anesthesia as having both scientific and psychological significance: "Thus the intro-duction of anaesthesia is a dramatic outward expression of Man's inner change from eighteenth-century brutality to our own more humane pattern of behaviour" (33). See also Rene Fulop-Miller, *Triumph over Pain*, trans. Eden and Cedar Paul (New York, 1938). The second phrase comes from Adrienne Rich, *Of Woman Born: Motherhood as Experience and Institution* (New York, 1977). For other feminist versions of this story, see Oakley, *Women Confined;* Ehrenreich and English, *For Her Own Good;* William Ray Arney, *Power and the Profession of Obstetrics* (Chicago, 1982).

8. For reports of unreported deaths, see *Lancet*, 1853, vol. 1: 523; *Lancet*, 1855, vol. 1: 496. Conflicting statistics can also be found in the latter article.

9. "The word *anaesthesia,* implying loss of sensation as a result of disease or injury, but not loss of consciousness, was quite frequently used during the eighteenth and early nineteenth centuries"; Duncum, *Inhalation Anaesthesia,* 562. For an account of the discovery of the anesthetic properties of ether and the establishment of chloroform, see ibid., 9–26 and passim.

10. *Lancet,* 1847, vol. 2: 549–50.

11. See Duncum, *Inhalation Anaesthesia,* 9–10. She quotes John Snow as stating: "Besides the great benefit conferred by chloroform in the prevention of pain, it probably confers still greater advantages by the extension which it gives to the practice of surgery" (10).

12. The *OED* cites instances of the adjective *obstetric* (or *obstetrical*) from the seventeenth and early eighteenth centuries. Interestingly, these early uses are almost all metaphorical and refer to a man aiding in the "delivery" of an idea, text, or event. Examples include: "There all the Learn'd shall at the labour stand, And Douglas lend his soft, obstetric hand" (1742; Pope, *Dunciad* 4.394); "This you protect their pregnant hour . . . exerting your obstetric pow'r" (c. 1750; Shenstone, *To the Virtuosi,* vii). One nonmetaphorical use depicts a male frog, the "obstetrical toad" *(Alytes obstetricans),* who aids the female in birth: "They spawn like frogs; but what is singular, the male affords the female obstetrical aid" (1776; Pennant, *Zoology,* 3:17). By the end of the eighteenth century, the word was generally used in its medical sense: "The obstetric art . . . began to emerge from its barbarity during the sixteenth century" (1799; *Medical Journal* 2:453). Instances of figurative usages continue to appear, however, as when Byron wrote to Scott in 1822 that "Mr. Murray has several things of mine in his obstetrical hands." The word *obstetrician* first appears in 1828, when Dr. Michael Ryan calls attention to its novelty: "It may be necessary to say a few words apologetic, for my adoption of the word obstetrician" (1828; *Man Midwifery,* v). In 1819, the word *obstetrics* already referred to a medical practice more extensive than the simple delivery in which even untrained women could assist: "*Obstetrics,* the doctrines or practice of midwifery. . . . Employed in a larger signification than mid-wifery in its usual sense" (1819; *Pantalogia*). The *OED* cites the first appearance of *accoucheur* as Laurence Sterne's *Tristram Shandy* (1759–67): "Nothing will serve you but to carry off the man-midwife," says Tristram's father. "*Accoucheur,*—if you please," responds Dr. Slop (2:12).

    It is interesting to note that W. Tyler Smith was intent upon eliminating the very word *midwife* from medical language and in sharply distinguishing between scientific, male-administered obstetrics and unscientific, female-dominated "midwifery": "We may confidently hope," he states in his first obstetric lecture, "that hereafter the sign of the escape of midwifery from the midwife will be . . . obscure and insignificant, and that the very term *midwifery* will be rejected on account of its derivation"; *Lancet,* 1847, vol. 2:371. See also "Obstetrics a Science, Midwifery an Art," *British and Foreign Medico-Chirurgical Review* 4 (1849): 501–10.

13. See Margarete Sandalowski, *Pain, Pleasure, and American Childbirth: From the Twilight Sleep to the Reed Method, 1914–1960* (Westport, Conn., 1984), 29–30. Simpson also acknowledged this when he stated that "the application of anaesthesia to midwifery involves many more difficult and delicate problems than its mere application to surgery"; ibid., 28.

14. See Oakley, *Women Confined,* 8–9.

15. Quoted by James Young Simpson, "Same Subject Continued, in a Letter to Dr. Protheroe Smith, of London," in *Anaesthesia; or, the Employment of Chloroform and Ether in Surgery, Midwifery, Etc.* (Philadelphia, 1849), 123.

16. *Lancet,* 1848, vol. 1:614. Simpson made the presumption of such "medical" arguments explicit when he called these speakers "London medical divines"; "Same Subject Continued," 125.

17. *Lancet,* 1848, vol. 1:614. Meigs states earlier, "I have been accustomed to look upon the sensation of pain in labour as a physiological relative of the power or force; and notwithstanding I have seen so many women in the throes of labour, I have always regarded a labour-pain as a most desirable, salutary, and conservative manifestation of life-force" (613).

18. Stanley Joel Reiser discusses the transformation of "theory-bound, patient-dependent scholastics" into "touch-oriented, observation-bound" practitioners who no longer depended on the patient's observations and accounts. See *Medicine and the Reign of Technology* (Cambridge, 1978), 4–29. See also M. Jeanne Peterson, *The Medical Profession in Mid-Victorian London* (Berkeley, 1978), 14.

19. James Young Simpson, "Answer to the Religious Objections Advanced Against the Employment of Anaesthetic Agents in Midwifery and Surgery," in *Anaesthesia,* 120.

20. Ibid., 122. This essay also cites many of Simpson's opponents.

21. Simpson, "Results of the Practice of Anaesthesia in Medicine," in *Anaesthesia,* 140–41.

22. Simpson, "Answer," 117.

23. Here is Simpson on the double nature of pain:

> Each so-called labour pain consists, as you well know, of two distinct and separate elements; viz. *first,* of contraction of the uterus and other assistant muscles; and, *secondly,* of sensations of pain, more or less agonizing, accompanying these contractions, and directly resulting from them. Now, I have been often struck, as you must have been, in chloroform labours, with the fact that, in the anaesthetic state, not only does the uterus contract powerfully, but that the abdominal muscles do so also, and even the face of the patient will sometimes betoken strong expulsive actions, while all accompanying suffering is quite annulled. We abrogate the second element of the so-called labour pain, without destroying the first. We leave intact the expulsive muscular efforts, but remove the sense and feeling of pain accompanying these efforts. It is only of late that these two elements or constituents of labour-pains have been recognised and studied by the Profession as *two* separate objects. But it is surely, as I have above stated, worthy of remark and wonder, that the language of the Bible is, on this as on other points, strictly and scientifically correct, and long ago made, with perfect precision, the very distinction which we are now-a-days only recognising. For the Hebrew noun, *'etzebh,* distinctly signifies the muscular contraction or effort, and the nouns, *hhil* and *hhebhel,* as distinctly signify the sensations of pain accompanying these efforts.

It is all right, of course, for the doctor to alleviate the latter, for *sorrow* is derived from the former, Simpson argues. See "Answer," 124–25.

24. Simpson, "Results," in *Anaesthesia,* 144. Simpson also states that the "manageableness" of an anesthecized patient can be "as perfect as if she had been a wax doll or a lay figure": *Lancet,* 1847, vol. 2:550.

25. For an account of Simpson's revulsion from the pain he had to inflict, see *Lancet,* 1847, vol. 2:625. Here he describes "that great principle of emotion which both impels us to feel sympathy at the sight of suffering in any fellow-creature, and at the same time imparts to us delight and gratification in the exercise of any power by which we can mitigate and alleviate suffering." Accounts of appreciative patients appear throughout "Report of the Results," in *Anaesthesia,* 151–79.

26. Ibid., 157.
27. Ibid., 159, 164, 156.
28. These are the "One Hundred Experiments on Animals, with Ether and Chloroform," conducted by Thomas Wakley in 1847 and reported in *Lancet*, 1848, vol. 1:19–25. The many variables in these experiments include different animals (ranging from horses to hedgehogs to pigeons), different amounts of chloroform or ether, different conditions of administration, and different periods of inhalation. Wakley concludes that chloroform is more dangerous than ether, but he offers no physiological explanation. Another unscientific set of experiments is reported in *Lancet*, 1851, vol. 1:505–6.
29. Snow stated: "I use chloroform for the same reason that you use phosphorus matches instead of the tinder box. An occasional risk never stands in the way of ready applicability"; quoted in Duncum, *Inhalation Anaesthesia*, 180. Duncum states that Snow "brushed aside evidence which ran counter to his theory (proved to his own satisfaction by experiments on animals in the laboratory), that if the vapour were sufficiently diluted with air then it could not cause death without warning" (203). In 1911, A. Goodman proved conclusively that Snow was mistaken. Light chloroform *could* kill without warning from ventricular fibrillations of the heart (203).
30. See Dr. S. Gower's judgment against chloroform in the *London Lancet* 1848, vol. 2:124. Gower admits that his preference for ether is primarily based on its odor. "Ether as inhaled as from a sponge not only acts on the patient, but diffuses a grateful fragrance around, which makes both Dr. and nurse—what doctors and nurses ought to be—cheerful." Gower's more "scientific" conclusions about ether and chloroform are, incidentally, wrong. Simpson's response to the argument that chloroform was unsafe was not to refer even to pseudoscientific experiments, but to attack the putative fallacy of the logic.

> If there were any soundness in the reasoning [he declaimed] a thousand things beside would require to be abandoned. Railways, steamboats, stage-coaches, &c., when used as substitutes for the natural and physiological function of human progression, are ever and anon attended with accidents to limb and life. But surely no one would, from this, maintain that these means of conveyance should in consequence be abandoned. Many persons are annually drowned in bathing.—Should bathing, therefore, be prohibited and this powerful means of maintaining and restoring health be entirely forsaken?

"Objections to Anaesthesia in Midwifery," in *Anaesthesia*, 187.
31. Simpson, "Discussion on the Employment of Chloroform in Midwifery and Surgery Before the Medico-Chirurgical Society of Edinburgh," in *Anaesthesia*, 189.
32. See *Lancet*, 1848, vol. 1:26; *Lancet*, 1847, vol. 2:389. Havelock Ellis, writing more than fifty years later, continued to assert that women were more likely to experience sexual excitation under anesthesia. He cites a series of experiments in which Dr. J. F. W. Silk administered anesthesia to 5119 patients, 3400 of whom were women. "Erotic phenomena occurred 18 times, but only once in a man; to preserve the male ratio they should only have occurred twice among the women"; *Man and Woman: A Study of Human Secondary Sexual Characters* (London, 1904; reprint ed., New York, 1974), 273.

Here is Dr. W. Martin Coates's description of his patient's and his own response to chloroform: "I own that I never witnessed the sudden suffused countenance, the foaming mouth, the injected conjunctivae, the dilated pupil, the convulsive movements of the extremities, the stertorous breathing, and, at a subsequent stage, the pallid face, the slow, laboured respiration, and the very feeble pulse of the patient under the ordinary dose inhaled, without a dread of a suddenly fatal result, and a conviction that chloroform, to be safely administered, must be inhaled in much smaller doses"; *Lancet,* 1851, vol. 1:505.

33. *London Lancet,* 1847, vol. 1:377. Smith allows a disturbing ambiguity to insinuate itself into this account when he fails to report that Dr. Dubois specified that the attendant the woman kissed was female. Dubois's account also emphasizes the woman's modesty.

> "What did you dream of?" was my question; but the patient turned her face aside with a smile, the peculiarity of which having drawn my particular attention, I renewed my question; but on her having again refused to let me know the nature of her dream, I had recourse, in order to ascertain it, to the intermediary communication of a respectable person of her own sex, and who was present at the operation of inhaling ether. To the same question being renewed, she answered, she had dreamt she was beside her husband, and that he and herself had been simultaneously engaged, going through those preliminaries which had led her to the state in which we now be-held her.

> *London Lancet,* 1847, vol. 1:411, 412. W. Tyler Smith, who had arrived in London in 1840 after scanty education in Bristol, had no influence or connections, yet he rose to such prominence that he became one of the founders of the Obstetrical Society in 1859. His degree was an M.B.; he was not a member of any of the Royal Colleges. See Youngson, *Scientific Revolution in Victorian Medicine,* 77–78; and W. Tyler Smith, "On the Founding of the Obstetrical Society of London (1859)," in *Transactions of the Obstetrical Society of London* (London, 1859), v–xiv.

34. *London Lancet,* 1848, vol. 2:207.

35. *London Lancet,* 1847, vol. 1:377.

36. *Lancet,* 1849, vol. 1:212. In 1853, Dr. Robert Lee and Dr. Gream were still making this point. See *Lancet,* 1853, vol. 1:611.

37. *Lancet,* 1849, vol. 1:212.

38. Ibid., 395. Dr. Syme added "that he had never witnessed any sexual excitement produced by the exhibition of chloroform, but that he and others had frequently heard patients in the operating theatre swearing, when excited by chloroform, and that, sometimes, in patients whose friends had seldom or ever heard using such language. Possibly these improper expressions were only a true exhibition of the state of the patients' mind, and it was always stopped by throwing him deeply asleep."

39. *Lancet,* 1855, vol. 1:499. One way of construing the quarrel about how to administer chloroform is to see it as part of the ongoing debate about whether Edinburgh-trained medical men were superior or inferior to London-trained men. The "Edinburgh method" of chloroform application was considered by many English doctors as irresponsible and unsafe; in England, lighter doses were applied, and often doctors used an inhaler—not a rag or handkerchief—to administer the anodyne. In Edinburgh, all medical men were trained in surgery and pharmacy and were therefore what would be called general practitioners in England. When they began coming to England in larger numbers in the second half of the eighteenth century, they helped swell the ranks of general practitioners, many of whom wanted—but were denied—representation in the Royal Colleges. Scottish physicians were not formally recognized in England, but the Royal Colleges had no mechanism for effectively limiting their practice. See Noel Parry and Jose Parry, *The Rise of the Medical Profession: A Study of Collective Social Mobility* (London, 1976), 105–7.

40. This phrase appears in the *Lancet,* 1856, vol. 1:424.

41. See Youngson, *Scientific Revolution in Victorian Medicine*, 78. In England, a medical student training for general practice was generally required to attend lectures on midwifery for three months (which would have included only a part of Smith's course) and to be present for at least six deliveries in a lying-in hospital. The latter part of this regulation was almost always curtailed because there were never enough women confined in the hospitals to enable each student to witness six births. See F. B. Smith, *The People's Health*, 24. By 1827, some training in midwifery was required by the Society of Apothecaries; by 1855, this was also true of the College of Surgeons; by 1884, midwifery and women's diseases were also part of the required curriculum of the Royal College of Surgeons. See Peterson, *The Medical Profession*, 62–63; and Ivan Waddington, "General Practitioners and Consultants in Early Nineteenth-Century England: The Sociology of an Intra-Professional Conflict," in *Health Care and Popular Medicine in Nineteenth Century England*, ed. John Woodward and David Richards (New York, 1977), 180.

It should also be noted that as late as the 1850s, licenses from all three Colleges could be obtained from extremely varied systems of training, including that provided by universities, hospitals, dispensaries, provincial schools, private schools, special institutions, and independent courses of lectures. See Ian Inkster, "Marginal Men: Aspects of the Social Role of the Medical Community in Sheffield, 1790–1850," in *Health Care and Popular Medicine*, 132–35. Inkster also discusses the institution of private lecturing. See pp. 133–34.

42. *Lancet*, 1847, vol. 2:544.

43. Ibid., 595.

44. Ibid.

45. Dr. M. L. Holbrook, *Parturition Without Pain: A Code of Directions for Escaping from the Primal Curse* (1892), quoted in Carroll Smith-Rosenberg and Charles E. Rosenberg, "The Female Animal: Medical and Biological Views of Woman and Her Role in Nineteenth-Century America," in *Women and Health in America: Historical Readings*, ed. Judith Walzer Leavitt (Madison, Wis., 1984), 13.

46. *Lancet*, 1847, vol. 2:371.

47. Thomas Laycock, *An Essay on Hysteria: Being an Analysis of Its Irregular and Aggravated Forms, Including Hysterical Hemorrhage, and Hysterical Ischuria* (Philadelphia, 1840), 63. Laycock differed from many other mid-nineteenth-century medical men in maintaining that "the uterus is an appendage to the ovaries" (64), but he agreed that the female reproductive system was central to the organism.

48. From Dr. Charles Taylor in 1882, quoted in Carl Degler, "What Ought To Be and What Was: Women's Sexuality in the Nineteenth Century," in *Women and Health in America*, 41.

49. See G. J. Barker-Benfield, "The Spermatic Economy: A Nineteenth-Century View of Sexuality," in *Feminist Studies* 1 (1972): 45–74; Smith-Rosenberg and Rosenberg, "Female Animal," 13–14; and Ehrenreich and English, *For Her Own Good*, 27. Here is Dr. Beard on reflex action:

> When any part or point of the body, external or internal, on the periphery, or at the center, is irritated, some other part is liable to be in some way changed for the better or worse; but there are *par excellence* three great centers of reflex action—the *brain*, the *stomach* and *digestive apparatus*, and the *genital* or *reproductive* system. When any one of these three reflex centers is irritated by over-use or direct abuse, the injury is likely to radiate or reverberate in any or in all directions; we can not tell just where, any more than we can tell where lightening will strike. . . . This accounts, in part, for

the immense number and variety of symptoms and abnormal sensations from which the nervously exhausted suffer. . . . Disorders of the genital apparatus in either sex are continually exciting disease in remote organs; and it is observed that as in women mild irritation—slight and limited disturbance—produces severer reflex trouble than coarse and grave lesions. In females, superficial disorder of the cervix, for example, often induces more annoying pains and distresses in the head than incurable cancers.

"The Nature and Diagnosis of Neurasthenia (Nervous Exhaustion)," *New York Medical Journal* 29, no. 3 (March 1879): 233–35. One of the most extensive treatments of reflex insanity in women is Horatio Storer, *The Causation, Course, and Treatment of Reflex Insanity in Women* (1871; reprint ed., New York, 1972). Storer was a student of Simpson's, and was surgeon to St. Elizabeth's and St. Francis's Hospitals for Women (in Boston) when he delivered this treatise to the AMA in 1865.

50. See Smith in *London Lancet*, 1848, vol. 2:326.

51. Thomas Laycock, *A Treatise on the Nervous Diseases of Women; Comprising an Inquiry into the Nature, Causes, and Treatment of Spinal and Hysterical Disorders* (London, 1840), 150.

52. In 1860, Dr. Stephen Tracy remarked of women: "The nerves themselves are smaller, and of a more delicate structure. They are endowed with greater sensibility, and, of course, are liable to more frequent and stronger impressions from external agents or mental influences"; *The Mother and Her Offspring*, quoted in Smith-Rosenberg and Rosenberg, "Female Animal," 13.

53. See Laycock, *Treatise*, 76, 126.

54. *London Lancet*, 1848, vol. 2:208.

55. Here is Dr. Robert Brudenell Carter, writing in 1853 on female emotionalism:

If the relative power of emotion against the sexes be compared in the present day, even without including the erotic passion, it is seen to be considerably greater in the woman than in the man, partly from that natural conformation which causes the former to feel, under circumstances where the latter thinks; and partly because the woman is more often under the necessity of endeavouring to conceal her feelings. But when sexual desire is taken into account, it will add immensely to the forces bearing upon the female, who is often much under its dominion; and who, if unmarried and chaste, is compelled to restrain every manifestation of its sway.

Quoted in Ilza Veith, *Hysteria: The History of a Disease* (Chicago, 1965), 201–2.

56. Here is Thomas Laycock (*Treatise*, 72) on female cunning:

One of the most remarkable of the faculties developed during the generative nisus, and peculiar to the females of the higher classes of animals, is their artfulness; and this seems to be given them in place of those weapons of offence and defence with which the males are so generally provided. Indeed the less muscular power, want of defensive weapons, and exalted perceptive faculties of females, would naturally excite into action timidity and cunning. This is strikingly obvious in the human female in general.

57. Horatio Storer remarks: "The wise old physician was not far wrong in his judgment: 'What is woman? Disease, says Hippocrates' "; *Reflex*, 152.

58. From W. C. Taylor, *A Physician's Counsels to Woman in Health and Disease* (1871), quoted in Ehrenreich and English, *For Her Own Good*, 21.

59. *London Lancet*, 1848, vol. 2:330.

60. From "Insanity Produced by Seduction" (1868), quoted in G. J. Barker-Benfield, *The Horrors of the Half-Known Life: Male Attitudes Towards Women and Sexuality in Nineteenth-Century America* (New York, 1976), 83. Storer refers to John Charles Bucknill as saying:

Every medical man has observed the extraordinary amount of obscenity in thought and language which breaks forth from the most modest and well-nurtured woman under the influence of puerperal mania; and although it may be courteous and politic to join in the wonder of those around, that such impurities could ever enter such a mind, and while he repudiates Pope's slander, that "every woman is at heart a rake," he will nevertheless acknowledge that religious and moral principles alone give strength to the female mind; and that, when these are weakened or removed by disease, the subterranean fires become active, and the crater gives forth smoke and flame.

For a view of twentieth-century ideas about hysteria, see Pierre Janet, *The Major Symptoms of Hysteria: Fifteen Lectures Given in the Medical School of Harvard University*, 2nd ed. (1920; reprint ed., New York, 1965); Thomas S. Szasz, *The Myth of Mental Illness: Foundations of a Theory of Personal Conduct* (New York, 1961), 21–163; and Alec Roy, ed., *Hysteria* (Chichester, Eng., 1982).

61. *London Lancet*, 1848, vol. 1:376.

62. *Lancet*, 1854, vol. 2:495.

63. Samuel Gregory, *Man-Midwifery Exposed* (1848), reprinted in *The Male-Midwife and the Female Doctor: The Gynecology Controversy in Nineteenth-Century America* (New York, 1974), 46. Here is George Gregory, writing in 1852: "The distinction of sex is laid in human nature, fixed by the creating hand, and on it are founded many of the most interesting relations and duties of life; it must, therefore, be preserved inviolate, or the social fabric will be overthrown. God has decreed that every man shall have his own wife free from mercenary or other pollution, and no tampering of the medical faculty can for a moment be permitted without destruction to the marriage compact"; *Medical Morals, Illustrated with Plates and Extracts from Medical Works; Designed to Show the Pernicious Social and Moral Influence of the Present System of Medical Practice, and the Importance of Establishing Female Medical Colleges, and Educating and Employing Female Physicians for Their Own Sex*, in *The Male-Midwife and the Female Doctor*, 47. See also Samuel Dickson, *The Destructive Art of Healing; or, Facts for Families*, 3rd. ed. (London, 1853), esp. 39–45; and John Stevens, *Man-Midwifery Exposed; or, The Danger and Immorality of Employing Men in Midwifery Proved; And the Remedy for the Evil Found* (London, 1865).

64. *Lancet*, 1847, vol. 2:371.

65. Ibid.

66. James Hobson Aveling cites an 1869 report of the Council of the Obstetrical Society of London as finding that among the agricultural poor "a large proportion, varying from thirty to ninety per cent., is attended by midwives." In small, nonmanufacturing towns, the percentage was lower; in large provincial and especially manufacturing towns, the rate was again 30 to 90 percent. In London, 30 percent to 50 percent of the poor were attended by midwives in the east, and in west London only 2 percent or even fewer women were attended by midwives. See Aveling, *English Midwives, Their History and Prospects* (1872; reprint ed., London, 1967), 164. For discussions of midwives, see also Jean Donnison, *Midwives and Medical Men: History and Inter-Professional Rivalries and Women's Rights* (London, 1977); and Jane B. Donegan, *Women & Men Midwives: Medicine, Morality, and Misogyny in Early America* (Westport, Conn., 1978).

67. *Lancet*, 1847, vol. 2:371. Margaret Versluysen argues that an important part of this transformation in obstetrics involved the doctors' access to lower-class patients in lying-in hospitals. These patients could not afford to exercise modesty to the same extent as women paying for the doctor's attendance, so medical men could develop techniques of "touching" and physical examinations in these hospitals that they then took to middle-class patients. See "Midwives, Medical Men and 'Poor Women Labour-

ing of Child': Lying-In Hospitals in Eighteenth-Century London," in *Women, Health & Reproduction*, ed. Helen Roberts (London, 1981), 18–49. The first lying-in hospitals in London were the British Lying-In Hospital (1749), the City of London Lying-in Hospital (1750), Queen Charlotte's (1752), the Royal Maternity Hospital (1759), and the General Lying-In Hospital (1765). For a discussion of admission procedures to these charity hospitals, see Smith, *The People's Health*, 34–40.

68. William Harvey, Peter Chamberlen, and William Hunter are the "fathers" of obstetrics, according to Smith; *Lancet*, 1847, vol. 2:458–60.

69. For a typical antimidwife account, see *Lancet*, 1848, vol. 1:122–23. Here the midwife, acting "in a supercilious, half-drunken ignorant manner," is unable to deliver the child because of its presentation. Dr. Moore is called in by worried neighbors, and, once he surveys the situation, he tries to leave to get his equipment. But "there was no egress for me, the door being locked, as they feared I should perhaps leave them in the lurch." Dr. Moore administers chloroform and delivers the child alive. He concludes his account by stating that "there can, I think, be scarcely a doubt that the midwife's conduct deserves the severest reprehension."

   W. Tyler Smith advocates "principles" in his first obstetric lecture, *Lancet*, 1847, vol. 2:373.

70. One correspondant to *Lancet* remarked in 1842 that "the information of the medical profession, generally, on matters of natural science, is very little greater than that of the people at large. This is an extremely humiliating fact"; quoted in Youngson, *Scientific Revolution in Victorian Medicine*, 16. On the limitations of the authority accorded to medical men, see ibid., 9–41; and Peterson, *Medical Profession*, 34–39.

71. See ibid., 5–29. For a discussion of the limits of power of various colleges and licensing bodies, see *Lancet*, 1847, vol. 2:480–81, 483, 507.

72. See Peterson, *Medical Profession*, 30–39. When the Medical Act was finally passed in 1858, it was not the reform generally hoped for by general practitioners. The act created a General Council of Medical Education and Registration, which for the first time united representatives of all three medical corporations and gave a single governing body responsibility for supervising medical education throughout Great Britain. But the act also left intact the hierarchical organization of the profession and the powers of the corporations because it left the power to grant licenses in the hands of the corporations. The General Medical Council's role was largely supervisory and advisory. See also *Lancet*, 1858, vol. 2:124–29, for an article on the Medical Registration Act.

73. See Peterson, *Medical Profession*, 5–39; and Waddington, "General Practitioners," 165–68.

74. Ibid., 170–72; and S. W. F. Holloway, "Medical Education in England, 1830–1858: A Sociological Analysis," *History* 49 (1964): 299–324.

75. Remarking on the importance of women to the general practitioner, J. H. Aveling noted that "women, as you know, enjoy, and always find time for, gossip with one another. . . .Woe to the unhappy practitioner who has failed in his treatment of their troubles; his condemnation will be widely heard. On the other hand he who has been successful will have the trumpet of fame sounded with extravagant force"; quoted in Peterson, *Medical Profession*, 129.

76. Quoted in Donnison, *Midwives and Medical Men*, 47. Here is Sir Henry Halford, president of the Royal College of Physicians, in 1834:

   I think it [midwifery] is considered rather as a manual operation and that we should be very sorry to throw anything like a discredit upon the men who have been educated at the Universities, who have taken time to acquire their improvement of their minds in literary and scientific acquirements, by mixing it up with this manual labour. I think it would rather disparage the highest grade of the profession, to let them engage in that particular branch, which is a manual operation very much.

Quoted in Waddington, "General Practitioners," 177. Aveling gives a sense of the longevity of this male aversion to female bodies when he cites the translator's introduction to Roesslin's *The Birth of Mankynde*, the first midwifery book to be translated from Latin to English (1540). "Many think that it is not meete ne fitting such matters to be intreated of so plainly in our mother and vulgar language, to the dishonour (as they say) of womanhood and the derision of their own secrets, by the detection and discovering whereof, men it reading or hearing, shall be moved thereby, the more to abhorte and loathe the company of women, every boy and knave reading them as openly as the tales of 'Robin Hood' "; *Midwives*, 10–11.

77. *Lancet*, 1847, vol. 2:451–54. See also ibid., 479–83, 533–36, and 559–63. Burrows's concern about money emerges most clearly on p. 482.

78. Ibid., 371.

79. The only quotation I have found from a woman that approaches a description of how labor or chloroform felt appears in 1848. "I give the patient's description of her feelings in her own words," John Beaumont writes. " 'Up to the time of inhaling, the pains were most severe, and were becoming insupportable; but they appeared to do no good. I felt as if there were an insuperable bar across, which effectually resisted the force of the pains, and I felt in despair; but from the moment that I became under its [chloroform's] influence, that resistance appeared to give way, and every effort seemed successful' "; *London Lancet*, 1848, vol. 2:398. Despite this quotation, this letter to *Lancet* is typical in Beaumont's assertion that it is the "province of the physician" to decide whether to administer chloroform *and* in his implicit anxiety that such control will not remain with the doctor if patients have their way. Note his final reference to "a lady of high moral and religious feeling" who "did not scruple to make [the administration of chloroform] almost the condition of [his] attending her." Luckily, Beaumont's compliance still left him authority, for it made the woman "thankful" rather than assertive.

The argument against asking women to report on their own sensations under chloroform was not, incidentally, based on a person's inability to narrate unconsciousness. Many patients were not anesthecized into complete unconsciousness, for insensibility to pain could be induced before the disruption of consciousness by administering a light dose. Moreover, some doctors do report on the sensations chloroform caused when they administered it to themselves, and these descriptions are certainly not distinguished by language more technical or detailed than an intelligent lay person might have been able to provide. See *London Lancet*, 1848, vol. 2:122.

80. See Simpson, "Report on the Results," 164; *Lancet*, 1847, vol. 2:122; *Lancet*, 1853, vol. 1:609.

81. Here, for example, is W. Tyler Smith:

In the higher mammalia, a true vascular connexion is formed between the ovum and the mother by means of . . . the mucous membrane of the uterus; and the embryo, after a prolonged term of inter-uterine development, is expelled to pass through another protracted phase of maternal nutrition from the mammae. . . . The generative organs reach their greatest state of development in the human species, and consist of parts adapted to coitus, ovulation, menstruation, impregnation, utero-gestation, parturition, and lactation—functions which are placed in relation to the highest affection and parental love.

Lancet, 1856, vol. 1:4. Thomas Laycock links reproductive physiology and maternal instinct with this statement: "The desire for sexual congress, the secretion of milk, and the love of offspring, are equally the results of the same reproductive effort"; *An Essay on Hysteria*, 64.

82. Here is Dr. John Conolly, whom Storer cites with approval, on the extension of a physician's domain: "The physician's office is assuming in these times a higher character in proportion as he ceases to be a mere prescriber of medicines, and acts as the guardian or conservator of public and of private health; studious of all agencies that influence the body and the mind, and which, affecting individual comfort and longevity, act widely on societies of human beings"; quoted in Storer, *Reflex*, 174. This extension of a physician's territory is also intimately connected to the definition of various nervous or mental afflictions as diseases. Thomas Laycock, for example, wants to treat a woman's bad temper as a medical disorder: "Irritability of temper in the nervous and delicate should always be treated *as a disease;* that is, by medicine, regimen, air and exercise, soothing kindness, and gentle authority. . . . Irritability of temper is as much a disease as insanity"; *Treatise*, 352. See also Vieda Skultans, *Madness and Morals: Ideas on Insanity in the Nineteenth Century* (London, 1975), 9–23.

83. *Lancet*, 1847, vol. 2:481. Burrows estimated that there were 400 to 500 unlicensed physicians practicing in London and the provinces; *Lancet*, 1847, vol. 2:561.

84. The threat perceived by the medical men who attended nervous or hysterical women is discussed by Carroll Smith-Rosenberg in "The Hysterical Women: Sex Roles and Role Conflict in 19th-Century America," *Social Research* 39, no. 4 (1972), esp. 663 and 674.

85. *Lancet*, 1855, vol. 1:205–6. Skey recommends examining a patient's spine for pain as a means of detecting true (organic) disorder.

86. Jules Falret, *Etudes cliniques sur les maladies mentales et nerveuses* (1890), quoted in Veith, *Hysteria*, 211.

87. Quoted in S. Weir Mitchell, *Fat and Blood: An Essay on the Treatment of Certain Forms of Neurasthenia and Hysteria* (1877; 4th ed., Philadelphia, 1885), 49.

88. *Lancet*, 1847, vol. 2:574.

89. Simpson, "Report of the Results," 165. See also pp. 160–63, 166, 169, and 170.

90. *Lancet*, 1848, vol. 1:163.

91. *Lancet*, 1847, vol. 2:677.

92. Ibid., 626. Protheroe Smith seconds this warning when he says: "Accoucheurs will, ere long, have to submit to the demand of their patients to be relieved from the agony of childbirth. . . . The question will no longer be whether anaesthetic agents shall be employed, but which of them shall be preferred"; ibid., 574.

93. *Lancet*, 1853, vol. 1:609.

94. Quoted in Veith, *Hysteria*, 204.

95. George Gregory, *Medical Morals*, 47.

96. I suggest that the debate about *whether* women experience sexual feelings, and orgasm in particular, emerges in this period because of the ambiguity inherent in conceptualizing female sexuality according to a model of male sexuality. Strictly speaking, if female sexuality is analogous anatomically, then women should have erections and ejaculate; many medical men, in fact, asserted that this is the case. But if women do not have these physical signs, as other medical men assert, then they must not experience sexuality at all. This is the position held by Dr. William Acton; see *The Functions*

and *Disorders of the Reproductive Organs in Youth, in Adult Age, and in Advanced Life: Considered in Their Physiological, Social, and Moral Relations* (London, 1857). See also Degler, "What Ought To Be," 40–53; Nancy F. Cott, "Passionlessness: An Interpretation of Victorian Sexual Ideology," *Signs* 4 (1978): 219–36; Peter T. Cominus, "Innocent Femina Sensualis in Unconscious Conflict," in *Suffer and Be Still,* ed. Martha Vicinus (Bloomington, Ind., 1972), 155–72; and Jean L'Esperance, "Doctors and Women in Nineteenth-Century Society: Sexuality and Role," in *Health Care and Popular Medicine,* 112–16.

97. For a related discussion from the point of view of epistemology, see Theresa de Lauretis, *Alice Doesn't: Feminism, Semiotics, Cinema* (Bloomington, Ind., 1984), esp. 5–6, 12–36.

98. Mid-nineteenth-century resistance to this ideology took several forms, which, while most often inchoate and even unconscious, suggest that spaces always existed within the dominant ideology. Hysteria, as Carroll Smith-Rosenberg points out, could be one form of resistance; see "Hysterical Women," esp. 671–74; and Ehrenreich and English, *For Her Own Good,* 42–43. So-called "passionlessness" could be another; see Cott, "Passionlessness," 219–36. One could also argue that a woman's requesting chloroform was an indirect rejection of the equation between woman and nature as set out in Genesis. Thus to refuse to suffer is to refuse both the "opportunity" or the "duty" to suffer and one's animal nature. This form of refusal, however, was probably almost never formulated as such by Victorian women, at least partly because a woman's moral "superiority" (however it was displayed) was the basis of what power she could exercise in society.

LAURA ENGELSTEIN

Morality and the Wooden Spoon: Russian Doctors View Syphilis, Social Class, and Sexual Behavior, 1890–1905

IN 1894 AMERICAN PHYSICIAN L. Duncan Bulkley published a book called *Syphilis in the Innocent* (Syphilis Insontium), *Clinically and Historically Considered, with a Plan for the Legal Control of the Disease.*[1] It was hailed by foreign colleagues as a timely confirmation of widely held views.[2] Bulkley showed in exhaustive detail that syphilis was not exclusively—perhaps not even primarily— a venereal disease. Genital contact was but one of a multitude of possible avenues of contagion. The shared cup, the casual hug, the dirty razor blade, the unwashed towel: these were the innocent ways in which innocent people disseminated a germ that was not intrinsically sexual. Only in the congested environment of urban life, with its surfeit of unwed and sexually hungry males, its abundance of destitute and unsupervised females, was sex a central cause for concern. Although there was no reason to infer from Bulkley's argument that the countryside should resist infection of such an all-pervasive kind, he nevertheless claimed the disease became less common "in a pretty direct ratio to the suburban or rural character of the people."[3]

While Bulkley denied that syphilis was inherently venereal, he considered it most frequent among people who lived in close proximity and who indulged their sexual appetites in a promiscuous way—that is, among the residents of big cities, the beneficiaries of modern civilization. Under certain circumstances, however, syphilis was both prevalent and unrelated to density of population or to cultural sophistication. Far from being rare in primitive agrarian societies, syphilis was often endemic to entire communities, in which it penetrated the fabric of everyday life. "It is difficult for us," Bulkley wrote, "amid the civilization of the nineteenth century, to fully understand the circumstances and surroundings which led to the rapid and extensive diffusion of syphilis in years gone by, and amid the crude modes of living belonging to earlier times; but we can better understand it if we consider, for a moment, some facts relating to its more recent extension among some of the less civilized portions of the earth, as in certain parts of Russia."[4]

European physicians invoked the threat of nonvenereal contagion to deter the educated from casual contact with the unhygienic poor and to emphasize the unintended ultimate consequences of original sexual delicts. Some employed the venereal threat to justify the police supervision of public women, while opponents of regulation used it to promote a uniform standard of sexual continence for women and men alike. The admission that sexual dereliction was not the only risk facing the urban population did not diminish the symbolic power of syphilis to represent the dangers of sex.

In examining the social function of syphilis in the medical scheme, one must first of all ask if indeed there was such a thing as nonvenereal syphilis, endemic or otherwise. Was the symbolic position of Russia, as an icon of primitive asexuality, a figment of the Western imagination, or could its backwardness truly be seen in the structure of its disease? The way physicians viewed syphilis reflected the medical profession's relation both to state power and to issues of class; it would not thus be surprising to find that Russian physicians, though trained in Western science, looked at syphilis in a different light and aspired to a different role in the policing of health and sexual comportment. Finally, one must explore the extent to which the medical interpretation of syphilis depended on cultural expectation, rather than clinical evidence, and proposals for its control on political, rather than medical, calculations. These are the questions this essay will address, pursuing the fate of European ideas about sexuality and social disease as they migrated onto Russian soil.

There is no doubt, at least, of Russia's place on the Western medical map, as a remnant of the past at civilization's outermost edge. Distinguished by "gross ignorance," to use Bulkley's phrase,[5] it shared with other marginal lands a vestigial pattern of disease, one which excluded the sexual component supplied by modern city life.[6] The risk of nonvenereal contagion was universal, as Russians, somewhat defensively, pointed out: "Culturally deprived Russia is not the only victim of nonvenereal syphilitic transmission," wrote Dr. Andrei Rozenkvist in 1898. "More enlightened peoples also contract syphilis in the unexpected way."[7] But the saturation of entire districts, the predominance of cases among women and children, among village craftsmen in their shops: these were peculiar to backwardness. In this guise, in fact, the disease appeared to Europeans as an exact index of cultural deprivation: its prevalence mirrored existing levels of filth, poverty, malnutrition, and overcrowding.[8]

Russian physicians, conscious of their national inferiority in so many other regards, did not disagree: "Endemic syphilis," asserted one at the end of the century, "is not found anywhere in Europe [but] constitutes the sad privilege of Russia alone."[9] Indeed, Russia's notoriety as a breeding ground of syphilitic contagion was due in no small part to the evidence supplied by Dr. Veniamin Tarnovskii, professor of dermatology and venereal disease at the St. Petersburg Academy of Military Medicine. "Syphilis of the innocent," he wrote, in a work often cited by European colleagues, "is the most serious, socially most harmful, and in Russia the most common form of syphilis."[10]

Venereal syphilis was widely thought to have arrived in Europe at the end of the fifteenth century, with the returning sailors on Columbus's ships, and then to have been diffused on an epidemic scale by the sexual activity of soldiers and public women.[11] Despite much expert controversy, even today still unresolved, about the actual origins of syphilis in Europe, the myth of venereal syphilis as the herald of the modern age has survived all learned disputes.[12] Convinced the disease had been in evidence under different names, and in nonvenereal form, since ancient times, Dr. Philippe Ricord, one of the founders of nineteenth-century syphilology, nevertheless recognized the virulent outbreak of 1493 as the start of a new era in medical and popular consciousness, akin to the political watershed marked by the Great Terror of 1793—"ce véritable 93 de la vérole," he called it.[13]

Russians interpreted their own national experience in light of this firmly entrenched idea. Dr. Eduard Shperk, son of an impoverished though well-born provincial doctor of German background, spent ten years in Siberia studying syphilis among the native population.[14] On the basis of this work, which he published as a doctoral dissertation in 1863, Shperk stressed the "enormous influence" exercised by "material life" on "manners and morals," citing in particular the effect of railroads in fostering demographic mobility and weakening traditional community bonds. Venereal syphilis, he argued, was least common in agricultural peasant villages, where family ties were strong and landed property the foundation of wealth. The growth of trade altered the character of the economic system, producing nonlanded wealth, or capital, and wage labor. People moved about more often and married later in life, the family lost its dominant role, and sex too became commercialized. Women, like other goods and personal services, became objects of exchange rather than items of permanent value and attributes of social status. "As the railroad enters a given locality," wrote Shperk, "it increases the number of rented apartments, rented carriages . . . and rented women."[15] The great fifteenth-century epidemic did not signal the appearance of a new malady, Shperk asserted, but rather the transformation of an old one. The historic turning point marked by crusades, invasions, and the growth of cities had provided the conditions that favored venereal over nonvenereal transmission and left contemporaries with the impression of confronting a totally different kind of disease. The continuing prevalence of endemic syphilis in Russian villages indicated that Russia had not fully entered the modern age.[16]

Other commentators linked the new form and level of contagion to the encroachment of alien values and social institutions. "In the West," asserted Dr. Petr Gratsianskii of the Academy of Military Medicine, "the main role in the spread of syphilis is played almost exclusively by prostitution."[17] Prostitution existed in Russia too, but it appeared as a foreign import, a product of urban commercial culture, inimical to traditional, native ways. "During the reign of Peter the Great," wrote Dr. Ivan Priklonskii, "we first entered into commercial relations with Western European states, and it was then that the concept of commercial prostitution also appeared in our society. Prostitution began to spread among the people, significantly lowering the moral level in all social strata."[18]

In 1897 the Ministry of Internal Affairs sponsored a congress in St. Petersburg on the prevention of syphilis in Russia. Shperk's contemporary, Veniamin Tarnovskii, delivered the prestigious opening address.[19] Though he did not share Shperk's social values, Tarnovskii nevertheless did not differ in his view of the social context of venereal disease. Whereas syphilis had, of course, existed in Russia since the end of the fifteenth century, he explained, it had only become a serious threat to the nation's well-being because "the intrusion of Western manufacture and commerce had increased the channels of infection a hundredfold, while the ability of the popular masses to defend themselves had not improved since the time of Ivan the Terrible." The danger lay in the "swift turn of agrarian Russia toward industrial development, when the external manifestations of Western civilization bore no relation to the cultural and economic level of the popular masses." "Under certain conditions," Tarnovskii reminded his listeners, "civilization elevates and enriches the people both morally and physically; under others it destroys them slowly but surely."[20]

Was the syphilis to which Russia was prone a product of change or a symptom of inertia, a mark of incorporation or of isolation from the ways of the modern world? Physicians seemed unsure. They could not decide whether the civilization they envied and feared had corrupted innocent bodies, leaving popular virtue intact, or whether health had departed in the wake of innocence itself. Unfortunately for lovers of medical and historical certainty, the scientific wisdom that might have decided the question on an "objective" basis, and in its updated form helped historians decipher the cultural bias of the past, has not become less ambiguous with the passage of time and the progress of that enviable sophistication. Syphilis remains a cultural puzzle to this day.

The Clinical Picture

The modern dermatology text informs us that syphilis is the work of the spirocete *Treponema pallidum,* a microorganism first isolated in 1905 that invades the bloodstream and other bodily fluids but is swiftly destroyed by sunlight, dryness, cold, soap and water, or simple exposure outside the living host.[21] Gone is the old notion of a "poison . . . endowed with the possibility . . . of being preserved for an indefinite period."[22] Genital contact, experts now explain, fosters transmission of the syphilis organism by providing the warmth and moisture in which it thrives and the friction that propels it through the vulnerable mucous membranes. The danger once said to be inherent in dirty cups, towels, and toilet seats belongs to the mythic catalog of the scientific past.[23]

Studies of disease in preindustrial societies present a different picture, however, one that saves Victorian medicine from some of the ridicule it has retrospectively earned. Genital contact is indeed the usual way for syphilis to spread in modern industrial nations for two reasons: intimate bodily contact is largely restricted in Western urban culture to sexual relations; penicillin, introduced during World War II, was able for the first time to eliminate the reservoir of contagion waiting to be dispersed through the infinitude of social interactions. In the peasant communities of twentieth-century Bosnia, or the Bedouin villages of Syria, however, where houses are crowded, notions of privacy and individuality different from our own, penicillin scarce, and folk traditions of shared drinking vessels and communal eating still unshaken, syphilis takes the form remarked in Russian villages over a century ago. Public health observers, using modern diagnostic tools, have confirmed that certain inanimate objects, such as cups and pipes, may convey infected fluid when passed quickly from mouth to mouth; that entire communities may harbor low levels of infection that inure them to the dangers of contagion by sexual means; that custom does not charge victims with sexual misconduct, because sexual activity is perceived as irrelevant to their case.[24]

Syphilis is a disease that adapts to the cultural environment.[25] Its shifting representation in the medical literature reflects not only the progress of clinical technique, or expanded knowledge of the biological world, but also the different manifestations of the disease itself. The shortness of our historical memory, combined with cultural self-centeredness, has allowed us to ignore present contrasts and discount past knowledge as myth. Though the timing and actual mechanism of communication were in many cases misconceived, and the scope of the danger vastly exaggerated, not all the perils enumerated by nineteenth-century physicians were necessarily the invention of sexual anxiety, or designed to fuel projects of sexual control.[26]

Imagination did certainly come into play, however, when it came to deriving the origin of a given case from its clinical symptoms. Syphilis typically passes through three stages: the primary chancre, which may appear anywhere on the body, though usually on the genitals, and whose secretions are highly contagious; the secondary lesions, or papules, which favor the moist mucous membranes and are also infectious; finally, after a long interval, the dread tertiary symptoms—the collapsed nose, the nervous and mental deterioration of Victorian medical demonology. Both the chancre and the secondary lesions vanish of their own accord without treatment; they are separated by an asymptomatic period, during which bodily fluids teem with the offending organism but the victim feels no distress. After the secondary eruption, the infection becomes less virulent, without entirely disappearing, and contagion no longer occurs. In only a minority of cases do the tertiary symptoms ever appear.[27]

Some nineteenth-century doctors believed, and modern authorities agree, that endemic syphilis may avoid the primary stage.[28] The Victorians had already correctly noted that infants may be born with the disease, although they misunderstood why;[29] they were also familiar with the possibility of infection being passed between a wet nurse and her charge. But in many more cases, circumstances are ambiguous and symptoms an uncertain clue.

The European texts to which Russian doctors turned left ample room for dispute. Some experts insisted that a chancre was inevitable at the initial point of contact, though it might be concealed (as on the cervix) or small and evanescent, and might escape the diagnostic eye.[30] Failure to spot one did not confirm innocence; finding one in some innocuous place did not exclude guilt. Oral chancres, for example, invited debate. There were so many things a mouth could do. "Honi soit qui mal y prête!" was the sanctimonious comment of Dr. Paul Diday, writing for the respectable, middle-class French audience.[31] But the eminent professor Dr. Alfred Fournier did not hesitate to put "genital-oral" contact at the top of his list.[32] Other organs were less versatile. Few texts denied that a chancre on the genitals meant sexual intercourse, on the anus anal penetration.[33] The latter, wrote French forensic specialist Dr. Ambroise Tardieu, was an almost certain proof of "unnatural acts," and even secondary lesions in that spot were to be accounted for in the same manner.[34] Fournier admitted that oral-anal contact was "much more frequent than one would dare to believe."[35] An American professor of genito-urinary diseases at the Columbia University College of Physicians and Surgeons baldly asserted that chancres on the anus, tongue, and mouth often resulted from "unnatural and beastly methods of indulgence between persons of the same and the opposite sex,"[36] what Dr. Bulkley referred to more chastely as *coitus preternaturalis*.[37]

Thus, whether doctors interpreted syphilis as venereal depended to a large extent on their notions of what constituted sexual activity; on a willingness to acknowledge the existence of nonstandard sexual practices, or of standard practice by the wrong people, such as children, pious peasants, or virtuous wives. While some authorities concluded from the abundance of nonsexual ways to contract it that syphilis "looked at in its largest sense . . . cannot, in the light of present knowledge, be any longer regarded as essentially a venereal disease,"[38] others were not so sure. The much respected Dr. Etienne Lancereaux remained, for one, uncertain that outbreaks, even on the marches of European civilization, could be as innocent as they seemed: crowding was a problem even there, he thought, because "density of population . . . does not fail, in general, to cause immorality."[39]

The Physician's Role

Russian physicians indulged in the same diagnostic squabbles as their European colleagues. Numerous articles in the medical press reported "rare cases of nonvenereal infection," primary chancres of nonsexual origin on a penis or on the vagina of a nine-year-old girl,[40] while discussions of prostitution and its relation to venereal syphilis were even more profuse. But clinical evidence, because of its very ambiguity, played a secondary role in distinguishing the two competing paradigms of syphilitic contagion. Instead of searching for primary lesions, Russian doctors looked to the social and cultural context for epidemiological clues.

This approach was no cultural innovation but drew heavily on the European medical tradition of environmental public health. Indeed, one of its leading advocates in Russia was the Swiss-born physician Friedrich Erismann, who practiced and taught in his adopted country from 1869 to 1896, holding the first chair of hygiene at Moscow University.[41] Viewing disease as a social problem, public health physicians devoted themselves to public, which is to say, administrative or political, solutions. Erismann's civic orientation, frustrated in the end by the stubborn hostility of an increasingly repressive regime, was matched by that of Russians such as Eduard Shperk, already established in a successful career when Erismann first arrived. Born in 1837, Shperk shared with the 1860s intelligentsia a belief in science as the key to social improvement and an ethic of commitment to the common welfare, without, however, endorsing the intelligentsia's more radical social critique. Active in Russia's largest and most influential public health organization, Shperk taught in the women's courses of the Academy of Military Medicine in the 1870s. He was known for his humanitarian treatment of hospital patients, including the registered prostitutes under his care, and later broke with the St. Petersburg syphilis society over the issue of regulation, which he had come more and more to oppose.[42] Though not all men of his generation shared his views (Tarnovskii, who also taught in the women's courses, provides the sharpest contrast), Shperk established a tone that dominated publicly conscious medical circles into the 1890s.

This outlook was congenial to physicians serving the urban poor, but it came to be associated in particular with those in rural practice, who fashioned for themselves a distinctive medico-political ethos. Most of the latter were employed by the zemstvos, local elective bodies created during the Great Reforms of the 1860s, which enjoyed relative autonomy from bureaucratic control and offered a rare chance for members of educated society to serve the public good and exercise a modicum of civic initiative.[43] The zemstvos, not surprisingly, acted as a focus of reform politics in the pre-1905 era.

Given the community context in which they worked, it was natural for zemstvo practitioners to adopt the view of disease as a demographic, or social problem, rather than a matter of individual pathology, whether physical or moral. "In private practice," explained Dmitrii Zhbankov, a leading zemstvo physician, "the doctor deals only with individual patients, unrelated one to the other. The task at hand is simple: to cure the patient, without a thought to the future or to surrounding circumstances. With the emergence of social medicine, doctors were obliged to deal with great numbers of patients and also with the healthy population among whom they lived. Doctors thus witnessed with their very own eyes the close links between the sick and the well, the way in which individual cases, as well as mass outbreaks, depended on environmental conditions." Programs aimed at education and prevention were thus the key to better health, as the case of village syphilis, the classic community scourge, clearly showed.[44]

The use of syphilis to illustrate a question of public policy was not original with Zhbankov, or unique to those who shared his critical views. The recurrent disappearance of symptoms, the mysterious process of congenital transmission, and the seeming disconnection between the various stages of the disease, made syphilis the perfect symbolic vehicle for the doctor's assertion of professional authority. It provided the ideal clinical channel, joining the private domain (meaning both personal and secret) and the public (meaning both civic and revealed). Veniamin Tarnovskii, for example, treated the question of syphilis control with the rhetoric of national honor and national self-defense. "No external, visible enemy can phase us," he announced to the St. Petersburg syphilis congress. "But we can be frightened by the secret, internal enemy that imperceptibly destroys the people's physical and moral well-being."[45] Syphilis, complained a staff physician at the Kiev military hospital, in identical terms, "is not a visible enemy one can fight with the obvious weapons; it sneaks up unnoticed and ruthlessly destroys whole families, whole generations."[46] Moscow University lecturer Dr. Nikolai Fedchenko echoed French expert Toussaint Barthélemy in complaining that syphilis caused less alarm than cholera only because "the harm wrought by syphilis, which is well known to doctors, does not catch the attention of the crowd."[47] The physician was to put his occult knowledge, acquired in the discreet examination of private parts, at the service of public policy.

Putting their skills to public use was nothing unusual for Russian physicians, the vast majority of whom were employed by the state bureaucracy or other public institutions.[48] They expressed their views and exchanged technical information in the pages of the numerous medical journals that promoted the discussion of social themes. Some 450 of them attended the 1897 congress, including 19 of the 35 people (31 men and 4 women) on whose observations and interpretations this essay draws.[49] Half of the 35 were over forty years old in 1897, which meant they belonged to a generation that had spent its youth in the 1860s, the optimistic early years of Alexander II's reign; the rest, their juniors, had trained during the repressive aftermath of his assassination in 1881. Most of the group had been content with the basic medical diploma, but a third had acquired the advanced degree of doctor of medicine. The sample is dominated by dermatologists, urologists, and specialists in venereal diseases and includes several pediatricians, but physicians typically held a variety of positions in the course of their careers, which widened the range of their social and clinical experience.[50] Whatever their philosophical and educational differences, all Russian doctors shared an acquaintance with European medicine, and all confronted the workings of a state determined to keep a tight reign on the process of social change and cede none of its authority to autonomous groups, a state on which they depended for their livelihood but that blocked the attainment of their professional goals.

In Europe questions of public health and public morality were closely intertwined as objects of state policy and of medical expertise. Enemies and partisans of regulated prostitution shared a common concern with lower-class sexual comportment and bolstered their devotion to middle-class decorum with a medical rationale. Despite similar (though not identical) standards of respectability, Russian physicians nevertheless found themselves in a different moral universe. In both Europe and Russia, judgments of sexual propriety were shaped by perceptions of social class and of gender; thus the peculiarities of the Russian class system produced distinctive moral expectations, which were in turn modified and increasingly confused by the turmoil in which the class system was caught.

In the vast majority of cases with which Russian physicians dealt, traditional mores seemed still intact and syphilis appeared not as the result of sexual promiscuity, the egotistic search for private pleasure in disregard of the collective norm, but as the result of social promiscuity, a reflection of collective tyranny and the weakness of self. This was a weakness the physicians deplored, for it inspired them with a sense of their own helplessness. Yet they persistently rejected evidence of sexual misbehavior that testified to the crumbling of traditional bonds. Eager for signs of personal autonomy that could be disciplined in nontraditional ways, through self-regulation guided by medical expertise, the sexualization of syphilis was nevertheless a strategy most Russian physicians did not willingly embrace.[51]

Syphilis in the Russian Countryside

Medical observers without exception all characterized syphilis as endemic to the peasant population and nonvenereal in origin.[52] If prostitution was "the main source of infection" in Russian cities, "in the countryside," said Dr. Konstantin Shtiurmer of the St. Petersburg medical police, "it plays only a minor role, and sometimes none at all."[53] "Rural syphilis," wrote zemstvo physician Pavel Govorkov, "is a misfortune that befalls the innocent. The statistics on this subject show that the number of people in the countryside who suffer from venereal forms of the disease, acquired as a result of sexual activity, is negligible."[54] On the basis of reports from towns and villages throughout the empire, the 1897 syphilis congress concluded that prostitution was a factor in the spread of syphilis only in large and medium-sized cities; smaller towns, like peasant villages, suffered from an epidemic of the disease in its nonvenereal form.[55]

Noted syphilologist Grigorii Gertsenshtein was typical in defending the moral integrity of peasant life:

Neither prostitution, nor soldiers, nor unmarried young men from urban factories and manufacturing centers transmit the disease, but rather innocent children and the women of impoverished towns and villages. The disease spreads not through sexual relations but in the course of everyday domestic contacts between healthy and diseased members of single families, neighbors, and casual visitors. The infection is spread even further by the sharing of bowls and spoons, by an innocent child's kiss, but not through dissolute behavior or unregulated prostitutes as is the case in the big cities.[56]

Not virtue but cultural deprivation was at issue. Rural practitioners blamed the prevalence of syphilis on poverty, ignorance, and traditional customs.[57] They called it "the Russian people's everyday disease" (*bytovaia bolezn' russkogo naroda*).[58] The word *bytovaia* expresses the two implications of this phrase: it means both "ordinary," in the sense of common, and "customary," reflecting a way of life (*byt*). Nonvenereal syphilis, said Gertsenshtein, "occurs only where the population is extremely ignorant and poor, at a relatively low level of civilization."[59] If the peasants did themselves harm it was not deliberately, through mistaken or ill-considered acts, but unknowingly, through blind adherence to "age-old popular habits."[60] "Without knowing it," wrote Shtiurmer, "the peasant is his own worst enemy. The remarkable carelessness toward his own and others' health, the positive savagery of certain customs cannot be characterized as anything other than ignorance."[61] Among these savage customs doctors counted the practice of spitting in a person's eye to cure sties, the feeding of children directly from the mother's own mouth, and the habit of sucking a baby boy's penis to calm him down.[62]

Doctors attributed the peasants' backwardness in part to the dominance of collective norms over personal development. "The patriarchal family, with its strict moral rules," wrote Dr. Mikhail Uvarov, one of the country's most prominent zemstvo physicians, was no defense against syphilis.[63] Indeed, the opposite was true: such "large, extended families encourage its rapid spread. . . . In the smallest little villages, with extensive kinship networks, in which the entire village sometimes bears a single family name and relations are close, syphilis occurs with greater intensity than in larger villages."[64] The peasants were sick because they lived cheek to jowl. A disease that "knows no bounds," syphilis flourished among people who respected no boundaries: they ate from one bowl, slept in the same beds, welcomed the itinerant beggar or tradesman. The disease thus "moved from one family to the next, sparing neither children nor old people, engulfing neighboring houses and nearby villages."[65] No one act—sexual or nonsexual—could be singled out as the first link in the fatal chain: "The original source of infection has long been forgotten, the agent that first introduced the poison has perhaps long been dead, but the sad consequences have nonetheless unfolded to their full extent."[66] Observers described the disease as spreading "passively," or "spontaneously," without conscious agency.[67] Often victims did not recognize their own disease, so little did the individual case stand out against the background of general ill health.[68]

Mothers played a central role in the spread of infection. Not only did they carry the disease in their blood, passing it to the unborn and the nursing child, but their unsanitary practices threatened all members of the family. Dmitrii Zhbankov described the domestic habits that perpetuated ill health:

The doctor will no sooner have finished explaining how to stop the spread of syphilis and is barely out the door, when the mother begins to feed her healthy child with the very same spoon she has just used to feed the sick one, or wipes the drooling saliva from the sick child's mouth with the same rag or kerchief she will then use to wipe her own face or the face of the healthy child. Better yet, a healthy family member will reach for a piece of bread with the hand he has just used to dry the sick child's running mouth.[69]

There is no implication in the medical literature that sexual indulgence on the part of peasant women might contribute to the spread of disease; indeed there is no suggestion that these women were sexually active outside the bounds of family life, where they were thought to perform an exclusively reproductive role. Dr. Aleksandr Efimov, studying the effects of syphilis on the "sex life" (*polovaia zhizn'*) of peasant women, did not discuss frequency of intercourse, or other modes of sexual pleasure, but examined menstruation, fertility, and pregnancy.[70]

To a certain extent these views mirrored observed social reality. But evidence gleaned from the direct experience of village life might reproduce illusions embedded in the culture itself. While one may safely conclude that the Russian village had not yet experienced the kind of demographic and cultural upheaval that had transformed the life of European peasants several decades before,[71] it was perhaps not as inert as it seemed. There is some reason to believe that extramarital sexual activity, whatever its actual extent, was obscured by the Russian peasants' high level of nuptiality, early marriage age, and the late onset of menstruation among women.[72] Few births occurred out of wedlock, even if conception had.[73] Contemporary observers, in any case, seemed reluctant to challenge appearances, as will become evident in their response to evidence that violated their cherished beliefs.

The most traditional element in a tradition-bound milieu, peasant women shone as unsullied examples of peasant virtue. They were so depicted even by men, such as Dmitrii Zhbankov, who held untraditional views of women's capacity for cultural advancement.[74] Such notions, as we have suggested, were not destroyed by prolonged personal contact with rural life. Himself the illegitimate son of a serf and her master, Zhbankov spent years in zemstvo practice, studying the effect of social mobility on the rural way of life.[75] Examining the moral impact of male seasonal labor in Kostroma Province, Zhbankov described the lonely wives of workers off in the city as faithful to their absent mates. Far from feeling the pangs of sexual frustration, the women lost every trace of sexual feeling from a combination of hard work and the lack of opportunity. Peasant women often failed to menstruate during the heavy work season, Zhbankov explained, because "the organism is so exhausted from hard labor that it has nothing to spare for the sexual functions; this is why during the work season and in the absence of their husbands women experience no sexual need. Moreover, seasonal labor has been practiced in this region for a long time, and the women may have therefore developed a *hereditary weakening of sexual desire*."[76] Zhbankov, like Efimov, equated menstruation, an aspect of female reproduction, with sexuality itself. He was not unusual in viewing both peasant men and women, while still in their villages, as modest and morally restrained. Grigorii Gertsenshtein complained that the peasants' "natural bashfulness" *(estestvennaia stydlivost')* prevented them from seeking medical aid for sexually marked disease.[77]

When faced with undeniable evidence of illicit sexual activity in the countryside, medical observers redefined it as an urban problem. St. Petersburg physician Aleksandr Vvedenskii assured the syphilis congress that "prostitution is completely alien to the patriarchal customs of our peasantry. There is no doubt that it appears in the small towns and villages only when the conditions of rural life have fundamentally altered. With the introduction of railroads, the growth of trade or manufacture, or the quartering of troops, the countryside loses its original character; it acquires the distinguishing features of urban life."[78] Then, Vvedenskii complained, formerly innocent customs became occasions for sexual debauch; local girls sold themselves for the sake of mere amusement; peasants massed in tobacco plantations and fisheries lost all moral restraint.[79]

Few joined him in believing that country mores had changed so profoundly for the worse. Most physicians clung to the prevalent notions of popular decorum, even when promiscuous sexuality was clearly a factor in spreading disease. Far from emphasizing the risks of sexual contact, they focused instead on environmental dangers, or on the consequences of purely social interaction. Prostitutes who congregated in local taverns, Dr. Mikhail Uvarov told the syphilis congress, were less of a health menace than the dirty tables, unwashed glasses, and stuffy, unventilated rooms in which customers rubbed shoulders and gave each other the disease. "Rural taverns have been singled out as breeding grounds of disorder and vice," Uvarov said, "but given the complete absence of sanitary controls, their filth and slovenliness are undoubtedly a much greater source of nonvenereal infection. It is enough to recall the eternal towels used to wipe dirty glasses which are then refilled with beer."[80]

Physicians were deeply concerned with the effect of syphilis on miscarriage, infant mortality, and childhood impairment, and considered the endemic form equally as dangerous in this regard as the venereal. Thus, Veniamin Tarnovskii blamed hereditary syphilis for physical deformity among peasant children, and a study of Tambov Province considered it a major cause of infant death.[81] Modern studies have shown that prenatal transmission does not occur when the disease is endemic, because women who themselves acquire it before puberty are not contagious by the time they reach childbearing age.[82] Of course, healthy nursing women were vulnerable to infection from syphilitic infants, posing a risk for later pregnancies. But if childhood infection had been common enough, women would rarely have embarked on the disease late enough in life to harm the unborn, and adults have rarely posed a danger to each other.

At least one observer, Dmitrii Zhbankov, declined to share the prevailing sense of alarm, offering evidence that is consistent with what modern medicine now knows about the disease in its endemic form. In contrast to the findings of experts in the West, his data did not show that syphilis increased the rate of miscarriages and premature births among Russian peasant women.[83] Two circumstances, however, may have sustained other observers in their contrary view: a tendency to confuse the symptoms of pre- and postnatal infant syphilis, which are in fact distinct; and the contribution of other diseases to high infant mortality in rural districts where syphilis was also widespread. If in retrospect one could somehow ascertain that congenital syphilis had indeed been rampant in the Russian countryside, then one would have to conclude that doctors in fact confronted a mixed case, in which true endemic syphilis coexisted with a certain frequency of adult acquisition, whether venereal or nonvenereal, and thus that venereal transmission (by definition involving postpubescent women) was at the least more common in peasant society than the doctors were willing to concede.

City Versus Country

Their reluctance, given their social expectations, to interpret the rural case as evidence of venereal transmission encouraged physicians to draw similar conclusions about peasants who had migrated to the cities. Nevertheless, the association of urban life with a different kind of social interaction produced a shift in the resulting medical picture. Because city life was "more individualized," explained Dr. Nikolai Fedchenko, the pattern of contagion was perceived in a different way:

Among the peasants nonvenereal contagion envelops entire families and social networks; in the cities even nonvenereal transmission affects individuals. Among those who live in town but still maintain the traditional peasant way of life, nonvenereal syphilis is as prevalent as in the countryside. Thus, cases of nongenital infection have been observed among artisans, soldiers, factory hands, servants, and others; but *such cases are nevertheless described as individual sicknesses.*[84]

City and country thus constituted, in medical eyes, two social and epidemiological models. Rural syphilis was a disease of community, not individuality; urban syphilis was the reverse. City life, culture, education—these were the forces that undermined the traditional communal structures, in which sexual behavior was neither a matter of choice, nor a means of personal gratification, but an obligation, a reproductive not an expressive function. But city and country were not simply stages in a cultural progression; they were locations on the map. What was their relationship in terms of the spread of venereal disease? To answer this question physicians were obliged to confront the issue of class, since population movement was the key both to the transformation of social categories and to the spread of social disease. Gender in turn modified class distinctions, producing an epidemiological grid that mirrored the process of social change.

In the village, men and women shared the same status, at one pole of the class-gender grid: instruments of reproduction, obedient to traditional collective norms, they lacked personal autonomy and hence sexual agency. At the other end of the scale, educated urban men bore full moral responsibility for their sexual acts. Respectable women of the same class, though shaped in some respects by urban culture, nevertheless, in sexual terms, fell into the same passive, hence morally irreproachable, category as peasants. As mothers and housekeepers, they figured, along with little children, as the archetypical victims of *syphilis insontium.*[85] In common with their male relatives, however, and unlike the lower-class casualties of collective disease, they each enjoyed their own personal afflictions, their private tragedies.

The sexual-epidemiological classification of male and female workers, by contrast, reflected their transitional place in the class hierarchy. As recent urban immigrants, they still enjoyed the moral immunity of villagers. Yet, under certain circumstances, both men and women earned the luxury of moral censure: the common soldier, the male seasonal worker, and the prostitute, like the educated male, were deemed capable of sexual license and hence responsible for the propagation of sexually defined disease. The dual identity of working-class men and women thus provided the key to the puzzle of urban-rural interaction.

Their uncertain status made them the objects of considerable diagnostic ingenuity and inconsistency. Some physicians proceeded from the conviction that all syphilis was in origin sexual to the belief that rural syphilis must owe its start to an urban germ. "Take any case of syphilis," said Veniamin Tarnovskii, speaking in the interests of his own favorite cause, "though apparently unconnected to prostitution, and trace it back through the chain of [infected] individuals, sometimes through generations, to the original source. You will always find a prostitute at the end of the line."[86] What began as venereal syphilis in the urban setting, Dr. Eduard Shperk had explained in 1869, evolved under rural conditions into the endemic form: "Los[ing] its capacity to spread in the chancre stage, it encounters the ideal conditions for spreading in the secondary stage."[87]

Others, less fixated on the role of prostitution, that is, of lower-class women, as the prime medical culprits, focused instead on the role of lower-class men. Male peasants who left the village for the factory or workshop might frequent prostitutes, or sleep with a female coworker or the dormitory cook.[88] "The [young] workers or soldiers are removed from their families at the moment of greatest sexual development and find themselves in the unfamiliar urban environment. . . . [They] contract syphilis and bring this sad product of 'civilization' home to their native backwoods."[89] Without necessarily contesting its sexual roots, other experts denied that syphilis started out in the cities. No causal link between factory work and rural syphilis had been established to the satisfaction of Dr. Mikhail Uvarov, though he suspected there might indeed be one.[90] More emphatically, Dr. Nikolai Speranskii concluded that "syphilis among the population of Moscow Province ha[d] no constant or direct relationship to the development of manufacture or seasonal work."[91]

Gregorii Gertsenshtein, for his part, rejected the hypothesis of urban origins on the grounds that sexual contact could not account for the extensiveness of the disease: "The enormous number of cases involving contagion through shared utensils, common dishes, and borrowed underclothing completely engulfs the relatively few cases of venereal transmission." Russia, he claimed, did not show the expected epidemiological patterns:

The army, which usually serves as the principal index of syphilis and venereal disease infection in a given locality, in Russia shows a lower level of syphilis than the civilian population. . . . Thus in Russia the normal direction of syphilis infection, from city to countryside, is reversed; here syphilis moves less often from factories, plants, soldiers, and cities to the villages, than the other way around.[92]

One could not at the same time, however, maintain the moral innocence of the village and the iniquity of the town if one was to avoid insuperable obstacles to consistent diagnosis. Most prostitutes, even in the big cities, were, as everyone knew, recent peasant immigrants. In the village context, as we have seen, peasant women were not perceived as sexually active, despite the routine conception of 8 to 10 children in the course of a married life;[93] constant childbearing symbolized rather their immunity from sexual desire. Upon arriving in the city, many worked as household servants before turning to the sexual trade.[94] Indeed, servants constituted the largest single group of lower-class women in urban syphilis wards.[95] But was their disease the result of moral corruption, or the stigma of innocent backwardness?

As prostitutes, servant women might indeed spread contagion through public sexual contact, yet the disease itself might still have been imported from the village, the familiar product of everyday domestic life. Infected perhaps by a neighbor's child, the woman might reach town while still in the contagious stage and contaminate her male partners. Of course, the reverse could also be true: she might just as easily start out with a clean bill of health and later carry a client's disease to her native village, where it would begin to circulate by nonvenereal means. Maids or shopgirls often earned extra money from sexual encounters; many spent the summers or holidays with families in the countryside. Yet most physicians persisted in viewing moral, or sexual, habits as a function not of person but of place. Women led astray by the town were said to recover their virtue upon returning home: "Those very same, simple women who constitute the overwhelming majority of prostitutes in the cities," wrote Dr. Konstantin Goncharov in his study of venereal disease in St. Petersburg, "rarely resort to prostitution in the countryside."[96]

Most physicians eschewed the more consistent, if no less improbable, position favored by Veniamin Tarnovskii. Following the Italian school of criminal anthropology, Tarnovskii solved the problem of moral ambiguity by classifying all prostitutes as an inherently degenerate type. The "predisposition to vice," a genetic trait, provided the organic subsoil for sociological growth:

It is a mistake to think that city life acts as the only corrupting influence on the large population of migrant peasant women that pours in from the small towns and villages. No! A certain number of rural girls, no longer virgin and predisposed to vice, arrive in the big city, ready material for the prostitutional class.[97]

The inborn prostitute might appear in any social milieu: "No matter what her social class, the girl with a predisposition to vice will find the opportunity to fall [from virtue] as soon as her sexual instinct comes to life, and will more or less gradually enter the ranks of active prostitution." That most prostitutes were poor did not prove that moral compunction had succumbed to economic need, but that the poor had no moral compunction. "Only the strong influence of middle- and upper-class family life, upbringing, and intellectual development" could prevent the degenerate from satisfying her biological urge.[98]

The essence of the prostitute's pathology, in Tarnovskii's view, was her sexual aggressiveness. Abolitionists, he complained, persisted in seeing these unfortunate women as victims of poverty, of circumstance, of male depredation. Whereas, in fact, they themselves were responsible for the seduction and downfall of many an innocent man. "The prostitute continuously, repeatedly, daily offers herself for sale. She does not do so at the customer's insistence, but herself seeks him out and inveigles him into the deal."[99] In the sense that she was the victim of her own pathological constitution, the prostitute was not mistress of her fate, but in the sense that this constitution endowed her with sexual desire, it granted her a subjectivity other women lacked. Even Tarnovskii faltered, however, before the implications of his own ruthless logic; even he could not abandon the conviction of rural chastity. Delinquency, he maintained, could not flourish in the traditional peasant community, which did not share the moral weakness of the urban lower class, but only in the context of modern, commercial life: "The prostitute brings to her trade all the active, commercial initiative [*aktivnaia, promyslovaia deiatel'nost'*] without which success is unthinkable, an initiative that responds to competition, demand, and the requirements of the marketplace."[100]

Thus, Tarnovskii created a special category that explained female sexual activity while allowing him to retain his conventional notions about female sexual passivity. In that respect he was no different from the majority of his colleagues who found it easier to think of peasant men than peasant women as disengaged from family or domestic ties. Outside the moral confines of the village, men were more likely to be viewed as free sexual agents. Even so, their habits and their diseases remained those of the countryside. In transition between communal and individual modes, they suffered the disadvantages of both. A study of syphilis in the Kiev garrison, for example, reported that commissioned and noncommissioned officers alike frequented prostitutes, but that only the socially more humble noncommissioned men, many of whom had risen from the ranks, contracted syphilis in other ways as well. Their crowded, unsanitary living quarters were as dangerous to their health as the freelance prostitutes in the local bar.[101] Career officers, by contrast, might engage in sexual promiscuity, but they kept their distance from each other and were more likely to wash. Their diseases were those of individuals not of the mass.

Another study reported that venereal syphilis was three times as common among officers as among enlisted men, because the latter were more likely to be married and faithful to their wives. Fresh recruits arrived with village virtues intact. "The purity of country ways is obviously so resilient, that even under circumstances in our opinion most favorable to infection, the young men are nevertheless the most virtuous in the garrison." First encountering prostitutes in the army, they did not immediately fall for temptation but only gradually succumbed. The common soldier, this observer insisted, wanted not sex but innocent diversion: frequenting the nearby tavern with its cheap beer, cheap prostitutes, and broken-down billiard tables, he was more likely to confine himself to a game and a drink than bother with the women.[102]

Like the raw recruits fresh to army life, unskilled workers, though transplanted to the city, had not yet assimilated its cultural values and still seemed to manifest the rural pattern of disease. "The less educated [*kul'turno*] the population," observed Moscow municipal doctor Aleksandr Petrovskii, "the worse the conditions in which it lives, the more likely that syphilis will be transmitted by nonsexual means."[103] Dr. Pavel Shiriaev, who treated Moscow workers, called the prevalent form "common" (*khodiachii*), or "communal" (*obshchezhitel'nii*) syphilis.

"This *everyday phenomenon*," he wrote, applying the familiar epithet, "has its *raison d'être* in the socioeconomic conditions of life in big cities, particularly among the laboring population." Like peasant syphilis, it was a sign not of depravity but of propriety and faithfulness to the family role: "This common syphilis is the disease of the average, one might say, respectable [*dobroporiadochnii*] worker, who still maintains close ties with his village and family home [*rodnaia sem'ia*]."[104]

If the educated classes had developed a strong sense of personal integrity that spared them the casual physical contacts so fatal to peasant health, they were nevertheless vulnerable to contagion in the general atmosphere of disease emanating from the slums. "The syphilis of our servants," Shiriaev warned, "of our workers, haunts us everywhere [*vsiudu presleduet nas*]: in the bosom of our family, in hotels, restaurants, theaters, on walks, in factories, plants, and so on."[105] The violation of class boundaries could have ominous results. The most obvious case in point was intercourse with prostitutes. But nonvenereal syphilis posed a more insidious threat: service personnel from the common ranks introduced the organism through everyday contacts of an intimate, if nonsexual, kind. Sales clerks, cab drivers, tailors, bakers, shoemakers, waiters, house porters, seamstresses, laundresses: "the urban element that is all too intimate and thus acts readily as an agent for the spread of venereal disease."[106] The three main culprits were servant women, wet nurses, and barbers. Cooks contaminated the food, nannies hugged the children, housemaids folded the linen, laundresses cleaned the underwear, wet nurses took the infant to their breast, and barbers shaved the unsuspecting gentleman with a dirty razor and wiped his cheek with a dirty rag.[107] "The syphilitic barber is no less dangerous to society than the [infected] prostitute," warned Dr. Nikolai Fedchenko, on the basis of a special study.[108]

Physicians emphasized that this was not a sexual threat. Nonvenereal syphilis must be seen, they argued, as a product of social conditions. Morality was not the key, wrote Dr. Andrei Rozenkvist of the Moscow women's venereal disease hospital, rejecting the popular idea " 'that only complete chastity can save us from syphilis.' . . . For centuries syphilis has been called the 'disease of sexual indulgence' [*liubostrastnaia bolezn'*], but contemporary knowledge has rendered this notion obsolete."[109] "The question of syphilis and the questions of sexual life, depravity [*razvrat*], and prostitution associated with it have been considered taboo and have never been discussed as widely and openly as they deserve to be," wrote Dr. Aleksandr Petrovskii. "This conception of the disease . . . must be radically altered."[110] Feminist public health physician and ardent foe of regulated prostitution Mariia Pokrovskaia argued in a similar vein that "syphilis is spread in a variety of ways . . . [a]nd thus . . . must not be tied to depravity and considered a shameful, secret disease."[111] Both she and Petrovskii objected to the focus on prostitution as a diversion from more serious, and basic, health issues.

Indeed, Pokrovskaia questioned whether the working class could reasonably be implicated in sexual transmission at all.

Since the very same population—which is to say, the so-called common folk [*prostoi narod*]—predominates in the big cities as well as the towns and villages, the question arises as to why this population should begin to spread infection through sexual channels in the city, when it has previously done so through domestic contacts alone. . . . Does the so-called common folk . . . suddenly change its customs and habits, becoming cleaner, more careful, and circumspect, and thus cease to transmit syphilis the way it does in the countryside? . . . In fact, the peasants who come to work in St. Petersburg live under identical, if not even worse, sanitary conditions than in the villages. They continue to share the same wooden spoons and the same towels, to sleep one on top of the other [*v povalku*], and so on. Why should these circumstances promote the spread of syphilis in the countryside and lose their meaning in the big city?[112]

The tendency to interpret similar data in opposite ways reflected both contrasting types of medical care, Pokrovskaia argued, and the investigating physicians' preconceived ideas. The rural zemstvo physician treated his patients in the context of their family and social networks: the grateful victims brought their "friends and relatives," and the doctor then "easily traced the origin of the disease." In the city, by contrast, adult men and women came singly to anonymous, specialized venereal disease hospitals, where physicians treated them out of context, as isolated individuals. The anonymity of urban medical facilities and the doctors' immersion in the professional rather than the social world meant that "the source of infection among the common folk of the big cities escaped calculation." Moreover, the urban physician tended to think in individualized, that is to say, sexual, terms: "The majority of medical specialists are convinced that the prostitute is the main cause of syphilis in the cities. This preconceived idea cannot help but influence the data they collect."[113] Because rural physicians understood the communal nature of peasant life, they avoided this bias and produced more reliable statistics.[114]

While it is true that some physicians, primarily associated with the Academy of Military Medicine or the medical police, focused on the prevalence of venereal syphilis as a problem linked to prostitution and moral disorder,[115] others downplayed the sexual connection by interpreting ambiguous symptoms as nonvenereal. Tarnovskii's assistant, Dr. Zinaida El'tsina, for example, described the case of an eight- or nine-year-old girl shoemaker's apprentice, who turned up with papular lesions of the secondary stage on her genitals and mouth. El'tsina explained them as the result of eating from the same bowl as the other girls and sleeping two to a bed on the same pillows.[116] While modern medicine might support her diagnosis as consistent with the disease in its endemic form,[117] contemporary texts warned not to exaggerate the danger of casual physical contacts such as these, insisting that sexual contact accounted for the overwhelming majority of such symptoms.[118] In short, scientific knowledge allowed—and still allows—considerable room for nonscientific judgment. Certainly, El'tsina's reading of the clinical signs does not confirm the innocence of her subjects but reflects instead the contemporary medical presumption of prepubescent asexuality.[119] Not all societies at all times have taken for granted the sexual innocence of children.[120] Indeed, the same Victorian culture that ignored or repressed precocious awakening was fixated, in the figure of the child prostitute, on the evidence that little girls were capable of sex.[121] The child prostitute was to childhood what the adult prostitute was to the virtuous peasant wife: contradictions to be explained away.

The presumption of chastity likewise governed the conclusions of the numerous observers who attributed sores on the lips and mouths of artisanal workers to communal eating habits.[122] The workers drank from the same cup, they explained, took puffs of the same cigarette, and greeted each other with a kiss,[123] thus spreading so-called "occupational [*promyslovyi*] syphilis."[124] Obviously aware of the other possible explanation, and eager to refute it, Dr. Andrei Rozenkvist was led to the improbable assertion that oral intercourse could not be to blame, because "*coitus per os* ('sapphism'), as far as I know, is not practiced in Russia."[125] While the risk of contagion had for centuries been associated with certain trades (in particular glassblowers), and is not rejected out of hand by all modern authorities, Rozenkvist's discomfort with sexual attribution is clear. Certainly he had read the passage in Parent-Duchâtelet describing the lesbianism common among Parisian prostitutes, and evidence of similar activity in Russian brothels was not lacking.[126] He had no doubt allowed himself to be convinced that this was an expression of the "tender female soul," as Dr. Boris Bentovin was to phrase it, and not an occasion for anything more serious than a passionate kiss on the lips.[127]

Interpreting various nongenital symptoms as sexual would, of course, have led to the admission that the "common folk" might not in fact confine themselves to the basics of heterosexual intercourse, any more than they confined themselves to producing children with wedded partners. Like prostitution, the perversions separated sexual pleasure from the "natural" process of reproduction. They had presumably resulted from the same excess of civilization that had corrupted Europe but gotten no more than a foothold in the Russian empire, still immersed in the natural, agrarian way of life typified by the peasant class. Such preconceptions made it hard for doctors to admit that alternate sexual practices were widespread in any social milieu. Most chancres on the perineum, anus, and buttocks must be sexual in origin, conceded Rozenkvist, "but not in the sense that all chancres on the anus, for example, have resulted from *coitus per anum* ('sodomy'). No, contagion in the majority of cases results from the overflow of secretions from the sexual organs *post actum coitus*."[128] Although one can find the same suggestion in Alfred Fournier's influential text,[129] other, equally respected, texts, like those by Ambroise Tardieu, Robert W. Taylor, and L. Duncan Bulkley cited above, would have confirmed a different view.

The Problem of Control

Despite frequent criticism of data on which the claim was based,[130] few medical reports in the 1890s challenged the perception that syphilis was an increasingly severe public health problem, a perception Russian physicians shared with—or borrowed from—their colleagues abroad. Because of its alleged demographic impact, the problem was said to have reached the proportions of a "question of state."[131] Mobilizing state resources in the medical war against syphilis, conceived as a venereal disease, was the key to the system of regulated prostitution in nineteenth-century Europe.[132] The classic exposition of this strategy, credited in virtually all subsequent treatments, was the work of French public health physician Alexandre Parent-Duchâtelet, *De la prostitution dans la ville de Paris, considérée sous le rapport de l'hygiène publique, de la morale et de l'administration.* First issued in 1836, its title underscored the link between health, morality, and state control that characterized the French approach. Here Parent struck the same anxious note that continued to sound throughout the century, across national boundaries, with undiminished alarm: "Of all the contagious diseases that affect the human species and cause society the greatest harm, none is more serious, more dangerous, or more to be feared than syphilis."[133]

In the classic tradition of enlightened despotism and the domestic tradition of paternalistic rule, the Russian state had been quick to claim jurisdiction over the medical terrain.[134] Following the European example, Catherine the Great established the first venereal disease wards for women in 1763, under the auspices of the St. Petersburg Admiralty Hospital.[135] Beginning in the 1840s the police in a number of major cities organized a system of licensed, medically approved brothels (*maisons de tolérance*, or *doma terpimosti*) on the French model.[136]

Discussion of syphilis control in the Russian medical press and at professional conferences centered on the question of the state's role in policing public behavior. But in contrast to their European counterparts, Russian physicians were more reluctant to sexualize public health questions, thereby defining sexuality itself as a medical problem. They tended instead to convert sexual into social issues and to extend their authority in an explicitly political direction. Both the preference for nonvenereal diagnosis and the profession's heated debates on public policy reflect the basic issues separating state and society in the fifteen years preceding the revolution of 1905.

Russia's leading advocates of regulated prostitution held posts in the Academy of Military Medicine (Veniamin Tarnovskii, Petr Gratsianskii, Grigorii Gertsenshtein), or on the police-medical committees (Aleksandr Fedorov, Konstantin Shtiurmer). Other supporters served in urban venereal disease hospitals (Oskar von Petersen, Ivan Priklonskii, Aleksandr Vvedenskii). Critics of the bureaucratic approach often worked, or had worked for significant periods, in zemstvo practice (Pavel Govorkov, Mariia Pokrovskaia, Dmitrii Zhbankov), or for city government (Aleksandr Petrovskii). Individual careers were not always so easily cataloged, however, and ideological divisions not always so neat: Eduard Shperk, chief physician at St. Petersburg's Kalinkinskaia Hospital from 1870 to 1891, had from the start expressed serious doubts about regulation; Petr Gratsianov, who had worked as a municipal physician as well as an army doctor, moved from ardent to qualified support of the system; Petr Oboznenko began as a zemstvo doctor, rose to a post in the Medical Department of the Ministry of Internal Affairs, served on the staff of the Kalinkinskaia Hospital, and evolved from moderate to highly critical endorsement.[137]

Regulation itself was hotly disputed throughout nineteenth-century Europe, but in Russia even its most energetic partisans found themselves in a quandry when it came to prescribing measures against nonvenereal contagion, particularly in the social environment of the countryside and of the newly emerging urban working class. Control over prostitutes had from the first been linked to the surveillance of migratory or criminal members of the lower orders. The original 1843 instructions called for the medical inspection of male factory workers, seasonal laborers, and "lower-class persons [litsa nizshego klassa] of both sexes arrested for sexual crimes."[138] Some physicians continued to endorse such measures in relation to artisans, factory workers, domestic servants, wet nurses, and barbers.[139] However, even the fierce, internationally renowned opponent of abolition, Veniamin Tarnovskii, conceded at the 1885 congress of Russian physicians that medical surveillance of factory workers was not a practical idea.[140]

Tarnovskii believed that prostitutes were a pathological element, combining the traits of inborn criminality with those of insanity. Lazy, immodest, and deceitful by nature, they knowingly spread evil and disease. As an impaired species, they did not deserve the same treatment as normal people: society, Tarnovskii wrote, "cannot allow them the freedom to harm other, healthy citizens, neither in the name of personal freedom, a concept applicable only to the normal person, nor in the name of morality, a concept they are constitutionally unable to grasp."[141] As a consequence of their "habitual depravity," these "morally depraved" and "physically abnormal" women "cannot enjoy full personal liberty, because such liberty harms society in two ways: on the one hand, by encouraging vice, and on the other, by spreading syphilis among the entire population."[142] "Free competition delivers prostitution into the power of capital," Tarnovskii warned, "and puts it on a par with the most immoral commercial operations."[143] Unregulated prostitution, like free enterprise, needed the discipline of paternal state control.

Having defined moral weakness as a biological deformity, Tarnovskii was then able to conclude, with a satisfying sense of paradox, that syphilis was not the product of immoral behavior, as everyone believed, but its cause. Syphilis was not the price society paid for the existence of prostitution, but the reverse: prostitution was the price of disease. Generations of "physically and morally crippled offspring," the damaged fruit of syphilitic wombs, supplied the male sexual demand and the female sexual inclination, without which prostitution itself would wither away.[144] Abolitionists might think regulation perpetuated the system of commercial sex; in fact, it was the key to its demise.

Many physicians rejected such arguments, even if they accepted the principle of state-administered syphilis control.[145] Defending his work on the St. Petersburg police-medical committee, Dr. Aleksandr Fedorov described the impulse behind male sexual demand as "natural [and] lawful [zakonnyi]," not abnormal and depraved.[146] Grigorii Gertsenshtein considered regulation a function of modern, not traditional, government. Prostitution, he argued, must operate under the same constraints as other businesses: "Everyone admits the government has the right to monitor hygiene conditions in factories and mills, to prevent them from poisoning the soil, the water, and the air. Naturally, it also has the responsibility to counteract the unhealthy consequences of the prostitution trade."[147]

But endemic syphilis was confined neither to outcast and dependent groups, nor to identifiable trades. The sacrifice of personal rights advocated by Tarnovskii in the case of the socially undesirable could not be justified in relation to the population at large.[148] Even Tarnovskii did not attempt to do so.[149] Gertsenshtein, for his part, was emphatic: "Can we subject the entire civilian population to similar surveillance, with the goal of detecting syphilitics, isolating, and curing them? The answer is self-evident!"[150] Under such circumstances, the use of force was ineffective as well as unethical, Gertsenshtein concluded, citing the words of a Novgorod zemstvo physician:

Measures such as the medical inspection of shepherds, itinerant shoemakers, wool-beaters, and returning seasonal workers, or the comprehensive examination of villagers, are in the first place always immoral, like all compulsion [nasilie], whatever its pretext, and in the second place they merely induce the victims to conceal their illness in every possible way.[151]

Pavel Govorkov, who had also served as a zemstvo doctor in Novgorod Province before being assigned to army work, used his military experience to demonstrate the futility of standard procedures even under the optimal conditions of army life. Well-policed prostitution in the vicinity of army camps and the compulsory medical inspection of supposedly "dissolute" enlisted men formed the basic elements of official policy, designed, in Govorkov's caustic words, "to reinforce [and] prohibit, with special attention to such-and-such; to seize [and] punish."[152] Such "coercive" [prinuditel'nye] tactics directed at "external causes" reflected the prevalent view of syphilis as the product of moral dereliction, a view Govorkov did not share: "Can one consider [the average soldier's] two to three acts of sexual intercourse per year licentiousness, especially among single men (except if one measures [their behavior] by the standards of rural virtue)?"[153]

The futility of a strategy based on these misconceptions proved how wrong they were. "Nothing is easier," Govorkov commented, "than to impose special regulations in the garrison." Trained to obedience, soldiers did not question orders; they had no influence on the course or conditions of their everyday lives. Nowhere else "can restrictive measures be applied with such force. If contagion nonetheless persists at its former rate, then one is fully justified in concluding that the officially listed causes [of syphilis] are either dubious, or ineradicable, or, finally, that coercive measures cannot achieve their goal."[154]

Physicians had insisted that syphilis was a "question of state," a matter of national importance to be tackled by the joint efforts of government and society. But in a period of increasingly strained relations between these two forces, they criticized the character of government intrusion into the business of popular health.[155] When it came to the problem of rural and working-class syphilis, coercive, bureaucratic measures were worse than useless. In the enduring tradition of the 1860s intelligentsia, physicians saw themselves as reaching out to the people with the power of enlightenment, not compulsion, which they identified with the repressive state.[156] They wished to have nothing in common with the callous official; to cultivate trust, not obedience, instill respect and knowledge, instead of fear. "One knows how the peasants react to any kind of inventories, or censuses," wrote Dr. Aleksandr Efimov, "to anything that smells of bureaucracy [kantseliarskoe svoistvo] intruding into their dark, frightened world. How many calamities have arisen in the peasant's world from this source! Thus, it is obviously critical when performing medical examinations to eliminate anything bureaucratic, official, and most important, anything coercive, so as not at the outset to undermine [the peasants'] confidence in what is going on."[157]

Physicians did not hesitate to underscore the political implications of their view. Without freedom of speech, the educated classes could not make their contribution to the general welfare; ignorance and ill health would remain the common lot. Delegates to the syphilis congress complained of the extreme difficulty in obtaining official permission to present educational material to popular audiences. The regime tolerated no free public expression, and therefore the physicians' attack on censorship conveyed not only a demand for professional autonomy but also a demand for political reform. "Our existing law allows us to give lectures, but only on the basis of prepared texts," complained Minsk municipal doctor Petr Gratsianov. "I may read, but not express myself in my own words. . . . I am merely asking," he assured his listeners, who included officials from the Ministry of Internal Affairs, "that the physician be granted the right to communicate with the element with which he deals." No doubt the rector of Kazan University and the representative of the Kharkov medical society, who endorsed this statement, understood the analogies they had been warned not to draw.[158]

Critics of regulated prostitution also aimed wide of the mark in sighting their chosen target. Many condemned the system as a feudal relic, incompatible with the modern principle of civil rights.[159] Such language also echoes in the rejection of proposals to submit the peasantry to compulsory examinations: "What is striking," wrote Efimov, "about such lack of respect [*bestseremonnost'*] toward the peasant folk is its origin in the old feudal attitude [*krepostnicheskii vzgliad*] which considers them some sort of lower species [*nisshaia poroda*], that one doesn't have to treat with kid gloves [*nezhnichat' s kotoroi nechego*]." Respect for the peasants' privacy and personal dignity, by contrast, acknowledged their individuality, that is to say, their humanity: a person, Efimov continued, "has an interior world, which is inaccessible to government authority."[160]

Plans to isolate infectious cases in special colonies were rejected as gross violations of individual rights.[161] The analogy between syphilis and other antisocial debilities such as insanity or criminality, promoted by Tarnovskii and his followers to justify their demands for quarantine, were equally condemned.[162] The entire process of selection, segregation, and penalization, argued Zhbankov, was incompatible with the values of the medical profession, not to speak of social justice: its logical conclusion, he pointed out, was "the death penalty, which [Ernst] H[a]eckel, if I am not mistaken, recommended as the suitable fate for criminals, the mentally ill, syphilitics, tuberculars, and others. Then, at least, we would *thoroughly* cure humanity of all its ills, if, that is, even a single person survived the strict enforcement of such measures."[163]

Doctors active in the rural context argued for integration, not segregation, of syphilitic patients as the most effective medical strategy. Similar arguments were made in relation to artisans and factory workers. Dr. Pavel Shiriaev, consultant to Moscow's working-class hospital, advocated treatment on an out-patient basis, a technique already successful among the middle class. Incarceration, he noted, was particularly hard on the poor, who could not afford to stop working. Hospitalization only emphasized the outcast status of lower-class syphilitics. It assumed they could not be responsible for their own treatment, but must be subjected to administrative constraint in this as in all else. Like Mariia Pokrovskaia, he deplored the social consequences of linking syphilis to sexual misconduct. Moral self-righteousness and exaggerated fear of infection, he argued, caused people to deny syphilitics the compassion they reserved for victims of other, equally dangerous, diseases, such as tuberculosis.[164] Dr. Petr Oboznenko, who had trained under Tarnovskii, nevertheless insisted that syphilis be treated no differently from other infectious conditions. Even in the big cities it was no cause for special alarm, he emphasized, but simply the "most commonplace" occurrence. Emergency measures, in any case, were never an appropriate response to medical problems but always a reflection of ignorance and fear.[165]

Thirty years earlier, Dr. Eduard Shperk had attacked police regulation for treating prostitutes as social outcasts, with no claim to personal or legal respect. The task of medicine, he warned, was to guard the public health, not to "punish the sins of individual persons or of society as a whole." If physicians raged against the horrors of "the evil disease" *(durnaia bolezn')* or against "fallen women," it was to disguise their shame at dealing with such an "indecent" subject.[166] "Shoe-makers should not bake pies," he admonished, and doctors should not meddle in legal and moral affairs.[167] However, meddling in public policy continued to function as a strategy of professional legitimization, inseparable from educated society's larger revolt against bureaucratic despotism. In the fight against syphilis, doctors argued, medical authority must replace official regulations; local and municipal organizations must substitute for the police.[168]

Oboznenko, for example, endorsed the majority resolution at the 1899 international syphilis congress in Brussels, calling for regulation to be reconstituted on a proper legal basis to eliminate the punitive role of the police.[169] In Russia, he said, the bureaucratic state machine *(kantseliarskaia mashina)* had preserved regulation, a remnant of serfdom *(krepostnoe pravo)*, into modern times as a rear-guard tactic against the progress of social and economic change. The influx of peasants into the cities had created a floating population of temporarily homeless, unemployed poor.[170] Women in this category were seized by the police on suspicion of moral impropriety and induced to regularize their situation by accepting the registered prostitute's yellow card. Thus did the authorities penalize a woman "for being poor, for having no job, and for living in a dirty corner, rather than in a first-class hotel."[171]

Class-differentiated justice was not exceptional in the Russian empire; it was a key to the official project of reinforcing class distinctions and inhibiting social change. The civil procedures introduced by the legal reforms of the 1860s did not extend to rural inhabitants: villagers remained under the jurisdiction of separate courts, administered by community leaders and household heads, usually male, following local custom, not the formalized legal code.[172] The original program of syphilis control targeted groups that had escaped the traditional, patriarchal institutions supposed to keep the dependent orders in line: peasants who had left the village, women who had left the family. Thus working-class men and women fell under state tutelage just at the moment when they first moved from patriarchal submissiveness to the exercise of personal choice.

Although they clung to notions of peasant virtue, physicians saw no special virtue in rural life; they were the first to criticize the traditional order for its hostility to individual expression and personal responsibility, yet they defended the importance of intermediate institutions as a buffer against the state's intrusion into civil society. As inconsistent as most Western liberals, they left the principle of familial (that is, patriarchal) authority intact. "If the husband cannot always look after his wife," wrote Oboznenko, "the father after his daughter, the brother after his sister, then how can police agents penetrate into the most secret corners in millions of lives? And is such penetration desirable? By virtue of the corrupting influence it exercises on the family and on society at large, is it not worse than any syphilis?"[173] In such a view, the state figured not as a liberating force but as another outmoded form of tyranny. Moreover, by confirming the status of women as merchants of sex, regulation contributed to the decline of popular morals: the prostitute was not defined in relation to father, brother, husband, but as a function of her own sexual agency.

Of the two errant groups—migrant peasants and independent women—it was the latter who incurred the more serious reprisals. Both the state and the medical establishment shared conventional assumptions about family life and the relative autonomy of men and women. The prostitute's clients were free to come and go without examination. Extreme regulationists, such as Tarnovskii, and feminists, such as Pokrovskaia, joined in condemning the inequity, of which their colleagues were guiltily aware. In her fight against the double moral standard, Pokrovskaia denounced prostitution itself, along with all schemes to control or improve it. She insisted that women were primarily the victims, not the agents, of venereal contagion.[174] Tarnovskii, by contrast, preached a reverse single standard of sexual debauchery. Certainly both partners in the commercial exchange of sex were "equally debased," he contended. Like the brothel inmates, its visitors were "morally insensitive, with an innately intensified sexual drive. . . . Just as the prostitutes infect the healthy population, so they are in turn, in the majority of cases, infected by these moral cripples, the true refuse of contemporary society." Medical surveillance was society's way of maintaining its normality, the equivalent of health. "Every psychologically healthy, normally developed person," Tarnovskii was sure, "will freely admit the injustice as well as the futility of limiting medical surveillance in regulated brothels to the prostitutes alone."[175]

The problem of allowing sexually active men to circulate freely and carry the infection so relentlessly tracked on female sexual parts bothered the profession enough to provoke a resolution at its 1885 congress in favor of pulling clients into the net.[176] The St. Petersburg syphilis society agreed, as did some officials in the Medical Department, but no such proposal ever became official policy, and the 1897 syphilis congress rejected the idea.[177] Few physicians accepted Tarnovskii's perverse egalitarianism, according to which sexual excess became a gender-neutral standard of social exclusion. The prevailing arguments against male inspection showed regulation for what it was: a system of controlling women, not disease. Those who accepted medical exams, for all their diagnostic inadequacy, as the only way to weed out sick prostitutes considered them too perfunctory to detect infection among men.[178] Clients were unlikely, in any case, to submit to such a humiliating procedure, it was argued, and would defeat the whole system by turning to nonbrothel prostitutes instead.[179] To Zhbankov, his colleagues were guilty of the same abuse of power they complained of at government hands: "By excluding from medical surveillance many individuals who spread syphilis by sexual means, whether deliberately or accidentally, the [1897 syphilis] congress is acting inconsistently and unjustly: compulsion only ceases to be compulsion if it *applies equally to all.*"[180]

The exempt individuals were exclusively men. The privilege of self-regulation was not reserved for the educated but was accorded to all males in their role as the customers of public sex. The same "dirty," disorderly factory hands covered by the 1843 instructions were free from interference at the brothel door. The very propensity for unthinking violence cited to justify police juris-diction over the lower classes in this case served to demonstrate the common man's capacity to assert his will and as an argument that his will must be respected.

> Houses of the lowest caliber . . . [are frequented by] drunken, brutalized hordes, resem-bling human beings only in outward appearance . . . [whose] victims . . . arrive at the hospital with bruises, bites, and scratches. . . . Clients at the better houses behave them-selves with greater tact, but even among them . . . sobriety is rare, and those who would submit to examination without making a scene are rarer still.[181]

If the gentleman was assimilated to the beast, so the beast was raised to the level of the citizen. Sexual agency, denied by definition to the female gender, was the mark of personal autonomy, the prerequisite for civic agency in its widest sense. To the extent that individuality was tolerated at all by the distrustful regime, it was in the person of the urban male. With few exceptions, the spokesmen of educated society, for all their critical views, shared this prejudice.

Self-regulation was possible, at least in theory, because sexual contact was a matter of choice. If control should fail, then prevention might succeed. Thus, the 1897 syphilis congress produced a series of resolutions calling for intensified moral vigilance: prohibition of alcohol, dancing, music, and singing in registered brothels; crackdown on street solicitation and independent prostitutes; educating youth in the spirit of "moral cleanliness," sexual continence, and respect for women.[182] The turn to moral purity reflected a current European trend.[183] But it failed to address the dominant Russian problem: endemic, rural syphilis.[184] In his enthusiasm for sexual continence, even Tarnovskii was obliged to admit it would do no good for the rural population.[185] The same congress agreed on the usefulness of compulsory examinations in regard to certain dependent groups: prostitutes, soldiers, prisoners, servants, and foundlings, but found them inap-propriate in the countryside. The congress did not, however, oppose the exam-ination of factory workers, a position some participants criticized on the grounds that rural and working-class living conditions were virtually the same.[186]

Physicians did not always agree on matters of public policy, and the 1897 congress produced a number of contradictory proposals.[187] One recommended the compulsory examination of all lower-class women without exception; another called for the enrollment of syphilitics in special regiments that would be mobi-lized to fight in time of war. Above all, however, the assembly emphasized the need for popular medical education. "What we need," said Dmitrii Zhbankov, "are not police ordinances, but the development of public self-awareness [*obshchestvennoe samosoznanie*]."[188] Self-regulation was in fact the only effective regulation, but an ignorant, oppressed populace was incapable of conducting itself in an enlightened way. Information was the key to autonomy, which was in turn the key to public health: "When it comes to limiting contagion by means of medical exams, no prohibitions or sanitary inspectors will be of any use. Without developing popular self-awareness and without information about the dangers and symptoms of the disease, it will be impossible to change those ordinary daily relations which are precisely the reason for its spread."[189]

Autonomy was desirable not only for the victims of disease but for those struggling against it. The congress insisted that medical programs be removed from police jurisdiction and placed in the hands of local "public institutions" (*obshchestvennye uchrezhdeniia*).[190] The defense of local initiative, of popular participation in administrative affairs, of corporate professional responsibility was not a theme peculiar to physicians alone; it was a dominant note in the growing chorus of political dissatisfaction in educated society at large, which was to coalesce after the century's turn in the organized Liberation Movement. The evolution of medical attitudes in accord with the dominant political mood may be charted, for example, in successive articles by Minsk municipal physician Petr Gratsianov. Writing in 1895, Gratsianov insisted on the need to restrict the prostitute's freedom of movement. Dishonest and deceitful, such women could not be expected to submit voluntarily to medical control. The police were therefore obliged, in the general public interest, to confiscate their passports, limiting the "personal liberty" that permitted them the luxury of harming others.[191] In 1904, Gratsianov criticized the system of police regulation as an abuse of the prostitutes' civic rights. Only in the hands of public, rather than bureaucratic institutions, would regulation be subject to the scrutiny of public opinion and would prostitutes be guaranteed the right of judicial self-defense.[192]

A passionate though nonrevolutionary radical of Populist outlook who stood outside party politics, Dmitrii Zhbankov was a leading figure in the Pirogov Society, Russia's most influential and progressive medical organization.[193] Zhbankov was acutely aware of the political dimension of the profession's claims. He objected to any violation of personal rights, whether the humiliating and intrusive compulsory medical exam or the degrading reference to stigmatized or underprivileged groups.[194] Syphilis, as the congress acknowledged, was no respecter of social class; yet physicians allowed themselves to be guided by the prejudices of the age, which brought dishonor to their calling and defeated their goals. "I am always struck," Zhbankov wrote, "by this amazing injustice: the propertied classes are allowed by law to demand medical certificates for their servants and nurses, but the employers themselves and their sick children may with impunity infect the nurses! The objection that the propertied are more cultured and restrain themselves from infecting others is hardly well founded, especially in regard to sexual transmission; otherwise husbands would not infect their own wives, a thing we often see among the middle and even the upper classes."[195]

Admitting that education and culture were not enough to transform the personal habits governing sexuality and health was, of course, fatal to the physicians' insistence that enlightenment was the key to disease control. It was not, however, inconsistent with their implied assumption that raising the populace to the level of autonomous individuality characteristic of the upper orders would have permitted it to err on a level that allowed for correction through self-control, though it might also foster self-indulgence. What doctors rejected was the objectification of the victims of misfortune, whether social, political, or physical, an attitude that left them hope neither of sin nor redemption.

After 1905, medical interest in nonvenereal syphilis as a matter of social policy seems to have succumbed to a new focus on clinical strategy. It is perhaps a coincidence, but the leading medical journal, *The Physician* (after the death of its founding editor in 1901 called *The Russian Physician*), which had teemed with articles on the social context of syphilis between 1890 and 1905, shifted thereafter to technical questions of individual diagnosis and treatment, especially following the discovery of the arsenical drug Salvarsan in 1910. It would not, however, be surprising to discover that increased peasant mobility and the extent of popular engagement in the revolution of 1905 had shaken the physicians' image of the common folk as victims, not agents, of misfortune, as well as of disease. Belief in the moral integrity of village life, which had sustained the diagnostic distinction between venereal and nonvenereal syphilis, could not long have withstood the evidence of upheaval and the sense of social crisis generated by the revolutionary events.

Medical interest in syphilis seems also to have peaked in Europe around the turn of the century, for reasons that are not entirely clear.[196] What is clear, however, is the distinctive symbolic function of syphilis in Russia, as opposed to continental Europe, during the heyday of rhetorical alarm. Insofar as Russian physicians adopted the European association between syphilis and illicit sex, it was in keeping with a view of their own cities as islands of Westernized culture.[197] These islands were colonized by wanderers from the domestic mainland of communal life, who acquired by virtue of their displacement attributes of autonomy they had never previously had. Regulated by biological rhythms and traditional norms, village sexuality had engulfed the traces of desire in the conspicuous cycle of conception, pregnancy, and lactation—the elements of reproduction and also of birth control. But cast adrift, or merely repositioned in the big city, the newcomers' sexual desire and its consequences leapt more readily to public view. Urban practitioners worried about the integrity of working-class family life, the risks of prostitution, and devised strategies of medical control. At the same time, however, Russian physicians maintained an alternate, desexualized interpretation of syphilis, which corresponded to notions of class and gender appropriate to the traditional framework of rural life. And just as they failed in such cases to link disease and moral disarray, so they rejected the role of moral arbiter assumed by their colleagues in the West.

Notes

1. I would like to thank Reginald Zelnik for his close, critical reading, William Bennett, M.D., for help with the modern medical literature, and Isabel V. Hull for her editorial comments. Mauri and Anna-Liisa Vihko, Marjatta Mustaniemi, and the staff of the Helsinki University Slavic Library sustained me in my research. The Mary Ingraham Bunting Institute of Radcliffe College provided support during the final stages of revision.

2. The concept itself was at least a century old, but it was widely popularized in the 1890s by Bulkley, who is cited, for example, in Alfred Fournier, *Traité de la syphilis*, vol. 1 (Paris, 1899), 134; A. I. Rozenkvist, "K statistike vnepolovogo zarazheniia sifilisom," *Biblioteka vracha* 5, no. 8 (1898): 532; M. A. Chlenov, "K kazuistike vnepolovogo sifilisa," *Russkii vrach*, no. 30 (1902): 1093–94.

3. L. Duncan Bulkley, *Syphilis in the Innocent* (New York, 1894), 3–4.

4. Ibid., 140.   5. Ibid., 4.

6. Leading authority Professor Alfred Fournier, who did not ignore the dangers of nonvenereal contagion, considered 90 percent of all cases in France to be venereal in origin; *Traité de la syphilis*, 1:20. "Endemic," nonvenereal syphilis was said to occur in contemporary Moravia, Sweden, Norway, Estonia, Courland, and Lithuania; Etienne Lancereaux, *Traité historique et pratique de la syphilis* (Paris, 1866; English ed., 1868; Russian ed., 1876), cited from English ed., *A Treatise on Syphilis: Historical and Practical*, 2 vols. (London, 1868–69), 1:29–43, 46; and Bulkley, *Syphilis*, 5–7. An influential French medical dissertation claimed that syphilis was brought to the countryside by peasant men who visited prostitutes in the towns. It cited the dangers of wet-nursing and congenital syphilis, but it largely ignored other forms of nonvenereal transmission, and it did not characterize the problem as endemic, a term it reserved for syphilis among the "Negroes" of North America. See Léon Issaly, *Contribution à l'étude de la syphilis dans les campagnes* (Paris, 1895), 7–8, 10–11, 13–14, 28; cited in Alain Corbin, "Le Péril vénérien au début du siècle: Prophylaxie sanitaire et prophylaxie morale," in *L'Haleine des faubourgs: Ville, habitat et santé au XIXᵉ siècle*, ed. Lion Murard and Patrick Zylberman (Fontenay-Sous-Bois, France, 1978), 250–51. Nelly Furman kindly found me a copy of Issaly. Doctors at the 1899 syphilis congress in Brussels insisted that European peasants were not afflicted with the same type of problem as Russian peasants; see P. A. Gratsianov, "Bor'ba s sifilisom, kak predmet obshchestvennoi gigieny," *Vos'moi pirogovskii s"ezd: Autoreferaty i polozheniia dokladov po sektsiiam*, vol. 6 (Moscow, 1902), 245.

7. Rozenkvist, "K statistike," 510.

8. Lancereaux, *Treatise*, 2:261–62.

9. Zemstvo doctor D. V. Imshenetskii from Chernigov Province, in *Trudy Vysochaishe*

razreshennogo s"ezda po obsuzhdeniiu mer protiv sifilisa v Rossii, vol. 2 (St. Petersburg, 1897), 150.

10. V. M. Tarnovskii, *Prostitutsiia i abolitsionizm* (St. Petersburg, 1888), 196. The German edition (Hamburg, 1890) is cited by Bulkley, *Syphilis,* 198, 204; Tarnovskii's work was also read by French physicians; Corbin, "Le Péril," 252.

11. Claude Quétel, "Syphilis et politiques de santé à l'époque moderne," *Histoire, économie et société* 3, no. 4 (1984): 543. This reference was a gift from Natalie Z. Davis.

12. For discussion of the origins of syphilis in Europe and the myth of the post-Columbus epidemic, see Ellis Herndon Hudson, *Nonvenereal Syphilis: A Sociological and Medical Study of Bejel* (Edinburgh, 1958), 14–25; also Corinne Shear Wood, "Syphilis in Anthropological Perspective," *Social Science and Medicine* 12 (1978): 47–55.

13. Philippe Ricord, *Lettres sur la syphilis,* 2nd ed., revised (Paris, 1856), 131.

14. For biographical information, see "Esquisse biographique," in Edouard Léonard Sperk [Shperk], *Oeuvres complètes: Syphilis, prostitution, études médicales diverses,* 2 vols. (Paris, 1896), vol. 1.

15. Eduard Shperk, "O merakh k prekrashcheniiu rasprostraneniia sifilisa u prostitutok," *Arkhiv sudebnoi meditsiny i obshchestvennoi gigieny,* no. 3, part 3 (1869), 68: ellipsis in original.

16. Eduard Shperk, "Signification des syphiloïdes dans la doctrine et dans l'histoire de la syphilis" (translation of "Znachenie sifiloidov v uchenii i istorii sifilisa," *Voenno-meditsinskii zhurnal* [August–September 1864]), in Sperk, *Oeuvres complètes,* 1:164–65, 167, 172.

17. P. I. Gratsianskii, "Nevinnye puti i sposoby zarazheniia i rasprostraneniia sifilisa," *Zhurnal russkogo obshchestva okhraneniia narodnogo zdraviia,* no. 11 (1892): 817.

18. I. I. Priklonskii, *Prostitutsiia i ee organizatsiia: Istoricheskii ocherk* (Moscow, 1903), 53.

19. Shperk lived 1837–94; Tarnovskii 1839–1906. Biographical information on Tarnovskii is in *Entsiklopedicheskii slovar' Brokgaus-Efron,* vol. 32A (St. Petersburg, 1901), 650–51.

20. Speech at the opening session, 15 January 1897; *Trudy Vysochaishe razreshennogo s"ezda,* 2:18–19.

21. Hudson, *Nonvenereal Syphilis,* 6.

22. Bulkley, *Syphilis,* 21.

23. In the words of a recent historian of venereal disease in America, "It is now known that syphilis and gonorrhea are almost never communicated in nonsexual ways." Allan M. Brandt, *No Magic Bullet: A Social History of Venereal Disease in the United States Since 1880* (Oxford, 1985), 22. See also Theodor Rosebury, *Microbes and Morals: The Strange Story of Venereal Disease* (New York, 1971), 250–51.

24. E. I. Grin, *Epidemiology and Control of Endemic Syphilis: Report on a Mass-Treatment Campaign in Bosnia,* World Health Organization Monograph Series, no. 11 (Geneva, 1953), 20, 30, 32; see also Hudson, *Nonvenereal Syphilis,* 9, 12–15, 80–81, 83.

25. Wood, "Syphilis," 47.

26. Lancereaux listed innocent kissing, sleeping two to a bed, breast-feeding, cupping, tattooing, shared linen, kitchen utensils, and pipes among the multiple hazards of everyday life. The dangers of suckling, ordinary physical contact, common household implements, and of congenital transmission were acknowledged, he notes, as early as the sixteenth century; *Treatise,* 2:214, 231–46; for French examples of sixteenth-century knowledge, see Quétel, "Syphilis," 545 and 549; on congenital syphilis, see R. C. Holcomb, "The Antiquity of Congenital Syphilis," *Bulletin of the History of Medicine* 10, no. 2 (1941): 164–65. For an exhaustive inventory, see Bulkley,

Syphilis, 209–40. For a Russian list of culpable everyday objects "too long to count," see Gratsianskii, "Nevinnye puti," 807; also Rozenkvist, "K statistike," 531. Corbin notes the popularity of such catalogs among French syphilologists of the period; "Le Péril," 250.

27. Stewart M. Brooks, *The V.D. Story* (South Brunswick, N.J., 1971), 37–39; Hudson, *Nonvenereal Syphilis,* 69.

28. Grin, *Epidemiology,* 32. Hudson explains that constant low-level exposure prevents extreme reaction to any single innoculation of the organism, of the kind that produces chancres in previously unexposed adults; *Nonvenereal Syphilis,* 64–65.

29. For mistaken views of congenital syphilis, see Fournier, *Traité de la syphilis,* 1:5–6; also, Elizabeth Lomax, "Infantile Syphilis as an Example of Nineteenth Century Belief in the Inheritance of Acquired Characteristics," *Journal of the History of Medicine* 34, no. 1 (1979): 23–39.

30. Fournier, *Traité de la syphilis,* 1:22, 25–26, citing Ricord.

31. P. Diday, *Le Péril vénérien dans les familles* (Paris, 1881), 319.

32. Fournier, *Traité de la syphilis,* 1:133.

33. For example, see Lancereaux, *Treatise,* 2:355–56.

34. Ambroise Tardieu, *Etude médico-légale sur les attentats aux moeurs,* 7th ed. (Paris, 1878), 230, 249.

35. Fournier, *Traité de la syphilis,* 1:189.

36. Robert W. Taylor, *A Practical Treatise on Genito-Urinary and Venereal Diseases and Syphilis,* 3rd ed., revised (New York, 1904), 496.

37. Bulkley, *Syphilis,* 240.

38. Ibid., 109.

39. Lancereaux, *Treatise,* 2:262.

40. E. A. Rotman, "K kasuistike vnepolovogo shankra: Vnepolovoi shankr na penis'e," *Russkii zhurnal kozhnykh i venericheskikh boleznei* 10 (1905); A. J. Tulinov, "Pervichnaia sifiliticheskaia iazva vnepolovogo proiskhozhdeniia na polovykh chastiakh devochki 9 let," *Detskaia meditsina* 4 (1899).

41. N. A. Semashko, "Friedrich Erismann: The Dawn of Russian Hygiene and Public Health," *Bulletin of the History of Medicine* 20 (June 1946): 1–9.

42. On 1887 break, see Sperk, *Oeuvres complètes,* xxvi–xxvii; on abolitionism, see B. Bentovin, *Torguiushchie telom: Ocherki sovremennoi prostitutsii,* 2nd ed., revised (St. Petersburg, 1909), 239.

43. For the European background, see George Rosen, "The Evolution of Social Medicine," in *Handbook of Medical Sociology,* ed. Howard E. Freeman, Sol Levine, and Leo G. Reeder (Englewood Cliffs, N.J., 1963). For the zemstvo medical philosophy, see Nancy Mandelker Frieden, *Russian Physicians in an Era of Reform and Revolution, 1856–1905* (Princeton, N.J., 1981), chap. 4; and Samuel C. Ramer, "The Zemstvo and Public Health," in *The Zemstvo in Russia: An Experiment in Local Self-Government,* ed. Terence Emmons and Wayne S. Vucinich (Cambridge, 1982), 279–82.

44. D. N. Zhbankov, *O deiatel'nosti sanitarnykh biuro i obshchestvenno-sanitarnykh uchrezhdenii v zemskoi Rossii* (Moscow, 1910), 2–3.

45. In *Trudy Vysochaishe razreshennogo s"ezda,* 2:21.

46. V. K. Borovskii, "K voprosu ob istochnikakh zarazheniia sifilisom," *Voenno-meditsinskii zhurnal,* no. 8 (August 1894): 412.

47. N. P. Fedchenko, "O zarazhenii sifilisom pri brit'e," *Meditsinskoe obozrenie* 33, no. 1 (1890): 25.

48. Frieden, *Russian Physicians,* 210–11.

49. On the congress attendance, see *Trudy Vysochaishe razreshennogo s"ezda*, 2:259–66.
50. Career and biographical data are taken from *Rossiiskii meditsinskii spisok* (St. Petersburg, 1890–1916).
51. The link between individuation and modern strategies for imposing behavioral norms is, of course, a central point of Michel Foucault's *Discipline and Punish: The Birth of the Prison* (New York, 1977).
52. Among the most authoritative expressions of this universal opinion: M. A. Chistiakov, *Protokoly sektsii sifilidologii na pervom s"ezde russkikh vrachei 1885 g. v S. Peterburge* (St. Petersburg, 1886), 41; G. M. Gertsenshtein, "Sifilis v Novgorodskoi gubernii i voprosy o bor'be s nim na VII i IX s"ezdakh zemskikh vrachei 1888–1895 gg.," *Vestnik obshchestvennoi gigieny, sudebnoi i prakticheskoi meditsiny* 30, no. 4 (1896): 25; Gratsianskii, "Nevinnye puti," 817–18; O. V. Petersen, "O sifilise i venericheskikh bolezniiakh v gorodakh Rossii," in *Trudy Vysochaishe razreshennogo s"ezda*, 1:127; A. I. Rozenkvist, "Redkii sluchai vnepolovogo zarazheniia sifilisom: Iz ambulatorii Miasnitskoi bol'nitsy v Moskve," *Vrach* 20, no. 9 (1899): 244; I. S. Speranskii, *K statistike sifilisa v sel'skom naselenii Moskovskoi gubernii* (Moscow, 1901), 125; V. M. Tarnovskii, quoted in Chistiakov, *Protokoly*, 6; M. S. Uvarov, "Sifilis sredi sel'skogo naseleniia," in *Trudy Vysochaishe razreshennogo s"ezda*, 1:73–85.
53. K. L. Shtiurmer, *Sifilis v sanitarnom otnoshenii* (St. Petersburg, 1890), 45.
54. P. A. Govorkov, "Polovaia zhizn' garnizona," part 1, *Vrach* 17, no. 37 (1896): 1016.
55. Congress resolution cited, for example, by A. G. Petrovskii, "Bor'ba s sifilisom v gorodakh," part 1, *Izvestiia Moskovskoi gorodskoi dumy*, no. 5 (1905), Obshchii otdel: 3.
56. Gertsenshtein, "Sifilis v Novgorodskoi gubernii," 47.
57. In the cryptic words of D. N. Zhbankov, "blagodaria bednote, temnote i tesnote"; quoted in K. V. Goncharov, *O venericheskikh bolezniakh v S. Peterburge* (St. Petersburg, 1910), 23.
58. Veniamin Tarnovskii, quoted in Chistiakov, *Protokoly*, 6; see also Shtiurmer, *Sifilis*, 44.
59. G. M. Gertsenshtein, *Sifilis v Rossii* (1885); quoted in Goncharov, *O venericheskikh bolezniakh*, 5.
60. G. M. Gertsenshtein, "Peredvizhnye vrachebnye otriady dlia bor'by s sifilisom," *Vestnik obshchestvennoi gigieny, sudebnoi i prakticheskoi meditsiny* 32, no. 10, book 1 (1896): 25.
61. Shtiurmer, *Sifilis*, 45; see also Gertsenshtein, "Sifilis v Novgorodskoi gubernii," 36 and 38.
62. Rozenkvist, "K statistike," 529.
63. Uvarov's career in zemstvo medicine is outlined in N. I. Afanas'ev, *Sovremenniki: Al'bom biografii*, 2 vols. (St. Petersburg, 1909–10), 2:427–30.
64. Uvarov, "Sifilis sredi sel'skogo naseleniia," 82–83.
65. Borovskii, "K voprosu," 413.
66. Gertsenshtein, "Peredvizhnye vrachebnye otriady," 26.
67. Ibid.; "Sifilis v Novgorodskoi gubernii," 47.
68. Fedchenko, "O zarazhenii sifilisom," 19. See also zemstvo physician D. D. Sandberg, cited in P. I. Messarosh, "K voprosu o rasprostranenii sifilisa v Rossii," *Vestnik obshchestvennoi gigieny, sudebnoi i prakticheskoi meditsiny* 31, no. 7, book 1 (1896): 50.
69. D. N. Zhbankov, *Materialy o rasprostranenii sifilisa i venericheskikh zabolevanii v Smolenskoi gubernii* (Smolensk, 1896); quoted in Rozenkvist, "Redkii sluchai," 245.

70. Appendix to A. I. Efimov, *Sifilis v russkoi derevne, ego kharakternye cherty i vliianie na sanitarnoe polozhenie naseleniia* (Kazan, 1902). Many physicians showed an interest in the "physiological aspects of peasant women's sex lives"; see the numerous studies cited in Dr. V. S. Sergiev, "K ucheniiu o fiziologicheskikh proiavleniiakh polovoi zhizni zhenshchiny-krest'ianki Kotel'nicheskogo uezda Viatskoi gubernii," in *Trudy antropologicheskogo obshchestva pri Imperatorskoi Voenno-Meditsinskoi Akademii*, vol. 5 (St. Petersburg, 1901), 175–99.

71. See J. Michael Phayer, "Lower-Class Morality: The Case of Bavaria," *Journal of Social History* 8, no. 1 (1974): 79–95.

72. For the demography of the traditional peasant village, see B. N. Mironov, "Traditsionnoe demograficheskoe povedenie krest'ian v XIX-nachale XX v.," in *Brachnost', rozhdaemost', smertnost' v Rossii i v SSSR: Sbornik statei*, ed. A. G. Vishnevskii (Moscow, 1977). Studies concluded that the average peasant woman began menstruating between the ages of sixteen and seventeen; see Sergiev, "K ucheniiu," 180.

73. David L. Ransel notes that illegitimacy figures were much higher in Russian cities than in the countryside, but he attributes this in part to the practice of peasant women bringing unwanted or illegitimate infants to urban foundling homes. Stricter rules for foundling home admission, introduced in 1890, produced a drop in illegitimacy statistics, which Ransel thinks conceals an actual rise in illegitimate births during the 1890s: "Problems in Measuring Illegitimacy in Prerevolutionary Russia," *Journal of Social History* 16, no. 2 (Winter 1982): 111–27.

74. See his argument for the admission of women to university education; D. N. Zhbankov, "O dopushchenii zhenshchin v universitet," *Russkii vrach* 1, no. 6 (1902): 209–13.

75. Zhbankov's background is given in S. I. Mitskevich, *Na grani dvukh epokh: Ot narodnichestva k marksizmu* (Moscow, 1937), 96.

76. D. N. Zhbankov, *Bab'ia storona: Statistiko-etnograficheskii ocherk* (Kostroma, 1891), 91; italics in the original.

77. Gertsenshtein, "Peredvizhnye vrachebnye otriady," 30.

78. A. A. Vvedenskii, "Prostitutsiia sredi sel'skogo (vne-gorodskogo) naseleniia," in *Trudy Vysochaishe razreshennogo s"ezda*, 1:1.

79. Ibid., 2.

80. Uvarov, "Sifilis sredi sel'skogo naseleniia," 85.

81. Tarnovskii, *Prostitutsiia i abolitsionizm*, 206, asserts that hereditary syphilis had the same impact among peasants as among the educated classes. See also D. D. Sandberg, "Sifilis v derevne," *Vrach* 15, no. 26 (1894): 741.

82. Hudson, *Nonvenereal Syphilis*, 150–152.

83. D. N. Zhbankov, "K voprosu o plodovitosti zamuzhnikh zhenshchin," *Vrach* 10, no. 13 (1889): 311.

84. Fedchenko, "O zarazhenii sifilisom," 19; italics mine.

85. That doctors viewed such women as lacking in personal autonomy is evident in the practice of concealing from them the nature of their disease while confiding the unpalatable news to their husbands. The deception was thought necessary to maintain "professional confidentiality" between physician and husband. For a critique, see Z. Ia. El'tsina, "K voprosu o rasshirenii mer bor'by s sifilisom," *Russkii vrach* 1, no. 26 (1902): 969–71.

86. Veniamin Tarnovskii, speech at the 1897 syphilis congress, in *Trudy Vysochaishe razreshennogo s"ezda*, 2:10.

87. Shperk, "O merakh k prekrashcheniiu," 69.

88. Shtiurmer, *Sifilis*, 41. Peasant women also worked in the factories (hence the availability of female coworkers with whom to have sex) but were not themselves designated as carriers of disease.

89. Borovskii, "K voprosu," 414.

90. Uvarov, "Sifilis sredi sel'skogo naseleniia," 56–58

91. Speranskii, *K statistike sifilisa*, 91.

92. Gertsenshtein, "Peredvizhnye vrachebnye otriady," 17 and 27. Shtiurmer, *Sifilis*, 45, agrees that infection moves from village to cities. For a modern assertion of the same principle, see Hudson, *Nonvenereal Syphilis*, 192.

93. This well-known figure is mentioned by D. D. Sandberg in the course of her description of syphilis among peasant women in Tambov Province; "Sifilis v derevne," 741.

94. Shtiurmer, *Sifilis*, 42.

95. Z. Ia. El'tsina, "Sifilis i kozhnye bolezni sredi zhenskogo rabochego naseleniia Peterburga," *Vrach* 17, no. 42 (1896): 1178–79; Gratsianskii, "Nevinnye puti," 806; M. M. Kholevinskaia, "Otchet ob osmotrakh prostitutok na Samokatskom smotrovom punkte Nizhegorodskoi iarmarki za 1893 god," *Vrach* 15, no. 17 (1894): 487.

96. Goncharov, *O venericheskikh bolezniakh*, 97; however, A. A. Vvedenskii disagreed; "Prostitutsiia," 2.

97. Tarnovskii, *Prostitutsiia i abolitsionizm*, 180.

98. Ibid., 179 (fall from virtue), 177 (poverty), 181 (upbringing). He continued to express this view of prostitution in 1897 at the syphilis congress: *Trudy Vysochaishe razreshennogo s"ezda*, 2:10–11.

99. Tarnovskii, *Prostitutsiia i abolitsionizm*, 133–34 (abolitionists); 159, 164 (seduction); 135 (quote).

100. Ibid., 179 (peasant community); 136 (quote).

101. Borovskii, "K voprosu," 417–18.

102. Govorkov, "Polovaia zhizn'," part 1, 1017; part 2, *Vrach* 17, no. 38 (1896), 1050–51.

103. Petrovskii, "Bor'ba s sifilisom v gorodakh," part 1, 3.

104. P. A. Shiriaev, "Organizatsiia vrachebnoi pomoshchi pri sifilise i venericheskikh bolezniakh sredi rabochego naseleniia v bol'shikh promyshlennykh i torgovykh tsentrakh," *Meditsinskoe obozrenie* 58, no. 13–14 (1902): 151–52.

105. Ibid., 152.

106. Goncharov, *O venericheskikh bolezniakh*, 87.

107. On servants, see Z. Ia. El'tsina, "Vybor prislugi," *Pervyi zhenskii kalendar' na 1903 god*, ed. P. N. Arian (St. Petersburg, 1903); Gratsianskii, "Nevinnye puti," 802 and 806; P. A. Pavlov, "Ob otnoshenii vnepolovogo zarazheniia sifilisom k polovomu mezhdu srednim klassom g. Moskvy," *Meditsinskoe obozrenie* 33, no. 1 (1890): 13–14; Shtiurmer, *Sifilis*, 42. The literature on wet nurses is extensive, for they were employed not only by private families, but also by state foundling homes; see for example Z. Ia. El'tsina, "Zhelatel'nye sposoby vskarmlivaniia grudnykh sifiliticheskikh detei," *Vrach* 15, no. 4 (1894); also Shtiurmer, *Sifilis*, 43; Gratsianskii, "Nevinnye puti," 779–88.

108. Fedchenko, "O zarazhenii sifilisom," 24.

109. Rozenkvist, "K statistike," 510 and 512.

110. Petrovskii, "Bor'ba s sifilisom v gorodakh," part 1, 2, 4, and 23.

111. M. I. Pokrovskaia, "Mery, preduprezhdaiushchie rasprostraneniia sifilisa," part 3, *Russkii vrach* 2, no. 12 (1903): 455.

112. Ibid., part 2, *Russkii vrach* 2, no. 11 (1903): 413.

113. Ibid. Pokrovskaia was not the only one to link the sexualization of syphilis to the

tendency to see it as a problem of individual behavior; see also Gratsianov, "Bor'ba s sifilisom," 247.

114. Pokrovskaia, "Mery," part 2, 414; part 3, 455. Shperk had earlier suggested that clinicians in urban hospitals fostered the venereal interpretation of syphilis, while provincial physicians drew different conclusions from their own, rural experience; "Signification des syphiloïdes," 186–87.

115. For the split between urban and zemstvo doctors at the 1897 syphilis congress, see A. A. Tsenovskii, *Abolitsionizm i bor'ba s sifilisom* (Odessa, 1903), 52.

116. Z. Ia. El'tsina, "Nedostatochnost' nadzora za maloletnimi v artel'nykh masterskikh i neobezpechennost' detei sifilitikov bol'nichnymi mestami," *Vrach* 21, no. 19 (1900): 579. El'tsina's career is described in Afanas'ev, *Sovremenniki*, 1:97.

117. Hudson, *Nonvenereal Syphilis*, 81–82.

118. Diday, *Le Péril vénérien*, 317.

119. Sander L. Gilman, *Difference and Pathology: Stereotypes of Sexuality, Race, and Madness* (Ithaca, N.Y., 1985), 41.

120. See injunctions issued by French clergymen between the sixteenth and eighteenth centuries against four-year-old peasant children sharing the same beds, for fear of their committing "horrible sins"; Jean-Louis Flandrin, ed., *Les Amours paysannes: Amour et sexualité dans les campagnes de l'ancienne France, XVIᵉ–XIXᵉ siècle* (Paris, 1975), 150.

121. In choosing a nonsexual explanation, doctors such as El'tsina were rejecting alternatives of which they could not have been unaware. A commission established by the Ministry of Internal Affairs in 1847 to investigate unregistered streetwalkers found "still innocent young girls" between the ages of nine and fourteen infected with syphilis, which it explained as either the nonvenereal result of living among syphilitic prostitutes or as the consequence of "inexcusable naughtiness [*shalosti*], bordering on prostitution [*blizkie prostitutsii*], that they commit with infected men"; "O prostitutsii v Rossii," *Arkhiv sudebnoi meditsiny i obshchestvennoi gigieny*, no. 1, part 3 (1869): 104–5.

122. Rozenkvist, "K statistike," 516; see also A. I. Pospelov, *O vnepolovom zarazhenii sifilisom sredi liudei chernorabochego klassa g. Moskvy* (St. Petersburg, 1889), 45.

123. Gratsianskii, "Nevinnye puti," 805.

124. Uvarov, "Sifilis sredi sel'skogo naseleniia," 61–67.

125. Rozenkvist, "K statistike," 528.

126. Western sources on lesbian prostitutes were reported in K. I. Babikov, *Prodazhnye zhenshchiny* (Moscow, 1870), 53–54.

127. Bentovin, *Torguiushchie telom*, 125–35.

128. Rozenkvist, "K statistike," 516 (workshops); 528–29 (sodomy).

129. Fournier, *Traité de la syphilis*, 1:189.

130. See remarks by L. F. Ragozin, director of the Medical Department of the Ministry of Internal Affairs, in *Trudy Vysochaishe razreshennogo s"ezda*, 2:2.

131. M. Kuznetsov, *Prostitutsiia i sifilis v Rossii* (St. Petersburg, 1871), 68. Among numerous similar statements, see Borovskii, "K voprosu," 412–13 ("a question of the first importance . . . for the state"); Gratsianskii, "Nevinnye puti," 775 ("constitutes a question of state"); Petrovskii, "Bor'ba s sifilisom v gorodakh," part 1, 2 ("direct government responsibility").

132. On the nineteenth-century French system, see Alain Corbin, *Les Filles de noce: Misère sexuelle et prostitution, 19ᵉ et 20ᵉ siècles* (Paris, 1978).

133. A. J. B. Parent-Duchâtelet, *De la prostitution dans la ville de Paris,* 3rd ed., vol. 1 (Paris, 1857), 603.

134. For the role of European states, see Rosen, "The Evolution of Social Medicine," 17–61.

135. Ia. A. Chistovich, *Istoriia pervykh meditsinskikh shkol v Rossii* (St. Petersburg, 1883), 452; John T. Alexander, "Catherine the Great and Public Health," *Journal of the History of Medicine* 36, no. 2 (1981): 186, 197–99.

136. See G. M. G[ertsenshtein], "Prostitutsiia," in *Entsiklopedicheskii slovar' Brokgaus-Efron,* vol. 25A (St. Petersburg, 1898), 479–86. For reference to France as the model for the Russian system, see N. B-skii, "Ocherk prostitutsii v Peterburge," *Arkhiv sudebnoi meditsiny i obshchestvennoi gigieny,* no. 4, part 3 (1868): 67, 82, 88; this author, along with many other Russian writers on the subject, makes frequent reference to Parent-Duchâtelet.

137. Most career information is taken from *Rossiiskii meditsinskii spisok* (St. Petersburg, 1890–1916).

138. Quoted in P. A. Gratsianov, "K voprosu o reorganizatsii nadzora za prostitutsiei v Rossii," *Vestnik obshchestvennoi gigieny, sudebnoi i prakticheskoi meditsiny* 28, no. 11 (1895): 141.

139. On artisans, see El'tsina, "Nedostatochnost' nadzora," 577–79. On servants and wet nurses, see Pavlov, "Ob otnoshenii," 17. On all groups, see Rozenkvist, "K statistike," 533. On barbers (under medical inspection in St. Petersburg since 1883), see Fedchenko, "O zarazhenii sifilisom," 25.

140. Quoted in Chistiakov, *Protokoly,* 50–51.

141. Tarnovskii, *Prostitutsiia i abolitsionizm,* viii (pathology); 136–39, 159, 161 (other epithets); 189 (quote).

142. Ibid., 243; see also his 1897 speech, *Trudy Vysochaishe razreshennogo s"ezda,* 2:10–11.

143. Tarnovskii, *Prostitutsiia i abolitsionizm,* 242.

144. Ibid., 210.

145. Gertsenshtein, "Sifilis v Novgorodskoi gubernii," 58.

146. A. I. Fedorov, "Prostitutsiia v S.-Peterburge i vrachebno-politseiskii nadzor za neiu," *Vestnik obshchestvennoi gigieny, sudebnoi i prakticheskoi meditsiny* 13, no. 1 (1892): 73.

147. Gertsenshtein, "Prostitutsiia," 486.

148. Tarnovskii, *Prostitutsiia i abolitsionizm,* 242, on personal rights sacrificed to "the people's welfare"; 1897 speech, in *Trudy Vysochaishe razreshennogo s"ezda,* 2:21, on compulsory treatment for "dangerous classes."

149. Tarnovskii, 1897 speech, in *Trudy Vysochaishe razreshennogo s"ezda,* 2:19.

150. Gertsenshtein, "Peredvizhnye vrachebnye otriady," 28.

151. A. A. Desiatov, quoted in Gertsenshtein, "Sifilis v Novgorodskoi gubernii," 37.

152. Govorkov, "Polovaia zhizn'," part 2, 1052.

153. Ibid., 1053.

154. Ibid., 1052–53.

155. On the radicalization of public health circles between 1895 and 1905, see E. I. Lotova, *Russkaia intelligentsia i voprosy obshchestvennoi gigieny: Pervoe gigienicheskoe obshchestvo v Rossii* (Moscow, 1962), 39.

156. What was needed, Dmitrii Zhbankov later wrote, was "the most active intervention in the people's life, not by means of force but through persuasion and trust"; Zhbankov, *O deiatel'nosti,* 3. On the intelligentsia tradition and opposition to state intervention, see Nancy M. Frieden, "Physicians in Pre-Revolutionary Russia: Pro-

fessionals or Servants of the State?" *Bulletin of the History of Medicine* 49, no. 1 (1975): 22–23, 28.

157. A. I. Efimov, "Sravnitel'naia otsenka raznykh sposobov izucheniia derevenskogo sifilisa," *Vrach* 21, no. 51 (1900): 1553.

158. P. A. Gratsianov, A. G. Ge, and A. Kh. Kuznetsov in *Trudy Vysochaishe razreshennogo s"ezda,* 2:28.

159. For example, see P. E. Oboznenko, *Podnadzornaia prostitutsiia S.-Peterburga* (St. Petersburg, 1896), 39.

160. Efimov, "Sravnitel'naia otsenka," 1552 (both quotes).

161. For such a proposal, see Uvarov, "Sifilis sredi sel'skogo naseleniia," 113.

162. For equation of the infected prostitute with an armed, homicidal maniac, see Tarnovskii, *Prostitutsiia i abolitsionizm,* 190; for the analogy condemned by Gertsenshtein, see "Sifilis v Novgorodskoi gubernii," 56. Julie Vail Brown notes that Russian folk tradition did not welcome incarceration, even of the insane, and that after 1905 the Russian psychiatric profession itself abandoned its earlier defense of incarceration as indispensable to treatment; *The Professionalization of Russian Psychiatry, 1857–1911* (Ph.D. diss., University of Pennsylvania, 1981), 331–33.

163. D. N. Zhbankov, "O s"ezde pri Meditsinskom Departamente po obsuzhdeniiu meropriiatii protiv sifilisa v Rossii," part 2, *Vrach* 18, no. 30 (1897): 832.

164. Shiriaev, "Organizatsiia vrachebnoi pomoshchi," 153–54.

165. P. [E.] Oboznenko, "Po povodu novogo proekta nadzora za prostitutsieiu v Peterburge, vyrabotannogo Komissieiu Russkogo Sifilidologicheskogo Obshchestva," *Vrach* 20, no. 12 (1899): 349.

166. Shperk, "O merakh k prekrashcheniiu," 77–81; quotes, 80.

167. Shperk, "Otvet na stat'iu: 'Zhenskii nadzor za prostitutsiei,'" *Arkhiv sudebnoi meditsiny i obshchestvennoi gigieny,* no. 1, part 5 (1870): 7.

168. See Pirogov Society petition in K. I. Shidlovskii, ed., *Svodka khodataistv Pirogovskogo obshchestva vrachei pered pravitel'stvennymi uchrezhdeniiami za 20 let (1883–1903 g.)* (Moscow, 1904), 19; see also discussion of debates in city administrations in Empe, "Neskol'ko slov o sifilise s sanitarnoi tochki zreniia i o polozhenii etogo voprosa v Peterburge," *Russki vrach* 2, no. 13 (1903): 498–500.

169. P. E. Oboznenko, "Vopros ob uporiadochenii prostitutsii i o bor'be s neiu na dvukh mezhdunarodnykh soveshchaniiakh 1899 goda," *Vrach* 21, no. 30 (1900): 910.

170. Oboznenko, "Po povodu novogo proekta," 348–49.

171. Oboznenko, *Podnadzornaia prostitutsiia,* 39.

172. Peter Czap, Jr., "Peasant Class Courts and Peasant Customary Justice in Russia, 1861–1912," *Journal of Social History* 1, no. 2 (1967): 149–78.

173. Oboznenko, "Po povodu novogo proekta," 348.

174. Pokrovskaia, "Mery," part 1, *Russkii vrach* 2, no. 10, (1903): 374.

175. 1897 speech, in *Trudy Vysochaishe razreshennogo s"ezda,* 2:13.

176. For congress resolution, see Chistiakov, *Protokoly,* 59.

177. Recommendation of A. I. Smirnov from the Medical Department, of K. L. Shtiurmer on behalf of the St. Petersburg Society, and rejection by special session of the congress, in *Trudy Vysochaishe razreshennogo s"ezda,* 2:39 and 136, respectively.

178. Oboznenko, "Po povodu novogo proekta," 348.

179. A. I. Fedorov, "Deiatel'nost' S.-Peterburgskogo Vrachebno-Politseiskogo Komiteta za period 1888–95 gg.," *Vestnik obshchestvennoi gigieny, sudebnoi i prakticheskoi meditsiny* 32, no. 11, book 2 (1896): 185; "Pozornyi promysl'," ibid., no. 8 (1900): 1183.

180. Zhbankov, "O s"ezde pri Meditsinskom Departamente," part 2, 833; italics in original.
181. Oboznenko, "Po povodu novogo proekta," 348.
182. Zhbankov, "O s"ezde pri Meditsinskom Departamente," part 2, 831–32.
183. Corbin, "Le Péril," 255–57.
184. Psychiatrist P. I. Kovalevskii counseled sexual abstinence and early marriage as a defense against venereal syphilis, but could offer no recourse against nonvenereal infection; "Sifilitiki, ikh neschast'e i spasenie," *Arkhiv psikhiatrii, neirologii i sudebnoi psikhopatologii* 30, no. 1 (1897): 64–65.
185. 1897 speech, in *Trudy Vysochaishe razreshennogo s"ezda*, 2:16.
186. Zhbankov, "O s"ezde pri Meditsinskom Departamente," part 1, *Vrach* 18, no. 29 (1897): 803; part 2, 833.
187. On "sharp" disagreements at the congress, see Petrovskii, "Bor'ba s sifilisom v gorodakh," part 1, 6.
188. Proposals in Zhbankov, "O s"ezde pri Meditsinskom Departamente," part 2, 832–33; quote, 832.
189. Ibid., 833.
190. Ibid., part 1, 801.
191. Gratsianov, "K voprosu o reorganizatsii," 166–67.
192. P. A. Gratsianov, "Po povodu proekta novogo 'Polozheniia o S.-Peterburgskom vrachebno-politseiskom komitete'," *Russkii meditsinskii vestnik* 6, no. 1 (1904): 5–7.
193. Mitskevich, *Na grani dvuch epokh*, 96–97; for Zhbankov's political activity in the 1890s, see Frieden, "Russian Physicians," 171–72, 191.
194. Zhbankov, "O s"ezde pri Meditsinskom Departamente," part 1, 802; part 2, 833.
195. Ibid., part 2, 833.
196. Corbin, "Le Péril," and Gérard Jacquement, "Médecine et 'maladies populaires' dans le Paris de la fin du XIXᵉ siècle," in *L'Haleine des faubourgs*.
197. Note the description of urban syphilis offered by G. M. Gertsenshtein: "taking the form common in Western European countries"; "K statistike sifilisa v Rossii," *Vrach* 7, no. 18 (1886): 335.

ALAIN CORBIN

Commercial Sexuality
in Nineteenth-Century France:
A System of Images and Regulations

IN THE EYES OF NINETEENTH-CENTURY abolitionists, especially Josephine Butler, France was the fatherland of regulation. The "French system," a mass of regulations developed during and after the Consulat, served as a model for all of Europe. Even in Great Britain, the Contagious Diseases Act of 1866 drew its inspiration from this system. Consequently, we cannot overestimate its importance.

In their respective discourses, municipal authorities, hygienists, the police, and the judiciary attempted to justify clearly (perhaps too clearly) their arrangements for the regulation of prostitution. They reiterated a small number of arguments that quickly became pat stereotypes. These arguments, which encumber denotative discourse, can be grouped in three categories.

—The most frequent ones appeal to the need for the protection of *public morality*. In particular, these arguments insist on the importance of protecting young girls' innocence and feminine modesty from the spectacle of vice, and of preserving male adolescents from precocious sexual contact and female adolescents from the snares of the seducer. The arguments emphasize the necessary tranquility of the passerby and aim to shield the family outing from erotic scenes; they also refer to the protection of sexual morality. The desire to prevent the spectacle of prosperous vice from offending the eyes of poor but honest women is cited less frequently.

—The second series of arguments centers around the protection of male prosperity. Commercial sexuality can devastate patrimonies; it can hasten and pervert the accepted stages of social mobility, if one is not careful, and can thwart the most cleverly contrived patrimonial strategies.

—The need to protect the population's health forms the third category of justification.

The relative importance of these arguments varies according to periods. The ascendancy of the sanitary alibi, although not linear, is obvious. The obsession with congenital syphilis contributed to reviving this argument at the end of the century. When, in 1960, France slowly endeavored to respect the United Nations' injunctions, only "sanitation" continued to require the preservation of certain regulations. During the rule of the party of order, just after the defeat of 1871 and the Commune, the importance of protecting wealth was ceaselessly stressed. Zola's novel, *Nana*, expresses the power of this obsession. After 1880, the number of allusions to the dangers presented by the spectacle of vice began to decline. By the beginning of the twentieth century, it had lost its essential import.

A series of images and perceptual schemas with numerous implications have made possible the social acceptance of French policies (in many ways, dreadful) toward prostitutes. These images and schemas, rather than collections of monotonously repeated arguments or denotative discourses, should be our object of study. It would be of little profit to examine the latter, even with the help of the most sophisticated quantitative methods. An ensemble of representations has authorized the preservation of the "French system," still viable after so much struggle and condemnation. This system of images is firmly rooted in what I will call pre-Pasteurian mythologies and is structured by an archaic definition of health and disease.

Certainly, one can also show the distant origin of French regulation in the first age of Judaeo-Christian civilization, or affirm that Solon devised the model for the regulated bordello. However, I will avoid this kind of historical bulimia and concentrate on the dawn of the contemporary epoch.

Five images, among others, have helped to inspire the need for regulation:
1) The prostitute is the *putain* (whore), whose body smells bad. The etymology that derives *putain* from the Latin *putida* remains uncertain, although the word originates in ancient literature (see Juvenal). This is of little consequence; what is essential is that this definition has been acknowledged for a long time. Restif de la Bretonne declared himself convinced of its accuracy. At the end of the eighteenth century, *putain* was an appropriate word to take literally. The humoral theory and the well-known rise of a neo-Hippocratism led to an emphasis on the importance of the coction of the humors of the human body.[1] At the same time as the "birth of the clinic" in France, the glandular theory of Théophile de Bordeu revived the earlier concern with organic fluids and emunctories.[2]

In vitalism, which in many ways marked a return to a pre-Cartesian mental universe, the notion, supported by Jean-Baptiste Silva at the beginning of the eighteenth century, that sperm confers an odor of flesh on females was defended.[3] In every area, it was repeated, coitus perfects the woman;[4] coitus particularly bestows its definitive olfactory seal on her, through a discharge into her humoral system and an impregnation of her flesh.

Still, excessive sexual relations threaten this equilibrium of internal "living" decay, whose importance had been stressed, after Bacon, by Beecher, Pringle, and Mac Bride. The *putain* does not just symbolize moral rot; she is literally a putrid woman, as demonstrated by the odor she emits. By frequenting her, one risks the living corruption of syphilis, just as the sailor risks scurvy or the prisoner risks "prison fever." An ancient belief was thus accepted and revived by a fraction of the medical profession. This image was to have a long life at the heart of traditional society. I have heard old women in the Norman groves of my childhood say, in speaking of men suspected of syphilis, "They have rotten blood."

Three other images are intimately related to this one:

2) The prostitute enables the social body to excrete the excess of seminal fluid that causes her stench and rots her. This indefensible image assimilates a category of women to both the emunctories, which, from the organicist perspective, discharge humors, secretions, and excretions and permit the survival of the social organism—here an ancient belief of the early Church Fathers is revived— and a drain, or sewer. Thus, Dr. Fiaux, one of the specialists on the problem during the nineteenth century, speaks of the "seminal drain."[5] The importance given to the notion of circulation since Harvey's discovery strengthens this image. The Physiocrats drew parallels between the necessary circulation and flux of air and water and that of products in the economy—this physical exigency should apply as well to the humors of the social organism.

This second image links the prostitute less to waste or ordure than to the sewer or drain that prevents a fatal congestion and assures the elimination of excess sperm. It is necessary to understand the prevalence of pre-Pasteurian mythologies; cleaning does not necessarily mean washing—water and dampness are distrusted—but rather the elimination of filth.

3) As putrid body and emunctory/sewer, the prostitute maintains complex relations with the *corpse* in the symbolic imagination of these times. This fact is not surprising; after all, psychoanalysts link the death drive with the desire that overwhelms the prostitute's client. In Alexandre Parent-Duchâtelet's writings, this connection is clearly revealed.[6] We have just seen how the stinking body of the prostitute, given over to living putrefaction, prefigures death; its very odor testifies to the victory of that living death whose concept will be refined by Xavier Bichat.

In nineteenth-century hygienists' discourse, the association between the prostitute and cadaverous flesh becomes a leitmotif. All through the Latin Quarter's dark alleys, they tell us, the dissection of cadavers, the flaying and dismembering of animals, and clandestine prostitution coalesce. Frances Finnegan remarks on this same association in the city of York.[7] The madames of houses of prostitution used purveyors to recruit girls; in a similar manner, the proprietors of dissection theaters relied on purveyors for their supply of corpses. The Faculté doctors used the prostitutes' bodies from the morgue. I will return to the similarity between the regulations that govern dead flesh and those with which the commercial woman must comply. These authorities—not I—have, in their municipal designs, identified the corpse with the prostitute, a confusion sanctioned in the vernacular when it names working-class houses of prostitution "slaughter houses" (*maisons d'abattage*).

Prostitutes, then, appeared dangerous for the same reason as corpses or carrion. In this period when "anticontagionism" flourished, the war against infection, or the miasma emanated by a rotting corpse, was of supreme importance.[8] From this perspective, regulating prostitution became a major objective.

These first three images indicate the ambiguous status of the woman's body, at once menace and remedy, agent of putrefaction and drain. The social authorities accepted these contradictions without question.

4) Of course, the prostitute symbolizes, and even incarnates, the ailment that testifies, more than a disgusting smell, to the infection of the social structure: *syphilis*, the only malady where one dare not deny the power of contagion. This scourge was believed to be particularly acute in the proximity of putrescence, an illusion that demonstrates the hold of moral considerations on the medical thought of the time. Parent-Duchâtelet, unlike his contemporaries but with the American Warren, was one of the few to reinvestigate putrefaction's deadly influence; in order to substantiate it, he went as far as to consume meat cooked over a fire fed with the remains of human corpses. However, he remained convinced that the proximity of latrines and the presence of sewers hastens the fatal result of venereal disease.[9] Such a conviction explains why, in his eyes, the privileged agent of transmission for the disease is the woman-sewer, the putrid woman, the *putain*.

This image evolved over the course of the century. The development of the modern theory of congenital syphilis between 1860 and 1885, and its subsequent propagation between 1885 and 1910, was to charge the prostitute's image with new anxieties in learned discourse.[10] The commercial woman henceforth threatens the genetic patrimony of the dominant classes. As the bearer of virulent syphilis, she infects the male bourgeois, who then transmits, as a risk of diseased inheritance, a still more terrifying hereditary disease that will devastate his posterity. The virus incubated by the prostitutes sets in motion a process of *degeneration* that threatens to annihilate the bourgeoisie. The alcoholic, syphilitic, and often consumptive prostitute, herself a victim, it was said, of a morbid heredity, represents woman's criminal inclination in the view of C. Lombroso and G. Ferrero.[11] In short, she becomes the symbolic synthesis of the tragedy of the times.[12]

But let us return to the end of the eighteenth century. The four images that I have just sketched combine with a more inclusive image of the diseased city. All things considered, prostitution is but one aspect of urban pathology, and the strategy adopted toward it should parallel those deployed to heal and purify the city. This explains the great attention paid to the prostitute by new social investigations, which were also concerned with those other urban untouchables who work with mire, ordure, excrement, and carrion.

5) The final image that I wish to evoke is of a completely different nature. It integrates the prostitute with that chain of resigned female bodies, originating

in the lower classes and bound to the instinctive physical needs of upper-class males—an image that, today, has started to come undone. To this series of submissive bodies belongs the nurse who lavishes her intimate care on the newborn; the nursery maid who toilet trains the child; the double-faced servant, both Martha and Mary Magdalen, whose body serves as an object of obsession in the master's house and who sometimes undertakes the adolescent's sexual initiation or sets out to conquer the marriage bed; and finally, the old servant maid, all self-abnegation, become nurse and waiting to play the role of layer-out. The lower-class woman, at the heart of the bourgeois household, is entrusted with all that is organic, the management of the body's needs—all the more so in that, over the decades, the young girl of good family and the wife show a growing disgust for the practice and the transmission of this somatic culture. One cannot overestimate the role of this social dichotomy in the formation of the male psyche. The recourse to the prostitute can be inserted logically into this series of female bodies at the beck and call of the bourgeois body.

Once these few decisive images have been enumerated, significant silences remain in the hygienic and regulatory discourses on prostitution. The image of pleasure never emerges. It is appropriate to question the function of this silence, just as it is important to decipher the meaning of the laughter that rocked the Chamber of Deputies in 1895 when it tried, unsuccessfully, to discuss a legal proposal on prostitution. One can imagine watching a Marshall Sahlins, returned from Tahiti, resting his anthropological gaze on this group of males with bulging bellies, the majority of which were clients of prostitutes, as they shook with irrepressible laughter.

Let us further note that, until recently, academic history in France has been emprisoned in such a system of images that structure its sources. In scholarly works, the rare allusions to prostitutes would be found in chapters dedicated to refuse dumps, sickness, and death.

This system of images suggests a series of principals that structure the policy toward prostitution. I will limit myself to five:

1) *Tolerance of prostitution.* Like everything that relates to bodily needs and everything dirty but necessary for the social body's survival, prostitution must be tolerated. For this reason, regulationists remained faithful to that Augustinian moral realism whose development can be traced from Aquinas, Pascal, and the doctrine of the lesser of two evils to the pretentious hygienics of the Restoration. The essential reference can be found in Augustine's *De ordine*:

What can one find that is more ignoble, more deprived of honor, more charged with turpitude, than commercial women, procurers and all such scourges. If one suppresses prostitutes, the passions will convulse society; if one gives them the place that is reserved for honest women, everything becomes degraded in defilement and ignominy. Thus, this type of human being, whose morals carry impurity to its lowest depths, occupies, according to the laws of general order, a place, although certainly the most vile place, at the heart of society.[13]

The pragmatic attitude toward a necessary evil not only prescribes tolerance of prostitution but governs everything that concerns the social physiology of excretion, drainage, the elimination of waste and filth—in brief, everything that attempts to prevent infection. Listen to Parent-Duchâtelet, a specialist in drains and cesspools, as well as in brothels under police supervision, whose career, by itself, speaks for the global coherence of regulation.

The dissection theater is a necessary evil that must be tolerated while alleviating, by all possible means, the unfortunate influences that we attribute to it.

The same tolerance is shown toward cesspools.

It is necessary that these cesspools exist; they are absolutely, inevitably necessary: they must be tolerated by the residents of the adjacent countryside.[14]

Such texts—and there are many others—underscore how decisive it is that the authorities had initially considered prostitution as a branch of public hygiene. "This is a question of refuse dumps," exclaimed Léon Gambetta indignantly in 1878, when the Chamber thought briefly of debating the problem. The victory of the Republic would have no effect on this issue.

2) *Isolate and circumscribe.* To ward off infection and to purify public space involves the emplacement and registration of sewers and the containment of vice. The first half of the nineteenth century is obsessed with the problem of refuse dumps. A vast literature is devoted to cesspools, filthy refuse dumps, and in particular to the sewer that developed at Montfaucon, to the northeast of Paris. The hygienists began to preach the establishment of a garbage dump in each township.

The "red-light district," a distant medieval legacy, no longer seemed appropriate to the exigencies of the new age: it was too large, and the display of vice and infection too open and unrestrained. With the project to destroy the disorder of the terrible Hôtel Dieu on the Île de la Cité, and the struggle to reform the disgusting compound at Montfaucon, it is too late to think of creating such a district in the center of Paris. A scattering of houses, a commercial archipelago pragmatically designed to respond to the city's sexual misery, presents itself little by little as the most efficacious solution. In 1829, Mangin, the Parisian prefect, would even try to enclose in this network all the prostitutes whom he had succeeded, for several months, in prohibiting from the streets of Paris.

3) *Enforce concealment and conduct close surveillance in order to control prostitutes.* During the first half of the nineteenth century, there is a growing intolerance toward the presence of excrement in the city; the place for defecation tends to be specified within the interior of the home. The development of the concept of

privacy leads to restricting lovemaking to the bedroom. The baroque death, surrounded by a weeping crowd, becomes henceforth an archaic spectacle. The bordello inscribes itself in this new sensibility. Like corpses, carrion, and excrement, prostitution must remain hidden as much as possible. The similarity of vocabulary here is revealing: thus, with regard to dissection, the ordinance of 17 October 1803: "The windows (will be) continuously covered by means of canvas nailed to the boards which form the hood outside of these windows." The same document concerning cadavers: "The cadavers will be carried to the dissection theaters in closed carriages." Flaying and cutting up of animals must also, as Parent-Duchâtelet emphasizes, remain hidden from the eyes of the public.[15]

But stagnation becomes dangerous unless it is accompanied by a permanent record of the putrefaction process. Everything that swarms in obscurity increases the threat of disease: the mire of swamps as well as virgin, muddy soil concealed by thick vegetation. The brothel must therefore remain permanently under the scrutiny of government administration. The first task of regulation is to bring the prostitute out of the foul darkness and remove her from the clandestine swarming of vice, in order to drive her back into an enclosed space, under the purifying light of power.

The model of the efficacious industrial technique of fabricating in retorts helps to fulfill this requirement. It was hoped that, thanks to new processes, industrial dangers could be eliminated. The slaughterhouse, the tallow foundries, and the desiccation of blood would lose their stench. Isolation and permanent control of the dissolution process would remove the deadly threat of nauseating miasma.

4) Still another series of images, which owes very little to those previously evoked, inspire the municipal authorities. I wish to speak of a respect for the functional, the rise of utilitarianism, and the concern to administer circulation. Once the function of prostitution is well analyzed, the need to organize it in such a way as to accelerate its rhythms is clear. A new, speedier time frame simultaneously assures the maximum profit from the enterprise, the best response to demand, and especially the prevention of pleasure, accommodation, and a consequent loss of the client's vitality. The libertarians at the end of the century would say that the aim is to conserve intact the constraints of labor over the prostitute's partner and thus to authorize a sexual relation that accommodates itself to the schedule of work without disturbing it. This interpretation is not without merit, but the acceleration of rhythms causes another moral concern— it is necessary to return the prostitute's client, the young man or husband, to his family or wife in a morally intact condition, appeased but not infected by vice.

The brothel under police supervision, a seminal drain, must be the antithesis of the house of clandestine debauchery where the absence of surveillance authorizes the practice of perversions, even group sex, or at least delectation and voluptuousness. Far from being this sort of school for pleasure, the brothel must act as a safety valve, without the temptation of erotic refinements.

I have read very carefully Parent-Duchâtelet's writings on the flaying and cutting up of animals, another problem he addresses.[16] He lyrically admits his fascination with the new Salmon and Payen process that, by accelerating the treatment of cadaverous flesh, upsets the natural rhythm of putrefaction and simultaneously disarms the threat of infection. As a consequence of this model, Parent-Duchâtelet cherishes the dream of a functional prostitution/meatworks, capable of exorcizing the prostitute's putridity.

5) This, of course, entailed the examination of the prostitute's sanitary condition. One cannot avoid observing, in this matter, several concurrent events. The anatomical-clinical doctor, then in full flight, leaves off investigating the truth of sickness in the depths of corpses; Recamier invents the speculum that permits him to penetrate the interior of living bodies; and the decision is made to open a *dispensary* dedicated to the examination of prostitutes. Nothing subterranean will remain obscure. At the same time, Parent-Duchâtelet and certain of his colleagues undertake that interminable exploration of drains and sewers which Victor Hugo echoes with fascination in his long evocation of the "Bowels of Leviathan."[17]

From this perspective, the dispensary, and the mapping and arranging it generates, appear indeed as symbols of modernity. The dispensary serves as a model for the dream of a prophylactic bordello, promised to a future that we now know.

The ensemble of measures that define the "French system," as sketched by Pasquier and gradually developed, chiefly under the direction of the Belleyme commissioners of police, Delavau and then Mangin, can be inferred from these principles. There is no longer need for lengthy enumerations.

After investigation, the "tolerated" house of prostitution is placed under the care of a woman who has filed her request at the Paris police headquarters. This "madame," after receiving the book in which she will register the prostitutes she employs, becomes, by delegation, an agent of the government. She is directly responsible for the establishment, which is subject to regular inspection.

The pragmatism shown by the authorities led them to tolerate the existence of registered independent prostitutes; it induced them even to tolerate a certain amount of secrecy, which the agents of morals tried to control by directly placing several registered prostitutes in clandestine operation.

Both the distribution of brothels under police supervision in the city and the existence of certain prohibited locations can be explained by pragmatic concern for the reconciliation of sequestered vice with dispersed establishments for drainage. The regulations forbid opening an approved brothel in the proximity of a

Catholic or Protestant church, a *lycée*, or a barracks. The registered independent prostitutes must not frequent cafés, taverns, or theaters. In a more general fashion, areas of male sociability are forbidden to them, as well as travel by open carriage.

Several time prohibitions complement these spatial restrictions. Prostitutes must respect the purity of day, but also the license of profound darkness. These hard-to-reconcile demands led to the authorization of solicitation only between the hours of seven and eleven at night. During this period of time, prostitutes must circulate. This enforced movement prevents them from forming groups and obstructing the strolls of passersby.

The windows of a brothel under police supervision must remain closed; the entry requires a double door. The isolated prostitute avoids exhibiting herself at her window, the privileged scene of intimate solicitation.

Thus restricted and confined, the prostitute must, however, continue to be recognizable in order to prevent any mistakes or misrecognitions. A large number designates the brothel under police supervision. Lamps light up the entrance as well as the staircase. There are no locks on the bedroom doors; windows permit the madame's control and the prostitutes' reciprocal surveillance. The establishment must remain permanently open to the inspectors of morals.

Previous marks of infamy have disappeared, but more discreet signs indicate sexual commerce. This growing subtlety of signs corresponds to a refinement of criteria for style of dress. In public spaces, the prostitute will not wear a hat; she must circulate bare-headed.

The regulations strive to exercise physical control over the streetwalker. Her posture, her gestures, her speech, and, with greater reason, her cry must lose their obscenity. This "training" was partially successful from the start of the July Monarchy, at least if one believes Parent-Duchâtelet. The nineteenth-century bourgeoisie had a phobia of tactile contact; consequently, it is hardly surprising if prostitutes are forbidden to clutch at passersby or to embrace or kiss a partner.

The madames are charged with regulating the tempo of sexual relations. Moreover, they have to take their "boarders" to inspection each week, before the administration decides to visit the prostitutes in their establishment.

The regulation of prostitutes was the mayor's concern. For this reason, regulations varied according to municipalities, and what I have just described applied essentially to Paris. However, the provincial authorities were hardly innovative. They were usually content with variations, stemming from regional traditions, on the model elaborated in Paris.[18]

The policies governing prostitutes are not immutable—they do not escape history; they accompany the evolution of customs. While Haussmannization (which can be read, not without exaggeration, as a social dichotomy of purification) strove to create in certain neighborhoods ennobled, well-lit, cleared, and purified public spaces where the bourgeoisie, and especially their wives, could represent themselves, a new prostitution proliferated that eluded the system of representation that I have just described. This was ordered as nothing more than a frequently clandestine popular commercial sexuality, which anticipated the development, in the twentieth century, of those working-class houses of prostitution (*maisons d'abattage*), the *Temps modernes* [Sartre's journal] of sex, for the sake of a new subproletariat, composed in large part of immigrant laborers.

The great turn-of-the-century bordellos under police supervision, such as the *Sphinx* or the *Chabanais*, symbolize the new practices rather well; the *maisons de rendez-vous*, then in full swing, are even better models.

What is essential for my purpose is that this "modern" prostitution responds to another, extremely complex, system of representations that I can only suggest. Here, there is no longer haste, no longer a question of the procreative instinct. In the *maison de rendez-vous*, the bourgeois eager for adultery can imagine himself seducing the wife of another. In the bordellos under police supervision, he seeks to satisfy fantasies that are often rooted in the libertine literature of the eighteenth century. The disguises, the profusion of false names, the sadism (often just simulated), the desire for young virgins, the technical refinement of caresses requiring, in this period obsessed by perversions, that one work at acquiring a repertory of techniques, the new relation between sex and money: ordure and decay are excluded from these new relations.

In the great "houses," temples of modernity, the corruption of light and the reign of "the enchantment of electricity" allows new and skilled stagings that create an increasingly large place for voyeurism and purely visual excitation.

The change in forms of desire forced the adoption of regulation. The prefect Lepine made this his project in the Paris of the "Belle Epoque"; meanwhile, the contemporary "sex shop" demonstrates the wish to reconcile the multiple social and psychological functions attributed to prostitution. A confluence of ancient dreams, a synthesis of two systems of representations long antagonistic, this establishment aims for purely prophylactic pleasure. In the new bordello, the prostitute has ceased to be a *putain* in the etymological sense of the term.

—Translated by Katharine Streip

Notes

1. On neo-Hippocratism's rise in eighteenth-century France, see Jean-Paul Desaive, et al., *Médecins, climat, et épidémies à la fin du XVIIIe siècle* (Paris, 1972).
2. See Michel Foucault, *The Birth of the Clinic* (New York, 1973).
3. Jean-Baptiste Silva, "Dissertation où l'on examine la manière dont l'esprit séminal est porté à l'ovaire," in *Dissertation et consultations médicales de MM. Chirac et Silva*, vol. 1 (Paris, 1774), 188ff.

4. On this subject, see Yvonne Knibiehler's writings.
5. Louis Fiaux, *La Police des moeurs,* vol. 1 (Paris, 1907), 212.
6. See our presentation of extracts from the work of Alexandre Parent-Duchâtelet in Alain Corbin, *La Prostitution à Paris au XIXe siècle* (Paris, 1981), 9–42.
7. Frances Finnegan, *Poverty and Prostitution: A Study of Victorian Prostitutes in York* (Cambridge, 1979).
8. See Erwin H. Ackerknecht, "Anticontagionism Between 1821 and 1867," *Bulletin of the History of Medicine* 22, no. 5 (1948): 562–93.
9. Alexandre Parent-Duchâtelet, "Essai sur les cloaques . . . ," in *Hygiène publique,* 2 vols. (Paris, 1836), 1:256.
10. Alain Corbin, "L'Hérédosyphilis ou l'impossible rédemption: Contribution à l'histoire de l'hérédité morbide," *Romantisme,* no. 31 (1981): 131–49.
11. C. Lombroso and G. Ferrero, *La Femme criminelle et la prostituée* (Paris, 1896).
12. Alain Corbin, *Les Filles de noce* (Paris, 1978), 386–453.
13. Augustine *De ordine* 2.12, as cited in Corbin, *La Prostitution,* 216.
14. See reference for the two citations in Alexandre Parent-Duchâtelet, "De l'influence et de l'assainissement de salles de dissection," in *Hygiène publique,* 2:1; and "Des obstacles que les préjugés medicaux . . ." (1835), 51.
15. Alexandre Parent-Duchâtelet, *Les Chantiers d'écarrissage de la ville de Paris* (1832), 108.
16. Ibid.
17. Title of the second book of part 5 of Victor Hugo's novel, *Les Miserables.*
18. See the thesis of Jacques Termeau, *Les Prostituées et la vénalité sexuelle dans le Centre-Ouest de la France au temps de réglementarisme* (Tours, 1985).

CHRISTINE BUCI-GLUCKSMANN

Catastrophic Utopia: The Feminine as Allegory of the Modern

Introduction

FROM THE YOUNG WALTER BENJAMIN'S first critiques in 1913 of the lack of culture in modern erotic civilization—the absence of an *experience* of a feminine culture—to his recognition of woman as *allegory of the modern* displayed in the great Baudelairean images (prostitute, barren woman, lesbian, androgyne), the motif of the woman imposes, by its constancy, its persistence and wealth of meanings, all its interpretive radicality. Certainly, this motif is never direct: it is subject to the oblique, the fragment, the interstice between concept and metaphor. More than any other theme, it links the fictive, materialist reformulation of a reconstructed history with our lack of presence. It remains, secret and concealed, as if in a labyrinth—a labyrinth we must find our way through once again.

In "A Berlin Chronicle," Benjamin wrote that in the Proustian Berlin of childhood and recaptured memory—this city/forest, city/maze and labyrinth— he had found "that Ariadne in whose proximity I understood for the first time (and was never entirely to forget) something that was to make instantly comprehensible a word that . . . I cannot have known: love."[1] And when, in "Central Park" and *Passagen-Werk,* the metaphor of the labyrinth becomes intrusive, this first engraved souvenir and the *arcana* of Paris of the Second Empire's modernity reappear together. "With the rise of the great cities prostitution came into possession of new secrets. One of these is the labyrinthine character of the city itself. The labyrinth, whose image had passed into flesh and blood in the *flaneur,* is at the same time colorfully framed by prostitution" (CP, 53).

Passing from the labyrinths of big cities to the labyrinths of commodities, without omitting the ultimate labyrinth, history ("the home of the hesitant" where "the way of the [sexual] drive in those episodes that precede its satisfaction" curiously meets "the way of mankind which does not wish to know where things are leading" [CP, 42]), the theme of the labyrinth, occupied by the "desire not to know," defines a complete web of thoughts. It is here that the symbolic and imaginary divisions of the feminine are caught. Should we admit, in our turn, that the feminine today might be one of Ariadne's threads for retracing these entangled routes?

The question of woman finds itself at the exact point of recovery of two scenes in Benjamin's historical work—the "sociological" determination of history (industrialization, the creation of large cities, the domination of commodity fetishism) and modernity as an ensemble of fantastic spectacles and as a progressive aesthetic. With the representations that emerge in Baudelaire, their origins in the utopian currents of nineteenth-century France (Saint-Simonianism, Claire Demar's feminism, the history of sects), and their descendents in Alban Berg's *Lulu* or the "female/flower/pubescence" of the *Jugendstil*, Benjamin reconstructs a system of feminine fictions that characterize modernity. We could name this system, recalling his expression, an unconscious of vision that parallels the Freudian unconscious of desire.

Of this we can be certain: the image engraved upon the *flâneur's* body, the Baudelairean passerby barely glimpsed in the intoxication of large cities, this multiplicity of emotions are only specific examples of what is characteristic of modernity: the cult of images, the secularization/sublimation of bodies, their ephemeral nature and reproducibility. Here, the feminine constitutes one of the nineteenth-century's "original historic forms" *(urgeschichtlichen Formen)*, an origin *(Ursprung)* where a "prehistory" and a "posthistory" *(Vor- und Nachgeschichte)*, the archaic and the modern, are dialectically articulated. The feminine becomes the inevitable sign of a new historic regime of seeing and "not-seeing," of representable and unrepresentable.

My purpose is to resurvey the scene of this "original historic form," to delineate it as *a tragedy (Trauerspiel) of modernity's woman-body,* to add in reflection certain implications of Benjamin's notion of "utopia" or a-topia, as affected by "that excess that accompanies the feminine" described by Maurice Blanchot in his writing on Marguerite Duras's *La Maladie de la mort*[2]—an excess seen as "the undefinable power of the feminine over all that wills or imagines itself as foreign to it."

The "feminine" could delineate certain scenes of modernity, certain of its negative or positive utopias, which appear close to the spaces of the baroque with their multiple entrances and doubled, ambiguous aspects:

1) *"Catastrophic" utopia,* the destructive tendency toward appearance and false totality, where the feminine body is an allegory of modernity.

2) *Anthropological utopia,* the exploration of the underground history of the nineteenth century: that of androgyny as traced through Saint-Simonianism, Claire Demar, Ganeau, the history of sects, and Baudelaire—the scene of a matrix bisexuality of "anthropological materialism" *(PW, 971)* that has broken with the bloodless humanism of the "man as totality," of universal man *(Allmensch).*

3) *Transgressive utopia,* the sudden appearance in writing, as in historical praxis, of an absolute imaginary space *(hundertprozentigen Bildraums)* that dislocates estab-

lished frontiers and forces apparent "opposites" together in thought: catastrophe and progress, messianism and Marxism, feminine and masculine, novelty and repetition. [The discussion that follows takes up the first of these aspects.—Ed.]

Modernity and the Redistribution of Feminine/Masculine

There emerges in all its dimensions in Baudelaire's work a symbolic redistribution of relations between feminine and masculine that is characteristic both of modernity and of the archeological double scene (sociohistorical and aesthetic) of Benjamin's work as historian of nineteenth-century France. In the realm of sociology, there is the new status of women in large cities, subjected by work and urbanization to a certain sexual uniformity. The violent insertion of women into commodity production collapses both material (division of labor) and symbolic differences of sex. Women become mass-produced, widely available commodities with the "massification" of industrial labor and society, simultaneously losing their "natural" qualities (a feminine essence, a nature determined by child-bearing) and their poetic aura (beauty as the sublimating idealization that surrounds Dante's Beatrice).

This social dynamic urgently requires that the symbolic distinctions separating feminine and masculine be redefined, a task becoming all the more pressing in that the beginning of the nineteenth century is marked by the historical development of the first feminist movements. In the aesthetic realm, new representations of the feminine body already appear at work in the lyric experience of Baudelaire, the "feminized" poet victimized by his androgyny and offered at the marketplace like a prostitute.[3] Here, allegory's destructive impulse with regard to "natural" appearances and the social order, its saturnine gaze over a history in which the alienation and *attenuation of experience* (spleen, melancholy, ennui, emptiness) characteristic of modernity unfold, shatter the integrity of the Baudelairean poetic Self, which hereafter finds itself, as in a drunken frenzy, in the grip of that same "dissolution of the I" (*Lockerung des Ich*).

In his own destructive rage, confronting this impotence in a Calvary of solitude, Baudelaire, captured in all his ambivalence (historical, psychic, poetic) in Benjamin's analysis, discovers his own "androgyny" and identifies in turn with the prostitute, the image of modernity, and the lesbian, the heroic protest against that modernity.

The relation between the historic and aesthetic dimension is so close that Benjamin did not hesitate to write that "Baudelaire produces in his lyricism the sexually perverse figure who seeks its object in the streets" (*PW*, 343). Woman, like the poet, becomes one of the privileged sites for a mythological correspondence, in which "the modern world of technology and the archaic world of the symbol" (*PW*, 617) will be in play. This interweaving precisely characterizes a kind of modernity which differs radically from that of "progress" and which almost always emerges out of the extremity of a crisis: in seventeenth-century baroque, Baudelaire, *Jugendstil*, Viennese and German culture during the twentieth century. . . . For this reason, the perspective of "catastrophe" in the face of progress allows us to clearly separate two forms of modernity.

The first form of the modern produces progress and is informed by it. It arises out of the great Hegelian synthesis and is characterized by linear, cumulative time; development "without barbarity" of culture and production; classic and romantic aesthetics of the Beautiful; and a historical vision stemming from a subject that, even if alienated, gives it meaning in Marxist evolutionary and historical interpretations. Benjamin dislodges the second modernity from the constellation of Baudelaire, Nietzsche, and Louis Blanqui, for whom the destruction of the appearance of totality, system, and historical specificity acts as the condition for the eternal return of a catastrophic utopia: the recognition of atrocity, fragmentation, and destruction as critical forces.

This second form of modernity, which I will call *untimely* in Nietzsche's sense, establishes itself against "modernist" or "historicist" versions of modernity. It rests not on the fullness of a meaning, of a unified, perfectly intelligible history, but on a loss, an emptiness, a lack: the power of an absence, in relation to the "actual" immediate, that links signification and death. The ravaging power of spleen, the loss of the aura or the nihilistic emptying of values, this non-Hegelian negativity inscribes in writing the "blank space" evoked by Benjamin in describing Baudelaire as "envisioning blank spaces which he filled in with his poems" (*CB*, 116).

That this loss "of love," leading to melancholy, can be expressed in the new status of the "feminine" and its *modern allegories,* that it is embodied with all its violence and ambivalence in the figure of the prostitute—from Georg Büchner to Berg without forgetting Baudelaire—says a great deal about the phantoms that haunt it.

Indeed, the prostitute is one of those monads that open the way for the archeological work of reconstructing history. Benjamin's interest in the "nameless" (*Namelosen*) and the depths of history as well as literature, his constant desire to *"fix the image* of history in the humblest crystallizations," will produce a constellation of thoughts and images, a chaos of metaphors around this figure of the feminine, the tragic form of modernity.

The Tragedy *(Trauerspiel)* of the "Prostitute-Body"

The urban development of prostitution as a mass phenomenon leading to legislation, along with the visible "massification" of feminine bodies, expresses a historical change even more typical of the middle of the twentieth century— expressed in new relations between the visible and the invisible, the representable and unrepresentable, and their consequent practices and discourses. The feminine body is the preeminent site of "that archeology of the look" Foucault describes and which is not unrelated to Benjamin's concerns. Here indeed is a new staging of bodies, henceforth irreducible to their literal visibility, that is affected by an obscure, mysterious factor.

The increasingly "profound" visibility of the feminine body is at the center of Benjamin's many analyses of the role of makeup, artifice, style and of the new "feminine fauna" of *Passagen-Werk* (*PW*, 617). In the most direct perspective, "woman becomes a commodity" in prostitution and is displayed in the street, then in bordellos, to be purchased and consumed. Such a "commodity" conveys a new correlation between sex and work—the prostitute claims "worth" as labor and has a price at the very moment "when work becomes prostitution" (*PW*, 439). There is much more than a superficial historical analogy between the prostitute, who obtains an increasingly well-accounted for, both profitable and exploitative, payment for her time and attentions, and a commercial economy where everything has its price. For if salaried labor and the general extension of commodities mark the "decline" of the qualitative, of use value, of distinctions for the benefit of a more generalized social submission to the universality of exchange—by the very abstraction of its universality—so prostitution expresses the end of the aura and the decline *(Verfall)* of love (*PW*, 617).

In this outline of a political economy of the prostituted body, Benjamin achieves a veritable permeation of appearances that carries his analysis far beyond a socioeconomic examination of prostitution. "The revolutionary character of the technical" presents itself in prostitution: serial and serialized bodies, interchangeable like those put to work in a factory. But it is not just a question of regimentation; in the very mechanism of prostitution, there is "an unconscious knowledge of man"—the performance "through all the nuances of payment" of even "the nuances of love play [*Liebesspiel*], sometimes intimate, sometimes brutal" (*PW*, 615). In the strict sense, one does not so much buy pleasure as purchase that which commands it—"the expression of shame," "the desire for fanatic pleasure" in its most cynical form. In mass prostitution—which does not end with prostitutes—new anthropological figures and new figures of the passions, characteristic of modernity, are defined. Eros links itself to Thanatos; the love of pleasure joins with perversion; and what appears to be the language of Christianity merges (even in the work of Baudelaire) with the language of commodities.

Here lies, then, one of the threads of Ariadne of our labyrinth: the masculine desire to immobilize, to *petrify* the feminine body. In Benjamin's words, "In the inanimate body, which can however, give itself to pleasure, allegory unites with commodities."

By this union, one must understand the entire series of imaginary and symbolic equivalents that Benjamin will establish around the "prostitute-body." As one example, there is an equivalence between love for prostitutes, the form of

mythical communion common to big cities, and empathy *(Einfühlung)* for commodities. A more decisive equivalence occurs between new markings of feminine
bodies, their *traces,* and the destructive violence of allegory, which creates a
second-degree allegory from the prostitute—that of "the allegory of commodities."

For this reason, the tragedy *(Trauerspiel)* of the prostituted body is organized
by the double movement characteristic of allegoric violence—a *disfiguration* and
devalorization of all reality, followed by its phantasmagoric *humanization.*

Disfiguration/devalorization—henceforth, the woman has lost her aura, her
religious and cultic presence, her absolute unity, her feminine body as an
announcement of the celestial beauty of love. Beauty herself no longer sees nor
speaks. Her eyes, pure and inexpressive mirrors, are from this point on closed
to every idealized and sublimated belief. *Beauty has become petrified* (PW, 411).

As Baudelaire writes in his poem "La Beauté":

> *Je suis belle, ô mortels! comme un rêve de pierre,*
> *Et mon sein, où chacun s'est meurtri tour à tour,*
> *Est fait pour inspirer au poète un amour*
> *Éternel et muet ainsi que la matière.*

> [I am beautiful, O mortals, as a dream in stone, and my breast, on which
> every man has bruised himself in his turn, is formed to inspire in poets
> a love as eternal and as silent as matter itself; author's italics.][4]

This dream of stone, this petrified, materialized love, mute as Benjamin's haunt-
ing images of allegory "as image of a *petrified* anxiety" (PW, 414) or as a "*petrified*
primordial landscape" (OT, 166), returns to the double movement that affects
the love object in modernity. If, since the civilization of the Middle Ages, there
is no love object but the unreal as reflected by the phantasm in what Erich
Auerbach calls the *figural* in relation to Dante, the loss of the aura can then only
be a double loss, to be read and seen in the scenographies of the feminine.

In one sense, this loss leads to that sublimation of love which links Beauty to
Truth and makes the figure of the female (such as Beatrice's image in the *Divine
Comedy*) the mediatress of another, more "celestial" love, that of Paradise. The
Beauty of the "immortals" becomes the "dream of stone" of *mortals.* The poet
deciphers contingency, mortality, his own "castration" in the feminine body; Baudelairean poetry is indeed, as Benjamin says in a striking formula, "a mimesis of
death." Thus the radical separation, always possible, between the erotic and love
that is represented by the prostitute.

But in another sense, this "dream of stone" also expresses an alteration of
desire: the inscription of a desire for its cessation in lyric experience. This perverse paralysis has, as an ultimate goal, precisely the love of prostitutes and
masculine impotence. From this derives the new polarization of desire so characteristic of Baudelaire: either a perverse pleasure or a mystical consummation—
if it is true that, as Benjamin observes, "masculine impotency feeds precisely on

the attachment to the seraphic image of the female." In this polarity of desire, Benjamin's analysis partially coincides with that of Lacan: "The body as final signified, this is the corpse of the *stone phallus*."[5]

Beauty petrified can only be a travesty of itself. Benjamin shows particular interest in artifice, disguise, and fashion, going so far as to see in the prostitute's rituals of makeup an anticipation of twentieth-century chorus lines. But these travesties do not succeed in dissembling the drawn-out labor of death that infests Eros. The Freudian *uncanny* finds a distant origin in the ontological aging of the body (e.g., the Baudelairean interest in the "petites vieilles") and the "erotology" of the skeleton where a "terrible and monstrous" beauty is found. As Baudelaire writes, "Ô charme d'un néant follement attifé" (O lure of nothingness so well tricked out!) and "Ô beauté, monstre énorme, effrayant, ingénu" (O beauty, huge, frightening, ingenuous monster).[6]

In this de-idealized beauty, stripped by the allegorist's destructive gaze at appearances, in this curious "ontology" of feminine absence "well tricked out," the woman's body, deprived of its maternal-body, becomes desirable only in its passage to the limit: as death-body, fragmented-body, petrified-body. It is as if the death of the organic body could only be represented as feminine in Baudelaire's interiorizing and subjectivizing of death, indeed to the point of being central to the perception of reality. John E. Jackson points out in his excellent book *La Mort-Baudelaire* that, since Büchner, the body's finitude, its characteristic ontological corruptibility and the aesthetic of fragmentation it induces, is crystallized in prostitution.[7] Witness Danton's love of prostitutes, as when he searches "for the Venus of Medici piece by piece among all the grisettes of the Palais Royal . . . making a mosaic, as he says. Heaven knows what limb he's at right now. It's a shame that nature has cut up beauty into pieces—like Medea her brother—and has put the fragments into our bodies."[8]

Prostituted, dispersed, and fragmented bodies themselves express the destructive impulse of allegory—with its loss of aura, veils, immortality. But this destructive utopia is also critical; though regressive, it admits of a positive aspect— "the dissipation [*Austreibung*] of appearances," the demystification of all reality that presents itself as an "order," a "whole," a "system" (PW, 411). From this point of view, modernity is a *mission*, a "conquest" (CP, 35).

Paradoxically, the prostituted body is not only a fragment, a ruin of nature, a disfigurement of the "sublime body." It is also staged by and in new fictions of style, play, image, all the "phantasmagoria" that provoke the myriad stimulations of modernity. It is thereby re-idealized and humanized: the prostitute represents the way "the commodity attempts to look itself in the face. It celebrates its becoming human in the [prostitute]" (CP, 42)—becoming human and something more: the plenitude of allegory itself. Thus, in Baudelaire's work "the prostitute could be the commodity that fulfills the allegoric vision of plenitude."

In this baroque approach to the feminine body, allegory presents itself in its *modern* interpretation. We wish to emphasize all the implications of this in this statement: *only the status of the feminine as a simultaneously real and fictive body permits a differentiation between modern and baroque allegory.*

The Woman-Body as Interpretive Principle of Modern Allegory

Like all allegory in Benjamin's sense, and contrary to the romantics', modern allegory shares certain features with baroque allegory, that origin (*Ursprung*) of modernity. To summarize:

—Allegory, as both rhetorical figure and as interpretation, simultaneously destroys and demystifies the real in its tidy, well-ordered totality. In its destructive intent, allegory *strips* the real by fragmenting it: reality appears as a ruin. In this process, history itself emerges in its most saturnine aspects and as representation.

—Such a development produces that *emotional writing* characteristic of allegory. This writing paralyzes itself in scenes; it represents itself. One of the key points in Benjamin's interpretation of allegory rests precisely on its visual character: allegory works with images, sight, scenes that link the visible and the invisible, life and dream. History presents itself to be *seen* with all its ambivalence fixed *in tableaux*. Like mysticism, history practices a language of bodies, and so "the observer is confronted with the 'facies hippocratica' of history as a petrified primordial landscape" (*als erstarrte Urlandschaft*; *OT*, 166).

—Because history emerges here in its catastrophic and fictive inclination (hence the theatrical models of Calderon, Shakespeare, and Gryphius), the alterity of tragedy, the perception of time as henceforth secularized, occurs in and through sentiment: mourning, affliction (*Trauer*), and play (*Spiel*). History refers back to a typology of passions and to a complete anthropology.

—In this distanced, passionate, and impassioning writing, the oxymoron is the dominant rhetorical figure, staging extremes and contradictions without ever exceeding them. "Nothingness" is "decked out," as in "icy fire" and "dark light."

One can say that allegory is an antidialectic, or to use Benjamin's expression *a dialectic at the state of arrest*, a frozen dialectic, fixed in images.

If these are the principal characteristics of allegory, its modernity, in contrast, is linked by Benjamin to a precise point: its relation to death. "Baroque allegory sees the corpse only from the outside. Baudelaire sees it also from the inside" (*CP*, 51). By leaving the exterior world for the interior, by creating an endopsychic (in Freud's terminology) image from death, *modern* allegory rids itself of certain of the limitations of the baroque, establishing itself henceforth on the foundation of a double disappearance. In the modern allegory, salvation, the present/absent redemption of the baroque, disappears. Modern time is radically secularized, occurring without transcendence or future, and is periodized by the always new and always the same. Likewise, the opposition nature/cosmos vanishes as a totality, a metaphoric, "objective" reserve—a disappearance already evident in romantic irony, particularly in Jean-Paul's works.

From now on, what "body" could give a "body" to the destructive impulse of an increasingly "feminized" poet, expelled from the great models of paternal filiation and mimicked by his own "depths"? The feminine body, which polarizes the sadistic and perverse impulse of the allegoric look: "For it [allegory] to touch things means to violate them, to know them means to unmask them." Literally. As proof:

—The woman's body presents itself, in Baudelaire's work, as a "baroque enumeration of details" *(barocke Detaillierung;* referring to "Beau Navire," *PW*, 415).

—The woman's body, as well, in particular the prostituted body, stands as a metaphor for extremes: desire/death, animating/agitating, life/corruption, skeleton . . . and serves to materially convert that "petrified anxiety" *(erstarrter Unruhe) that is the same formula as "the Baudelairean image of life"* (Lebensbild), the image "that knows no development" *(PW*, 414).

—Finally, it is always the real/fictive body that provides modern allegory with the conditions of its existence, its visibility, and all that turns around the "image" *(Bild)*. For this reason, as we have seen, the scenarios of the "feminine-body" serve as metaphors for those of the "commodity-body."

One could multiply these practices, which doubtless all refer to the most secret and pregnant one, that of the *abyss*. This Baudelairean abyss—an inclination for chasm-like ruin and nothingness—accompanied by modern figures of mourning (spleen and melancholy) lives through a *continuous metaphor,* that of the feminine sex. An abyss without end exciting anguish and impotence, an abyss where the poet henceforth undergoes pregnancy as "a disloyal competition." As Benjamin remarks in his most beautiful fragment, "The abyss-like meaning is to be defined as signification. It is always allegorical" *(PW*, 347). However, if in Blanqui "the abyss is a star," defining itself in the space of the world and finding its historical index in the natural sciences, in Baudelaire's works "it is without a star." It is not even "the exoticism of theology; it is secularized: an abyss of knowledge and of signification" *(PW*, 347).

In this suggestive parallel, Benjamin questions himself on the historical index of the Baudelairean abyss, connecting it to fashion, its twin, and suggesting that this index could be "the arbitrariness of allegory itself" *(PW*, 348). In our turn, we suggest here that this historical index is not without a connection to the change in relations between feminine and masculine that emerged in mid-century in Baudelaire's work.

—Translated by Katharine Streip

228 CHRISTINE BUCI-GLUCKSMANN

Notes

This article is comprised of the introduction and the first section of "L'Utopie féminin," part 2 of the author's *La Raison baroque: De Baudelaire à Benjamin* (Paris: Editions Galilée, 1984)—Ed.

1. Walter Benjamin, *One-Way Street and Other Writings,* trans. Edmund Jephcott and Kingsley Shorter (London, 1979), 294. Other works by Benjamin cited in the text: "Central Park" (CP), trans. Lloyd Spencer, *New German Critique* 34 (Winter 1985): 32–58; *Charles Baudelaire: A Lyric Poet in the Era of High Capitalism (CB),* trans. Harry Zohn (London, 1973); *Das Passagen-Werk (PW),* ed. Rolf Tiedemann (Frankfurt, 1983); *The Origin of German Tragic Drama (OT),* trans. John Osborne (London, 1977).
2. Maurice Blanchot, *La Communauté inavouable* (Paris, 1983), 87 and 91.
3. On Baudelaire's androgyny, see Michel Butor, *Histoire Extraordinaire,* trans. Richard Howard (London, 1969); and Leo Bersani, *Baudelaire and Freud* (Berkeley, 1977). Bersani links this androgyny to the loss of virility and the dislocation of the Baudelairean subject.
4. Francis Scarfe, ed. and trans., *Baudelaire* (Baltimore, 1961), 26.
5. Jacques Lacan, "La Relation d'objet," unpublished seminar cited by Monique David-Ménard in *L'Hysterique entre Freud et Lacan* (Paris, 1983).
6. Richard Howard, trans., *The Flowers of Evil* (Boston, 1983), 102; Scarfe, *Baudelaire,* 223.
7. John E. Jackson, *La Mort-Baudelaire* (Neuchâtel, 1982). The book concentrates on this "interiorization" of death.
8. Georg Büchner, *The Complete Collected Works,* ed. and trans. Henry J. Schmidt (New York, 1977), 31.

List of Contributors

THOMAS LAQUEUR is the author of *Religion and Respectability: Sunday Schools and Working-Class Culture, 1780–1850* (New Haven, 1976); his current interests are in medical history and the history of discourses connected with the body and with sexuality. He is Professor of History at University of California, Berkeley.

LONDA SCHIEBINGER teaches in the Program in Values, Technology, Science, and Society at Stanford University; she received her Ph.D. in 1984 from the Department of History, Harvard University. She was recently awarded a grant from the Rockefeller Foundation (Gender Roles Program) to work on her book, *Women and the Origins of Modern Science*.

CATHERINE GALLAGHER's *The Industrial Reformation of English Fiction* was published in 1985 by University of Chicago Press. She is Associate Professor of English at University of California, Berkeley. Her current research focuses on the connection between economic and sexual ideologies in women's fiction.

D. A. MILLER is Associate Professor of English and Comparative Literature at University of California, Berkeley. He is the author of *Narrative and Its Discontents: Problems of Closure in the Traditional Novel* (Princeton, N.J., 1981).

MARY POOVEY is Associate Professor of English at Swarthmore College. She is the author of *The Proper Lady and the Woman Writer: Ideology as Style in the Works of Mary Wollstonecraft, Mary Shelley, and Jane Austen* (Chicago, 1984) and is currently working on a book entitled *Uneven Developments: Social and Literary Representations of Victorian Women*.

LAURA ENGELSTEIN has published *Moscow 1905: Working-Class Organization and Political Conflict* (Stanford, Calif., 1982) and is currently writing a book on the Sexual Question in Russia, 1860–1914. She teaches history at Princeton University.

ALAIN CORBIN is the author of *Les Filles de noce: Misère sexuelle et prostitution, 19ᵉ et 20ᵉ siècles* (Paris, 1978), *Le Miasme et la jonquille: L'Odorat et l'imaginaire social, XVIIIᵉ—XIXᵉ siècles* (Paris, 1982), and *Archaisme et modernité en Limousin au XIXᵉ siècle, 1845–1880* (Paris, 1975). He teaches at Université de Tours.

CHRISTINE BUCI-GLUCKSMANN is Director of Research at the Centre national du recherche scientifique, Paris. She is the author of *La Raison baroque: De Baudelaire à Benjamin* (Paris, 1984), from which the present essay is taken, and *Walter Benjamin und die Utopie des Weiblichen*, among other works.

Index

Abortion cases, 49
Abyss, allegorical, 228
Academy of Military Medicine, Russia, 189
Ackermann, Jakob, 51–53, 59, 62, 64, 70, 75
Adler, L., 31
Albinus, Bernhard Siegfried, 52, 53–54, 58, 60–61, 62, 76
Albucasis, 16
Alexander II, 176
Allegory of the modern, feminine as, 221, 227–29
Anal contact, syphilis spread by, 174, 188
Anatomie of the Body of Man, 15–16
Anatomy, 3–16. *See also* Skeleton studies
Anatomy (Cheselden), 58
Anatomy of the Humane Bones, 56, 58
Androgyny, 13, 221, 222, 229
Anesthesia, 137–61 passim, 166, 168
Animals: female reproductive organs compared with, 5, 16, 76; human skeletons compared with, 62; male-female similarities among, 13; reproductive biology of, 3, 25–31, 34, 38
Anthropological utopia, 221
Anthropologie, 71
Apollo, 49, 58
Apothecaries, Victorian, 149
Apothecaries' Society, 149, 150, 162
Appeal of One-Half the Human Race, 22–23
Aquinas, Thomas, 213
Araeteus the Cappadocian, 9
Aristotle, 2, 7, 13, 53; on semination, 36–37; on women, children, and slaves, 66, 78–79; on women's natures, 46, 74, 79
Arnott, James, 144
Ascetic traditions, 86
Astell, Mary, 47, 53

Asylum, in *Woman in White*, 113–14, 119–22, 124–25
Auerbach, Erich, 225
Augustine, 213–14
Authority, 18
Aveling, James Hobson, 164, 165–66
Aversion therapy, for homosocial desire, 131, 133
Avicenna, 7, 9

Bacon, F., 210
Baglio, 53
Barbers, Russian syphilitic, 186
Barchester Towers, 113, 118–19
Barclay, John, 59, 61, 62, 63, 64–65, 77
Barrenness, pleasure and, 9
Barrows, Susanna, 18
Barthélemy, Toussaint, 176
Barthes, Roland, 116, 126
Baudelaire, Charles, 221–29
Bauhin, Gaspard, 13–14, 54
Beard, Dr., 162–63
Beast, Malthus's, 97, 100, 103
Beaumont, John, 166
"Beauté," 225
Beauty: prostitute-body and, 225–26; Soemmerring's norm of, 62
Beecher, 210
Bell, Andrew, 77
Benjamin, Walter, 220–29
Bentovin, Boris, 188
Berg, Alban, 221, 223
Berlin, Proustian, 220
"Berlin Chronicle," 220
Bersani, Leo, 229
Biblical tradition, male dominion in, 66
Bichat, Xavier, 211
Bidloo, Godfried, 49–50, 54, 58
Biology. *See* Body
Birth of Mankynde, 166
Bischoff, Theodor L. W., 26, 28, 33, 41, 67, 71, 72
Blacks, 64, 70–71, 80

Blackwell, Antoinette Brown, 81
Blanchot, Maurice, 221
Blanqui, Louis, 223, 228
Bleak House, 113
Bleeding, 8–9, 37. *See also* Menstruation
Blumenbach, Johann Friederich, 25, 28
Bodard, Pierre-Henri-Hippolyte, 77
Body, 18–19; and social body, 4, 12, 16, 19, 35, 66, 83–106. *See also* Anatomy; Female body; Healthy bodies; Male body; Physiology; Reproduction
Boerhaave, Herman, 9, 37
Bonaparte, Marie, 15
Borie, Jean, 29
Bosnia, syphilis in, 173
"Bowels of Leviathan," 216
Braddon, Mary Elizabeth, 121–22
Brains, 78–79, 81, 89–90; sex differences in, 43, 46–47, 64–81 passim
Brontë, Charlotte, 120
Brooks, Peter, 117
Brotherhood, 131–32
Brown, Julie Vail, 207
Browne, Thomas, 13, 38
Büchner, Georg, 223, 226
Buci-Glucksmann, Christine, 220–29
Bucknill, John Charles, 163–64
Buffon, Georges-Louis Leclerc de, 76, 148
Bulkley, L. Duncan, 169, 170, 174, 188
Burdach, Karl, 75
Burrows, George, 150–51, 152, 166, 167
Butler, Josephine, 209

Cabinis, Pierre-Jean-Georges, 36
Canon, 7
"Care in the Use of Chloroform," 147–48
Carlyle, Thomas, 99
Carpenter, Edward, 135
Carter, Robert Brudenell, 155, 163
Catastrophic utopia, 221–29
Catherine the Great, 189
Cats, in heat, 30
Censorship, syphilis prevention and, 192
"Central Park," 220
Cesspools, 214
Chabanais, 218
Chamber of Deputies, 213, 214
Chamberlens, 138
Chereau, Achilles, 27
Cheselden, William, 49, 54, 58
Childbirth, 146–47, 156–57; with anesthesia, 137–38, 139–43, 147, 151,

159, 166. *See also* Labor, child-birthing; Midwives/Midwifery
Childlikeness, of women, 63–66
Children: sexual activity of, 187–88; and skeleton studies, 63, 64–65, 66; syphilis effects on, 181
Chloroform, 137–48 passim, 153–56, 160–61, 166, 168
Choulant, Ludwig, 58
Christian ascetic traditions, 86
Circulation, social/body, 97–98, 100, 102
Circumscription, of prostitution, 214, 216–217
Cities. *See* Urban areas
Class, social: Russian, 169–99. *See also* Lower classes; Middle class
Class conflict, 102
Classical ascetic traditions, 86
Clinic, birth of, in France, 210
Clitoris, 1; homologies of, 3, 14–16
Coates, W. Martin, 160–61
Codpiece, 15, 16
Collins, Wilkie, 107–36
Colombus, Readolus, 14, 16
Commercial sexuality. *See* Prostitution
Commodities: value of, 95–96, 102–3; women as, 222, 224, 228
Comte, Auguste, 69
Concealment, of prostitution, 214–15
Conception, 1–2, 3, 7, 10–11
Condorcet, M., 1, 67, 83, 87–88, 92
Conolly, John, 167
Consultants, Victorian medical, 150, 152
Contagion, syphilis, 169–208, 212
Contagious Diseases Act (1866), 209
Control, of women, 147, 151–53, 155. *See also* Incarceration
Corbin, Alain, 209–19
Costermongers, Mayhew's, 91, 97, 99–102, 103–5
Cott, Nancy, 39
Councils, of Royal Colleges, 150
Cours de philosophie positive, 69
Cowper, William, 49–50
Crooke, Helkiah, 15, 16, 78
Cruickshank, William, 25
Culpepper, Nicholas, 15
Cunning, female, 163
Cuvier, Georges, 69

d'Alembert, J., 67
d'Arconville, Marie-Geneviève-Charlotte Thiroux, 43, 54–64 passim, 73, 77, 78
Darwin, Charles, 65, 81

Death: from chloroform, 137–38; in
    modern allegory, 227–28; in pros-
    titute image, 211–12, 225–26
de Bordeu, Théophile, 210
De corporis humani fabrica, 48–49
de Gouges, Olympe, 68
de Graaf, Regnier, 2, 25
De humani corporis fabrica, 12
de la Bretonne, Restif, 210
De la prostitution dans la ville de Paris, 189
Delavau, Commissioner, 216
Demar, Claire, 221
Democracy, 18, 67
Democritus, 7, 36, 53
De ordine, 213–14
Desire/Passion, 4, 9–11, 20–30 passim,
    35, 88–89. *See also* Pleasure
d'Héricourt, Jenny, 81
Dickens, Charles, 113, 120
Diday, Paul, 174
Diderot, Denis, 21, 76
Diets, women's, 66, 79
Differentiation, of sexes, 2–4, 16–24,
    30–35 passim; in skeleton studies,
    4, 42–82
Discourse on Inequality, 19–20
Disease/Disorder, 41; nervous, 146–47,
    150–51, 153, 154, 163, 167, 168;
    syphilis, 41, 169–208, 209, 211,
    212; woman as, 41, 146–47, 155,
    163–64
Dispensary, for prostitute examination,
    216
Dissection, 49, 74, 211, 214
Doctors. *See* Physicians
"Doctrine of crisis," 146
Dogs, reproductive biology of, 3, 25, 26,
    30
Dohm, Hedwig, 72
Domestic ideology, 22, 23, 24, 40
Douglas, Mary, 4
Drugs, heat-producing, 10
Dubois, Baron, 142–43, 144, 161
Duncan, Mathews, 28
Duncum, Barbara M., 160
Duras, Marguerite, 221
Duval, Jacques, 15, 16

Economy. *See* Political economy
Edinburgh method, of chloroform ap-
    plication, 137, 144, 161
Education, syphilis prevention, 196–97,
    198
Efimov, Aleksandr, 179, 192, 193
Egg, 27, 39, 75

Eisenstein, Zillah, 23
Ellis, Havelock, 16, 32, 160
Ellis, Sarah, 22, 24
Elshtain, Jean, 19
El'tsina, Zinaida, 187, 205
Embryology, 3–4
Emile, 20, 67
Emotionalism, female, 163
Encyclopédie, 68
Engelstein, Laura, 169–208
England: female skeleton drawings in,
    42, 53, 54, 68; land in, 96, 99;
    medical practice in, 141, 142, 149,
    161, 162, 164; population growth
    in, 93. *See also* Victorians
Enlightenment, 1–41, 83, 86, 90
Enquiries into Vulgar and Common Errors, 13
Epitome, 48
Equality. *See* Inequality, sexual
Erismann, Friedrich, 175
Essay on the Principles of Population,
    83–87, 91–98, 103, 105
Estrous, 31, 41
Ether, 137, 139, 141–44, 147, 160
Europe: medicine in, 170, 174, 175,
    177, 189, 198; problematization/
    valorization of body in, 90;
    syphilis in, 171, 196; women's po-
    sition in, 42–43, 46, 63–72 passim,
    222. *See also individual countries*
Exchange, economic, 93–96, 102, 103
Excitation, under anesthesia, 142–44,
    147–48, 160, 161
Experimentation, chloroform use and,
    141

Falret, Jules, 153, 154
Fedchenko, Nikolai, 176, 181–82, 186
Fedorov, Aleksandr, 189, 191
Female body, 1–18 passim, 24, 27–35,
    222, 223–28; orgasm in, 1–12 pas-
    sim, 17, 35, 37, 167; prostitute
    submissive, 212–13; sexual ho-
    mologies of, 2–16 passim, 27, 35,
    38, 74, 75, 76; skeleton studies of,
    4, 42–82; Victorian medical practi-
    tioners and, 144–47, 151–55,
    165–66. *See also* Nervousness, fe-
    male; Reproduction
Female Reader, 23–24
Females. *See* Women
Female Spectator, 71
Femininity: as allegory of modernity,
    220–29; nature defining, 62, 70,
    72; in *Woman in White,* 110–12,

Femininity (*cont.*)
 115, 118, 121, 130–31, 136. *See also* Differentiation, of sexes
Feminism, 1; on childbirthing practices, 138; early movements of, 46–47, 222; of fictional madwoman, 120; and passionlessness, 24, 35; Rousseau and, 67; science related to, 72; on sex differences, 18, 19, 32–33, 46–47
Ferrero, G., 212
Fertility: period of, 36; and pleasure, 9
Fiaux, Louis, 211
Figural, 225
Finnegan, Frances, 211
Fluids, body, 8–9, 37. *See also* Bleeding; Semen
Food: production of, 93, 95–96, 99, 102, 103–4; for women, 66, 79
Forceps, 138, 148
Foucault, Michel, 224
Fournier, Alfred, 174, 188, 199
France, 36, 220, 222; female skeleton drawings in, 42, 53, 54, 58, 68; midwives required at dissections in, 49; prostitution in, 199, 209–19; sex differences explored in, 18, 42, 51, 53, 67–68, 69; syphilis in, 199, 209, 211, 212
Franklin, Benjamin, 105
Frederick the Great, 9
Freedom of speech, syphilis prevention and, 192
French Revolution, 18, 36, 67
Freud, Sigmund/Freudianism, 129, 133, 221, 226
Functional organization, of prostitution, 215–16, 217

Galen/Galenism, 53, 78; Aristotle and, 36–37; homologies of, 2, 3, 4, 5, 12, 14, 16, 74; on sex differences, 46, 48, 74, 75, 76; on sexual pleasure, 4, 5, 7, 9; on women's child-likeness, 66
Gall, F. J., 64
Gallagher, Catherine, 22, 83–106
Gambetta, Léon, 214
Ganeau, 221
Ganong, W. F., 34–35
Gardner, Augustus, 27
Garnier, Germain/Marie, 13
General Council of Medical Education and Registration, Great Britain, 165

General practitioners, Victorian, 150, 151, 152
Genital contact, syphilis spread by, 172–73, 174. *See also* Reproductive organs
Germany: female skeleton drawings in, 42, 53, 54; Proustian Berlin in, 220; and sex differences, 42, 51, 53, 68–69
Germ-layer theory, 3
Gertsenshtein, Grigorii, 178, 180, 183, 189, 191
Gilbert, Sandra M., 119, 120
Girdwood, G. F., 30
Gladstone, W. E., 157
Glandular theory, 210
Godwin, William, 22, 83–94 passim
Goldfinger, 128
Goncharov, Konstantin, 184
Goodman, A., 160
Govorkov, Pavel, 177–78, 190, 191–92
Gower, S., 160
Gratsianov, Petr, 190, 192, 197
Gratsianskii, Petr, 171, 189
Gream, G. T., 143–44
Great Britain: medical professions and practices in, 141–49 passim, 161, 162, 165; regulation of diseases in, 209; skeleton drawings in, 42, 53, 54, 68; women's suffrage movement in, 18. *See also* England
Gregory, George, 148, 164
Gregory, Samuel, 148
Gubar, Susan, 119, 120

Haeckel, Ernst, 193
Haighton, John, 25
Halford, Henry, 165–66
Haller, Albrecht von, 9, 17, 28, 39, 53
Handbuch der Physiologie, 27
Hares, sexual homology of, 13, 38
Harvey, William, 48, 75, 211
Haussmannization, 217–18
Haywood, Eliza, 71
Health, public, 169–208, 209–10, 214
Health manuals, 69, 80
Healthy bodies, 83–86, 93, 97. *See also* Disease/Disorder
Heape, Walter, 31–32, 41
Heat, sexual, 4–13 passim, 20, 27–37 passim, 75
Hegel, G., 64, 70
Height, sex differences in, 66
Helvétius, C. A., 67

Hemorrhoidal bleeding, 9, 37
Henle, Jakob, 10
Hensen, V., 26–27
Hermagoras, 66
Hermann, L., 27
Herophilus, 2
Hierarchy, 46; by sexual homologies, 3, 4–16, 35. *See also* Inequality, sexual
Hippel, Theodor, 68
Hippocrates, 9, 46
Hippocratic school, 4, 7, 8, 36, 210
Hips, women's, 58, 59
Historicism, 223
Hitschmann, F., 31
Hobbes, T., 18, 19, 24
Hocquenghem, Guy, 115
Hoffmann, Paul, 46
Holmes, Oliver Wendell, 153
Holst, Amelia, 81
Homologies: body/society, 84–86, 100; sexual, 2–16 passim, 27, 35, 38, 48–49, 74, 75, 76
Homosexuality: female, 128, 136, 188, 222; male, 112, 115, 118, 131–36 passim
Horses, male skeletons like, 62
Hugo, Victor, 216
Humboldt, Wilhelm von, 70
Hume, David, 83, 84
Humors, doctrine of, 42, 46, 48, 75, 210
Huxley, Aldous, 25
Hydrogen-oxygen ratio, sex differences in, 75
Hysteria, 146–47, 153, 154, 168

Illegitimacy, in Russia, 179, 203
Images, of prostitutes, 210–13
Incarceration: for disease, 193, 207; female, 113–14, 119–22, 124–25, 130–31, 135; for insanity, 113–14, 119–22, 124–25, 207
Incommensurability, of women and men, 72; biology of, 3, 18, 19, 24, 30, 31, 35
Inequality, sexual, 1, 73; and brain equality, 46–47; sex differences justifying, 18–21, 32–34, 43, 53, 66, 67–72
Insane, incarceration of, 113–14, 119–22, 124–25, 207
Intelligence, 43, 46–47, 64–81 passim, 89–90
Irish women costermongers, 101
Isolation, of prostitution, 214, 216–17

Itching, 7

Jackson, John E., 226
Jacobi, Mary Putnam, 32–34
John Chrysostom, Saint, 38
Jouard, G., 75
Jove, 4
Jugendstil, 221, 223
Juno, 4

Kant, Immanuel, 43, 71
Klose, Carl Ludwig, 53, 75
Kovalevskii, P. I., 208

Labia, homologies of, 3, 14
Labor, childbirthing: anesthesia during, 139–40, 147, 159, 166; pain during, 12, 142–43, 157, 159; sexual excitement during, 143, 147; sexual pleasure consoling for, 12
Labor force: productive, 91–103 passim; unproductive, 91–92, 95, 97, 99–100. *See also* Value, theory of; Working class
Labyrinths, 220–21, 224
Lacan, Jacques, 2, 226
Lady Audley's Secret, 121–22
Lancereaux, Etienne, 174, 200
Lancet: chloroform debate in, 137, 138, 139, 142, 147–48, 154, 160, 165, 166; on menstruation, 27
Laqueur, Thomas, 1–41
Latin Quarter, prostitution and death in, 211
Law of Diminishing Returns, 105
Laycock, Thomas, 145, 146, 162, 163, 167
Lee, Robert, 154
Legal judgment, in *Woman in White*, 112–13, 114–15
Leonardo da Vinci, 6, 12
Lepine, Prefect, 218
Lesbianism, 128, 136, 188, 222
Lettres Persanes, 43
Liberalism, 19, 23, 43
Locke, John, 43, 73
Lombroso, C., 212
London Labour and the London Poor, 90–91
London Medical Dictionary, 2
London midwives, 164
Lotichium, J. P., 46
Love, 220, 225
Lower classes: English, 90–105 passim, 164; Russian, 177, 182–83 (*see also*

Lower classes (*cont.*)
  Rural syphilis, Russian); women
  of, 213 (*see also* Prostitution). *See
  also* Working class
Lulu, 221

Mac Bride, 210
Maclean, Ian, 46, 48, 74, 76
Maisons de rendez-vous, 218
Maladie de la mort, 221
Male body, 1, 2–18, 24, 31; orgasm in,
  5–7, 9–12; sexual homologies of,
  2–16, passim, 27, 35, 38, 74, 75,
  76; skeleton studies of, 46–50 pas-
  sim, 56–57, 63–71 passim
Male bonds, 131–32; homosexual, 112,
  115, 118, 131–36 passim
Males. *See* Men
Malthus, Thomas, 22, 83–90, 91–98,
  102–6 passim
Mangin, Commissioner, 214, 216
Manual of Obstetrics, 144
Manuals, medical, 69, 80
Maria Theresa, Princess, 16–17
Marriage, 23, 84, 85, 151, 164
Masculinity: nature defining, 62, 70, 72;
  in *Woman in White,* 127, 129, 130.
  See also Differentiation, of sexes
Maturity, of women, 63–66, 78
Mayhew, Henry, 90–91, 97–98, 99–102,
  103–5
Medical Act (1858), 165
Medical manuals, 69, 80
Medical Question, 51
Medicine: Russian, 169–208; Victorian,
  137–68, 173–74. *See also*
  Anatomy; Midwives/Midwifery;
  Physicians; Physiology
Medici Venus, 49–50, 58
Meigs, Dr., 140, 141, 149
Men, 1; homosexual, 112, 115, 118,
  131–36 passim; and prostitution,
  182, 195–96, 209, 224, 225–26;
  studying women, 32, 43, 64, 72,
  137–68 (*see also* Anatomy; Physiol-
  ogy). *See also* Male body; Maculin-
  ity; Sexuality
Menstruation, 8–9, 10, 27–37 passim,
  146, 180
Mental capacities, 43, 46–47, 64–81 passim, 89–90
Michelet, J., 9, 26, 32
Middle class: childlike women in, 66;
  medical treatment of, 164; nervousness marking, 110; prostitutes

serving, 213; Russian, 177; work-
  ing class view by, 104
Midwives/Midwifery, 81, 150, 151, 152,
  162, 164, 165–166; and anesthe-
  sia, 137, 139, 140, 149, 158, 165;
  dissections to be attended by, 49;
  (W. T.) Smith on, 144, 148–49,
  158; and women's scientific capac-
  ities, 70
Mill, J. S., 69
Mill, James, 22
Millar, John, 21–22
Miller, D. A., 107–36
Miller, John Hawkins, 156
Miscarriages, syphilis and, 181
Mitchell, S. Weir, 153
Modernity, women as allegory of,
  220–29
Modesty, female, 20, 21, 143, 147
Mole eyes, female reproductive organs
  like, 5, 16
Money, Malthus on, 93–97
Monro, Alexander, 56–58
Montaigne, M., 13
Montesquieu, C., 43, 105
Montpellier Codex (1363), 49
Moonstone, 112
Moore, Dr., 165
Moore, Philip, 38
Moral anthropology, 2–3
Morality: and prostitution, 169–208,
  209, 213–14; versus scientific
  credibility, 71–72, 81; of sensation
  fiction, 118–19; sex differences in,
  2–3, 22–24, 29–30, 68, 71, 72, 80,
  168; of women writers, 22, 39–40,
  72
More, Hannah, 22
Moreau, Edmond Thomas, 51
Moreau, Jacques-Louis, 53, 60, 78, 80
Moreau, Thérèse, 32
Mort-Baudelaire, 226
Motherhood, 43, 53, 68. *See also* Repro-
  duction
Muller, Johannes, 26, 29

Nana, 210
Natural law, 43, 67–72, 168. *See also*
  Body
"Natural reason," 43, 64, 72. *See also* In-
  telligence
Negroes, 64, 70–71, 80
Nemesius, 2
Neo-Hippocratism, 210. *See also* Hippo-
  cratic school

Nervousness, female: disorders of, 146–47, 150–51, 153, 154, 163, 167, 168; in male homosexual, 134–35; in sensation novel, 107–11, 114
Nietzsche, F., 223
Nomadic movement, 90–91, 99–100
"Nurture" versus "nature," 68
Nutrition, menstrual, 33, 34

Oboznenko, Petr, 190, 193–95
Obstetrical Society, 142, 161, 164
Obstetric (term), 158
Offen, Karen, 81
Oliphant, Margaret, 111
On the Seed, 4
On the Usefulness of the Parts of the Body, 4
"On the Utility and Safety of the Inhalation of Ether in Obstetrical Practice," 142–43
Oral contact, syphilis spread by, 174, 188
Orgasm: female, 1–12 passim, 17, 35, 37, 167; male, 5–7, 9–12
Orgasme (term), 41
Origin of the Distinctions of Ranks, 21
Ostéologie, 77
Ostriches, female skeleton like, 62
Ovaries, 12, 27–28, 29, 30, 34, 41; homologies of, 2, 3, 6, 76
Ovulation, 3, 25–35 passim, 41
Oxygen-hydrogen ratio, sex differences in, 75

Pain, labor, 12, 142–43, 157, 159
Paranoids, 115, 117, 118
Paraurethral glands, 7
Pare, Ambroise, 11, 13
Parent-Duchâtelet, Alexandre, 188, 189, 211, 212, 214, 216
Paris: Benjamin and, 220; prostitution in, 211, 214, 217, 218
Paris Commune, 18
Parliament, British, 149
Parturition. *See* Childbirth
Pascal, B., 213
Pasquier, E., 216
Passagen-Werk, 220, 224
Passion. *See* Desire/Passion
Passionlessness, 24, 35, 39, 168
Pechey, John, 14
Pelvis, in skeleton studies, 43, 62, 63, 65
Penicillin, 173
Penis, homologies of, 3, 5, 14, 16
Penisneid, 129

Periodicity, female, 146
Petersen, Oskar von, 189
Petrification, of prostitute-body, 224, 225–26
Petrovskii, Aleksandr, 185, 186, 190
Pfluger, E. F. W., 32
Physician, 198
Physicians: English, 149–50, 167; Russian, 169–208
Physiocrats, 211
Physiology: of Mayhew's costermongers, 100; reproductive, 1, 3, 8–16, 20, 25–35, 75, 166–67; of sex differences, 3, 30–35 passim, 71, 75
Physiology (Haller), 28
Pirogov Society, 197
Plague, 41
Plato, 20–21, 53
Pleasure, 1, 3, 4, 27; locale of, 14–15, 17, 28; Malthus on, 88–89; and prostitution, 213, 215–16, 224; reproductive capacity dependent on, 1, 4, 5–7, 9–12, 35, 37. *See also* Orgasm
Pliny, 13, 28
Pockels, Carl Friedrich, 69, 71
Pokrovskaia, Mariia, 186–87, 190, 193, 195
Political economy: Malthus and Mayhew on, 92–104 passim; of prostituted body, 224
Politics: "nature" in, 43; of reproductive biology, 1, 16–24, 35, 152; of syphilis prevention, 192, 197. *See also* Feminism
Pontormo, Jacobo, 15
Poor laws, 94
Poovey, Mary, 137–68
Population size, 53, 83–90, 93, 94, 105
Posner, E. W., 65–66
Pouchet, F. A., 26, 27, 29, 33
Poullain de la Barre, François, 46, 53
Pre-Pasteurian mythologies, 210
Priklonskii, Ivan, 172, 189
Pringle, 210
Privacy: concept of, 215; in *Woman in White*, 116–17
Problematization, of body, 90, 97
Productive labor, 91–103 passim. *See also* Working class
Propriety, 143–44, 147, 151–52, 177
Prostitution, 222, 223–27; French, 199, 209–19; Russian, 171–72, 177–78, 180, 182–185, 186, 188, 189–95, 197, 205; state regulation of,

Prostitution (*cont.*)
189–96, 197, 206, 209–19
Psychiatrists, Russian, 207
Public health. *See* Health, public
Pudenda: drawings of, 10, 12; sexual
pleasure in, 28
Putain (term), 210–11, 212, 218

Question of Rest for Women During Menstruation, 32–33

Rabbits, ovulation by, 25
Race, 63, 64, 66, 70–71, 80
Raciborski, Adam, 33, 41
Ransel, David L., 203
Rape, in *Woman in White,* 116, 117,
127–29
Ravoth, Friedrich, W. H., 72
Ray, Isaac, 146–47
Ray, W. Fraser, 135
Recamier, 216
"Red-light district," 214
Reflex action, 145–46, 162–63
Refuse dumps, and prostitution, 214
Regulation. *See* State sexual regulation
Reiser, Stanley Joel, 159
Religion, 24, 139–40
Remak, Robert, 28–29
Renaissance, 1–41, 47–48
Reproduction, 166–67; biology of, 1–41,
53, 146 (*see also* Reproductive organs); healthy body indicated by,
83, 85; of lower classes, 93, 105;
and sexuality, 1–12 passim, 32–37,
88, 143–44, 147, 152, 167, 180,
188; women governed by, 18–21,
32–34, 43, 68, 145–46, 151,
156–57, 162. *See also* Childbirth
Reproductive organs, 162; homologies
of, 2–16 passim, 27, 35, 38,
48–49, 74, 75, 76. *See also* Ovaries;
Testes; Uterus
Review of Medical Physiology, 34–35
Ribs, women's, 58–59
Ricord, Philippe, 171
Riehl, Wilhelm, 72
Roesslin, Euchar, 166
Rosenmüller, Johann Christian, 75, 76
Rousseau, Jean-Jacques, 19–21, 24, 67,
69, 70
Roussel, Pierre, 2, 36, 51, 63, 68, 69, 80
Royal College of Physicians, 149, 161
Royal College of Surgeons, 149, 150,
161, 162
Royal Medical and Chirurgical Society
of London, 137
Rozenkvist, Andrei, 170, 186, 188
Rueff, Jacob, 10
Rural syphilis, Russian, 170, 171, 175,
177–88, 192–99 passim
Russian medicine, 169–208
Russian Physician, 198
Ryan, Michael, 158

Sachs, J. J., 51, 69
Sade, Marquis de, 1, 24
Sadler, John, 11
Sahlins, Marshall, 213
St. Petersburg Admiralty Hospital, 189
Saint-Simonianism, 221
Salvarsan, 198
Sarthe, Jacques Moreau de la, 2
Schiebinger, Londa, 42–82
Schreber, 115, 129
Science, 175; and intelligence, 43,
64–65, 67, 70–72, 81. *See also*
Anatomy; Medicine; Physiology
Scotland, chloroform use in, 137, 142,
144, 161
Scottish Enlightenment, 21
Scrotum, homologies of, 3, 6, 16
Sects, history of, 221
Sedgwick, Eve Kosofsky, 131
Seed, 7
Self-regulation, against syphilis, 196–97
Semen: men's, 9; women's, 7, 9, 36–37
"Seminal drain," prostitutes as, 211,
215–16
Sensation novel, 107–19, 123, 130, 134
Servant women, Russian syphilitic, 186
Sex differences. *See* Differentiation, of
sexes
Sex organs. *See* Reproductive organs
"Sex shop," 218
Sexuality, 167; under anesthesia,
142–44, 147–48, 160, 161; as disorder, 155; Malthus on, 88–89,
105; reproduction and, 1–12 passim, 32–37 passim, 88, 143–44,
147, 152, 167, 180, 188, society
mirrored in, 4, 12, 16, 35; and
syphilis, 169–208, 209, 211, 212;
in *Woman in White,* 112, 115, 116,
117, 118–19, 127–29, 131–36 passim. *See also* Desire/Passion; Homosexuality; Prostitution
Sharp, Jane, 14
Shiriaev, Pavel, 185–86, 193
Shperk, Eduard, 171, 172, 175, 183,
190, 193–94

Shtiurmer, Konmain, 177, 178, 189
Silk, J. F. W., 160
Silva, Jean-Baptiste, 210
Simpson, James Young, 137–63 passim
Skeleton studies: of children, 63, 64–65, 66; of females, 4, 42–82; of males, 46–47, 48, 49–50, 56–57, 63, 65, 68
Skey, F. C., 153, 167
Skulls, in skeleton studies, 43, 58, 63, 64–65, 78
Smell, of prostitutes, 210–11
Smith, Adam, 83, 92, 94, 95, 96, 98
Smith, Hilda, 47–48
Smith, Protheroe, 167
Smith, W. Tyler, 142–67 passim
Smith-Rosenberg, Carroll, 168
Snow, John, 141–42, 144, 158, 160
Socialists, 22
Society, 43, 64; body and, 4, 12, 16, 19, 35, 66, 83–106; prostitute as seminal drain for, 211, 215–16; syphilis and, 169–208, 209, 211, 212; women's roles in, 18–22, 30, 32, 43, 46, 53, 66–73 passim, 138–46 passim, 151, 164, 168, 222. See also Class, social; Morality; Politics; individual countries
Soemmerring, Samuel Thomas von, 42, 54–71 passim, 78, 80
Solon, 210
Soranus, 4
Southey, Robert, 105
Speculum, 155, 216
Speenhamland system, 94
Speranskii, Nikolai, 183
Sperm, 39, 75
"Spermatical vessels," 38
"Spermatic economy," 146
Sphinx, 218
State sexual regulation: French, 209–19; Russian, 189–96, 197, 206
Sterne, Laurence, 158
Stewart, James, 105
Stopes, Marie, 36
Storer, Horatio, 163–64, 167
Strong bodies, 83–86, 93, 97
Subordination, female, 66, 67–72, 73
Sue, Jean-J., 58, 59, 62, 64, 73, 77
Suffrage movement, women's, 18
Surgeons, Victorian, 149–50
Surgery, chloroform in, 139
Surveillance, of prostitution, 214–15
Sydenham, Thomas, 48
Syme, Dr., 161

Syphilis, 41, 169–208, 209, 211, 212
Syphilis in the Innocent, 169
Syria, syphilis in, 173

Tabulae sex, 12
Tanner, Dr., 144
Tardieu, Ambroise, 174, 188
Tarin, Pierre, 54
Tarnovskii, Veniamin, 171–71, 172, 175, 176, 181–96 passim
Taylor, Barbara, 22, 24
Taylor, Robert W., 188
Taylor, W. C., 146
Testes, 78; homologies of, 2, 3, 6, 76
Thompson, William, 22–23
Timaeus, 4, 12
Tiresias, 4
Tocqueville, Alexis de, 18
Tolerance, of prostitution, 213–14, 216
Townsend, Joseph, 105
Tracy, Stephen, 163
Transgressive utopia, 221–22
Treponema pallidum, 172
Trollope, Anthony, 113, 120
Trotulla, 9

Ulrichs, Karl, 112
Unconscious of desire, 221
Unconscious of vision, 221
Unproductive labor, 91–92, 95, 97, 99–100
Urban areas: disease in, 169, 175, 181–88, 212; labyrinthine, 220
Uterus, 10, 12, 75; as animal, 76; centrality of, 53, 145–46, 162; homologies of, 5, 6, 16; menstruation and, 28, 31–32, 33, 35
Utopianism, 83–93 passim, 220–29
Uvarov, Mikhail, 178, 180, 183

Vagina: drawings of, 10, 12; homologies of, 14
Valorization/Devalorization, of body, 90, 97, 225
Value, theory of, 91, 92–96, 98, 102–6 passim
Venus, 49–50, 58
Versluysen, Margaret, 164
Vesalius, Andreas, 74; drawings by, 8, 10, 12, 38, 43–54 passim; successor of, 14
Vicary, Thomas, 15–16
Victoria, Queen, 137, 157
Victorians: on child prostitution, 188; and lower classes, 90–105 passim,

Victorians (*cont.*)
164; medicine of, 137–68,
173–74; sensation novel of,
107–36
Virchow, Rudolph, 32
Vitalism, 210
Voltaire, F., 80
von Baer, Karl Ernst, 25
Vvedenskii, Aleksandr, 180, 189

Wakley, Thomas, 160
Wanderers, 90–91, 99–100
Warren, 212
Weib und das Kind, 65
Wenzel, Joseph, 62, 66
Wet nurses, Russian, 186, 204
Wheeler, Anna, 22–23
White males, 63, 64, 66
Wilde, Oscar, 132
Willis, Thomas, 48
Wives of England, 24
Wollstonecraft, Mary, 22, 23–24, 40, 68
Woman in White, 107–36
Womb. *See* Uterus
Women, 1; as disease/disorder, 41,
146–47, 155, 163–64; homosex-
ual, 36, 128, 188, 222; Russian,
179–80, 182, 183–85, 186, 195,
203, 204; social roles of, 18–22,
30, 32, 43, 46, 53, 66–73 passim,
138–46 passim, 151, 164, 168,
222; Victorian medical treatment
of, 137–68. *See also* Female body;
Femininity; Feminism; Prostitu-
tion; Sexuality
Woolf, Virginia, 1
Working class: French prostitute, 218;
Russian, 182, 186–87, 190, 192,
193, 204; Victorian, 91–105 passim, 164

York, prostitution and death in, 211
Young, Arthur, 105

Zemstvos, 175–76, 180, 187, 189–90
Zenocrates, 66
Zhbankov, Dmitrii, 176, 179–80, 181,
190–97 passim, 206
Ziegenbien, Johann, 68–69
Zola, E., 210